FAITHFUL MEASURES

Faithful Measures

New Methods in the Measurement of Religion

Edited by

Roger Finke and Christopher D. Bader

NEW YORK UNIVERSITY PRESS

New York

NEW YORK UNIVERSITY PRESS
New York
www.nyupress.org

Several chapters in this volume were made possible through the support of grants from the John Templeton Foundation. The opinions expressed in this publication are those of the authors and do not necessarily reflect the views of the John Templaton Foundation.

Library of Congress Cataloging-in-Publication Data
Names: Finke, Roger, 1954– editor.
Title: Faithful measures : new methods in the measurement of religion /
edited by Roger Finke and Christopher D. Bader.
Description: New York : NYU Press, 2017. | Includes bibliographical references and index.
Identifiers: LCCN 2017003767| ISBN 9781479875214 (cl : alk. paper) |
ISBN 9781479877102 (pb : alk. paper)
Subjects: LCSH: Religion—Methodology. | Religion—Statistics.
Classification: LCC BL41 .F355 2017 | DDC 200.28/7—dc23
LC record available at https://lccn.loc.gov/2017003767

New York University Press books are printed on acid-free paper, and their binding materials are chosen for strength and durability. We strive to use environmentally responsible suppliers and materials to the greatest extent possible in publishing our books.

Manufactured in the United States of America

10 9 8 7 6 5 4 3 2 1

Also available as an ebook

Dedicated to Rodney Stark,
our mentor and friend and a master
of innovative measures and designs

CONTENTS

Introduction

The Art and Science of Studying Religion

ROGER FINKE AND CHRISTOPHER D. BADER

In most areas of life, we take stable and accurate measures for granted. When buying food, land, or almost any commercial product, buyers assume that standard units of length, weight, or some other measure will be used, and the seller assumes that a standard measure of currency will be given in return. Likewise, there is an assumption that the tools used for measuring these products will be highly standardized and accurate. The expectations for clear standards and precise measures are even higher when applied to the sciences.

This has not always been the case. Indeed, the history of developing and adapting measures has an interesting overlap with religious history. Adapting standardized measures was often justified as a religious or moral imperative. One of the best-known efforts to impose standardization is the 1215 Magna Carta of King John of England, requiring that "there be one measure for wine throughout our kingdom, and one measure for ale, and one measure for corn. . . . Let it be the same with weights as with measures" (Halsall 2011 [1215]). Centuries before the Magna Carta, however, Caliph 'Abd al-'Aziz decried the "wicked practices" of tax collectors and charged them to "take in taxes only the weight of seven" (Wright 1997:33); and in the book of Amos, the Jewish Bible warns against "skimping on the measure, boosting the price and cheating with dishonest scales."[1] Guillaume Budé, famous for his treatise on ancient coins and measures, summarized the close link between measurement and morality in 1514: "Let there be one single faith, one measure, one weight, and the order of the world shall be free from harm" (as quoted in Stecchini 1961).

Yet, standardized measures did far more than preserve the moral order or curb social harm; they quickly became the foundation of scientific discovery. Plato noted that if number, weight, and measure are taken away from a discipline, little remains (Stecchini 1961). The ability to assign a numerical value to the observable unit measured became the expectation for any scientific venture.

This scientific standard was initially applied to the young social sciences. In the early twentieth century, an influential group of logical positivists proposed that we could infer an external reality based on the score of a single measure (Campbell and Russo 2001). Such optimism was short lived. By the middle of the twentieth century, the highly regarded psychologist Donald Campbell labeled this as "positivism's worst gift to the social sciences" (Campbell and Russo 2001:1). Campbell and others noted that human characteristics are far too complicated, and confounded by external factors, to allow the measurement of a person's character with a single measure. No single measure can clearly define a single trait, much less measure it with precision.

This problem is evident in the study of religion. Religion is a particularly sensitive and intricate domain that packages together religious practices with beliefs about the nature of the deity or deities, morality, literalism, visions of the afterlife, ideas about the meaning of life, and a host of other factors. No single measure can hope to capture the totality of an individual's belief or provide a single "number" that represents religion. As Dougherty et al. (2009) found, members of the same rural, conservative Baptist congregation may share a religious denomination, belief in the existence of God, and high levels of church attendance, yet exhibit a surprising diversity in their beliefs about God's tendency to judge humans, about who will get into Heaven, and about the so-called paranormal, such as haunted houses and UFOs. Consequently, any single religion measure will only represent a single aspect of religiosity. It probably includes more beliefs than those targeted, but also fails to include all of the beliefs intended or to paint a complete picture of religion. When the uncertain range of the measures is combined with the lack of clear standards for assessing measures, social science measures suffer from multiple sources of error.

To make matters worse, the values assigned to each measure can be distorted by the methods used for gathering data. Social surveys, the dominant method for collecting social data, suffer from a long list of "artifacts" that can alter outcomes, such as question ordering, the response categories offered, the interviewers used, and the question wording. Moreover, asking respondents to reveal intimate experiences with the sacred requires a trust seldom established in a ten-minute phone interview.

Other methods raise their own problems (Schuman 1982; Bradburn, Sudman, and Wansink 2004). Experiments often fail to simulate a real-world setting, and researchers observing social settings can distort the outcomes merely by their presence.[2] Official documents or government reports also suffer from measurement error, frequently introducing selection and reporting biases. Further, religious experiences typically fall outside of everyday experience, are difficult to recreate in laboratory settings, and are completely absent from government data sources. In sum, it is safe to conclude that social science measures of religion and religiosity are plagued with serious errors.

Despite this apparent state of hopelessness, Campbell and his colleagues (Webb et al. 1966; Campbell and Stanley 1963; Campbell and Russo 2001) pointed to a relatively simple solution to single-measure and single-method approaches. They proposed that the use of multiple measures and multiple research methods could help to uncover the very content we are trying to understand. They suggested that the limitations of social science measures were "demoralizing . . . only as long as one set of data, one type of method, is considered separately" (Webb et al. 1966:29). They explained that the strengths of one measure and method could complement the weaknesses of another. The solution was to include multiple measures for the character, trait, or content of interest and to use multiple research designs to study the topic. For the complex topic of religion, this is sage advice.

When applied to surveys, multimeasure approaches quickly produced a long list of multi-item scales that attempted to capture some underlying concept or content of interest. In their 531-page volume on *Measures of Religiosity*, Peter C. Hill and Ralph W. Hood Jr. (1999) review 126 scales and indexes developed to measure religion, and they concede that this is still incomplete. Along with this proliferation of new multi-item scales arose a vast literature on how to evaluate scales and indexes, with researchers developing sophisticated techniques and procedures for understanding and evaluating sources of measurement error in these multi-item measures (Alwin 2007).[3]

Despite this proliferation and evaluation of survey scales, however, developing new items to place in scales remains more art than science. Scholars have provided guidelines on how to write survey items (Sudman and Bradburn 1982; Bradburn, Sudman, and Wansink 2004), and research has illustrated how these items can be evaluated (Schuman and Presser 1996), but the vast majority of the individual survey items undergo little systematic evaluation. What they are measuring or how they compare to similar measures used in the past is often poorly understood.

Along with advocating for a multimeasure/multimethod approach to understanding phenomena, Campbell and his colleagues also encouraged researchers to utilize "unobtrusive" measures, or means of collecting data that do not require direct interaction with the subject of study. For example, their book on *Unobtrusive Measures* demonstrated how seating patterns in lecture halls could be coded to measure racial attitudes, how the erosion of floor tiles could help to measure floor traffic, and how the shrinking diameter of children seated in a circle could measure fear induced by a ghost story. They also used archives, official records, and public data sources. To measure the impact of TV being introduced to a community, they charted the rate of library withdrawals, noticing a drop in fiction titles, but no change for nonfiction. In the age of social media, online role-playing games, and websites that track user clicks and purchases, there has never been a better time for social scientists to gather unobtrusive measures. Yet more than thirty years after *Unobtrusive Measures* was published, one of Campbell's coauthors lamented that "like so many other of Campbell's ideas, those underlying unobtrusive measures are more honored by being talked about than [practiced]" (Sechrest 1998:404).

The social scientific study of religion has unfortunately fallen far short of Campbell's ideal of a multimethod approach. The use of unobtrusive measures and methods, such as quasi-experimental designs, remains the exception in social scientific research. Surveys remain the design that generates most of our social science knowledge, including our knowledge of religion. Approximately 95 percent of the data files currently held in the Association of Religion Data Archives (theARDA.com) were generated by surveys.

This book is a venture into the art and science of measuring religion. This venture evaluates existing measures of religion and unveils new methods for tapping into religion's many dimensions. Some of these new methods and measures offer revisions to past research accounts or supplement existing knowledge, while others explore new areas of religion and offer new revelations. The sources for our new and revised measures vary. Some rely almost entirely on recent technology such as online networks, new software tools, and expanded databases. Other approaches wed old designs with new technologies, such as online surveys using experimental designs or survey collections relying on smartphones. Still others suggest new measures or approaches to measurement that utilize existing information in new ways.

We recognize, of course, that innovative and new measures face many obstacles. Two of the most obvious are continuity and cost. Replicating past findings and charting trends over time require a continuity of survey measures that discourages the introduction of new items. The high cost of collecting new data results in efforts to reduce risk by using the tried and accepted measures and methods of the past. Yet, each of these efforts, improving continuity and decreasing risk due to costs, increases the temptation to replicate past measures even when they suffer from weaknesses.

But if continuity and cost are the most obvious obstacles to introducing new measures, institutional barriers are perhaps the most formidable. Editors and reviewers are often skeptical of novel measures, making researchers wary of trying innovative methods or measures. Ethical concerns are heightened when institutional review boards cannot point to a clear precedent. Moreover, many of these same reasons make it more difficult to secure funding for new and novel measures. In an effort to address these concerns, we carefully assess the promise and the limitations of the methods and measures introduced, as well as demonstrate how they can be effectively used.

This volume is our attempt to both improve upon existing methods and encourage use of new approaches. Put another way, we hope to inspire creativity and exploration among social scientists of religion—to improve upon the science and art of measuring religion in everyday life. It is our hope that this enterprise will both advance the social scientific study of religion and, perhaps more importantly, act as a call and encouragement for religion researchers to think creatively about our own "sacred cows."

We believe that religion scholars should learn from Campbell and his colleagues and be more willing to explore new methods and measures.

In this book we follow their lead by attempting to learn from our past as we build for the future. We learn from the past by devoting some time to evaluating existing survey measures, as well as proposing new ones. We also explore new methods for evaluating and designing survey measures. Using online surveys and quasi-experimental designs, we explore alternative ways of wording questions and the results of differing response categories. Further, we introduce methods for designing measures for cross-national surveys.

Much of our effort, however, is devoted to testing end exploring new, or underutilized, methods for measuring religion. Many of the methods are unobtrusive in nature, and like Campbell's research teams, we often rely on existing records, documents, and observations to generate measures. However, we have several advantages. Unlike these earlier scholars, we have access to far more information and can search this information in ways that were, at best, deemed possible in only the wildest science fiction of the 1960s. Moreover, with response rates falling and the diversity of the samples increasing, traditional survey measures are facing more challenges at providing data that accurately represent the population of interest. There has never been a better time for scholars to pull together data from disparate sources.

Throughout this process, we document the new outcomes we find. We introduce new technologies and methods for collecting data, but in the end, our interest is not in technology or even measurement design alone. Rather, we are interested in how new measures can help us to better understand a topic of interest. In our case, we ask if these measures produce a new understanding of, and offer new stories about, religion. By developing survey measures that offer an accurate reflection of what we are attempting to discover, by creating new measures that tap into religious dimensions untouched by surveys, and by exploring new methodologies, we offer new findings and new stories on religion.

Why Religion?

Clearly, the problems and concerns we have raised about measures and methods would apply equally to all topics within the social sciences. So why did we select religion?

One reason is that we relish the challenge. Perhaps no other substantive area faces greater measurement challenges than religion (Finke, Bader, and Polson 2010).[4] From defining the content studied to choosing the method and measures for studying it, each step of the process is filled with hurdles that threaten to introduce error. As the diversity of religions and irreligion increase in the United States and global studies become increasingly common, the measures of the past are in need of careful review and revision. For example, when multiple world religions are included in a sample, survey questions and the methods used for administering the survey must be revised. Because each world religion uses different sacred texts and the meaning of worship varies from one group to the next, survey questions about biblical inerrancy or church attendance no longer generalize across all respondents. Even the seemingly obvious concepts of god(s), prayer, and many other religious terms (including "religion" itself) can pose challenges. Each needs to be defined and measured with a clarity and consistency that can cross diverse religions and cultures.

There are many areas of religion, however, that surveys cannot address. For these areas, we need to think creatively about alternative methods for tapping into religious beliefs, behaviors, and organizations. We want to explore alternative methods and measures that provide a historical backdrop, offer new profiles of religious organizations, and allow us to observe religious behaviors and networks from new vantage points. Regardless of the research method used, religion remains one of the most challenging topics to measure.

A second reason for selecting religion, closely related to the first, is need. There is a need for new measures and methods and a need for improving the way we assess past measures and methods. Whereas government agencies collect data on education, income, immigration, crime, health, and many other topics, religion is not included in official government collections.[5] The most heavily used national data collection on religious organizations, the Religious Congregations and Membership Study, relies on volunteers, a modest budget, and the goodwill of the organizations collecting and submitting the data. Some government funding agencies, such as the National Institutes of Health, now support surveys including items on religion, but the focus of the study is seldom religion. A few private foundations, most notably the Sir John Templeton Foundation, the Pew Trust, and the Lilly Endowment, have supported data collections in this area. Yet, when compared to other areas of the social sciences, the study of religion receives only modest support.

As a result, data are completely lacking in some areas, and opportunities to evaluate new and past measures are often limited. In a few of the areas where data are lacking, we introduce new methods for collecting data. We find that unobtrusive measures are especially well suited for the study of religion because they can often be collected on low budgets and require minimal interference in the lives of those being studied. In areas where measures do exist, we introduce new methods for evaluating and improving these measures.

Our relationship with the Association of Religion Data Archives (www.theARDA.com) is a third reason we selected religion. Serving as director and associate director of the ARDA, we have helped to assemble more than one thousand data collections into a single database. For each of these collections, we include the complete wordings and response categories used to collect these data. This has resulted in an archive of measures, as well as data, that are supported with multiple online tools. Along with giving us immediate access to the thousands of existing measures, our positions also have introduced us to the most recent measurement innovations and have embedded us in a community of scholars who are actively developing and using new measures. It is from this community that we have recruited the talented group of scholars included in this volume. Although the authors have very diverse research interests, each of the authors has been actively engaged in evaluating past measures of religion and developing new ones. The result is a diverse array of exciting research projects with new insights on measuring religion.

Plan of the Book

Innovation in the social scientific study of religion will require both the refining of current methodologies and the exploration of new approaches. To this end we have organized this volume into two sections.

Quantitative studies in research on religion remain largely dependent upon the analysis of survey data. Therefore, our first section focuses upon the evaluation and refinement of our survey measures of religion.

Philip S. Brenner opens section 1 by addressing one of the most fundamental issues about survey questions on religion: are respondents telling us the truth when they report their religious beliefs and behaviors? It is well known among religion researchers that survey respondents tend to exaggerate levels of religious service attendance. In "How Religious Identity Shapes Survey Responses," Brenner uses identity theory to explain this pattern. Respondents are not simply lying, or merely attempting to look virtuous to the interviewer, he argues. Rather, the respondent's religious identity exerts a powerful influence on his/her response patterns, leading the respondent to draw upon self-concepts of the way someone with a particular religious identity is *expected to behave* when answering related questions. Brenner concludes by recommending specific techniques, such as time diaries, that can help to avoid the overreporting of religious behaviors.

One means by which researchers can protect themselves from biased responses to individual questions is to utilize multiple measures of religiosity. Psychologists have long recognized the importance of developing multi-item scales to measure religious and spiritual beliefs, attitudes, values, and behaviors. In their chapter "Measurement Tools and Issues in the Psychology of Religion and Spirituality," psychologists Peter Hill and Kenneth Pargament note that multi-item scales of religiosity and spirituality face their own measurement issues. They then provide guidelines for selecting religiosity and spirituality scales and provide examples of several such scales that meet their criteria. Hill and Pargament conclude by suggesting some alternatives to the standard strategy of collecting religion data using self-report surveys.

Jonathan Jong, Bonnie Zahl, and Carissa Sharp's chapter, "Indirect and Implicit Measures of Religiosity," builds upon Hill and Pargament by further advocating for alternatives to standard self-report surveys when studying religion. Specifically, Jong et al. argue that religion researchers should utilize *indirect* and *implicit* measures of religion to complement standard self-report measures. For example, researchers might note the speed with which respondents categorize or evaluate religious concepts, providing insight into the underlying religiosity of the individual without asking him/her to self-report. Jong et al. summarize several such indirect and implicit approaches to religion measurement, urging the reader to add them to his or her methodological tool kit, as they could provide insight into those aspects of religiosity that are unconscious.

Clearly, religion researchers need to be aware of weaknesses with our existing indicators of religion and strive to strengthen those measures. However, we must also face the challenge of developing *new* measures when necessary. For example, the ranks of the religiously unaffiliated (often called "nones") have been increasing in the United States over the last several decades, but we have little understanding of the beliefs and practices of the nones or the motivations behind disaffiliation or lack of religious affiliation.[6] Understanding the nones will require the development of new survey questions, but the cost of fielding new questions can be high, discouraging such innovations. Thankfully, there are cost-effective means of testing new survey questions, as Joseph Baker, Jonathan Hill, and Nathaniel Porter discuss in their chapter, "Assessing Measures of Religion and Secularity with Crowdsourced Data from Amazon's Mechanical Turk." Baker et al. provide an overview of Amazon's Mechanical Turk (MTurk) platform, which provides a pool of potential participants for completing simple online tasks, including survey instruments, in a cost-effective manner. In their chapter, the authors use the MTurk platform to demonstrate both the problems of using existing religion measures with the nonaffiliated and how new measures could provide useful descriptive information on the rationales individuals give for being either religious or secular.

Developing new measures of religion can be deceptively difficult. As religion in America becomes more diverse, both from increasing disaffiliation and from immigration, finding a shared vocabulary that taps into concepts of interest and selecting response categories that capture the full range of choices become ever more challenging. In "Evaluating Survey Measures Using theARDA's Measurement Wizard," we draw upon our experience as directors of the Association of Religion Data Archives (www.theARDA.com) to discuss how looking to the past can help us both improve existing measures and develop new ones. As of this writing, theARDA.com hosts more than a thousand different data collections with religion measures. A new software tool, the Measurement Wizard, treats this massive collection of measures as meta-data, allowing the user to compare the way different surveys have asked about the same underlying concept. Using this tool, we explore the manner in which surveys have addressed issues such as human origins, personal religiosity, and images of God—and how responses to such questions are very sensitive to question wording, response category wording, and even the number of response categories provided.

As our research projects become more global, we will need to address many of the issues discussed in previous chapters, but on a wider scale. How do we conduct cross-cultural religion research, when many of the "sacred cows" in our measurement tool kits, such as church attendance, prayer, biblical literalism, and images of God hold widely different meanings across major world religions and in some cases are not even applicable? Tom W. Smith draws upon his extensive experience with the International Social Survey Programme to provide guidance in his chapter "Using the Total Survey Error Paradigm to Improve Cross-National Research on Religion." As Smith describes, the Total Survey (TSE) is a very useful paradigm for describing and improving surveys. TSE provides an outline of the various sources of error that a survey instrument can produce, ranging from sampling problems such as the unintentional exclusion of types of respondents, systematic patterns of nonresponse often arising from problems with noninclusive wording and content, statistical errors due to weighting, and a host of other issues. While TSE can help to reduce errors in survey instruments, it was designed to apply to only a single, stand-alone instrument. Smith provides a methodology by which TSE could be used to compare across multiple surveys, with a particular focus upon using this method to improve cross-cultural surveys about religion. He concludes by assessing some of the problems that have emerged in using religion measures in cross-national surveys.

The remaining chapters, Section II of this volume, move us beyond surveys. Each chapter attempts to outline novel (or certainly underutilized) research methods in the hope of spurring creative work in the study of religion. The authors are not proposing that we abandon the venerable survey. Rather, they illustrate how the use of multiple methods and several new techniques can offer new and diverse measures that increase our understanding of religion.

Christopher P. Scheitle exemplifies the use of creativity in our research on religion in his chapter "From Documents to Data." Religion researchers have long referenced government censuses, original/source documents, and other non-survey-based documents. As Scheitle notes, such work typically required spending months in remote locations poring through dusty filing cabinets. But the increasing digitization of documents and a plethora of websites, electronic databases, and search tools have made it increasingly feasible for a researcher to access and code a wealth of data from governments and religious groups. Scheitle provides a number of examples of how he has used such tools in his own work, including using tax returns of religious nonprofits to generate creative measures of finances, identity, and mission, as well as examining the mission statements of congregational websites to assess attitudes about gays and lesbians.

William Sims Bainbridge further highlights the benefits of the rapid expansion of online archives and tools in his chapter "Historical Research: Oneida Online." Even though the Oneida community dissolved before 1900, the Internet still provides a wealth of resources for creatively researching the group. Bainbridge utilizes Google Books and an online genealogy website to assess claims about sexual predation of young women by the group's founder, John Humphrey Noyes. He then draws upon Wikipedia, online newspaper archives, Ancestry.com, blogs, the online archives for an academic journal, and census data to paint a portrait of three key members of Oneida and the changing demographics of the group.

With the exception of surveys of organizational leadership, an interest in researching religious organizations of any form is going to require methods beyond the survey, as Scheitle and Bainbridge demonstrate. However, conducting research on organizations (religious or otherwise) *also* requires having a strict definition of the organizational type. Most religion researchers have a clear understanding of what qualifies as a denomination and what meets the criteria for a congregation. Other organizations are slightly more challenging to define, as Evelyn L. Bush addresses in her chapter "What Is a Religious NGO? Conceptual and Classificatory Challenges in Research on Transnational Religion."

Simply put, an NGO (nongovernmental organization) is any nonprofit, voluntary group that is not directly associated with a government agency. NGOs are often organized around some form of advocacy (such as women's rights) or development projects (such as providing access to clean water). While most NGOs are secular, Bush notes that there are a growing number of explicitly religious NGOs. However, there are many problems that emerge when attempting to classify an NGO as religious or nonreligious, and the way in which such groups are coded will have great impact on our understanding of the boundaries between the religious and the secular and between government and civil society. Bush provides a number of different classification schemes for distinguishing between religious and nonreligious NGOs, discussing the strengths and weaknesses of each. Ultimately she advocates for the usage of multiple coding schemes as reflected by a number of different criteria and variables in a dataset, allowing the researcher to examine the extent to which different selection criteria impact results.

One clear benefit of utilizing nonsurvey methodologies is the ability to gather unobtrusive measures. When we code original documents or classify organizations, we do so without the individuals/groups in question being aware of that classification.[7] Therefore, we need not worry that the respondents have answered questions or behaved in certain ways based on the desire to please the researcher or to maintain positive self-images. Chapters 10 and 11 highlight two rich sources of unobtrusive data on religion that have recently become available.

In chapter 10, "Reviewing Millions of Books: Charting Cultural and Religious Trends with Google's Ngram Viewer," Roger Finke and Jennifer McClure discuss how the recent digitization of more than twenty million books by Google and an associated feature, Google Ngram Viewer, can be used to generate vast amounts of trend data on religion and to locate primary historical sources. Allowing users to conduct sophisticated word and phrase searches, Google's Ngram Viewer quickly quantifies the usage of the inputted words/phrases in published books for each year from 1800 to 2000. Finke and McClure discuss and illustrate the strength of this tool by charting significant events in the history of the Mormon Church and showing subtle shifts in the meaning of the terms "fundamentalist" and "Pentecostal" over time; but they also demonstrate the limitations of the tool in charting other religion measures. Finke and McClure conclude by reviewing how Google's Ngram Viewer can be used to locate and code primary historical documents, resulting in even more historical measures of religion.

Nathaniel Porter and Christopher Bader's chapter, "Pathways to Discovery and Enlightenment: Amazon's Recommendation System as a Source of Information on Religious and Paranormal Consumption

Patterns," also utilizes data from books in an attempt to understand religion, in this case focusing upon purchasing data from online retailer Amazon.com. For each item in its catalog, Amazon recommends similar items by computing how many customers bought specific items together. Such copurchase data, Porter and Bader argue, could prove particularly useful in improving our understanding of small religious and cultural groups and ideas that lack clear boundaries or formal organizational structures. One religious/spiritual category well known for its lack of clarity is the New Age/paranormal. Using copurchase data on books related to Bigfoot, UFOs, psychic powers, and other subjects, Porter and Bader find three identifiable belief clusters represented within New Age/paranormal purchasing patterns that align with previous qualitative research on the paranormal. The authors conclude by providing examples of the visualization of purchasing networks.

Amazon may have changed the way in which people buy books and a host of other products, but no recent piece of consumer technology has reshaped everyday lives as much as smartphones. The chapter by Bradley Wright and colleagues, "Lessons Learned from SoulPulse: A Smartphone-Based Experience Sampling Method (S-ESM) Study of Spirituality," describes his ongoing study of spirituality that uses participants' smartphones to collect data over a two-week period. Wright's team administered two short surveys a day over two weeks to participants in the SoulPulse study who downloaded an associated phone app. The questions on these surveys were a mixture of items about religion and spirituality (such as asking the respondent their level of awareness of God's presence "right now"), items about daily activities, and questions about current emotional states. SoulPulse provided a unique opportunity to gather data on how religion and spirituality fit into everyday life. Wright discusses the lessons his team learned while conducting this study, providing concrete guidance on how to administer surveys, create suitable measures, design an appealing software interface, recruit participants, and analyze the uniquely structured, multilevel data generated by this approach.

Together these chapters respond to the challenges posed by Campbell and his colleagues more than sixty years ago by using multiple different methods to propose multiple new measures. No one measure, or one method, provides all the information needed, but the wealth of measures and the different methods reveal new insights into and understanding of religion. The authors also address the challenge of developing unobtrusive measures by using techniques that Campbell and his colleagues could never have imagined. This book is about measuring religion, but the most exciting outcomes are the stories these new measures tell.

NOTES

1 Quoted from Amos 8:5 (New International Version translation). The translation from the Stone Edition of the Tanach (Brooklyn, NY: Mesorah Publications, 1996) warns against efforts to "reduce the ephah and increase the shekel, and distort scales of deceit."

2 Festinger, Riecken, and Schachter's (1956) classic study of a failed prophecy, *When Prophecy Fails*, raises concerns about the impact observers can have upon the very phenomena they wish to document. Festinger and colleagues witnessed *increased* excitement and proselytization among the members of a small flying-saucer cult after a failed prophecy about the arrival of extraterrestrials, resulting in the concept of "cognitive dissonance." Bainbridge (1997, 137) is very skeptical of these findings, noting that at some group meetings, a third of the fourteen people in attendance were observers. Bainbridge argues that the very attention the group received from Festinger and colleagues may have produced the excitement that allowed them to continue for a time after failed prophecies.

3 Campbell and Fiske (1959) were early contributors with their introduction of the "Multitrait-Multimethod Validity Matrix."

4 In the early 1990s, a group of scholars exploring the connections between religion and politics advocated for the use of a set of improved measures of religious belief, behavior, and belonging. A few were integrated into the NES. For a discussion, see Wald and Smidt (1993).

5 From 1906 to 1936, the U.S. Census Bureau collected the Census of Religious Bodies. The bureau is no longer allowed to collect religion data.

6 See Baker and Smith (2015).

7 We oversimplify here in the interest of making a point. When working with nonpublic documents or information, permission of some form is sometimes required to access that information. There is also the possibility that organizations only provide documents to the researcher that support a certain perspective. But in most cases, we can circumvent concerns about social desirability by coding secondary documents and reports.

BIBLIOGRAPHY

Alwin, Duane. 2007. *Margins of Error: A Study of Reliability in Survey Measurement.* Hoboken, NJ: Wiley.

Bainbridge, William Sims. 1997. *The Sociology of Religious Movements.* New York: Routledge.

Baker, Joseph O., and Buster G. Smith. 2015. *American Secularism: Cultural Contours of Nonreligious Belief Systems*. New York: NYU Press.

Bradburn, Norman M., Seymour Sudman, and Brian Wansink. 2004. *Asking Questions: The Definitive Guide to Questionnaire Design*. San Francisco: Wiley.

Campbell, Donald T., and Donald W. Fiske. 1959. "Convergent and Discriminant Validation by the Multitrait-Multimethod Matrix." *Psychological Bulletin* 56: 81–105.

Campbell, Donald T., and M. Jean Russo. 2001. *Social Measurement*. Thousand Oaks, CA: Sage.

Campbell, Donald T., and Julian C. Stanley. 1963. *Experimental and Quasi-Experimental Designs for Research*. Chicago: Rand McNally.

Dougherty, Kevin D., Christopher D. Bader, Paul Froese, Edward Polson, and Buster Smith. 2009. "Religious Diversity in a Conservative Baptist Congregation." *Review of Religious Research* 50(3): 321–34.

Festinger, Leon, Henry W. Riecken, and Stanley Schachter. 1956. *When Prophecy Fails*. San Francisco: Harper & Row.

Finke, Roger, Christopher D. Bader, and Edward C. Polson. 2010. "Faithful Measures: Developing Improved Measures of Religion." ARDA Guiding Paper Series. State College, PA: Association of Religion Data Archives at Pennsylvania State University, from www.theARDA.com.

Gorsuch, R. L. 1988. "Psychology of Religion." *Annual Review of Psychology* 39: 201–21.

Halsall, Paul, ed. 2011 [1215]. *Magna Carta of King John of England*. Internet History Sourcebooks Project. Accessed January 26, 2013, www.fordham.edu.

Hill, Peter C., and Ralph W. Hood Jr. 1999. *Measures of Religiosity*. Birmingham, AL: Religious Education Press.

Malinowski, Bronislaw. 1954. *Magic, Science, Religion*. New York: Doubleday.

Presser, Stanley, Jennifer Rothgeb, Mick Couper, Judith Lessler, Elizabeth Martin, Jean Martin, and Eleanor Singer, eds. 2004. *Methods for Testing and Evaluating Survey Questionnaires*. New York: Wiley.

Schuman, Howard. 1982. "Artifacts Are in the Mind of the Beholder." *American Sociologist* 17: 21–28.

Schuman, Howard, and Stanley Presser. 1996. *Questions and Answers in Attitude Surveys: Experiments on Question Form, Wording, and Context*. Thousand Oaks, CA: Sage.

Sechrest, Lee. 1998. "Don Campbell and Measurement in the Social Sciences." *American Journal of Evaluation* 19: 403–6.

Shafranske, E. P. 1996. "Religious Beliefs, Affiliations, and Practices of Clinical Psychologists." In E. P. Shafranske (ed.), *Religion and the Clinical Practice of Psychology* (pp. 149–62). Washington, DC: American Psychological Association.

Smith, Tom. 2004. "Developing and Evaluating Cross-National Survey Instruments." In Stanley Presser, Jennifer Rothgeb, Mick Couper, Judith Lessler, Elizabeth Martin, Jean Martin, and Eleanor Singer, eds., *Methods for Testing and Evaluating Survey Questionnaires*. New York: Wiley.

Stecchini, Livio C. 1961. "A History of Measures." *American Behavioral Scientist* 18: 4–7.

Sudman, Seymour, and Norman M. Bradburn. 1982. *Asking Questions: A Practical Guide to Questionnaire Design.* San Francisco: Jossey-Bass.

Upal, M. Afzal. 2005. "Simulating the Emergence of New Religious Movements." *Journal of Artificial Societies and Social Simulation* 8(1), jasss.soc.surrey.ac.uk.

Wald, Kenneth D., and Corwin E. Smidt. 1993. "Measurement Strategies in the Study of Religion and Politics." In David C. Leege and Lyman A. Kellstedt, eds., *Rediscovering the Religious Factor in American Politics.* Armonk, NY: Sharpe.

Webb, Eugene J., Donald T. Campbell, Richard D. Schwartz, and Lee Sechrest. 1966. *Unobtrusive Measures: Nonreactive Research in the Social Sciences.* Chicago: Rand McNally.

Wright, Benjamin D. 1997. "A History of Social Science Measurement." *Educational Measurement: Issues and Practice* 16: 33–45.

SECTION I

Survey Measures of Religion

1.

How Religious Identity Shapes Survey Responses

PHILIP S. BRENNER

Introduction

According to survey findings released in January 2015, only about 20 percent of American churchgoers would skip church to watch their favorite football team.[1] As you might expect, the report noted that women are even less likely than men (10 and 22 percent, respectively) to play hooky from church to watch football. These findings were included in a press release that hit newspapers and the blogosphere not long before the Super Bowl (notably played in 2015 by teams from two of the least religious regions in the country: the Seattle Seahawks and the New England Patriots). By itself, this press release is an interesting tidbit, worthy of a colorful beneath-the-fold infographic in *USA Today* and a perhaps humorous dinner party anecdote. But what does it say about the state of American religion, or about survey research on religion? And to what extent does this statistic reflect how we *actually* behave?

The products of survey research can give us invaluable insight into ourselves and our society, informing policymaking and public debate and contributing to an educated and engaged public. However, they can also bias and muddle our knowledge if we consume them without due diligence by failing to understand the nature of survey measurement and its potential errors.[2] This chapter aims to clarify the nature of survey measurement of religious service attendance. It reviews the current state of the field, focusing primarily on the measurement of religious behaviors, like religious service attendance and prayer, and its distal source of error: our religious identities.

My main argument in reviewing the literature is borrowed from an important article by C. Kirk Hadaway, Penny Long Marler, and Mark Chaves (1998). They suggest that the cause of measurement bias in survey estimates of church attendance is rooted in the survey respondent's religious identity, "generated by the combination of a respondent's desire to report truthfully his or her identity as a religious, church-going person and the perception that the attendance question is really about this identity rather than about actual attendance" (Hadaway et al. 1998, 127). From this perspective, survey respondents are not making a simple recall mistake—misremembering what they did or didn't do. Nor are survey respondents giving us a bald-faced lie about what they accurately remember *not* doing. Rather, the error they make in reporting behavior is motivated by a desire to report the truth about how they see themselves. That is, while they may not be telling us the truth about what they *did*, they are telling us the truth about *who they are* or, perhaps closer to the point, *who they think they are*. Maybe these self-reported churchgoers in Boston, Seattle, and elsewhere are actually sitting in the pews when their favorite NFL team is playing (or for our Seventh-day Adventist friends, sitting in the pews when their favorite college team is on the field). On the other hand, maybe some of these self-reported churchgoing football fans are actually watching the game but see themselves as being more like their fellow churchgoers (who are piously sitting in the pews) than their fellow fans (who are not-so-piously sitting on their sofas, drinking beer, and raucously cheering on their favorite teams).

Thus, this chapter synthesizes and extends the research on the measurement—and mismeasurement—of religious behavior. The research on religious service attendance is highlighted given its primacy in the literature, although, as will be suggested, the attention paid to church attendance is a function of the practicalities of survey measurement. Compared to other potential research foci (i.e., religious behaviors like prayer, meditation, scripture study, religious affiliation, or beliefs), attendance is commonly measured, regularly and frequently performed, and potentially verifiable. Thus, this chapter focuses primarily on errors in survey estimates of religious service attendance but also draws connections to biases in other religious measures. The main thrust of this research points to the tendency of survey respondents to *overreport* their religious behavior—that is, claim a higher rate of behavior than is warranted. In this investigation, we look to the more recent work that digs behind these statistics in an attempt to understand why overreporting occurs. In synthesizing this recent work, this chapter offers a theoretical approach we can use to think about how and why survey respondents misreport religious behavior generally and church attendance specifically. Rather than assuming that survey respondents intentionally dissemble to look virtuous for a survey interviewer, I offer an explanation rooted in the survey respondent's identity as a religious person. This approach, based in Sheldon Stryker's identity theory (1980), proposes that the divergence between actual and self-reported behavior is motivated by the importance of the survey respondent's religious identity. In sum, respondents reflect not only on past behavior when answering the survey question about religious behavior but also on their self-concept as a religious person regardless of the data-collection mode, whether interviewer or self-administered. Finally, this chapter applies this identity-based model of measurement (and mismeasurement) to the analysis of respondents' own narratives about their survey reports from a series of cognitive interviews highlighting their own understandings about why they report the way they do.

Religious Identity as a Cause of Measurement Bias

Human life is not inherently meaningful. Rather, our lives achieve meaning from our connections with others. Many of us gain meaning through connections with family and friends. Relationships between partners or spouses, parents and children, grandparents and grandchildren, aunts and uncles and their nieces and nephews, and so on give us a sense that we matter (Rosenberg and McCullough 1981). For others, a profession provides a sense of meaning. Being a physician, politician, or professor links us to our patients, constituents, or students, and can lend a sense of purpose to our lives. Of course, these sources of meaning are not mutually exclusive. Individuals gain meaning and a sense of purpose from multiple and varied connections with others.

In each of these examples, familial and professional, the individual is connected to others via role-relationships. These role-relationships link individuals in roles and counter-roles, each performing role-identities that define the self and provide meaning. Mothers and fathers achieve meaning from nurturing and raising their children; professors, from educating students and watching their intellectual development; physicians, from treating sick patients and preventing others from becoming ill. Each identity helps us to define who we are and, importantly, who we are not (McCall 2003).

The religious identity provides another such pathway to meaning. A group of like-minded individuals cooperatively or concordantly engaged in prayer, meditation, song, or another form of worship can provide a sense of collective effervescence (Durkheim 1995 [1915]). In addition (or even in lieu) of relationships with other living humans, the religious identity can also connect the individual to spirits, saints, ancestors and the souls of those passed, and the divine. These connections link the individual in his or her religious role to an imagined other in a counter-role through prayer and meditation, recitation or reading of scripture, or other religious performances. In addition to a fleeting sense of togetherness or awe gained from sacred performances designed to connect with the divine, relationships with other coreligionists in a congregation and community also provide a powerful sense of meaning. These connections may link the individual to his or her ancestors reaching back in history and provide a sense of continuity through the millennia. Thus, like other role-identities, religious memberships or affiliations can give individuals a sense of meaning that helps the individual to define who s/he is (e.g., Catholic or Jewish) and who s/he is not (e.g., adherent of some other faith or none at all).

Whether the role-identity is familial, professional, religious, or some other type, identity theory proposes two constructs useful for understanding the performance of an identity and survey reports of it. Prominence is the subjective value placed on the identity (McCall and Simmons 1978) and is highly related to, or even synonymous with, the concepts of identity importance (Ervin and Stryker 2001) and psychological centrality (Rosenberg 1979). Survey measures of prominence are typically direct and subjective, asking respondents to report how much they value the focal identity, how important it is to their daily life, or the extent to which they would miss it if they could not hold that identity.

Individuals place their identities in a hierarchy of prominence. Identities that are more subjectively important to the individual and more central to his or her self-concept (e.g., spouse, parent) are higher in the prominence hierarchy than are identities that are less important and peripheral to his or her self-concept (e.g., amateur tennis player or member of a knitting circle). Prominence is consequential because it has a strong influence on the propensity to perform an identity. The more prominent the identity, the more likely the individual is to perform it (Brenner, Serpe, and Stryker 2014) or to define a situation as one in which identity performance is relevant (Stryker and Serpe 1994). This performance propensity (Stryker 1980), referred to as identity salience, is often measured as survey self-reports of behavior in realistic but hypothetical situations or as self-reports of recent behavior.

As their definitions suggest, prominence and salience are typically in concordance. An identity that is highly prominent is also likely to be highly salient. For example, many professors both strongly value and are very likely to perform their professor identities. This identity is paradigmatically performed in the classroom in front of undergraduates, as well as during interactions with colleagues during faculty meetings and academic conferences. Moreover, other situations outside the direct purview of the professor identity can be defined as an opportunity to perform that valued identity. For example, during a cocktail party or some other gathering with friends and family, the professor might discuss the details of his or her current research or the findings of a recent study. In this example, the individual both values the professor identity and is very likely to perform it.

Alternatively, prominence and salience may be mismatched. For example, a prisoner may be highly likely to perform his or her prisoner identity, even though s/he does not value that identity and may actively disvalue it (Asencio and Burke 2011). Perhaps more common, however, is the alternate pattern: an identity that is highly prominent but unlikely, or less likely to be performed than would be expected given the value placed on it. For many Americans, the religious identity is a paradigmatic example of this form of prominence-salience discrepancy.

To be sure, Americans report strongly valuing their religious identities. Anecdotal evidence of this abounds throughout the entire history of the country. Joas (2009) suggests that the importance placed on religion spanned from the time of the Puritans to the presidency of George W. Bush through the nearly four centuries in between, making reference to the reports of de Tocqueville (2002) that commented on the importance of religion during his visit to the United States in the 1830s. Recent data supports these anecdotes and suppositions for the present day. A study by the Pew Research Center (2015b) notes that two-thirds of Americans report that their religious identity is very important.

But attitudes, religious or otherwise, do not always result in behavior (Chaves 2010). Many self-reported religious individuals cannot or do not regularly perform their religious identities in terms of their religious service attendance or other religious behavior. The mismatch between prominence and salience can result in a discrepancy between actual behavior and the survey report of it. This problem can be understood from the perspective of identity theory.

Burke notes that most measurement situations, like the survey interview or self-administered survey questionnaire, lack normal situational constraints, making it "very easy for a respondent to give us that idealized identity picture, which may only seldomly be realized in normal interactional situations" (1980, 27). In other words, as we ask questions about role-identities and their behavioral expectations, we prime the respondent to think not only about his or her actual behavior but also about idealized notions of the self—including the prominence of the identities upon which the survey questions focus. Stryker and Serpe add to Burke's warning, noting that measurements of prominence and salience are easily conflated in the measurement situation, yielding potentially biased measurement of the latter "when actors, by whatever process, become aware of the salience of given identities" (1994, 34).

It is from this perspective that we can begin to understand the overreporting of religious behavior in general and religious service attendance in particular. And it is this phenomenon to which we now turn our attention.

Establishing the Phenomenon

There is nothing magical about church attendance or its measurement. A goodly number of measures of religiosity could be the focus of research instead of attendance, including other behaviors, affiliation, belief, etc. But attendance is a handy subject for research into survey error for a few good reasons. Unlike affiliation, attendance is a behavior. It requires that the individual actually do something—a "something" that is potentially verifiable. Unlike other behaviors we could ask survey respondents about, attendance is typically frequent, regular, and lasts long enough to be recalled. Other behaviors do not readily allow for this type of analysis. For example, in many Christian denominations,[3] prayer is also frequent, but hardly regular and long lasting. Prayers can be fleeting, lasting only seconds, and do not necessarily occur at regular intervals. And finally, from a simply pragmatic standpoint, religious service attendance works well because it is perhaps the most commonly measured religious behavior on surveys (Brenner, 2016).

Thus, much of the research on the validity of religious measures has dealt primarily with religious service attendance, and most of this research has centered on the United States. The American focus makes a good deal of sense as, correctly or incorrectly, the United States has long been viewed as religiously exceptional: a still strongly religious country among secularized and secularizing developed countries (Demerath 1998; Voas and Chaves 2016). Hadaway, Marler, and Chaves (1993) were the first to rigorously investigate the phenomenon of overreporting of religious service attendance in the United States. Their study focused on the internal validity of survey self-reports, comparing them to a set of criterion measures including head counts of parishioners from Catholic dioceses around the country and counts of cars in church parking lots (multiplied by an average number of persons per car) in a purposively selected county in Ohio. These comparisons yielded an important finding: the real attendance rate is probably half that reported on surveys.

These findings proved to be contentious. Glenn Firebaugh's editorial note opening a 1998 symposium on rates of American church attendance in *American Sociological Review* observed that "the central claim of that [1993] article—that survey data greatly exaggerate actual church attendance in the United States—has proven to be controversial. It challenged conventional wisdom about church attendance, and reprised the questions about the reliability of survey data generally" (Firebaugh 1998:111). Hout and Greeley (1998) criticized Hadaway et al.'s criterion measure—counts from administrative records and estimates based on tallies of automobiles— using correlations with other survey variables to call into question Hadaway et al.'s finding. Caplow (1998) accused Hadaway et al. of including "phantoms" in their survey estimates: survey respondents who are not church members but claim attendance. Woodberry (1998) agreed with Hadaway et al.'s finding that surveys generally yield inflated estimates of attendance, but differed on the magnitude and cause of the bias. He proposed that the overestimation (which he estimated to be closer to 10 percentage points) is probably caused by survey nonresponse, arguing that the mechanisms that motivate participating in a survey and attending services are highly related or even are one and the same. In short, those sample elements most likely to respond to a survey are also those most likely to attend religious services.

In the face of these criticisms, continuing research by Hadaway, Marler, and Chaves (1998) and others has replicated the findings of Hadaway et al.'s 1993 study with samples from the same and different populations as well as with similar and different methods as criterion measures. Chaves and Cavendish (1994) extended their analysis of Catholic churches, including attendance records from an additional thirty dioceses. Their analysis nearly perfectly matched the findings from Hadaway et al. (1993). Marcum (1999) replicated this finding in the Presbyterian Church (USA) using three years of data from the 1990s. He found overreports that inflated attendance rates by about 40 percent.

In response to the critique that administrative records are just as prone to error as the survey responses to which they have been compared, Marler and Hadaway (1999) focused their attention on validating the survey reports of a sample of congregants from a single large evangelical church. As their highly circumscribed sampling design suggests, Marler and Hadaway's purpose "was not to establish a universal rate of church attendance overreporting, but to compare self-reports to the behavior of specific individuals" (1999:185). They found a rate of overreporting over 80 percent—nearly equal to that reported by Hadaway et al. (1993).

Presser and Stinson (1998) extended the extant research to improve its external validity, using nationally representative survey data in conjunction with time diary data as a criterion to establish the population rate of overreporting.[4] They estimated overreporting as the difference between survey estimates of church attendance from two conventional sample surveys—the 1993 and 1994 General Social Survey (GSS) and the 1994 Gallup Poll—with those from a time diary study conducted in 1992–1994 by the University of Maryland. Their conventional survey estimates of religious service attendance in the "last week" range from 41 to 45 percent from Gallup, and 37 to 41 percent from the GSS, whereas diary estimates fall at 29 percent. Presser and Stinson's finding, that self-reports inflate attendance by nearly 50 percent, are a bit lower than those from Hadaway et al. but do support their conclusion: "[R]espondents in conventional surveys substantially overreport their religious attendance" (1998:140).

The research to this point has focused primarily on establishing the existence and magnitude of the overreport rather than on explaining why it occurs. Taken together, these studies present a strong portfolio of persuasive evidence for the existence of the phenomenon of overreporting. However, this research has not focused on hypothesizing and testing the cause of the phenomenon. And it is this topic to which we now turn our attention.

Explaining the Phenomenon

Conventional wisdom explains the overreporting of normative behaviors (including religious behavior, as well as voting, recycling, and getting preventative medical and dental care) and the underreporting of counternormative behaviors (like illegal, illicit, and sexual activity) as a function of impression management in the presence of the interviewer. This approach understands overreporting as a measurement bias generated from the interaction of the survey respondent and the interviewer. The respondent feels threatened to admit illegal behavior, embarrassed to admit sensitive sexual behavior, or ashamed to admit not having performed a normative behavior (Tourangeau and Yan 2007). Thus, survey respondents manage the impression they present to the interviewer by reporting less negative behavior and more positive behavior than is warranted by actual behavior.

This explanation appears to work reasonably well for counternormative behavior. Moving to a self-administered data collection mode, like a web or mail survey, tends to result in higher self-reported rates of counternormative activity compared to interviewer-administered survey modes (Tourangeau and Yan 2007). However, shifting to a self-administered mode does not alter the way respondents report on many normative behaviors (Kreuter, Presser, and Tourangeau 2008). A recent study by the Pew Research Center (2015a) found no significant or substantive difference in rates of church attendance between random subsamples of respondents assigned to a phone interview or web survey. Moreover, other conventional methods often used to improve the validity of survey responding have failed to eliminate or even reduce bias in measures of attendance. For example, the American National Election Study tested an experimental question with an altered wording to allow respondents to feel more comfortable admitting their nonattendance. The experiment failed to reduce overreporting and actually made the problem worse, increasing the self-reported rate of attendance (DeBell and Figueroa 2011).

Clearly, impression management is not the (sole) problem generating overreporting. Following Hadaway et al.'s (1998) supposition, Brenner proposed and investigated an alternative explanation based in religious identity. This research started at the macro level, comparing overreporting between countries before moving to the micro level and attempting to understand intrapersonal processes that lead to this form of measurement bias.

At the macro level, Brenner (2011a) put American overreporting in a cross-national context, examining variation in the size of the difference between survey and time diary estimates among countries to begin to investigate its cause. If overreporting is a common feature of survey measurement of attendance—a function of the way memory works or the way humans answer questions—overreporting should occur widely if not universally. In this case, overreporting would operate essentially like a tide, raising all boats equally. In this case, high survey rates of American attendance would remain relatively equidistant from lower European rates after overreporting is taken into consideration. However, if Americans overreport in a manner and magnitude that does not occur elsewhere, the picture could change dramatically. In this case, accounting for American overreporting (but encountering valid reporting elsewhere) would make the United States look more similar to other countries in Europe. Thus, this cross-national comparison opens the door to understanding why overreporting occurs.

To investigate these possibilities, Brenner (2011a) expanded the population defined by Presser and Stinson temporally and spatially to include four decades of data (1970s through the early 2000s) from fourteen countries (United States, Canada, Great Britain, Ireland, France, Spain, the Netherlands, West and East Germany, Italy, Austria, Slovenia,

Norway, Finland). Taking advantage of newly collected time use data from the American Time Use Study as well as older studies, he extended the investigation of Presser and Stinson backward and forward in time, showing that the magnitude of the overreport in the United States remained relatively stable at about 40 percent (about 15 percentage points) over four decades. The magnitude of this overreport, along with a slight negative trend in attendance estimates over this period (Chaves 2011; Presser and Chaves 2007), yields a decline in the actual rate of American attendance from over 30 percent to just over 20 percent.

Because the United States is the only country with a highly consistent, substantively large, and statistically significant overreport, overreporting cannot be described as a tide, but rather as a more localized phenomenon. This finding means that the actual rate of American church attendance is similar to, or even on par with, that of many countries in Europe, like the Netherlands, Spain, Italy, and Slovenia. While this finding further undermines American religious exceptionalism (Demerath 1998; Hadaway et al. 1998; Voas and Chaves 2016), it also opens a new chasm of difference between the United States and Europe. Even if Americans are not different in religious behavior, they are different in the way they claim religious behavior, raising an important question: why do Americans overreport?

Brenner (2012b) tried to explain where overreporting occurred and where it did not using a set of demographic variables often associated with religious service attendance. He included age (older adults are typically more religious than younger adults), education (more educated adults are typically less religious than less well-educated adults), gender (women more than men), family status (married individuals and those with children are more religious than the single and childless), and income (which has a more complex relationship that varies by place). He found no consistent pattern that would explain why overreporting occurs when and where it does. This finding importantly suggests that, while marginal statistics (estimates of population rates of attendance) are positively biased, correlations between self-reported church attendance and important demographic covariates may remain unbiased (Finke, Bader, and Polson 2010).

Brenner then shifted to the micro level, digging into the two cases in which he had discovered evidence of overreporting: the United States

(Brenner 2011b), where a significant, substantive, and consistent overreport was discovered; and Canada (Brenner 2012a), where the evidence for an overreport was significant but inconsistent.[5] In the United States, he combined conventional survey data from the General Social Survey with time diary data from the American Time Use Survey using a statistical technique proposed by Gelman, King, and Liu (1998) and Rendall et al. (2013). Using the diary report of church attendance as a criterion measure, he estimated the validity of the survey report for each respondent and then predicted response validity using a survey measure of the importance[6] of the religious identity. He found that religious identity importance predicted overreporting among those respondents who did not attend. Put plainly, respondents who strongly value their religious identities are more likely to overreport than those who do not. Importantly, religious identity importance could not differentiate those who overreported from those who did attend. In other words, importance appears to motivate both actual attendance as well as invalid reports of attendance. In the Canadian case, Brenner (2012a) replicated these findings using data from the Canadian General Social Survey, which contained both conventional survey measures of attendance as well as those from time diaries. Nearly identical findings provided support for the identity explanation.

The main limitation of these studies is their use of correlational models with observational data. While the regression models with survey data support the identity explanation, causal inference must be taken with a grain of salt. Survey data can be used to generalize to a population and to establish associations between measured concepts, but other methods can present stronger, more defensible causal claims.

Moving in an experimental direction, Brenner and DeLamater (2016) tested a novel data collection procedure similar to a time diary. They recruited a sample of undergraduates to take a web survey, ostensibly about daily life, in the spring of 2011. Questions asked about use of campus facilities, patronage of other establishments in the city, and other typical student activities, including attending religious services. The students were then asked to complete a diary-like data collection procedure using short message service (SMS) text messaging. Respondents were asked to send a text message whenever they changed their current major activity (e.g., going to work, going to class, going to church), and instructions explained the types of activities respondents should report. Findings were quite clear. Even respondents who reported weekly or more frequent church attendance in response to the conventional survey question failed to actually go to services during the field period, which, notably, included Passion Palm Sunday. Moreover, this overreport occurred in a self-administered mode.

The second component of this study included an important manipulation. A second independent sample of undergraduates was randomly assigned to receive instructions that either did or did not mention the focus of the study: religious behavior. The manipulation was just one additional clause in boldface font near the beginning of the instructions informing students that the study was particularly interested in religious behavior. Nevertheless, it generated a large difference in rates of church attendance. The respondents who received the manipulation were much more likely to attend services during the reference period than were those in the control group.

In both components of the study, overreporters looked much more similar to those students who accurately reported their attendance than they did to the other students who did not attend and admitted their nonattendance. Students who overreported their attendance reported a rate of religious identity importance that was on par with those students who actually attended. Those students who did not attend and did not misreport their attendance claimed a much lower level of religious identity importance.

To further dig into this identity-based cause, Brenner (forthcoming) conducted twenty-five cognitive interviews with survey respondents in Boston. Cognitive interviewing is a technique used by survey methodologists to evaluate a survey instrument to identify potentially difficult question wordings, unclear terminology, or any other problem that could introduce error (Willis 2004). Typically, the interviewer reads the survey question and then uses cognitive probes to help look inside the cognitive "black box" to understand how respondents interpret the question being asked and how they arrive at the answer they give. But in this particular study, Brenner used cognitive interviewing to try to discern the cause of measurement bias in a typical measure of church attendance. Respondents were first asked a series of conventional survey questions on religious behavior in a standardized survey interview. The interviewer recorded the respondent's answers before the cognitive interview began. Then, for each of the original questions, the interviewer reread the question, reminded the respondent of his or her answer, and used a standard probe to ask the respondent to verbalize how he or she chose the answer he or she gave. In about half of the cases, the respondent changed his or her answer as a result of the cognitive probe—and in every case of change, the modified report was lower than the original report.

Each of these interviews was reviewed and the narratives qualitatively analyzed. Four main themes emerged. Respondents expanded the definition of "religious services" to include other types of activities, like private prayer, Bible study, and other religious events and activities. Respondents also extended the reference period further back in time than was intended by the question. This form of telescoping[7] allowed respondents to report on religious activity during a period of time that they thought more closely matched their intended behavior or the "kind of person" they see themselves to be. Expansion of the reference period often operated in conjunction with situational constraints—the reasons that respondents were not able to perform behavior they had reported. Constraints ranged from attending school to transportation problems to employment issues. Finally, respondents reported that they felt pressure to attend religious services, and to report attendance, given the demands, real or imagined, of important others, both living and dead.

In these narratives, respondents made it clear that their original response to the survey question was closer to the "real truth" than their actual frequency of behavior constrained by the other demands of life. When respondents reflected on an idealized past, gave themselves credit for other nonservice activities, or adjusted their report for situational constraints, they were reflecting on *who they think they are*, which they believe to be a more accurate reflection of their true selves than what they did. Thus, these respondents are doing exactly what Hadaway et al. (1998) posit that survey respondents do in answering the church attendance question—they reflect on their religious identity rather than their actual religious behavior.

These findings lend support to the supposition that religious identity has a strong role to play in motivating religious behavior as well as in the biases that arise when measuring religious behavior. To further test this supposition, I return to the cognitive interview data to examine how respondents understand a survey question about religious identity importance and how it relates to religious behavior. I look at respondents' answers to cognitive probes aimed at understanding how they answer—what they think about in specific or generic memory to generate an answer, and the judgment process they use in weighing one response option (e.g., "very important") over another (e.g., "extremely important").

Probing Importance

In addition to cognitively testing the religious service attendance question, the religious importance question was also investigated. This question asked, "How important is religion in your life? Extremely important, very important, somewhat important, not too important or not at all important?" Cognitive probing of the respondents' answers started with, "Why did you choose the answer you did?"

In line with the supposition of Stryker and Serpe (1994), respondents commonly reflected on behavior, conflating identity salience and importance when answering this question. Some respondents mentioned relatively vague levels and types of behavior, referencing a sense of living religion throughout each day. Erica, a thirty-three-year-old member of the Church of Jesus Christ of Latter-day Saints, noted that the importance of religiosity is reflected in how enmeshed it is for her in her daily life: "It's like something I do every day basically, is live my religion." Monica, a thirty-four-year-old Catholic, sounded a similar note. She reported that her religious identity is "very important because for me personally it's, you know, I act on it, it's my life."

Anthony, a sixty-seven-year-old nondenominational Christian, offered more concrete examples for how an important religious identity manifests itself in behavior:

> If it's extremely important to you, then you should do everything the Bible says. You should be in church and you should be praying and you should be fellowshipping and you should be worshiping. It's extremely important to me because it's a way to live your life. That's what makes it extremely important.

Henrietta, a forty-one-year-old Baptist, offered comments that reflected on her religious behavior, but also distinguished between belief as her primary focus and behavior as a salutary effect of belief.

> I just—it's extremely important because religion is kind of, like, a—a guidance sort of. It's—it's a way to live, it's a way to act, it's the way to be. It doesn't *have to be* the whole structure of going to church and doing it, that's not religion to me. It's believing in something. Strongly enough that it changes your life, it changes how you think, it changes how you feel, it changes your actions, and so—that's it, for me.

Kathleen, a fifty-four-year-old Christian, also stressed the causal link between religious identity and behavior, although she switched their order. When the interviewer asked her to clarify why she chose "very important" rather than "extremely important," Kathleen responded, "Because I don't—maybe I don't practice it enough. And I think that the more I do it the more important it becomes for me."

Seth, a twenty-four-year-old Jehovah's Witness, noted that "[religion is] an action, it's a form of habits and—and rituals and different things you have to do to, you know, to heighten and experience that I'm religious." But when the interviewer asked why he chose "very important" rather than "extremely," Seth echoed Henrietta's comments about behavior being a side effect of belief, rather than the primary focus.

> Because I don't want to put myself in a—in a category where I say it's extremely important and—I'm not saying that it's not extremely important, but it's a part of my life. It's not my whole life, you know? So, you know, I think it's important that everybody should be aware that there is a greater power, there's a higher self, but at the same time, don't get so bogged down into the activities and—and more focus on your way of lifestyle. It's your lifestyle reflecting what you're teaching and what you're going to learn at these churches and it's your lifestyle reflecting that, or is it just lip service? It's just a way of impressing people, saying oh, look at—look at my big Bible. It's marked up and—you know?

Like Seth, other respondents commented on behavior being a secondary effect, although for the purposes of explaining their lack of religious behavior. Anna Maria, a forty-two-year-old Catholic, was one of the only respondents to report that her religious identity was "somewhat important." When probed why she chose "somewhat" rather than "very important," she explained,

> Because it is important, you know, I go by church, I do an Our Father, I was always brought up as a Catholic, and I wanted—I mean I just don't see any other religion for me. Because it, like, I'm not at church, like, every Sunday at seven a.m. or twelve in the afternoon. I'm not, like, at church every Saturday. I'm not, like, a holy roller. But it's—it's somewhat important, you know. I believe in God and, you know, I pray to God, but I'm not at the church every Sunday. But the priest still knows my name.

Vanessa, a fifty-year-old nondenominational Christian, somewhat differently reflected on her religious behavior, or lack thereof, when responding to the cognitive probe. "Even though I've gotten away from praying as much as I think I should, reading the Bible as much as I think I should, he's right here twenty-four/seven and infinite."

These comments that the importance of one's religious identity prescribes behavior (even if the individual fails to perform it) also rang true for other respondents in another way: by proscribing behavior. Noreen, a thirty-three-year-old Christian, responded to a question asking why she reported that her religious identity was "very important" with a comment on behavior: "I follow a certain path, I should say, so there's certain things that I wouldn't really do, when I think about it, that probably would not happen because of that. So it—it's—yeah it's a big influence on my decisions."

Willow, a twenty-four-year-old Catholic, outlined in much greater detail where the fine line between allowable and disallowable behavior was laid for her. In response to the interviewer's probe to expand on why she reported that religion is "extremely" important for her, Willow responded,

> Because almost everything that I do in my daily life, I have to look at—or I have to compare what the Bible says or what I have learned through religion in order for me to do it. For example, I love piercings. I would pierce any part of my body, but I would not put a tattoo because in the

> Bible, it says something about you're not supposed to put anything under your skin or something like that. So there are a lot of things that I—that's just an example. There are a lot of things the Bible talks about that I try not to do it in my daily life.

Other respondents drew limits on the extent to which the religious identity affects their life and behavior. Jillian, a forty-two-year-old Catholic, noted,

> I couldn't imagine life without it, again, it—it comforts me and—and—but I didn't go for the next one ["extremely important"] because it's not—it doesn't rule my life, it doesn't dictate how things are going to happen, you know what I mean? I don't follow it to the letter. I don't let it rule my life.

James, a fifty-year-old Catholic, neatly summed up the behavioral prescriptions and proscriptions, and his lack of will or ability to live up to them. He noted, "I consider myself a religious person, you know. Do I swear and drink? Yeah, I do. Maybe if I was a—if it was extremely important I wouldn't do those things."

James's brief comment makes two important points worth noting. First, he reemphasizes the link between the religious identity and behavior—that the importance of the religious identity makes demands on one's behavior, even if they go unmet. Second, he comments about people with higher religious identity importance than himself and says that they are more likely to more closely follow the behavioral prescriptions and proscriptions of their religion. Probes asked respondents why they chose the rating that they did, e.g., "very" rather than "extremely" or "somewhat." In response, a number of respondents commented that "extremely" was just that: extreme. Patricia, a thirty-year-old Baptist, noted that those who are extremely religious have nearly ascetic behavior:

> I guess extremely, to me, means, like, okay, praying constantly or for long periods of time, you go to church every week, you are, like, the perfect, you know, Christian, Buddhist, whatever, like, you know, you don't drink, smoke, swear, none of that, you know. I feel like if it was extremely, I would definitely be a lot more strict.

Other respondents were somewhat less charitable in their characterization of an individual with an extremely important religious identity:

> I think extremely is too—almost saying perfection, and perfection is a touchy thing. And I think just "very important" is satisfactory. (Bernard, fifty-two, Catholic)

> I'm not a fanatic, so I wouldn't say—I wouldn't say "extremely." That sounds fanatic. (Noreen, thirty-three, Christian)

> Well, I'm not a radical, so therefore I don't like extremes. (Sharon, sixty-seven, Christian)

Respondents, all from the Boston area, may have an understanding influenced by the relative irreligion of the region. However, even outside New England, it may be easy to understand their motivation to distance themselves from the religiously "extreme." Examples of individuals who claim a high level of religiosity but act in a way that is counter to religious tenets are easy to recall. Respondents may have considered relatively minor moral infractions of religious politicians (e.g., David Vitter, Mark Sanford) or grievous acts of violence, ostensibly in the name of religion (e.g., the World Trade Center bombing). Regardless of their mental comparator, many respondents were careful to distance themselves from being seen as extremely religious.

The important thing for studies of religious identity and its effect on measurement is that respondents reflected on behavior when asked about identity. Moreover, they explicitly discussed this connection when discussing why they reported the level of importance they did. In combination with previously discussed findings from these data linking identity to overreporting (Brenner, forthcoming), these narratives help us understand a relatively simple fact that creates a difficult problem: respondents do not necessarily answer the question we think we are asking.

Discussion and Conclusion

The goal of this research program is a better, more complete understanding of the sources of measurement bias in survey reports of religious behavior, including, but importantly not limited to, religious service attendance. While the measurement and mismeasurement of attendance is a substantive subject of study in its own right, the focus on attendance is also a pragmatic one given various measurement features that make it a practical choice for study. Unlike other behaviors, affiliations, and beliefs, it is potentially verifiable and performed with a regularity and frequency that make it a good measurement choice.

Rigorous investigation of the phenomenon of overreporting of church attendance by Hadaway et al. (1993, 1998) and others has established the reality of the phenomenon: positive systematic variation in survey estimates of attendance from actual rates of attendance. This work suggested, but did not test, a cause based in the survey respondent's religious identity. More recent work by Brenner (2011b, 2012b, 2014) focused on establishing both why overreporting occurs and what it means. This chapter synthesizes and builds on this recent work, focusing on how respondents interpret and answer the religious service attendance question, what their answers—which may include measurement bias—mean, and, finally, how we may use and improve these measures.

A better understanding of the source of this measurement bias will help us to predict where and when it, and perhaps other similar measurement biases, will emerge. The importance placed on religion in American society suggests that overreporting will be significant and consistent in the United States, whereas the relative irreligion in many countries in Europe suggests that overreporting will be negligible or nonexistent in European surveys—with Canada falling somewhere in the middle of these two extremes. Research findings (Brenner 2011b) have supported this conjecture. Moving from a macro- to a micro-level approach, analyses focusing on predicting overreporting at the respondent level have found that religious identity importance can be a powerful predictor of this form of measurement bias (Brenner 2011a, 2012b).

Moreover, this identity-based understanding of measurement bias will help us understand how and when to use the church attendance measure appropriately. While overreporting biases marginal statistics, skewing our view of population-level rates and change, it does not appear to affect some of the most common and important uses of the church attendance question. The attendance measure may still be valid if used as a general control for religiosity. If respondents are treating the church attendance question as a measure of religious identity, then using an attendance variable to "control" for religiosity in a general or generalized linear model and their extensions may still be appropriate. For example, using a measure of religious service attendance to predict intention to vote, actual turnout, or preference for one candidate over another may be appropriate as long as researchers do not assume that the attendance measure is a valid, unbiased measure of actual attendance but rather understand the measure within these limitations. While other measures of religious identity may be preferable, many surveys contain few measures of religiosity and religious behavior, and attendance is one of the most common. Thus, as long as research uses this measure as an indicator of religiosity in general, it may be defensible.

Note, however, that the growth in the unaffiliated may alter this relationship. The percentage of Americans claiming no religious affiliation ("nones") has increased dramatically in the past four decades, from about 2 percent in the 1950s to about 8 percent in the 1980s (Glenn 1987), and from 14 percent in the 1990s (Hout and Fisher 2002) to nearly a quarter of Americans today (Hout and Fisher 2014; Pew 2015b). It is possible that this remarkable change in religious affiliation could soon alter how many respondents answer the attendance question. If the increase in the percentage of unaffiliated leads to reduced claims of attendance, the smaller pool of self-reported attenders may change (perhaps more religious and more religiously conservative).

But more than just predicting where measurement biases affecting attendance and religious measures will emerge and how to cope with them, this work may help us to develop techniques to prevent these biases from occurring in the first place. This research is needed as conventional understandings based in question sensitivity, social desirability, and impression management have failed to yield solutions. The typical solution to combat social desirability biases, moving to a self-administered mode like a web or mail survey, does not alter the way respondents report on their church attendance or other religious behaviors (Pew 2015a). Revising question wording to invite reports of nonattendance has also failed to reduce overreporting and in some cases made the problem worse, increasing the self-reported rate of attendance (DeBell and Figueroa 2011).

Instead, an understanding rooted in identity offers a better and more complete explanation. The respondent hears the question about religious behavior and reflects, not only on current behavior but also on his or her identity as a religious person. The more important the respondent's religious identity, the more likely s/he is to reflect on an idealized conceptualization of his or her religious behavior, such as a time when s/he believes s/he lived up to this idealized self-view, a rate of intended behavior that exceeds his or her actual rate of religious behavior, or the like. The respondent has a strong desire to report behavior concordant with who s/he sees himself or herself to be without the constraints that may prevent quotidian religious behavior. In essence, respondents alter the question about behavior to one about identity: "What do you do?" becomes "What kind of person are you?"

The primary solution to this problem has been to avoid direct survey questions. Presser and Stinson (1998) and Brenner and DeLamater (2013, 2014, 2016) demonstrate the efficacy of chronological measurement. Calendrical and other chronologically based approaches—e.g., time diaries, ecological momentary assessment/experience sampling, event history calendars—may allow sociologists and survey researchers to measure normative behaviors, like church attendance and perhaps other religious behaviors, without the identity-rooted bias that affects conventional direct survey questions. By eschewing a direct question that focuses the respondent's attention on the focal behavior, these measurement techniques can help us to avoid the biasing effect of identity.

Unfortunately, these techniques can be much more time-consuming and expensive than conventional survey questionnaires. In a time of abysmally low rates of success for grant applications and shrinking budgets for those social scientists lucky enough to be awarded funding, these techniques may be out of reach for most researchers and studies. Moreover, they may not be appropriate for use as a criterion measure for comparison with every religious behavior, especially those that are infrequently or irregularly performed or are very brief in their duration (e.g., prayer in many Christian religious traditions). What is needed is essentially a unicorn—a version of the standard direct survey question that avoids the biasing effect of identity. Is such a question even possible? Honestly, it is unclear—but that will not stop those of us in the field, survey researchers and sociologists of religion alike, from trying.

Church attendance is probably not the only survey measure affected by measurement bias. Other measures of religiosity, including other religious behaviors like prayer, affiliation, belief in God, and the like, may also be overreported although research has not pursued these given the difficulty or even impossibility of validating them. Prayer, for instance, is potentially verifiable, but not universally so. Because Christian prayer may be performed erratically, the only research study validating survey reports of prayer used data from three predominantly Muslim countries: Pakistan, Palestine, and Turkey. The study found overreporting of prayer in all three countries, although more consistently for women than for men (Brenner 2014). But shifting from a validation study of behaviors like attendance and prayer to one in which we attempt to validate beliefs and identities presents a tricky methodological problem. Validating a claim of belief in God, or some other tenet of faith, would be difficult indeed. Either in light or in spite of these difficulties, the validation of other measures of religiosity is clearly a potential focus of future research.

While the primary and relatively straightforward (if difficult to achieve) goal of this research program is the creation of the perfect survey measure of religious service attendance, as well as the improvement of other religious measures (and those of other normative behaviors), this research program has a parallel purpose. Investigating the cause of overreporting of religious behavior is important as a substantive topic on its own. As Howard Schuman wrote, understanding survey artifacts allows us to understand ourselves (1982). Religious respondents are not making a simple mistake (or, more technically, a random or stochastic error). Their overreports are systematic: their reports include bias. And like most forms of measurement bias, these overreports are meaningful. Respondents may not be telling us about their actual behavior with veracity and validity, but they are telling us about how they see themselves. Moreover, as we view these reports and their biases over time and in the context of our changing society, not only can we see how our behavior has or has not changed; we can also see how we have changed the way we see ourselves, and what we see is important. With such a perspective, bias too can yield insight.

NOTES

1 LifeWay Research, "Most Churchgoers Won't Skip Church for Football," factsandtrends.net, 2015.

2 Cathy Lynn Grossman, "Religion Survey Babble Confuses 103% of Readers: Here's Why," *Religious News Service*, November 18, 2014.

3 Prayer in Islam is different—highly routinized, occurring frequently at regular intervals. Thus, for Muslims, prayer is arguably a better behavior for potential verification (Brenner 2014).
4 Presser and Stinson were estimating the rate of overreporting for the adult population of the United States.
5 Subsequent work by Rossi and Scappini (2012) has found evidence for an overreport in Italy as well.
6 Brenner used "importance" as a synonym for the concept of identity prominence discussed earlier.
7 Telescoping is a phenomenon in survey responding in which respondents report on a salient activity or occasion that happened before the intended reference period.

REFERENCES

Asencio, Emily K., and Peter J. Burke. 2011. "Does Incarceration Change the Criminal Identity? A Synthesis of Labeling and Identity Theory Perspectives on Identity Change." *Sociological Perspectives* 54: 163–82.

Brenner, Philip S. 2011a. "Exceptional Behavior or Exceptional Identity? Overreporting of Church Attendance in the U.S." *Public Opinion Quarterly* 75(1): 19–41.

Brenner, Philip S. 2011b. "Identity Importance and the Overreporting of Religious Service Attendance: Multiple Imputation of Religious Attendance Using American Time Use Study and the General Social Survey." *Journal for the Scientific Study of Religion* 50(1): 103–15.

Brenner, Philip S. 2012a. "Identity as a Determinant of the Overreporting of Church Attendance in Canada." *Journal for the Scientific Study of Religion* 51(2): 377–85.

Brenner, Philip S. 2012b. "Investigating the Effect of Bias in Survey Measures of Church Attendance." *Sociology of Religion* 73(4): 361–83.

Brenner, Philip S. 2014. "Testing the Veracity of Self-Reported Religious Behavior in the Muslim World." *Social Forces* 92(3): 1009–37

Brenner, Philip S. 2016. "Cross-National Trends in Religious Service Attendance." *Public Opinion Quarterly* 80(2): 563–83.

Brenner, Philip S. Forthcoming. "Narratives of Error from Cognitive Interviews of Survey Questions about Normative Behavior." *Sociological Methods & Research.* doi: 10.1177/0049124115605331.

Brenner, Philip S., and John DeLamater. 2013. "Predictive Validity of Paradata on Reports of Physical Exercise: Evidence from a Time Use Study Using Text Messaging." *Electronic International Journal of Time Use Research* 10(1): 38–54.

Brenner, Philip S., and John DeLamater. 2014. "Social Desirability Bias in Self-Reports of Physical Activity: Is an Exercise Identity the Culprit?" *Social Indicators Research* 117(2): 489–504.

Brenner, Philip S., and John DeLamater. 2016. "Measurement Directiveness as a Cause of Response Bias: Evidence from Two Survey Experiments." *Sociological Methods & Research* 45(2): 348–71.

Brenner, Philip S., Richard T. Serpe, and Sheldon Stryker. 2014. "The Causal Ordering of Prominence and Salience in Identity Theory: An Empirical Examination." *Social Psychology Quarterly* 77: 231–52.

Burke, Peter J. 1980. "The Self: Measurement Implications from a Symbolic Interactionist Perspective." *Social Psychology Quarterly* 43: 18–29.

Caplow, Theodore. 1998. "The Case of the Phantom Episcopalians." *American Sociological Review* 63: 112–13.

Chaves, Mark. 2010. "Rain Dances in the Dry Season: Overcoming the Religious Congruence Fallacy." *Journal for the Scientific Study of Religion* 49: 1–14.

Chaves, Mark. 2011. *American Religion: Contemporary Trends*. Princeton, NJ: Princeton University Press.

Chaves, Mark, and James C. Cavendish. 1994. "More Evidence on U.S. Catholic Church Attendance." *Journal for the Sociology of Religion* 33: 376–81.

DeBell, Matthew, and Lucila Figueroa. 2011. "Results of a Survey Experiment on Frequency Reporting: Religious Service Attendance from the 2010 ANES Panel Recontact Survey." Paper presented at the Sixty-sixth Annual Conference of the American Association for Public Opinion Research, Phoenix, AZ.

Demerath, N. J., III. 1998. "Excepting Exceptionalism: American Religion in Comparative Relief." *Annals of the American Academy of Political and Social Science: Americans and Religions in the Twenty-First Century* 558: 28–39.

Durkheim, Emile. 1995 [1915]. *Elementary Forms of Religious Life*. New York: Free Press.

Ervin, Laurie H., and Sheldon Stryker. 2001. "Theorizing the Relationship Between Self-Esteem and Identity." Pp. 29–55 in *Extending Self-Esteem Theory and Research: Sociological and Psychological Currents*, edited by T. J. Owens, S. Stryker, and N. Goodman. New York: Cambridge.

Finke, Roger, Christopher D. Bader, and Edward C. Polson. 2010. "Faithful Measures: Developing Improved Measures of Religion." ARDA Guiding Paper Series. State College, PA: Association of Religion Data Archives at Pennsylvania State University, www.theARDA.com

Firebaugh, Glenn. 1998. "A Symposium on Church Attendance in the United States: Editor's Note." *American Sociological Review* 63: 111.

Gelman, Andrew, Gary King, and Chuanhai Liu. 1998. "Not Asked and Not Answered: Multiple Imputation for Multiple Surveys." *Journal of the American Statistical Association* 93: 846–57.

Glenn, Norval D. 1987. "The Trend in 'No Religion' Respondents to U.S. National Surveys, Late 1950s to Early 1980s." *Public Opinion Quarterly* 51(3): 293–314.

Hadaway, C. Kirk, Penny Long Marler, and Mark Chaves. 1993. "What the Polls Don't Show: A Closer Look at U.S. Church Attendance." *American Sociological Review* 58: 741–52.

Hadaway, C. Kirk, Penny Long Marler, and Mark Chaves. 1998. "Overreporting Church Attendance in America: Evidence That Demands the Same Verdict." *American Sociological Review* 63: 122–30.

Hout, Michael, and Claude S. Fischer. 2002. "Why More Americans Have No Religious Preference: Politics and Generations." *American Sociological Review* 67: 165–90.

Hout, Michael, and Claude S. Fischer. 2014. "Explaining Why More Americans Have No Religious Preference: Political Backlash and Generational Succession, 1987–2012." *Sociological Science* 1: 423–47. doi: 10.15195/v1.a24.

Hout, Michael, and Andrew M. Greeley. 1998. "What Church Officials' Reports Don't Show: Another Look at Church Attendance Data." *American Sociological Review* 63:113–19.

Joas, Hans. 2009. "The Religious Situation in the United States." Pp. 317–34 in *What the World Believes: Analysis and Commentary on the Religion Monitor 2008*, edited by M. Reiger. Gütersloh, Germany: Bertelsmann.

Kreuter, Frauke, Stanley Presser, and Roger Tourangeau. 2008. "Social Desirability Bias in CATI, IVR, and Web Surveys: The Effects of Mode and Question Sensitivity." *Public Opinion Quarterly* 72: 847–65.

Marcum, John P. 1999. "Measuring Church Attendance: A Further Look." *Review of Religious Research* 41: 122–30.

Marler, Penny Long, and C. Kirk Hadaway. 1999. "Testing the Attendance Gap in a Conservative Church." *Sociology of Religion* 60: 175–86.

McCall, George. 2003. "The Me and the Not-Me: Positive and Negative Poles of Identity." Pp. 11–26 in *Advances in Identity Theory and Research*, edited by P. J. Burke, T. J. Owens, R. T. Serpe, and P. A. Thoits. New York: Kluwer.

McCall, George J., and J. L. Simmons. 1978. *Identities and Interactions: An Examination of Human Associations in Everyday Life*. New York: Free Press.

Pew Research Center. 2015a. "From Telephone to the Web: The Challenge of Mode of Interview Effects in Public Opinion Polls." Accessed May 21, 2015, www.pewresearch.org.

Pew Research Center. 2015b. "U.S. Public Becoming Less Religious." Accessed December 1, 2015, www.pewforum.org.

Presser, Stanley, and Mark Chaves. 2007. "Is Religious Service Attendance Declining?" *Journal for the Scientific Study of Religion* 46: 417–23.

Presser, Stanley, and Linda Stinson. 1998. "Data Collection Mode and Social Desirability Bias in Self-Reported Religious Attendance." *American Sociological Review* 63: 137–45.

Rendall, Michael S., Bonnie Ghosh-Dastidar, Margaret M. Weden, Elizabeth H. Baker, and Zafar Nazarov. 2013. "Multiple Imputation for Combined-Survey Estimation with Incomplete Regressors in One but Not Both Surveys." *Sociological Methods and Research* 42: 483–530.

Rosenberg, Morris. 1979. *Conceiving the Self*. New York: Basic.

Rosenberg, Morris, and B. Claire McCullough. 1981. "Mattering: Inferred Significance and Mental Health." *Research in Community and Mental Health* 2: 163–82.

Rossi, Maurizio, and Ettore Scappini. 2012. "How Should Mass Attendance Be Measured? An Italian Case Study." *Quality and Quantity* 46: 1897–1916.

Schuman, Howard. 1982. "Artifacts Are in the Eye of the Beholder." *American Sociologist* 17: 21–28.

Stryker, Sheldon. 1980. *Symbolic Interactionism: A Social Structural Version.* Caldwell, NJ: Blackburn.

Stryker, Sheldon, and Richard T. Serpe. 1994. "Identity Salience and Psychological Centrality: Equivalent, Overlapping, or Complementary Concepts?" *Social Psychology Quarterly* 57: 16–35.

Tocqueville, Alexis de. 2002. *Democracy in America.* Chicago: University of Chicago Press.

Tourangeau, Roger, and Ting Yan. 2007. "Sensitive Questions in Surveys." *Psychological Bulletin* 133: 859–83.

Voas, David, and Mark Chaves. 2016. "Is the United States a Counterexample to the Secularization Thesis?" *American Journal of Sociology* 121: 1517–56.

Willis, Gordon B. 2004. *Cognitive Interviewing: A Tool for Improving Questionnaire Design.* Thousand Oaks, CA: Sage.

Woodberry, Robert D. 1998. "When Surveys Lie and People Tell the Truth: How Surveys Oversample Church Attenders." *American Sociological Review* 63: 119–22.

2.

Measurement Tools and Issues in the Psychology of Religion and Spirituality

PETER C. HILL AND KENNETH I. PARGAMENT

Measurement Tools and Issues in the Psychology of Religion and Spirituality

In the name of gaining scientific legitimacy, psychologists of religion have long been intentional in developing sound scientific measures of religiousness and spirituality, to the point that Gorsuch (1984) declared in a seminal *American Psychologist* article over three decades ago that the dominant paradigm in the psychology of religion was one of measurement. The focus on measurement in the psychology of religion is a *boon*, Gorsuch (1984) argued, in that it helps establish scientific credibility and provides an infrastructure that will move the field forward. But, Gorsuch warned, it could also be a *bane* to the field's progression by directing research efforts away from more substantive and theoretically driven issues.

Despite this strong emphasis on measurement from *within* the psychology of religion field, psychology from *without* has, until recently, demonstrated little enthusiasm toward the study of religion or spirituality. In 2003 we suggested that the tendency to keep religion and spirituality at arm's length was greatly hindering the ability to study the whole of human experience (Hill and Pargament 2003). We documented the extent to which religion and spirituality were understudied variables in psychology and related disciplines such as psychiatry and gerontology. This neglect, we proposed, was curious given what was then a small but emerging literature demonstrating the importance of religion and spirituality to both physical and mental health (e.g., Koenig, McCullough, and Larson 2001). Furthermore, we pointed out that religion, especially when viewed as a variable in relation to some other domain of interest (such as health) and not as the primary object of study in itself, has often been treated as an add-on variable to other research questions, resulting in the utilization of brief and imprecise measures such as church attendance, denominational affiliation, or single-item self-ratings of religiousness and spirituality that are limited in terms of reliability and validity. We made the case that advances in measuring the complexity of religion and spirituality are necessary to move the field forward.

Indeed, the complexity of religion and spirituality has been increasingly acknowledged by researchers, and this has resulted in many new measures that have been developed since the publication of Hill and Hood's (1999) compendium of 125 scales. Our purpose here is to selectively review some of the more promising measures that represent a number of centrally important domains in the psychology of religion and spirituality. Before delving into specific matters of measurement, however, we wish to clarify how the terms "religion" and "spirituality" are used in this chapter.

We will use both the terms "religion" (or "religiousness") and "spirituality" in this chapter. Our choice of terms will depend largely on the particular construct that represents the focus of measurement. When discussing specific measures, we will utilize the term that the developer(s) of the scale used. However, in so doing, we recognize that there has been considerable discussion in the literature surrounding the two terms. Both of us have been involved in this discussion (Pargament 1997, 1999; Hill et al. 2000), and our own usage of the terms in this chapter will utilize the guidelines recommended by Pargament, Mahoney, Exline, Jones, and Shafranske (2013). Therefore, we will use

> *the language of religion* when emphasizing (a) the search for significant psychological, social, or physical destinations within established institutional contexts designed to facilitate spirituality; or (b) beliefs, practices, experiences, or relationships that are embedded within established institutional contexts designed to facilitate spirituality. (pp. 16–17; emphasis in original)

We will use

> *the language of spirituality* when emphasizing (a) the search for the sacred; or (b) sacred beliefs, practices, experiences, or relationships that are embedded in nontraditional contexts. (p. 17; emphasis in original)

We also concur with Pargament et al. (2013) that the language of both religion and spirituality can be used "inclusively in a nonpolarized fashion" since the two "are neither independent nor opposed to each other" (p. 17). This will occur when the search for significance involves a full range of significant destinations and experiences (including beliefs, practices, and relationships) that can be embedded and facilitated within both traditional and nontraditional contexts.

Furthermore, it is important to note that the measures reviewed here are almost exclusively self-report measures, the limitations of which are well known and, as noted by Jong, Zahl, and Sharp (this volume), fall into two broad categories: (1) an intentional or strategic misrepresentation motivated by social desirability; and (2) an inability to fully access and accurately report cognitive elements, especially attitudes. There have been in the past two decades extensive efforts, largely theoretically driven by the social mind's dual processes of implicit and explicit knowledge (see Sherman, Gawronski, and Trope 2014), to develop implicit measures of social cognition that attempt to assess what the intentional mind is either unable to introspect or unwilling to report with honesty (either to others or to oneself). The application of implicit measures to the psychology of religion is the focus of the chapter in this volume by Jong et al., so the reader is directed to that chapter if interested. However, because of practical limitations in conducting research, self-report measures will continue to be foremost in the arsenal of measurement tools.

Here is the plan for this chapter. We will first discuss some general measurement issues in terms of three criteria as they apply to the psychology of religion and spirituality. We will then distinguish between substantive and functional measures of religion and spirituality and will discuss examples of measures that fit within common categories of each type. Following a brief section whereby we consider future measurement challenges and opportunities, we conclude this chapter by considering the implications for measurement in light of five integrative themes recommended for the field of the psychology of religion and spirituality as a whole.

General Issues Related to Measurement

Measurement challenges, especially those inherent to self-reports, in the psychology of religion and spirituality are no different than those found in virtually any domain in psychology. There are, however, unique aspects of religious and spiritual experience that may clarify the criteria for a good measure. Here we briefly consider three general measurement issues as they apply to the psychology of religion: theoretical considerations, psychometric issues, and sample representativeness.

Theoretical Considerations

A primary "bane" of the measurement paradigm was the lack of a sound theoretical grounding to many of the concepts being measured (Gorsuch 1984). In general, research programs are not well maintained without well-defined conceptual frameworks. In fact, the lack of overall broad theoretical frameworks in the field is a major underlying reason why the field is so fragmented today (Pargament et al. 2013). Even the single most influential theoretical framework in the psychology of religion, Allport's (1950) distinction between intrinsic and extrinsic religious orientation, became prematurely enmeshed in measurement issues to the point that researchers lost sight of its theoretical foundation (Kirkpatrick and Hood 1990).

The emergence of systematic research programs that are well grounded in conceptual and theoretical terms is most noted in understanding the *functional* aspects of religion and spirituality. The term "functional" refers to the way religion or spirituality operates in the life of an individual. Examples in the psychology of religion and spirituality literature include attachment processes (Granqvist and Kirkpatrick 2004, 2013; Kirkpatrick 2005) and religious coping (Pargament 1997, 2007). As expected, measures grounded in good theory tend to be among the most robust measures in the psychology of religion and spirituality, and it is in such domains that scientific progress is most easily observed.

However, theoretical clarity also requires serious attention to the *substantive* aspects of religion and spirituality, and it is here that the field's conceptualization and measurement, especially beyond Protestant

Christianity, has somewhat lagged. The term "substantive" refers to the specific beliefs, experiences, and practices that comprise one's religiousness or spirituality. Creating measures that are as generalizable as possible is indeed a desirable goal; however, as objects of study, religion and spirituality are often formed and maintained within a particular social and cultural context. Thus, the specific substantive aspects of *what* a person believes or practices should also be taken into account.

This concern about the neglect of religion and spirituality's substance is especially relevant to the preferential pull of many to study spirituality free of any religious context. The tendency to conceptualize spirituality in such broad terms—such that it forfeits many distinguishing characteristics and is assessed, for example, only by indicators of good mental health or character (e.g., meaning or purpose in life, general well-being, forgiveness)—will result in "meaningless and tautological" (Koenig 2008:349) correlations between measures of spirituality and measures of mental health. Thus, for example, to define spirituality simply as "finding meaning" in life is to strip spirituality of its unique characteristics and does not advance the field. To investigate the uniqueness of religious or spiritual meaning requires a conceptualization and measure of how one finds meaning as part of a search for significance in relation to what one perceives as sacred (Hill et al. 2000; Pargament 1997). Finding meaning in life is a process that is important to psychological makeup, but it should not, in and of itself, be called "spirituality" unless the substance of the meaning making is uniquely religious or spiritual in nature.

We cannot stress enough the importance of theoretical clarity for good measurement. This is true not only for scale development but also for research to which the measure is applied. Not only should the focal research concept be well represented in the measure, but the conceptual framework used to design the measure should be compatible with the research at hand.

Psychometric Considerations

Measurement in the psychology of religion and spirituality must meet acceptable scientific standards in terms of two basic psychometric considerations: reliability and validity. Reliability, the extent to which a scale is consistent in its measurement, is most frequently assessed via

Cronbach's *alpha* (α) as an indicator of the degree of internal consistency (i.e., the extent to which the scale's items are measuring the same thing). Less frequently used indicators of reliability measure consistency over time (*test-retest* reliability, frequently around one to two weeks apart).

A scale's *construct validity* is the extent to which a scale actually measures what it is intended to measure. Construct validity is especially important in a field involving complex phenomena such as religion and spirituality. Construct validity in the psychology of religion and spirituality utilizes virtually all common forms of validity: the correlation between a given scale and some other standard or measure of the construct (*criterion validity*), the degree to which a given scale includes all the facets of the construct (*content validity*), the extent to which a given scale correlates with measures of related constructs (*convergent validity*), and the degree to which a given scale is not correlated with measures from which it should be independent (*discriminant validity*).

As already noted, a scale that is well grounded in theory is more likely to be reliable and valid across samples representing different populations. After reviewing the literature, Hill (2013) proposed that measures demonstrating internal consistency reliability above .70 in at least two studies can be considered reliable measures in the psychology of religion and spirituality. He also recommended that significant correlations across multiple samples on at least two types of validity be enough to consider the measure as valid.

Sample Representativeness

In 2003 we pointed out that we know much about religiousness and spirituality but only if we limit our population to young, college-educated, middle-class European American individuals within a Judeo-Christian heritage (Hill and Pargament 2003). This is not to say that researchers should avoid conducting research (or developing new measures) on Western Christians or other well-studied religious groups. Important research questions still remain. However, what was a serious limitation in 2003 is rapidly changing as we have increasing access to culturally and religiously diverse populations. The key challenge is to determine the extent to which our current measures, largely based upon a Western Christian population, can or should be applied to other populations.

Sometimes measures initially created and tested within a singular cultural setting have been used successfully in other cultures (e.g., Ai, Peterson, and Huang 2003). However, the appropriateness of measures across various cultures and religious traditions should not be assumed. At the very least, researchers should demonstrate cultural sensitivity in making this call.

There are clearly some cases where scales, or at least individual items within scales, are inappropriate because they are designed to measure specific content within a religious tradition (e.g., belief in the divinity of Christ) or use terms that are religiously designated (e.g., "mosque," "church," "nirvana"). However, beyond such obvious needs for revision, there may be subtle implicit assumptions underlying a measure that might make it inappropriate for use beyond a specific religious tradition. Even Allport's (1950) longstanding intrinsic-extrinsic concept and subsequent scale (Allport and Ross 1967) of what he believed to be a measure of a mature religious sentiment (which is perhaps the single most influential theory in the psychology of religion to date) was subject to an individualist Protestant bias and is therefore less applicable even to American Catholics and Jews (Cohen and Hill 2007). A single definition or measure of religiousness or spirituality that is independent of its cultural or religious context may be misleading, at best.

Consider, for example, the care involved in creating the Chinese version of Underwood and Teresi's (2002) sixteen-item Daily Spiritual Experiences Scale (DSES) (Ng, Fong, Tsui, Au-Yeung, and Law 2009):

> While finding that all 16 items . . . make sense and are common spiritual experiences to Chinese, the team encountered problems with the term "God." In Chinese, "God" can be a "humanized" or "philosophical" higher power. Confucianism, Buddhism, and Daoism, all have religious ritual toward "humanized Gods." On the other hand, the term "God" can refer to spiritual transcendence, such as the notions of selfless social responsibility in Confucianism, enlightenment in Buddhism, and "merging with the way of nature" in Daoism. As such, the concept "God" had to be expanded to embrace both humanized and philosophical higher power in Chinese translation. To take care of this point, the team added an explanatory note to the term "God" while keeping the word "God" in translating the 16 items into Chinese. (pp. 92–93)

Such efforts demonstrate the care necessary in making a successful application of a measure to a different culture (see Ghorbani, Watson, and Khan 2007).

We recommend an indigenous approach to religious and spiritual measurement when conducting research in a culture different than the Judeo-Christian West. This will require an understanding of the religious and spiritual beliefs, experiences, and practices from *within* the culture to fully understand the phenomenon of interest (Cohen 2009). Only then can one make a careful and informed decision as to whether the underlying construct and its measure should be used, perhaps with some pilot testing. Many investigators have used this exact approach, and throughout this chapter we will identify several measures that have been developed for use beyond the Judeo-Christian tradition.

An indigenous approach should be considered not only in relation to broad cultural differences but also with regard to specific religious and spiritual groupings, whether traditional or not, that vary within a given culture. In this sense, as Cohen (2009) points out, religion and spirituality are in themselves cultural variables. An indigenous approach will value the substance of a tradition's beliefs, values, and practices, and it is to that point that we first turn our attention in our review of specific measures of religion and spirituality.

Substantive Measures of Religiousness and Spirituality

We will briefly review some representative measures of what is currently available by making a distinction between substantive and functional approaches to the study of religiousness and spirituality. We will first review measures that focus on religious or spiritual beliefs, behavioral tendencies, and practices—the substance of one's faith. We will then look at measures of how religious and spiritual activities and characteristics function in the lives of individuals. Some measures could be described in either category; substance and function are not independent of each other. This is a selective review that is far from exhaustive. The reader is directed to Hill (2013), Hill and Edwards (2013), and Hill and Hood (1999) for a more thorough listing and discussion of measures that have been established in the field. All of the measures reviewed here meet or surpass Hill's (2013) criteria of "good" measures in terms of theoretical grounding, sample representativeness, reliability, and validity. Furthermore, all of these measures have at least some track record of use in subsequent research, thus further establishing scale validity and generalization.

General Religiousness or Spirituality

Piedmont's (1999) notion of *spiritual transcendence* as "the capacity of individuals to stand outside of their immediate sense of time and place to view life from a larger, more objective perspective" (1999:988) is the strongest claim that spirituality could be considered a dimension of personality, even a sixth factor comparable to the other factors in the Five Factor Model (McCrae and Costa 2008). He has developed the three-factor (Universality, Prayer Fulfillment, and Connectedness), twenty-four-item Spiritual Transcendence Scale, which assesses individuals' search for a connection with the sacred. The scale is able to uniquely predict a number of psychological outcomes (e.g., positive affect, prosocial behavior, interpersonal orientation, perceived social support, vulnerability to stress, internal health locus of control) beyond the Five-Factor Model of Personality. The scale has been validated for cross-cultural use (Rican and Janosova 2010), including such contexts as the Philippines (Piedmont 2007) and India (Piedmont and Leach 2002).

Paloutzian and Ellison's (1982) twenty-item Spiritual Well-Being Scale (SWBS; also see Ellison 1983) has been one of the most widely used measures of spirituality over the last three decades. Developed to assess a need for transcendence, the SWBS provides an overall spiritual well-being score and scores on two subscales that moderately correlate with each other: Religious (RWB) and Existential (EWB). It should be noted, however, that the EWB subscale is confounded with general well-being and the RWB subscale is subject to ceiling effects among Christian respondents (Genia 2001).

Yet another dispositional measure is Hood's (1975) thirty-two-item scale of mysticism. Mysticism reflects intense spiritual experiences and felt connection or unity with either the outside world, something beyond oneself (be it God, Ultimate Reality, or some other transcendent notion), or "nothingness" (Stace 1960). According to Hood, the twenty-item first factor is the "single core" of mystical experience—"an indicator of intense experience [with unity], not interpreted religiously and not necessarily positive" (p. 34). The twelve-item second factor was conceived by Hood as "an indicator of a joyful expression of more traditionally defined religious experiences which may or may not be mystical but which are interpreted to indicate a firm source of objective knowledge" (p. 34).

Religious or Spiritual Commitment

Among measures of religious commitment meeting our criteria is the ten-item Religious Commitment Inventory (RCI-10; Worthington et al. 2003). This carefully developed instrument is highly recommended for researchers on several counts: solid psychometric qualities, brevity, and potential use in non-Christian traditions. The measure has been tested on both Christian samples and sizable samples of Hindus, Muslims, and Buddhists. The scale's two factors (intrapersonal and interpersonal) are highly correlated and thus the measure may be most useful as a full-scale assessment.

Plante and Boccaccini's (1997) ten-item Santa Clara Strength of Religious Faith Questionnaire (SCSRFQ) is worth consideration for populations where the term "faith" is appropriate. A short five-item version of the scale was later developed (SCSFQ-SF; Plante, Vallaeys, Sherman, and Wallston 2002) with similarly strong psychometric properties.

Beliefs/Religious Preferences

Many scales, especially those developed prior to the 1980s, have focused on religious beliefs. Our review here is brief and selective since most of these measures were more thoroughly reviewed in the Hill and Hood (1999) volume.

Most measures of Christian religious orthodoxy have strong psychometric qualities. One example is Fullerton and Hunsberger's (1982) twenty-four-item Christian Orthodoxy (CO) Scale. A short version of the scale has also been published (Hunsberger 1989). Other scales assessing belief in traditional Christian teachings include Brown and Lowe's (1951) Inventory of Religious Belief as well as Stellway's (1973) seven-item Christian Conservatism Scale and six-item Christian Liberalism Scale.

With the exception of Islam, few measures of religious belief outside of Christianity have been established. Emavardhana and Tori (1997) developed the eleven-item Buddhist Beliefs and Practices Scale, which assesses the importance of Buddhist teachings, the observation of the five precepts of Buddhism, the affirmation of the theory of karma and rebirth as well as the doctrine of *anatta* (the lack of souls), and the practice of meditation. Ji and Ibrahim's (2007) Islamic Doctrinal Orthodoxy Scale is one of several recently developed scales within Islam, many of which measure religious beliefs (see Abu-Raiya and Hill 2014). This eight-item scale demonstrates excellent psychometric properties grouped into two factors: a three-item Cognitive-Abstract Orthodoxy factor (sample item: "I believe there is no other God but Allah") and a five-item Ritualistic-Judgmental Orthodoxy factor (sample item: "Salah is crucial to the life of a Muslim").

Relational Measures: God Concept, God Image, Attachment to God

A relational theoretical framework works especially well for understanding religious or spiritual experiences within a monotheistic orientation. Such measures may assess cognitive understanding or beliefs regarding God's attributes or characteristics (e.g., God concept scales), emotional or experiential understandings of God (e.g., God image scales), or underlying interactional dynamics (e.g., attachment to God scales). Indeed, the distinction between a substantive and functional religiousness or spirituality is somewhat blurred in that these relational constructs and measures can be used to identify not only the substance of one's experience but also how such experiences function in one's life.

One of the more frequently used measures of God Concept is Benson and Spilka's (1973) ten-item Loving and Controlling God Scales, where each scale is rated on five seven-point semantic differential dimensions (e.g., rejecting-accepting for the Loving God scale; demanding-not demanding for the Controlling God scale). Such variables as religious or spiritual coping as well as clinically relevant constructs such as self-esteem or locus of control have been shown to be associated with this measure. It should be noted that reliability estimates for the Controlling God scale have been marginal in the .60 to .70 range.

A less commonly used measure, but one with good psychometric properties, is Gorsuch's (1968) ninety-one-item Adjective Ratings of God Scale. Designed as an alternative to the single-item measures of religiousness often used at that time, such as church attendance or self-rated religiousness, this measures requires respondents to rate a series of adjectives on a three-point scale (1—not describing God; 2—describing God; or 3—describing God particularly well). Scores are then summed on five dimensions: Traditional Christian, Deisticness, Wrathfulness, Omni-ness (i.e., omnipresence, omniscience, omnipotence, and infinite nature of God), and Irrelevancy.

Measures of God image assess an affectively laden experience of God in contrast to a largely cognitive representation of God. Hall and Edwards (1996, 2002) developed the forty-nine-item self-report Spiritual Assessment Inventory (SAI). Based on object-relations and attachment theories, the SAI consists of five subscales: Awareness of God, Realistic Acceptance (of God), Disappointment (with God), Grandiosity (excessive self-importance), and Instability (in one's relationship to God). All five subscales have shown good internal consistency (.73 to .95), and the overall scale shows incremental validity beyond religious orientation or motivation.

Within an attachment theory framework, individual differences in the security of emotional bonds between individuals and God can be assessed. Most of the measures have been developed largely on the basis of corresponding measures of adult attachment. Rowatt and Kirkpatick (2002) have developed a nine-item Attachment to God scale that contains two factors of insecure attachment (avoidance and anxiety, with three secure items negatively loading on the avoidant factor). The two factors correlate moderately with each other ($r = .56$), but correlate only with anxious and not-avoidant adult romantic attachments. It also correlates in expected directions with several of the Big Five factors of personality, most notably negatively with agreeableness and positively with neuroticism.

Modeled after the Experiences in Close Relationships Scale (ECR; Brennan, Clark, and Shaver 1998), a common measure of adult attachment, Beck and McDonald (2004) developed a twenty-eight-item Attachment to God Inventory (AGI). The measure has a stable two-factor structure of avoidance (lack of intimacy with God and strong self-reliance) and anxiety (lack of intrinsic lovability and concern of potential abandonment), and demonstrates strong psychometric properties. However, as with other measures of attachment to God, the AGI, without revision, is limited to a Judeo-Christian population.

Religious or Spiritual Development

Religiousness and spirituality may change over time. James Fowler's (1981) model of faith development, where faith is understood as a meaning-making process through commitment to a set of organizing principles or values, has served as an important theoretical grounding for much research. Fowler proposed that faith typically progresses through a sequence of stages ranging from concrete systems in the early stages to more complex, abstract, and autonomous processes in later stages. Individuals vary on how far they progress in this process. Of several measures of Fowler's model that have been developed, two will be mentioned here. The Faith Development Scale (Leak, Loucks, and Bowlin 1999) is an eight-item forced-choice measure with adequate reliability and validity. Fowler himself developed the Faith Development Interview Guide, a semistructured interview format. The measure has demonstrated high inter-rater reliabilities and internal consistency, and the measure's validity has been shown in its differentiation of various populations and positive correlations with ego development measures. The complete measure can be found in Hill and Hood (1999).

Aside from Fowler's theory, several other measures of faith development or maturity have been created. One example is the thirty-eight-item Faith Maturity Scale (Benson, Donahue, and Erickson 1993), which measures values, behaviors, commitments, and viewpoints that are "characteristics of vibrant and life transforming faith, as these have been understood in 'mainline' Protestant traditions" (p. 3). The measure seeks to assess both vertical (one's relationship with God) and horizontal (one's relationship with others) dimensions. The measure has excellent psychometric properties (see Hill and Hood 1999).

The substance of one's faith is only part of the picture. Failure to measure the way one employs that substance to life functioning would make the study of religion and spirituality irrelevant to many psychological interests. The way religion operates within the lives of individuals is often the focal point. It is therefore not surprising that numerous functional measures of religion have been developed.

Functional Measures of Religiousness and Spirituality

Just as in our discussion of substantive measures, we will have to be selective in our review of functional measures. Again, the reader is referred to other, more thorough discussions (Hill 2013; Hill and Hood 1999; Hill and Edwards 2013).

Religious Orientation as Motivation

INTRINSIC-EXTRINSIC RELIGIOUS ORIENTATION

The single dominant theoretical framework for the past half-century in the psychology of religion has been Gordon Allport's (1950) intrinsic-extrinsic (I-E) theory of religious orientation. Eleven measures of this topic were reviewed in the Hill and Hood (1999) volume, including the original measure by Allport and Ross (1967).

According to Allport (1950), people differ in the motivations that underlie religious experience and behavior. For some, religion is a master motive, a supreme value to address life's most important questions. Such an *intrinsic* orientation provides meaning and functions as an integrative framework from which all of life is lived. In contrast, one may take a starkly utilitarian approach focusing on the personal benefits that religion can provide (e.g., a sense of belonging or security, personal fulfillment, or community status). Such an *extrinsic* orientation calls upon religion only when beneficial and thus one's religiousness or spirituality may not be a central organizing feature in the person's life. Pargament (1992), however, has cautioned against the polarization of intrinsic and extrinsic orientations, noting that it is possible for people to both "live" and "use" their religion.

The original twenty-item Allport and Ross (1967) measure remains widely used, though the many scales subsequently developed have the benefit of the voluminous research findings and efforts devoted to this topic. For example, Kirkpatrick (1989) discovered two categories in the extrinsic scale: a personally oriented (Ep) and a socially oriented (Es) extrinsic orientation, which Gorsuch and McPherson's (1989) fourteen-item revision of the Allport and Ross scale took into account. Their revised scale, the I/E-R, shows sufficient reliability for the eight-item intrinsic measure (.83 in the original study) but lower reliability (.65) for the six-item extrinsic measure. The scale's lower reliability may be offset by the ability to employ larger samples due to its brevity, thereby retaining its statistical power (Gorsuch and McPherson 1989). However, if brevity is key, the three-item intrinsic religion subscale of the Duke University Religion Index (DUREL; Koenig, Patterson, and Meador 1997) is recommended as the measure of choice for the intrinsic religious orientation. The authors report sufficient reliability ($\alpha = .75$), and the three-item scale correlates strongly with Hoge's (1972) ten-item scale, from which the three items were drawn.

The intrinsic-extrinsic religious orientation concept is an excellent example of how one must be careful in considering cultural factors in religious experience and expression. On the one hand, the concept itself—religion as an integrative end in itself versus the use of religion as a utilitarian means to some other end—appears so basic and perhaps universally applicable. However, as pointed out earlier, at both a conceptual and an empirical level, Cohen and Hill (2007) questioned the extent to which Allport's notion applies equally well to Jews, Catholics, and Protestants. When applied to an Indonesia Muslim context, Hill and Dwiwardani (2010) found that the Religious Orientation Scale (ROS; Allport and Ross 1967) needed revising beyond simple language modification (e.g., changing "church" to "mosque"). They discovered that the extrinsic social dimension, originally conceptualized in relation to institutional religion (e.g., the church or mosque), was better understood in that context in relation to the broader culture. The Muslim-Christian Religious Orientation Scale (MCROS; Ghorbani, Watson, Ghramaleki, Morris, and Hood 2002), which has taken into account such cultural variation, has demonstrated incremental validity beyond the Allport and Ross measure among Iranian and Iranian American Muslims (Ghorbani, Watson, and Mirhasani 2007).

QUEST RELIGIOUS ORIENTATION

Based on concerns that intrinsic orientation measures may reflect only a devout endorsement of religious orthodoxy at the expense of Allport's

(1950) fuller, richer conceptualization, the *quest* construct was designed to address three factors from Allport's original ideas about mature religion that were neglected in subsequent measures and research: (a) acknowledging the complexity of existential questions, (b) characterizing doubts as healthy, and (c) holding religious views tentatively with openness to change. The quest construct may reflect the change in the religious landscape in the past half-century such as that described by Wuthnow (1998) as a shift from a dwelling to a seeking spirituality.

Given the complexity of the construct and its relevance to changes in contemporary society, it is not surprising that many scales of quest or related constructs have been developed. Batson and Schoenrade's (1991b) twelve-item Quest Scale is among the most widely used measures and has been shown to be distinct not only from intrinsic and extrinsic motivational measures (Batson and Schoenrade 1991a) but also from measures of anti-orthodoxy, religious liberalism, and agnosticism (Burris, Jackson, Tarpley, and Smith 1996).

Genia's (1997) revised Spiritual Experience Index (SEI-R; 1997) includes a distinct ten-item measure of spiritual openness that correlates strongly ($r = .55$) with the Batson and Schoenrade (1991b) measure of quest. Despite this strong relationship, spiritual openness appears to be distinct from quest in that it correlates with religious and spiritual well-being even when controlling for quest scores. Spiritual openness correlates negatively, as expected, with fundamentalism, intolerance of ambiguity, and dogmatism, but also with other measures of spirituality, such as God consciousness, participation in formal religious practices, and intrinsic religious orientation.

FUNDAMENTALIST RELIGIOUS ORIENTATION

Most discussions of religious orientation limit the concept to intrinsic, extrinsic, and quest religious categories. However, religious fundamentalism can be considered a fourth religious orientation, especially when considered in motivational terms (Hill, Smith, and Sandage 2012). Fundamentalism should not be confused with orthodoxy in general or with Christian evangelicalism in particular. Although fundamentalists and evangelicals do hold similar foundational beliefs, they differ in terms of how sacred texts are to be treated, both in terms of their relationship with other sources of knowledge and in terms of culture in general

(Hood, Hill, and Williamson 2005). Fundamentalists hold a more exclusive and privileged view of what is considered authoritatively sacred and are more suspicious of other sources of knowledge, especially those that may be seen as potential conflicts with the sacred authoritative source.

The motivational nature of a fundamentalist religious orientation is captured well by Altemeyer and Hunsberger's (1992) following definition:

> the belief that there is one set of religious teachings that clearly contains the fundamental, basic, intrinsic, essential, inerrant truth about humanity and deity; that this essential truth is fundamentally opposed by forces of evil which must be vigorously fought; that this truth must be followed today according to the fundamental, unchangeable practices of the past; and that those who believe and follow these fundamental teachings have a special relationship with the deity. (p. 118)

Their twenty-item (and, later, twelve-item; Altemeyer and Hunsberger 2004) Religious Fundamentalism Scale (RFS) has become the standard measure of religious fundamentalism and has been tested in Western Christian samples and also with Hindus, Jews, and Muslims. Both the longer and the shorter versions of the scale demonstrate strong psychometric properties.

An alternative measure, the Intratextualism Fundamentalism Scale (IFS), has been recently developed (Williamson, Hood, Ahmad, Sadiq, and Hill 2010) based on the Hood et al. (2005) intratextual theory of fundamentalism. The intratextual theory suggests that fundamentalist motivation is less characterized by militancy or right-wing authoritarianism than by an allegiance to a sacred text (usually written, but sometimes oral) through which objective truth is defined and the interpretive process for finding such truth is derived. The scale contains five six-point Likert items and is suitable for testing (with minor wording changes) across religious traditions, though initial analyses suggest that the psychometric properties of the scale hold better for a U.S. Christian sample ($\alpha = .83$) than a Pakistani Muslim sample ($\alpha = .65$).

Religious Coping

Religion's ability to help people cope with physical, psychological, and social stressors has been a focal point of interest for many psychologists. The most widely used measure, the brief religious coping measure (Brief RCOPE; Pargament, Smith, Koenig, and Perez 1998), consists of seven positive coping items (e.g., "sought God's love and care") and seven negative coping items (e.g., "wondered whether God had abandoned me"). Each positive coping item represents a different subscale of the Pargament, Koenig, and Perez (2000) more comprehensive 105-item RCOPE measure (spiritual connection, seeking spiritual support, religious forgiveness, collaborative religious coping, benevolent religious reappraisal, religious purification, and religious focus). The seven negative items represent five of the RCOPE subscales (spiritual discontent, punishing God reappraisal, interpersonal religious discontent, demonic reappraisal, and reappraisal of God's power). The scale has repeatedly demonstrated strong psychometric properties in numerous populations. Ano and Vasconcelles's (2005) meta-analysis of forty-nine studies of religious coping, the vast majority of which used items from the RCOPE or Brief RCOPE, found that positive and negative forms of religious coping are moderately related to positive and negative psychological adjustment to stress, respectively. Based on the Brief RCOPE, coping measures have been developed among Muslims (Khan and Watson 2006), Hindus (Tarakeshwar, Pargament, and Mahoney 2003), Jews (JCOPE; Rosmarin, Pargament, and Flannelly 2009), and Buddhists (Falb and Pargament 2013).

Religious Struggle

Though religion can provide resources for coping, it can also be a source of struggle with substantial ramifications for mental health and well-being. Of several measures assessing the experience of religious and spiritual struggle, the twenty-six-item Religious and Spiritual Struggles Scale (Exline, Pargament, Grubbs, and Yali 2014) is in one sense the most comprehensive in that it measures six domains: divine, demonic, interpersonal, moral, doubt, and ultimate meaning. Other measures of struggle worth considering tend to focus on one domain, such as God (e.g., Hall and Edwards 1996, 2002; Wood et al. 2010) or intrapersonal issues such as religious doubt (Altermeyer and Hunsberger 1997). Yet another scale worth consideration is Exline, Yali, and Sanderson's (2000) twenty-item Religious Comfort and Strain (RCS) measure, which includes three religious strain subscales (Alienation from God, Fear and Guilt, and Religious Rifts) that can be averaged together.

Other Categories of Measures

The listing of categories is somewhat arbitrary, and space limitations force us to discuss only some types of measures, whether substantive or functional. For example, not discussed here but covered in other reviews (Hill 2013; Hill and Edwards 2013) are measures of private religious or spiritual practices, social support, how religion functions as a source of meaning and values, and multidimensional measures. Researchers are directed toward those reviews as well as the Hill and Hood (1999) volume for a more complete listing.

Looking Ahead

Hill and Edwards (2013) identify five areas where measurement progress has been made, but important future development is necessary. We have touched upon each of these topics throughout this chapter and simply refer to them here as a reminder of how measurement in the psychology of religion and spirituality can be further improved. First, there is the need for *futhe development of theoretically driven measures.* Not only should religion or spirituality no longer be just an "add-on" variable to other research programs, but its importance and complexity demand strong theoretical bases that are capable of sustaining robust empirical research programs. Measurement quality depends on a solid conceptual foundation. Second, there must be *further development of culturally sensitive measures.* Religion is a cultural variable (Cohen 2009) that provides a contextual surround for understanding beliefs, attitudes, and experiences that must be taken into account in measurement. While it is certainly desirable to have measures that are as broadly generalizable as possible, specific religious and spiritual traditions will often have unique elements that should be honored (Belzen 2010). At the very least, researchers should not assume that a given measure is easily portable from one culture to another.

Third, we need to continue to *work on alternative measures to self-reports*, especially since religion and spirituality often involve issues of considerable personal investment. The momentum in developing such alternative measures (see Jong et al., this volume) should be maintained. Fourth, we must *keep up our measurement efforts in new domains*. New ideas in the field will abound and will provide the need for further measures. Fifth, it is important that researchers *develop clinically relevant measures* that can be applied to specific populations.

Even if these future measurement challenges are met, there is still concern that several hurdles facing the entire field of the psychology of religion and spirituality will remain. While the challenges to the field as a whole are not explicitly measurement related, they do have measurement implications.

The Vision of an Integrative Paradigm in the Psychology of Religion: Implications for Measurement

As a field, the psychology of religion and spirituality has experienced rapid growth in the past few decades. Though it is encouraging that the study of religion and spirituality is far less neglected than it was at the time of our 2003 article (Hill and Pargament 2003), the growth carries with it some major hurdles. Suggesting that the terms "mutlitplicity" and "diversity" best describe the current status of the field, Pargament et al. (2013) express concern that "the rapid growth, multiplicity, and diversity in the field . . . is accompanied by the danger of fragmentation—a field that becomes so large, so ill-defined, and so unwieldy that it carries a serious risk of fracture among researchers and practitioners who can pursue their own particular interests while remaining unaware of the relevant work of others" (p. 5). Such diversity is reflected in its concepts and methods, including measures.

Pargament et al. (2013) answered their concern about the field's fragmentation by proposing an *integrative paradigm* in terms of five themes as an organizing perspective for our rapidly growing field of study. We will complete our measurement review by considering their five themes in terms of their implications for measurement.

Theme 1: Integrating the Multiple Dimensions and Multiple Levels of Religion and Spirituality

Religion and spirituality often speak of life metaphorically as a journey that includes pathways and destinations (Pargament 1997, 2007). Psychological measurement must take into account the varied pathways and destinations of religion and spirituality. Such multiplicity should be considered in terms of both religious tradition and individual beliefs and practices, including how such beliefs and practices function in the life of individuals, families, intimate relationships, communities, and cultures.

Theme 2: Integrating the Multiple Valences of Religion and Spirituality

Researchers must develop measures that assess both the good and the bad in religion. While much of the research points to the benefits of religion and spirituality, it is equally true that religion and spirituality can often be used in unhealthy forms to deny reality, to justify bias or prejudice, or to promote intergroup tension. As Pargament et al. (2013) point out, "The critical question is not *whether* religion and spirituality are good or bad, but rather *when*, *how*, and *why* they take constructive or destructive forms" (p. 7, emphasis original). For example, there are both positive and negative forms of religious coping (Pargament et al. 1998). Furthermore, religion and spirituality may create personal tension and struggle, both intra- and interpersonally, that the nonreligious person may not have to face (Exline et al. 2014). Some motivations, such as some forms of extrinsic religiosity and fundamentalism, that underlie religion and spirituality may not be healthy and deserve the same empirical attention as research demonstrating the effective use of religion (Hill, Smith, and Sandage 2012). Such challenges require measurement flexibility that considers not only the benefits of religion and spirituality but also their liabilities.

Theme 3: Integrating Theory, Research, and Practice

As we have noted several times in this chapter, measures in the psychology of religion and spirituality must be conceptually grounded, thus avoiding a piecemeal research approach that keeps the field from progressing forward. However, that is only part of the integration story. Though research, in and of itself, is valuable in terms of furthering our understanding, it is especially useful if it can have important implications for practice, broadly defined to include clinical activities (e.g., pastoral counseling, psychotherapy), education (e.g., early education, prevention, correctional training), applications across a variety of settings (e.g., the workplace, family life, the church as a social institution), as well as a focus on specific issues (e.g., prejudice, violence, physical health). This may require that measures be designed for specific practice purposes. The ideographic nature of some practice applications, with a focus on the particular individual or case at hand, may require a greater openness to qualitative methodologies (e.g., a semistructured interview) than the more commonly used nomothetic measures designed to uncover the generalizable aspects of human functioning.

Theme 4: Integrating the Psychology of Religion and Spirituality with the Broader Field

Integration is a bidirectional process. On the one hand, the psychology of religion and spirituality should draw from the discipline as a whole and perhaps can utilize already existing measures as a starting point from which to modify. For example, the field has effectively utilized theories from mainstream psychology to investigate such domains as religious attachment, religious meaning making, religious coping, religious fundamentalism, religious attribution, and the like to further our understanding of both substantive and functional aspects of religiousness and spirituality (see Hill and Gibson 2008). With the exception of religious fundamentalism, each of these domains within the broader field has provided measurement tools that have been revised for application to the religious or spiritual domain.

On the other hand, the study of religion and spirituality may have something to offer the field of psychology as a whole. Hill (1999) suggested that the study of religious and spiritual experience, as a domain that is heavily affect laden, has the capacity to further our understanding of emotions since it, unlike so many topics of interest to psychologists, is often something about which people feel strongly

(Abelson 1988). Religion may also be uniquely capable of advancing our knowledge of experiential knowing. For example, in developing his Cognitive-Experiential Self-Theory of knowing (CEST), Epstein (1994) maintained that

> religion provides perhaps the most impressive evidence of all that there are two fundamentally different modes of processing information. . . . For many individuals, rational, analytical thinking fails to provide as satisfactory a way of understanding the world and of directing their behavior in it as does religious teaching. . . . [R]eligion is better suited than analytical thinking for communicating within the experiential system. (p. 712)

Other topics, such as the recently emerging interests of psychologists in virtue, can be promoted through an understanding of religion and spirituality. An individual's conceptualization of virtue is often based in a religious worldview that requires measures that account for the substance, and not just the function, of one's religious or spiritual beliefs and practices.

Theme 5: Integrating Perspectives on the Meanings of Religion and Spirituality

The parameters of what it means to be religious or spiritual must be acknowledged. Not everything is spiritual; if it were, then the field has no boundaries. But neither should the field be restricted to a narrow sectarian understanding of the terms. Though earlier we identified and made operational our understanding of the terms "religion" and "spirituality," it is beyond the purposes of this chapter to delve into all of the complex issues surrounding the use of these two terms (or their derivatives). The reader is encouraged to consult a number of resources identified by Pargament et al. (2013) to gain further definitional clarity regarding these terms and, especially for the focus here, to grasp the implications for measurement. It is safe to conclude that measures that are overly narrow and measures that know no bounds will be of little use to the field as a whole.

Conclusion

The discipline of psychology is filled with constructs that are difficult to measure, from attitudes and intelligence to personality and prejudice. Nevertheless, measurement is particularly challenging in the domain of religion and spirituality. Why? Because, as William James (1902) noted, these phenomena are by definition ineffable, difficult to put into words. How can psychology capture, in concrete form, experiences that are as inherently elusive and mysterious as religion and spirituality? Daunting as the task may be, it cannot be sidestepped. An empirical psychology of religion and spirituality can be no stronger than its capacity to measure its central phenomena of interest.

In this chapter, we have tried to highlight the progress that has been made in the measurement of these constructs. This progress has grown in part out of advances in theory, research, and practice in the field more generally. In turn, developments in measurement have helped to spur the growth in the scientific study of religion and spirituality. We believe that the field will continue to progress through interrelated advances in measurement, theory, research, and practice. Having said that, we admit that current approaches to religious and spiritual expressions cannot provide a complete accounting of these experiences, which will probably remain, in part, mysterious and ineffable. Even so, psychologists of religion and spirituality are shedding some valuable light on what may be one of the least understood but most important dimensions of human experience.

REFERENCES

Abelson, R. P. (1988). Conviction. *American Psychologist, 43*, 267–75.

Abu-Raiya, H., & Hill, P. C. (2014). Appraising the state of measurement of Islamic religiousness. *Psychology of Religion and Spirituality, 6*, 22–32.

Ai, A. L., Peterson, C., & Huang, B. (2003). The effects of religious-spiritual coping on positive attitudes of adult Muslim refugees from Kosovo and Bosnia. *The International Journal for the Psychology of Religion, 13*, 29–47.

Allport, G. W. (1950). *The individual and his religion*. New York: Macmillan.

Allport, G. W., & Ross, J. M. (1967). Personal religious orientation and prejudice. *Journal of Personality and Social Psychology, 5*, 432–43.

Altemeyer, B., & Hunsberger, B. (1992). Authoritarianism, religious fundamentalism, quest, and prejudice. *The International Journal for the Psychology of Religion, 2*, 113–33.

Altemeyer, B., & Hunsberger, B. (1997). *Amazing conversions: Why some turn to faith and others abandon religion.* Amherst, NY: Prometheus.

Altemeyer, B., & Hunsberger, B. (2004). A revised Religious Fundamentalism Scale: The short and sweet of it. *The International Journal of the Psychology of Religion, 14,* 47–54.

Ano, G. G., & Vasconcelles, E. B. (2005). Religious coping and psychological adjustment to stress: A meta-analysis. *Journal of Clinical Psychology, 61,* 461–80.

Batson, C. D., & Schoenrade, P. A. (1991a). Measuring religion as quest: I. Validity concerns. *Journal for the Scientific Study of Religion, 30,* 416–29.

Batson, C. D., & Schoenrade, P. A. (1991b). Measuring religion as quest: II. Reliability concerns. *Journal for the Scientific Study of Religion, 30,* 430–47.

Beck, R., & McDonald, A. (2004). Attachment to God: The Attachment to God Inventory, tests of working model correspondence, and an exploration of faith group differences. *Journal of Psychology and Theology, 32,* 92–103.

Belzen, J. A. (2010). *Towards cultural psychology of religion: Principles, approaches, applications.* Dordrecht: Springer.

Benson, P. L., Donahue, M. J., & Erickson, J. A. (1993). The Faith Maturity Scale: Conceptualization, measurement, and empirical validation. In M. L. Lynn & D. O. Moberg (eds.), *Research in the social scientific study of religion*, vol. 5 (pp. 1–26). Greenwich, CT: JAI Press.

Benson, P., & Spilka, B. (1973). God image as a function of self-esteem and locus of control. *Journal for the Scientific Study of Religion, 12,* 297–310. doi: 10.2307/1384430.

Brennan, K. A., Clark, C. L., & Shaver, P. R. (1998). Self-report measurement of adult romantic attachment: An integrative overview. In J. A. Simpson & W. S. Rholes (eds.), *Attachment theory and close relationships* (pp. 46–76). New York: Guilford.

Brown, D. G., & Lowe, W. L. (1951). Religious beliefs and personality characteristics of college students. *Journal of Social Psychology, 33,* 103–29.

Burris, C. T., Jackson, L. M., Tarpley, W. R., & Smith, G. (1996). Religion as quest: The self-directed pursuit of meaning. *Personality and Social Psychology Bulletin, 22,* 1068–76.

Cohen, A. B. (2009). Many forms of culture. *American Psychologist, 64,* 194–204.

Cohen, A. B., & Hill, P. C. (2007). Religion as culture: Religious individualism and collectivism among American Catholics, Jews, and Protestants. *Journal of Personality, 75,* 709–42.

Ellison, C. W. (1983). Spiritual well-being: Conceptualization and measurement. *Journal of Psychology and Theology, 11,* 330–40.

Emavardhana, T., & Tori, C. D. (1997). Changes in self-concept, ego defense mechanisms, and religiosity following seven-day Vipassana meditation retreats. *Journal for the Scientific Study of Religion, 36,* 194–206. doi: 10.2307/1387552.

Epstein, S. (1994). Integration of the cognitive and psychodynamic unconscious. *American Psychologist, 49,* 709–24.

Exline, J. J., Pargament, K. I., Grubbs, J. B., & Yali, A. M. (2014). The Religious and Spiritual Struggles Scale: Development and initial validation. *Psychology of Religion and Spirituality, 6,* 208–22.

Exline, J. J., Yali, A. M., & Sanderson, W. C. (2000). Guilt, discord, and alienation: The role of religious strain in depression and suicidality. *Journal of Clinical Psychology, 56*, 1481–96.

Falb, M., & Pargament, K. I. (2013). Buddhist coping predicts psychological outcomes among end-of-life caregivers. *Psychology of Religion and Spirituality, 5*, 252–62.

Fowler, J. W. (1981). *Stages of faith: The psychology of human development and the quest for meaning.* San Francisco: Harper & Row.

Fullerton, J. T., & Hunsberger, B. (1982). A unidimensional measure of Christian orthodoxy. *Journal for the Scientific Study of Religion, 21*, 317–26.

Genia, V. (1997). The Spiritual Experience Index: Revision and reformulation. *Review of Religious Research, 38*, 344–61.

Genia, V. (2001). Evaluation of the Spiritual Well-Being Scale in a sample of college students. *The International Journal for the Psychology of Religion, 11*, 25–33.

Ghorbani, N., Watson, P. J., Ghramaleki, A. F., Morris, R. J., & Hood, R. W., Jr. (2002). Muslim-Christian Religious Orientation Scales: Distinctions, correlations, and cross-cultural analysis in Iran and the United States. *The International Journal for the Psychology of Religion, 12*, 69–91.

Ghorbani, N., Watson, P. J., & Khan, Z. H. (2007). Theoretical, empirical, and potential ideological dimensions of using Western conceptualizations to measure Muslim religious commitments. *Journal of Muslim Mental Health, 2*, 113–31.

Ghorbani, N., Watson, P. J., & Mirhasani, V. S. (2007). Religious commitment in Iran: Correlates and factors of quest religious orientations. *Archive for the Psychology of Religion, 29*, 245–57.

Gorsuch, R. L. (1968). The conceptualization of God as seen in adjective ratings. *Journal for the Scientific Study of Religion, 7*, 56–64. doi: 10.2307/1385110.

Gorsuch, R. L. (1984). Measurement: The boon and bane of investigating religion. *American Psychologist, 39*, 228–36. doi: 10.1037/0003-066X.39.3.228.

Gorsuch, R. L., & McPherson, S. E. (1989). Intrinsic/extrinsic measurement: I/E-revised and single-item scales. *Journal for the Scientific Study of Religion, 28*, 348–54.

Granqvist, P., & Kirkpatrick, L. A. (2004). Religious conversion and perceived childhood attachment: A meta-analysis. *The International Journal for the Psychology of Religion, 14*, 223–50.

Granqvist, P., & Kirkpatrick, L. A. (2013). Religion, spirituality, and attachment. In K. Pargament (ed.-in-chief), J. Exline, & J. Jones (assoc. eds.), *APA handbooks in psychology: APA handbook of psychology, religion, and spirituality*, vol. 1 (pp. 51–77). Washington, DC: American Psychological Association.

Hall, T. W., & Edwards, K. J. (1996). Initial development and factor analysis of the Spiritual Assessment Inventory. *Journal of Psychology and Theology, 24*, 233–46.

Hall, T. W., & Edwards, K. J. (2002). The Spiritual Assessment Inventory: A theistic model and measure for assessing spiritual development. *Journal for the Scientific Study of Religion, 41*, 341–57.

Hill, P. C. (1999). Giving religion away: What the study of religion offers psychology. *The International Journal for the Psychology of Religion, 9*, 229–49.

Hill, P. C. (2013). Measurement assessment and issues in the psychology of religion and spirituality. In R. F. Paloutzian and C. L. Park (eds.), *Handbook of the psychology of religion and spirituality*, 2nd ed. (pp. 48–74). New York: Guilford Press.

Hill, P. C., & Dwiwardani, C. (2010). Measurement at the interface of psychiatry and religion: Issues and existing measures. In P. J. Verhagen, H. M. van Praag, J. J. Lopez-Ibor, J. L. Cox, & D. Moussaoui (eds.), *Psychiatry and religion: Beyond boundaries* (pp. 319–39). New York: Wiley.

Hill, P. C., & Edwards, E. (2013). Measurement in the psychology of religiousness and spirituality: Existing measures and new frontiers. In K. Pargament (ed.-in-chief), J. Exline, & J. Jones (assoc. eds.), *APA handbooks in psychology: APA handbook of psychology, religion, and spirituality*, vol. 1 (pp. 51–77). Washington, DC: American Psychological Association.

Hill, P. C., & Gibson, N. J. S. (2008). Whither the roots? Achieving conceptual depth in the psychology of religion. *Archiv für Religionspsychologie/Archive for the Psychology of Religion, 30*, 19–35.

Hill, P. C., & Hood, R. W., Jr. (1999). *Measures of religiosity*. Birmingham, AL: Religious Education Press.

Hill, P. C., & Pargament, K. I. (2003). Advances in the conceptualization and measurement of religion and spirituality. *American Psychologist, 58*, 64–74.

Hill, P. C., Pargament, K. I., Hood, R. W., McCullough, M. E., Swyers, J. P., Larson, D. B., & Zinnbauer, B. J. (2000). Conceptualizing religion and spirituality: Points of commonality, points of departure. *Journal for the Theory of Social Behaviour, 30*, 51–77.

Hill, P. C., Smith, E., & Sandage, S. J. (2012). Religious and spiritual motivations in clinical practice. In J. Aten, K. O'Grady, & E. Worthington Jr. (eds.), *The psychology of religion and spirituality for clinicians: Using research in your practice* (pp. 69–100). New York: Routledge.

Hoge, D. R. (1972). A validated intrinsic religious motivation scale. *Journal for the Scientific Study of Religion, 11*, 369–76.

Hood, R. W., Jr. (1975). The construction and preliminary validation of a measure of reported mystical experience. *Journal for the Scientific Study of Religion, 14*, 29–41.

Hood, R. W., Jr., Hill, P. C., & Williamson, W. P. (2005). *The psychology of religious fundamentalism*. New York: Guilford Press.

Hunsberger, B. (1989). A short version of the Christian orthodoxy scale. *Journal for the Scientific Study of Religion, 28*, 360–65.

James, W. (1902). *The varieties of religious experience: A study in human nature*. New York: Random House.

Ji, C. H. C., & Ibrahim, Y. (2007). Islamic doctrinal orthodoxy and religious orientations: Scale development and validation. *The International Journal for the Psychology of Religion, 17*, 189–208. doi: 10.1080/10508610701402192.

Khan, Z. H., & Watson, P. J. (2006). Construction of the Pakistani Religious Coping Practices Scale: Correlations with religious coping, religious orientation, and reactions to stress among Muslim university students. *The International Journal for the Psychology of Religion, 16*, 101–12.

Kirkpatrick, L. A. (1989). A psychometric analysis of the Allport-Ross and Feagin measures of intrinsic-extrinsic religious orientation. In D. O. Moberg & M. L. Lynn (eds.), *Research in the social scientific study of religion*, vol. 1 (pp. 1–31). Greenwich, CT: JAI Press.

Kirkpatrick, L. A. (2005). *Attachment, evolution, and the psychology of religion.* New York: Guilford Press.

Kirkpatrick, L. A., & Hood, R. W., Jr. (1990). Intrinsic-extrinsic religious orientation: The boon or bane of contemporary psychology of religion. *Journal for the Scientific Study of Religion, 29*, 442–62.

Koenig, H. G. (2008). Concerns about measuring "spirituality" in research. *Journal of Nervous and Mental Disease, 196*, 349–55.

Koenig, H. G., McCullough, M. E., & Larson, D. B. (2001). *Handbook of religion and health.* New York: Oxford University Press.

Koenig, H., Patterson, G. R., & Meador, K. G. (1997). Religion index for psychiatric research: A 5-item measure for use in health outcome studies. *American Journal of Psychiatry, 154*, 885–86.

Leak, G. K., Loucks, A. A., & Bowlin, P. (1999). Development and initial validation of an objective measure of faith development. *The International Journal for the Psychology of Religion, 9*, 105–24. doi: 10.1207/s15327582ijpr0902_2.

McCrae, R. R., & Costa, P. T., Jr. (2008). The Five-Factor theory of personality. In O. P. John, R. W. Robins, & L. A. Pervin (eds.), *Handbook of personality: Theory and research*, 3rd ed. (pp. 159–81). New York: Guilford Press.

Ng, S-M., Fong, T. C. T., Tsui, E. Y. L., Au-Yeung, F. S. W., & Law, S. K. W. (2009). Validation of the Chinese version of Underwood's Daily Spiritual Experience Scale: Transcending cultural boundaries? *International Journal of Behavioral Medicine, 16*, 91–97. doi: 10.1007/s12529-009-9045-5.

Paloutzian, R. F., & Ellison, C. W. (1982). Loneliness, spiritual well-being, and quality of life. In L. A. Peplau & D. Perlman (eds.), *Loneliness: A sourcebook of current theory, research, and therapy* (pp. 224–37). New York: Wiley Interscience.

Pargament, K. I. (1992). Of means and ends: Religion and the search for significance. *The International Journal for the Psychology of Religion, 2*, 201–29.

Pargament, K. I. (1997). *The psychology of religion and coping.* New York: Guilford Press.

Pargament, K. I. (1999). The psychology of religion and spirituality? Yes and no. *The International Journal for the Psychology of Religion, 9*, 3–16. doi: 10.1207/S15327582ijpr0901_2.

Pargament, K. I. (2007). *Spiritually integrated psychotherapy: Understanding and addressing the sacred.* New York: Guilford Press.

Pargament, K. I., Koenig, H. G., & Perez, L. M. (2000). The many methods of religious coping: Development and initial validation of the RCOPE. *Journal of Clinical Psychology, 56*, 519–43.

Pargament, K. I., Mahoney, A., Exline, J. J., Jones, J. W., & Shafranske, E. P. (2013). Envisioning an integrative paradigm for the psychology of religion and spirituality. In K. Pargament (ed.-in-chief), J. Exline, & J. Jones (assoc. eds.), *APA handbooks in psychology: APA handbook of psychology, religion, and spirituality*, vol. 1 (pp. 51–77). Washington, DC: American Psychological Association.

Pargament, K. I., Smith, B. W., Koenig, H. G., & Perez, L. (1998). Patterns of positive and negative religious coping with major life stressors. *Journal for the Scientific Study of Religion, 37,* 710–24.

Piedmont, R. L. (1999). Does spirituality represent the sixth factor of personality? Spiritual transcendence and the Five-Factor Model. *Journal of Personality, 67,* 985–1013.

Piedmont, R. L. (2007). Cross-cultural generalizability of the Spiritual Transcendence Scale to the Philippines: Spirituality as a human universal. *Mental Health, Religion, and Culture, 10,* 89–107.

Piedmont, R. L., & Leach, M. M. (2002). Cross-cultural generalizability of the Spiritual Transcendence Scale in India: Spirituality as a universal aspect of human experience. *American Behavioral Scientist, 45,* 1888–1901.

Plante, T. G., & Boccaccini, M. (1997). Reliability and validity of the Santa Clara Strength of Religious Faith Questionnaire. *Pastoral Psychology, 45,* 429–37.

Plante, T. G., Vallaeys, C. L., Sherman, A. C., & Wallston, K. A. (2002). The development of a brief version of the Santa Clara Strength of Religious Faith Questionnaire. *Pastoral Psychology, 50,* 359–68.

Rican, P., & Janosova, P. (2010). Spirituality as a basic aspect of personality: A cross-cultural verification of Piedmont's model. *The International Journal for the Psychology of Religion, 20,* 2–13.

Rosmarin, D. H., Pargament, K. I., & Flannelly, K. J. (2009). Religious coping among Jews: Development and initial validation of the JCOPE. *Journal of Clinical Psychology, 65,* 670–83.

Rowatt, W. C., & Kirkpatrick, L. A. (2002). Two dimensions of attachment to God and their relation to affect, religiosity, and personality constructs. *Journal for the Scientific Study of Religion, 41,* 637–51.

Sherman, J. W., Gawronski, B., & Trope, Y., eds. (2014). *Dual process theories of the social mind.* New York: Guilford Press.

Stace, W. T. (1960). *Mysticism and philosophy*. Philadelphia: Lippincott.

Stellway, R. I. (1973). The correspondence between religious orientation and socio-political liberalism and conservatism. *Sociological Quarterly, 14,* 430–39.

Tarakeshwar, N., Pargament, K. I., & Mahoney, A. (2003). Initial development of a measure of religious coping among Hindus. *Journal of Community Psychology, 31,* 607–28.

Underwood, L. G., & Teresi, J. A. (2002). The Daily Spiritual Experience Scale: Development, theoretical description, reliability, exploratory factor analysis, and preliminary construct validity using health-related data. *Annals of Behavioral Medicine, 24,* 22–33.

Williamson, W. P., Hood, R. W., Jr., Ahmad, A., Sadiq, M., & Hill, P. C. (2010). The Intratextual Fundamentalism Scale: Cross-cultural application, validity evidence, and relationship with religious orientation and the Big Five Factor markers. *Mental Health, Religion & Culture, 13*, 721–47.

Wood, B. T., Worthington, E. L., Jr., Exline, J. J., Yali, A. M., Aten, J. D., & McMinn, M. R. (2010). Development, refinement, and psychometric properties of the Attitudes toward God Scale (ATGS-9). *Psychology of Religion and Spirituality, 2*, 148–67. doi: 10.1037/a0018753.

Worthington, E. L., Jr., Wade, N. G., Hight, T. L., Ripley, J. S., McCullough, M. E., Berry, J. W., . . . O'Connor, L. (2003). The Religious Commitment Inventory—10: Development, refinement, and validation of a brief scale for research and counseling. *Journal of Counseling Psychology, 50*, 84–96.

Wuthnow, R. (1998). *After heaven: Spirituality in America since the 1950s.* Berkeley: University of California Press.

3.

Indirect and Implicit Measures of Religiosity

JONATHAN JONG, BONNIE POON ZAHL, AND
CARISSA A. SHARP

The Problem of Psychological Measurement

The fundamental problem in psychology as a scientific discipline is that of measurement. How can we access (and assess) what people are feeling and thinking? The most commonsensible answer to this question is, of course, to *ask* them. We ask people questions and make inferences about their mental states from their verbal responses, either spoken or written. We conduct opinion polls, structured interviews, and focus groups; we construct psychometric scales and other kinds of questionnaire-based measures. It is no exaggeration to say that most of what we know—*or think we know*—in the social sciences comes from self-report data, either taken at face value or interpreted through some theoretical or hermeneutical lens. The social scientific study of religion is no exception to this generalization. It is, and has been for over thirty years now, a truism in the psychology of religion that there is a preponderance of self-report measures of religiosity (Gorsuch 1984). To this point, Hill and Hood (1999) managed to compile a list of 126 self-report measures; and many more have since been published (Hill and Pargament, this volume).

Well-formed questionnaires are very useful tools in a psychologist's repertoire; at the same time, however, researchers have also long acknowledged the limitations of such *direct* or *overt* or *explicit* measures. We begin this chapter with a brief overview of the limitations of self-report measures of religiosity. We then describe and review a number of *indirect* or *implicit* measures of religiosity that have been designed specifically to circumvent these limitations. Finally, we conclude with recommendations for how these indirect or implicit measures may be adapted for use by social scientists to supplement more traditional measures of religiosity.

Self-Report Measures and Their Discontents

There are, broadly speaking, two classes of problems with self-report measures. The first is the "strategic responding" (Wittenbrink and Schwarz 2007:2) problem: participants might not always be honest when asked directly about their feelings, beliefs, and desires. Indeed, people also often misreport their behavior: for example, sociologists have consistently found that American Christians overreport their religious activity, such as religious service attendance (Brenner 2011; Brenner, this volume; Hadaway and Marler 2005). The standard interpretation of such trends is that people bias their responses in *socially desirable* ways, either because they want to manage others' impressions of them or because they are engaging in self-enhancing self-deception, or both. Indeed, researchers have linked social desirability tendencies to religiosity, finding that religious people—particularly intrinsically religious people (Allport and Ross 1967)—have a greater tendency toward socially desirable responding (Gillings and Joseph 1996; Leak and Fish 1989; Sedikides and Gebauer 2010; Trimble 1997; see also Brenner, this volume). Furthermore, this relationship between religiosity and socially desirable responding is particularly strong in contexts that place a higher value on religiosity (e.g., USA > UK; Christian universities > secular universities). To complicate matters, explicit self-report measures might also serve as *demand characteristics*: cues that lead participants to respond on the basis of beliefs that they form about researchers' expectations (Orne and Whitehouse 2000). When participants think (rightly or wrongly) that they know the purpose of a study, they may change their responses in order to affect the outcome of the study. This is one reason why psychologists are often reluctant to inform participants of the true purposes of any study.

The second class of problems is that of the limits of introspective access: even if we can guarantee honest responses from participants about their *explicit* attitudes, there might be *implicit* attitudes, or aspects of attitudes, of which participants are not aware, and therefore *unable* to report.

Over the last two decades, the view that there are aspects of human psychology that are not fully accessible to introspection has established itself as orthodoxy among social and cognitive psychologists. The literature is now replete with dual-process models of cognition, which variously distinguish between the implicit and explicit (e.g., Nosek 2007), or the automatic and controlled (e.g., Bargh and Chartrand 1999), or the unconscious and conscious (e.g., Dijksterhuis and Nordgren 2006), or the heuristic and systematic (e.g., Chen and Chaiken 1999), or the associative and the propositional (Gawronski and Bodenhausen 2006). This theoretical interest in dual processing has come with methodological developments: the past twenty years have seen remarkable growth in the number of *indirect* and/or *implicit* measures, as well as studies using such measures (see Sherman, Gawronski, and Trope 2014; Chaiken and Trope 1999; Wittenbrink and Schwarz 2007). Explicit and indirect (or implicit) measures of attitudes have been shown to independently predict behavior (Greenwald, Smith, Sriram, Bar-Anan, and Nosek 2009), to predict different kinds of behaviors (e.g., verbal v. nonverbal; Dovidio, Kawakami, and Gaertner 2002; Dovidio, Kawakami, Johnson, Johnson, and Howard 1997; spontaneous v. deliberative; Perugini 2005), and to be influenced by different causal factors (Gawronski and Strack 2004; Rydell, McConnell, Mackie, and Strain 2006). In the domain of religiosity, researchers have investigated how believers behave differently when asked directly about their propositional beliefs compared to when their beliefs are assessed via tasks that require more intuitive responses (Barrett and Keil 1996; Barrett 1998, 1999). In spite of significant unresolved disagreements about the precise nature of implicit cognitions, it is clear that our traditional self-report measures only provide a partial picture of what is going on in people's minds.

What Are Indirect and Implicit Measures?

We have already implied that the terms "indirect" and "implicit" are not synonymous; before we proceed to consider various examples of such measures, it is important to clarify the distinction. Indirectness refers to a property of the measurement procedure: a measure is indirect insofar as it does not rely on participants' self-assessment, but involves inference about participants' mental states and traits from some other behavior.

For example, a direct measure of racial prejudice might involve asking someone about his or her attitudes toward racial outgroups, whereas as indirect measure might involve observing the person's body language when interacting with racial outgroup members. All the measures described in this chapter are, to different extents, indirect in this way. Implicitness, on the other hand, refers to some feature of the psychological process that produces the responses in any given measurement procedure, whether indirect or otherwise. More specifically, a measure may be said to be implicit insofar as responses to it are made unconsciously, unintentionally, uncontrollably, and/or resource efficiently (Gawronski and De Houwer 2014; Moors, Spruyt, and De Houwer 2010).

Consciousness is notoriously difficult to define, but it will suffice for our purposes to say that a response is conscious to the extent that it involves the respondents' awareness and, concomitantly, unconscious to the extent that the respondent is unaware of some element of his or her response. For example, measures that involve *subliminal priming*—presenting stimuli in such a way that the participant does not realize that he or she has been exposed to them—can be said to be unconscious; however, participants' responses to the task (e.g., keypresses) might still be conscious. Intentionality and controllability are related properties that apply to the relationship between goals and behavioral outcomes. To intend an outcome is to have a goal to produce that outcome; to control an outcome is to successfully produce the intended outcome. It is important to note that unintended outcomes are not just random *accidents*: for an unintended outcome to be psychologically meaningful, it has to be related to a person in some stable way. An accidental fall on a wet floor does not tell us as much about a person as repeated unintentional falls under different circumstances. Similarly, a one-off slip of the tongue does not count as a measure of implicit attitudes unless it is replicable in some reliable way. Finally, resource efficiency pertains to the extent to which a response requires attention: thus, measures that are immune to distraction are implicit in this sense.

These four properties—dubbed the Four Horsemen of *automaticity* by social psychologists (Bargh 1994)—are related but distinct; furthermore, psychological measures, including indirect measures, vary to the extent that they involve each of them. In other words, not all indirect measures are implicit measures, and not all implicit measures are implicit in the same way. Both of these principles apply to the methods we describe in the remainder of this chapter, and we will revisit them when we discuss best practices in the use of indirect and implicit measures. In the next two sections, we will introduce a series of indirect and implicit measurement paradigms that have appeared in the research literature before concluding with some guidelines on how to adapt these paradigms for use in social scientific research.

"Low-Tech" Options

In their attempt to measure religiosity indirectly (and/or implicitly), some psychologists have adopted and adapted techniques that allow them to infer participants' psychological traits and states through measuring and interpreting participants' responses to certain (and sometimes seemingly unrelated) cues. We call these "low-tech" measures because their administration does not require any advanced technology like computers or special equipment. Two good examples of these are partially structured measures and assimilation bias measures.

Partially Structured Measures

Traditional projective measures, such as the Rorschach test (Rorschach 1927) and the Thematic Apperception Test (Murray 1943) require participants to respond to images—ambiguous visual patterns in the former case, and drawings of events in the latter—and testers to interpret participants' responses to infer personality characteristics and other psychological traits and states. In this particular form, results are heavily reliant on the tester's subjective (and potentially idiosyncratic) interpretations of participants' responses, and often reveal more about the tester than about the participant. Recently, however, Vargas, von Hippel, and Petty (2004) attempted to revive and reform partially structured measures, designing a narrative-based (as opposed to image-based) version to assess participants' personal religiosity. Consider the following vignette:

> Mary didn't go to church once the whole time she was in college but she claimed that she was still a very religious person. She said that she prayed

occasionally and that she believed in Christian ideals. Sometimes she watched religious programs on TV like the 700 Club or the Billy Graham Crusade. (Vargas et al. 2004:197)

In Vargas et al.'s (2004, Study 4) study, participants were presented with twenty such vignettes describing a character's religiosity, and were asked in each case, "How religious was the behavior [Mary] performed?" and "How religious do you think [Mary] is in general?" Participants' judgments about Mary's religiosity depend in part on their *own* religiosity: specifically, participants who are very religious will perceive Mary to be much less religious than those who are themselves relatively nonreligious. On the basis of this idea, Vargas et al. (2004) asked participants to respond to both questions on an eleven-point scale anchored at "not at all religious" and "extremely religious." Given that religious participants are expected to rate Mary as relatively *non*religious, their scores were reversed-coded so that higher scores implied that participants were very religious. The forty ratings were averaged together to form a single religiosity score. As predicted, participants' scores on this measure predicted their self-reported religious behavior; they were also correlated with participants' self-reported religious attitudes. Crucially, they predicted unique variance in religious behavior beyond what was accounted for by the self-reported attitude measure. Thus, this partially structured measure has incremental validity; it does not merely serve as an alternative to its self-report counterpart, but can also supplement it.

Partially structured measures have also been used to assess particular theological beliefs. Barrett and Keil (1996) designed a series of vignettes to assess the extent to which participants held *anthropomorphic* representations of God. They presented eight vignettes, such as the following:

A boy was swimming alone in a swift and rocky river. The boy got his left leg caught between two large, gray rocks and couldn't get out. Branches of trees kept bumping into him as they hurried past. He thought he was going to drown and so he began to struggle and pray. Though God was answering another prayer in another part of the world when the boy started praying, before long God responded by pushing one of the rocks so the boy could get his leg out. The boy struggled to the river bank and fell over exhausted. (Barrett and Keil 1996:224)

These vignettes were designed to be ambiguous. In the case above, the vignette—or so Barrett and Keil (1996) argue—neither states nor necessarily implies that God is at one particular place at any given time, or that God moves at any point, or that God answered the two prayers sequentially. The measure of theological anthropomorphism relies on this ambiguity. Unlike in Vargas et al.'s (2004) measure, Barrett and Keil's (1996) participants were not asked to make any particular judgments, but instead to recall information from these vignettes. Participants' recollections were then coded for the extent to which they featured anthropomorphic interpretations of the vignettes. To the extent that participants (mis)remembered that God moves from one place to another or answers prayers sequentially, Barrett and Keil (1996; Barrett 1998) inferred that they displayed anthropomorphic beliefs about God (e.g., being limited by space and time). Indeed, their study showed that religious believers held these "theologically incorrect" beliefs even while denying them in a direct self-reported measure. Admittedly, however, Barrett and Keil's (1996) partially structured measure has not been assessed for its psychometric properties; their studies demonstrated a phenomenon that could be exploited to construct an indirect measure, but we do not yet have a fully developed measurement tool here.

In summary, partially structured measures seem like promising tools, adaptable for measuring different aspects of religiosity: Vargas et al. (2004) assessed individuals' levels of religious commitment, and Barrett and Keil (1996) assessed individuals' anthropomorphic representations of God. However—as with other indirect and implicit measures—they remain controversial as it is still unclear whether participants' responses reliably indicate underlying attitudes, or reflect some extraneous artifact of the task or the context of measurement. It is also unclear whether these measures count as *implicit* measures, as defined earlier. Vargas et al. (2004) and Barrett (1998; Barrett and Keil 1996) do claim that these measures assess implicit attitudes, but they do not clearly fulfill the criteria for automaticity (Bargh 1994; Gawronski and De Houwer 2014). More psychometric research needs to be done for these understudied and underutilized measures.

Assimilation Bias Measures

The *assimilation bias*, sometimes known as the *confirmation bias*, is the tendency of people to search for and evaluate evidence in ways that maintain their current attitudes. Social psychologists have exploited this bias to infer individuals' attitudes in an indirect way. Saucier and Miller (2003), for example, designed their Racial Argument Scale (RAS) in this way. The RAS consists of a series of sixteen short paragraphs, some of which presented arguments with pro-black conclusions and others of which presented arguments with anti-black conclusions. The participants were asked to evaluate each paragraph by rating how well each argument supported its conclusion on a five-point scale ranging from "not at all" to "very much." Participants were not asked to rate how much they agreed with the conclusion, only the extent to which the conclusion followed from the premises in the argument. Saucier and Miller (2003) found that test-retest reliability for the RAS was high ($r = .81$); RAS scores were moderately correlated with various explicit measure of racial prejudice ($r = .42$ to $.57$) and uncorrelated with social desirability measures. Furthermore, RAS scores predicted respondents' willingness to provide their contact details to a black student organization for the purposes of completing a phone survey, and also their willingness to provide negative feedback about black authors' work beyond the contribution of explicit measures. As with the partially structured measures in the previous section, this demonstrates incremental validity.

There is, as yet, no religiosity measure that exploits the assimilation bias in this way. The closest approximation is Norenzayan and Hansen's (2006, Experiment 2) measures of people's beliefs in supernatural agency. They presented participants with (what was ostensibly) a *New York Times* article describing an experiment on the efficacy of prayer, which purportedly showed that women who were prayed for were far more likely to successfully conceive a child than those who were not prayed for. Participants were then asked to rate their agreement with a series of statements. Some of these statements were directly about participants' supernatural beliefs (e.g., "God/a higher power exists"), but others were about the article itself (e.g., "The study was scientifically rigorous"). Norenzayan and Hansen (2006) did not analyze responses to the latter statements, but Saucier and Miller's (2003) work strongly suggests that such items might serve as good indirect measures of supernatural belief (or, more specifically in this case, belief in the causal efficacy of intercessory prayer).

Response Latency–Based Measures

In contrast to the "low-tech" measures described above, by far the most commonly used indirect measures are those that use computers or other equipment to record participants' response latencies or reaction times in some task and, from these latencies, infer participants' attitudes and other psychological states and traits. These response latency–based measures are also generally considered to be *implicit*, in the sense that they involve automaticity to varying degrees. For the remainder of this chapter, we will consider three classes of measures that rely on participants' response latencies. The basis of each of these is the *simple choice reaction time* task, which requires participants to respond to stimuli by categorizing them into one of two options as quickly as they can. An example of this is the *lexical decision task*, which requires participants to categorize strings of letters as either words or nonwords: "key" is a word, whereas its anagram "yek" is not. Another common example involves categorizing words as either positive or negative: "delightful" is positive, whereas "awful" is negative. The stimuli in these tasks are not limited to words, though they are typically presented visually: thus, images of particular objects or types of objects may also feature. In each case, psychologists are interested in how *quickly* (and accurately) individuals perform these tasks: the speed (and accuracy) of making these classifications is taken as an indication of how information is cognitively stored or processed. The simple choice reaction time task forms the basis for all the other implicit measures of religiosity that we will consider below.

Property Verification Measures

A *property verification task* measures the links or associations, in participants' minds, between some stimuli and some property of the target objects to which the stimuli refer. If, for example, the researcher is interested in participants' positive or negative evaluations of Christianity, she might choose target stimuli like "church," "priest," and "cross," and property words like "good" and "pleasant" on one hand and "bad" and "unpleasant" on the other. The way in which participants categorize the targets—as positive or negative—is likely to closely reflect their *explicit* attitudes, but the *speed* at which they perform the task may tell us more: speedier responses indicate stronger attitudes. This task therefore potentially includes both an explicit and an implicit measure at the same time. For any given task of this kind, researchers have to determine what the targets are as well as what the properties are: this depends on the psychological construct of interest.

Let us turn to actual examples of property verification tasks applied to religiosity. Cohen, Shariff, and Hill (2008) presented participants with a series of nouns, which participants simply had to categorize as quickly as possible as either "real" or "imaginary." Some of these words referred to things that were uncontroversially real (e.g., car, water); others referred to things that were uncontroversially imaginary (e.g., Darth Vader, Superman); others still referred to objects of religious faith (e.g., God, Devil); and yet others referred to objects of secular faith (e.g., black hole, Socrates). There were eight stimuli for each category, and each stimulus was presented twice: stimuli were presented one at a time in random order, with a five-hundred-millisecond gap between each trial. Clearly, the category of interest was one referring to the objects of religious faith: furthermore, given the properties—real and imaginary—Cohen et al. (2008) were not evaluating how positively or negatively people felt about these objects, but the extent to which people believed in them. Cohen et al. (2008) found that individuals' classification of religious items as real or imaginary was highly reliable ($\alpha = .95$), and response latencies for religious items showed moderately good test-retest reliability (after seven days), even controlling for overall response speeds ($\beta = .24$). Furthermore, only response latencies for religious items were correlated with self-reported religiosity: indeed, there was a *curvilinear* relationship between them. That is, very religious people categorized objects like "God" and "Devil" as real faster than did more nominally religious people; similarly, very nonreligious people categorize those objects as imaginary more quickly than did more nominally nonreligious people.

More recently, Jong, Halberstadt, and Bluemke (2012, Study 3) ran a modified and simplified version of this measure, and found evidence for

Table 3.1. Stimuli for Jong et al. (2012) simple choice reaction time measure

Category	Stimuli
Supernatural	angel, demon, devil, god, heaven, hell, miracle, prophet, soul, spirit
Real	eagle, helicopter, otter, Puerto Rico, turtle
Imaginary	batmobile, fairy, genie, mermaid, Narnia

discriminant validity relative to a self-report measure of religious belief, while studying the relationship between religiosity and death anxiety. In their version of the task, they had twenty stimuli: ten referred to objects of religious belief, five referred to patently real objects, and five referred to patently imaginary objects (see table 3.1). Each stimulus was presented thrice, and the order of presentation was randomized for each participant. Prior to each trial, a fixation cross was presented for 750 milliseconds; the fixation cross reappeared immediately after participants made their response about whether each object was real or imaginary. Jong et al. (2012) found that thinking about death reduced nonreligious participants' scores on a self-report measure of religious belief, but *increased* their scores on this implicit measure: the experimental manipulation had diverging effects on explicit and implicit religious belief, thus showing the added value of assessing both types of belief.

Property verification tasks have also been used to measure other aspects of religiosity besides belief in the supernatural. Gibson (2006), for example, has constructed a yes/no task in which participants are asked to determine whether or not certain adjectives describe God; Sharp, Rentfrow, and Gibson (2015) then adapted this task to compare Christians' representations of the three "persons" of the Trinity. Other researchers have also extended this work to examine individuals' positive or negative evaluations of God (Yarborough 2009; Zahl 2013).

There is a sense in which property verification tasks are not indirect measures at all, given that they *directly* ask participants to make judgments about religious concepts. However, they are indirect in the sense that strength of religious belief is inferred not from participants' categorization responses, but from participants' response latencies on the critical target stimuli. Similarly, these tasks do not unambiguously fulfill the four criteria of implicitness or automaticity. The categorization task itself is performed intentionally, consciously, controllably, and not particularly resource efficiently, though Järnefeldt, Canfield, and Kelemen (2015) provide some evidence that speeded responses are less than perfectly amenable to conscious control. Using a yes/no task, they asked professed atheists whether a series of natural phenomena were "purposefully made by some being" or not. Approximately half the participants were told to answer "as quickly as possible" (with a maximum time of 865 milliseconds per trial), while the other half were given as much time as they needed. They found that those in the speeded condition categorized more phenomena as having been created than those in the unspeeded condition. Furthermore, while responses to property verification tasks are not necessarily automatic in principle, participants are usually unaware that their response latencies are being measured, and are thus also unlikely to attempt to intentionally control their speed.

Sequential Priming Measures

A sequential priming task essentially involves a simple choice reaction time task, with additional stimuli that participants are meant to ignore ("primes"); the primes may be presented either above the threshold of conscious awareness (supraliminally) or below (subliminally). Furthermore, the primes may be presented prior to or simultaneously with the target stimuli, which participants have to categorize. As a measure of attitudes, this task exploits the *congruency effect*: participants tend to respond more slowly to targets when they are paired with *incongruent* primes, and more quickly when paired with *congruent* primes. Broadly speaking, pairs of stimuli can be *semantically* or *evaluatively* congruent or incongruent, though there is some overlap between the two.

The classic example of semantic priming is that, in a lexical decision task, the stimulus "doctor" is more easily and quickly recognized as a word when it is paired with "nurse" than when it is paired with "bread." Conversely, "butter" is more easily and quickly recognized as a word when it is paired with "bread" than when it is compared with "nurse" (Meyer and Schvaneveldt 1971). From this, we infer that the cognitive associations between the concepts *doctor* and *nurse* are stronger or closer to each other than they are to *bread* and *butter*, which are conversely more strongly associated to each other than they are to the previous pair. An evaluative priming task (sometimes known as an affective priming task) is an extension of the semantic priming phenomenon, but relies on a valence congruency effect (Fazio 2001; Fazio, Sanbonmatsu, Powell, and Kardes 1986), and concomitantly requires participants to categorize target stimuli as either positive or negative. Thus, in their seminal studies, Fazio et al. (1986) showed that positive primes facilitate the categorization of positive stimuli, whereas negative primes facilitate the categorization of negative stimuli. Sequential priming tasks—both semantic and evaluative—have long been used as measures of attitudes; there is therefore considerable evidence of their reliability and validity. For example, Cameron, Brown-Iannuzzi, and Payne (2012) ran a meta-analysis of 167 studies involving sequential priming measures and found that they were both correlated with explicit attitude measures ($r = .2$), as well as with behavioral measures ($r = .28$); implicit measure scores continued to predict behavior even when controlling for explicit measure scores. Evaluative priming measures thus show incremental validity.

There are, as yet, no validated implicit measures of religiosity based on the evaluative priming task. However, Wenger (2004) has designed a task that is potentially useful as such a measure. In this task, participants were primed with the words "Christian" (religious prime), "student" (neutral prime), and "housetop" (nonhuman neutral prime); they then categorized a series of phrases as describing behaviors that are either "possible" or "impossible" to perform. The stimuli consisted of sixteen phrases, four describing religious behaviors (e.g., worship God), four, academic behaviors (e.g., take tests), and eight, nonsensical nonactions (e.g., open sand). Wenger (2004) theorized that the extent to which the "Christian" prime facilitated responses to the religious actions indicated close correspondence between religious ideas and religious practice; indeed, he found that performance on this task predicted *intrinsic* religiosity but not *extrinsic* religiosity (see Hill and Pargament, this volume). Wenger (2004) interpreted this task as "indicating a kind of internalization of beliefs for intrinsically oriented individuals" (p. 12), but with different stimuli, the evaluative priming task may be adapted to measure other religiosity constructs. With measures of religious belief like Cohen et al.'s (2008) and Jong et al.'s (2012) property verification tasks, for example, researchers may use the word "god" (and other words related to religion) as the prime, and positive (e.g., genuine, actual) and negative (e.g., bogus, fictional) existential concepts as targets, to be categorized either as positive/negative existential concepts (i.e., real/imaginary) or as words/nonwords in a lexical decision task.

So far, we have been describing congruence—whether semantic or evaluative—as if it were an objective property of the pairs of stimuli, but whether two concepts are cognitively associated is bound to vary somewhat from person to person, and even from situation to situation. For some stimuli, there is so much stable intersubjective agreement that we can assume, for example, that "bread" and "butter" go together, and that words like "delightful" are positive and words like "awful" are negative. But when we are using a sequential priming task as a measure of attitudes, we are trying to *assess* rather than assume the extent to which stimulus pairs are congruent or incongruent for any given individual in any given situation. And given that personal religiosity is a highly subjective topic, the degree of variation between people in their individual perception of the degree of congruence between religious primes and specific targets will result in meaningful differences in performance on these tasks.

Implicit Association Test and Its Variants

The Implicit Association Test (IAT; Greenwald, McGhee, and Schwartz 1998) and its descendants are among the most commonly used implicit measures of psychological constructs, including prejudice (Rudman, Greenwald, Mellott, and Schwartz 1999), self-esteem (Greenwald and Farnham 2000), anxiety (Egloff and Schmukle 2002), aggression (Lemmer, Gollwitzer, and Banse 2015), consumer attitudes (Maison, Greenwald, and Bruin 2004), and attitudes toward alcohol (Ostafin and Palfai 2006). As the name suggests, IATs measure the strength of cognitive *associations*; in particular, they compare two target-attribute pairs on the basis of relative response times.

IATs consist of two critical categorization tasks, implemented across five phases. Phases 1 and 2 are both practice phases, in which participants learn to respond to the *target* and *attribute* stimuli as quickly and accurately as possible by pressing two keys. For example, participants might first be asked to categorize target images of Pepsi-Cola and Coca-Cola by pressing the "Z" and "M" keys of a keyboard, respectively. Then, in Phase 2, they would be asked to categorize positive (e.g., "delightful") and negative (e.g., "awful") attribute words using those same keys. Phase 3 is the first critical categorization task, in which both kinds of stimuli—targets and attributes—are presented, randomly interspersed, and participants have to categorize each of them accordingly ("Z" for Pepsi OR positive; "M" for Coke OR negative). Given the valence congruence effect described earlier, we would expect people who prefer Pepsi-Cola over Coca-Cola to find this task easier (and therefore to respond faster) than those who prefer Coca-Cola over Pepsi-Cola. Phase 4 is another practice round like Phase 1, but now the key presses are reversed ("Z" for Coke, "M" for Pepsi). Finally, Phase 5 is identical to Phase 3, except that the target responses correspond to Phase 4 ("Z" for Coke OR positive, "M" for Pepsi OR negative). For this phase, we might expect Coke fans to outperform Pepsi fans. The critical phases are 3 and 5, when participants have to categorize both targets and attributes. The response latencies observed in Phases 3 and 5 allow us to compute the *relative* strength of one pair of associations ("Coke good, Pepsi bad") with another pair of associations ("Pepsi good, Coke bad"). There are multiple ways to compute an implicit association score from raw response latencies, but the basic idea is to compare between Phases 3 and 5 (see Greenwald, Nosek, and Banaji 2003 for detailed algorithm), thereby producing a score that assesses the implicit attitude toward one object in relation to another object. Greenwald, Poehlman, Uhlmann, and Banaji's (2009) meta-analysis of 184 independent samples found that IAT scores were correlated with explicit measures ($r = .36$) and behavioral measures ($r = .27$), and also provided evidence for incremental validity as we have seen with other implicit measures.

An example of an IAT in the domain of religiosity is the Religiousness-Spirituality IAT (RS-IAT; Labouff, Rowatt, Johnson, Thedford, and Tsang 2010). This IAT measures the extent to which people consider themselves religious relative to others. Participants were asked to categorize words as belonging to "self" ("I," "me," "my," "mine," "self") or "other" ("they," "them," "their," "it," "other"), and to "religious-spiritual" ("religious," "spiritual," "faithful," "theistic," "believer") or "not religious–not spiritual" ("nonreligious," "nonspiritual," "faithless," "atheistic," "agnostic"). Higher scores on the RS-IAT indicate that people are faster at categorizing self/religious-spiritual and other/not religious–not spiritual than at categorizing self/not religious–not spiritual and other/religious-spiritual. Scores on the RS-IAT were found to be positively correlated with self-report measures of religiosity, and to account for unique variability in predicting people's attitudes toward gay men and lesbian women.

Despite being a tried-and-true measure of implicit attitudes, one common criticism of the classic IAT is that it requires two contrasting targets (e.g., Pepsi v. Coke), and therefore that it is a measure of *relative* attitudes: the classic IAT does not tell us how someone feels about Pepsi, so much as about how he or she feels about Pepsi compared to Coke. This limitation is particularly problematic for assessing some religiosity variables, such as religious beliefs, because it is not clear what the contrasting target would be, given that researchers are not necessarily interested in individuals' religious beliefs relative to their secular beliefs. Fortunately, there is a variant of the IAT, the Single Target IAT (ST-IAT, Wigboldus, Holland, and van Knippenberg 2006; also Karpinski and Steinman 2006; Penke, Eichstaedt, and Asendorpf 2006; and see Nosek and Banaji 2001 on the Go/No Go Task). It is largely similar to the classic IAT, but assesses only one target. For example, if we were to assess implicit attitudes toward Coca-Cola, the first critical categorization task might involve classifying images of Coca-Cola OR negative words with the left key, and positive words with the right key. The second critical categorization task would involve classifying negative words with the left key, and positive words OR images of Coca-Cola with the right key. Just as with the IAT, the implicit association score is the difference between the two critical test phases (see Bluemke and Friese 2008 for more information on computing ST-IAT scores, and for a psychometric evaluation of the ST-IAT).

Together with the property verification task described earlier, Jong et al. (2012, Study 2) also designed a Religious Belief ST-IAT to assess strength of implicit religious belief. In Phase 1, participants categorized attribute words connoting "real" and "imaginary" by pressing the "Z" and "/" keys on their keyboard, respectively (see table 3.2 for stimuli). Each stimulus was presented thrice, in random order, preceded by a five-hundred-millisecond fixation cross. In Phase 2, words referring to supernatural entities were also presented, interspersed with the "real" and "imaginary" words; participants responded to "real" OR "supernatural" words (presented thrice each) by pressing "Z," and to "imaginary" words (presented six time each) by pressing the "/" key. In Phase 3,

Table 3.2. Stimuli for Jong et al. (2012) ST-IAT Measure

Category	Stimuli
Supernatural	god, demon, devil, angel, heaven, hell, soul
Real	real, genuine, existent, actual, true, valid, factual
Imaginary	imaginary, fake, false, fictional, bogus, untrue, illusory

the key for "supernatural" words was switched such that participants responded to "real" words by pressing "Z" and "imaginary" OR "supernatural" words by pressing "/".

As mentioned earlier in our discussion of the property verification task, Jong et al. (2012) found that thinking about death decreased nonreligious participants' self-reported religious beliefs, but *increased* their implicit religious beliefs. This finding was replicated using the Religious Belief ST-IAT: thinking about death increased both religious and nonreligious participants' ST-IAT scores. This is not to say that explicit and implicit beliefs *always* diverge. For example, Shariff, Cohen, and Norenzayan (2008) also employed an ST-IAT, and found that reading essays that criticized religion reduced both explicit and implicit religious belief. This shows that the relationship between explicit and implicit beliefs depends at least in part on the experimental manipulation. This, along with the fact that explicit and implicit measures of religious belief are positively correlated ($r = .27$, Jong et al. 2012; .31, Shariff et al. 2008), is also consistent with the view that explicit and implicit cognitions are not totally dissociated from one another, but are related albeit nonidentical constructs.

Constructing and Using Indirect and Implicit Measures

There is one obvious difference between self-report measures of religiosity and indirect or implicit measures of religiosity: whereas there are dozens upon dozens of more or less *fixed* versions of the former that have been psychometrically evaluated, this is not the case for the latter. Rather, we have various *paradigms*—partially structured tasks, tasks involving the assimilation bias, simple choice reaction time tasks, sequential priming tasks, Implicit Association Tests, and so forth—that form the basis for constructing specific implicit measures. Indeed, researchers are much more likely to construct their own implicit measures of religiosity than to reuse one that has been used before; this is in stark contrast to the general tendency to prefer established self-report scales over ad hoc ones. Accordingly, in this final section, we provide some basic guidelines for how to construct, use, and evaluate implicit measures of religiosity from the sort of paradigms described above.

Why (and Why Not) Indirect and Implicit Measures?

Before considering the question of which indirect/implicit paradigm should be used, researchers should first ask a more basic question: why use indirect/implicit measures at all? As we have discussed earlier, indirect and implicit measures were developed to overcome self-report biases and the limits of human introspection. We therefore recommend using implicit measures under the following conditions:

1. there is good reason to believe that self-report measures cannot yield any meaningful data (e.g., because participants have limited introspective access on the trait in question); and/or
2. the researcher is interested in the effects of religiosity on some outcome variable, but does not want participants to know that their religiosity is being assessed (e.g., because awareness is likely to affect their behavior in undesirable ways); and/or
3. there is good reason to expect a divergence between explicit and implicit religiosity.

Insofar as there is good theoretical reason to assume that an implicit measure can illuminate some aspect of religiosity that would meaningfully contribute to the research question, then the paradigms we have presented can be valuable: they should not supplant but support (and perhaps even be meaningfully contrasted with) self-report measures or observational studies of religiosity. There is no question that the richness of religious experience and the depth of conviction that people hold about their religious beliefs could never be adequately reflected in response latencies or performance on a comprehension task with fictitious narratives. Nevertheless, the measures we have introduced are based on empirically grounded theories about human cognition, and we have every reason to think that these theories and paradigms will enhance our ability to study religiosity scientifically.

Our enthusiasm for indirect and implicit measures should not be confused with the naïve belief that they are panaceas that swiftly and straightforwardly cure us of our methodological weaknesses. First, it would be a gross oversimplification to say that indirct and implicit measures are completely immune to those self-presentational effects that they seek to avoid. It is not impossible to "fake" responses to implicit measures (e.g., Fiedler and Bluemke 2005; Röhner, Schröder-Abé, and Schütz 2013; Steffens 2004), though they are much harder to fake than traditional self-report measures. It is similarly unjustified to assert that implicit measures provide privileged and unequivocal access to "the unconscious," as if this were a mysterious mental realm far beyond the reach of our introspective powers, nor is it correct to value implicit attitudes as somehow *more* true or more genuine than explicit attitudes. Against the view of radical independence is the fact that the correlations between explicit and implicit measures tend to be nonzero and positive, albeit only moderately so (e.g., .24 in a meta-analysis by Hofmann, Gawronski, Gschwendner, Le, and Schmitt 2005 on the Implicit Association Test). Furthermore, the fact that different implicit measures can and sometimes do diverge from one another indicates not only that they vary in quality but also potentially that different implicit measures are assessing different psychological constructs, or different aspects thereof (e.g., Bosson, Swann, and Pennebaker 2000; Fazio and Olson 2003). A more reasonable attitude toward implicit measures is perhaps to say that, under certain circumstances, they help us to access and assess aspects of human cognition that are related to but nevertheless distinct from those aspects that are more easily measured via self-report measures.

Having decided to use indirect or implicit measures, the researchers must choose which paradigm to use. This choice will largely depend on both theoretical and practical considerations.

Which Paradigm? Theoretical Considerations

The first theoretical decision to be made concerns the aspect of religiosity that is of theoretical relevance or interest. As the theoretical and methodological research on the multidimensionality of religiosity has amply shown, it is simply too vague to say that we are interested in measuring "religiosity." Not only are there important differences between religious *identity* and *belief* and *behavior*, but there are different kinds and levels of each. "Religious beliefs" may include attitudes toward God, which may be entirely independent from one's attitude toward organized religions, beliefs about angels and demons, and beliefs about the afterlife. It is therefore important for the researcher to clearly identify a conceptual framework for what precisely he or she wishes to study (including how implicit cognition comes into play in the particular framework), before choosing the most appropriate methodology. Fortunately, the paradigms we have introduced in this chapter are flexible with respect to content, and can therefore be adapted to measure a wide variety of religious cognitions.

The second theoretical decision pertains to the measurement problem at hand. The tasks we have described vary on whether they were designed to solve the strategic-responding problem, the limitations-of-introspection problem, or both. In other words, they vary on the extent, as well as the sense, in which they involve automaticity. Recall that a measure is automatic insofar as responses do not require intention, can occur without conscious awareness, are difficult or impossible to control, and do not require much attentional resource. These four criteria of automaticity are neither binary properties, nor do they always co-occur. The fact that the criteria are dissociable means that different measurement techniques might capture psychological constructs that are automatic in different ways. It also means that a single task can be an implicit measure in one sense, but not in another. Thus, a valid interpretation of what any particular implicit measure tells us requires additional information about the precise sense in and extent to which a measure is implicit. For example, as we have already discussed, property verification tasks are implicit to the extent that they manage to bypass participants' conscious, intentional control; however, given that participants may, with some ease, respond in such a way as to "fake" their responses, it is fairer to conclude that property verification tasks are only minimally implicit on these aspects of automaticity. In contrast, studies have shown that while IATs are not immune to faking, they are much more difficult to fake than traditional questionnaire measures, particularly for novice participants. Furthermore, participants completing IATs are less consciously aware of what is being measured than participants completing property verification tasks: the latter might not realize that their response latencies are being used as measures, but the former might not even know that the task measures attitudes at all. That said, the categorization tasks involved in IATs might arouse participants' suspicions about the true purpose of the IAT; there is indeed some evidence to that effect (De Houwer and Moors 2012), showing also that IATs for some attitudes (e.g., racial prejudice) arouse more suspicion than IATs for others (e.g., political attitudes). Sequential priming techniques seem even less amenable to faking, though it is again not impossible (Degner 2009; Klauer and Teige-Mocigemba 2007; Teige-Mocigemba and Klauer 2008). To reduce fakeability—that is, intentionality and controllability—researchers can reduce the time between the presentation of the prime and the presentation of the stimulus (even to the point of subliminality; e.g., Wittenbrink, Judd, and Park 1997), and also impose a deadline by which a response must be made in order to be counted as valid (e.g., six hundred milliseconds; Degner 2009). Furthermore, while there is no direct evidence that sequential priming techniques can access cognitions about which participants are themselves unaware, the fact that subliminal priming is effective in this context means that sequential priming can access cognitions without participants' awareness that this is being done at all.

There is still insufficient evidence regarding indirect measures in general, let alone measures of religiosity more specifically, for us to make firm conclusions, but sequential priming techniques seem to most completely fulfill the automaticity criteria, relative to other paradigms (cf. Moors, Spruyt, and De Houwer 2010; for a more detailed comparison, see De Houwer, Teige-Mocigemba, Spruyt, and Moors 2009). Thus, if *implicitness* is crucial, all else being equal, researchers should use sequential priming tasks (see Wentura and Degner 2010 for more practical recommendations on this task). However, there may be other reasons for preferring other techniques, such as the IAT. For example, given that sequential priming tasks do not require participants to attend to the category of the stimuli—this is a feature that increases its implicitness—it is, under some circumstances, more likely to be affected by idiosyncratic features of individual stimuli: that is, sequential priming measures might tell us more about participants' attitudes toward the particular *stimuli* in the task than about their attitudes toward the *categories* they are intended to represent (Livingstone and Brewer 2002; Olson and Fazio 2003). As with the choice between paper- and computer-based tasks, practical considerations like the feasibility of subliminal priming or the familiarity of potential participants with any given technique may also influence a researcher's decision about which paradigm to employ.

Which Paradigm? Practical Considerations

If the researcher determines that indirect or implicit measures would indeed produce meaningful and valuable data to answer specific research questions, then the second set of considerations concerns the practical administration of indirect/implicit measures. In this chapter, we have introduced five measurement paradigms, two of which are "low-tech" options that can be done on paper, and three of which are based on participants' response latencies. The former category can be easily administered in a range of contexts, though some measures may need to be administered in a quiet space that is free of distraction. For example, a task that measures a participant's memory of certain types of stimuli as an indirect measure of religious beliefs may need to be administered in a quiet room that is free of distraction in order ensure that the data are valid. Response latency–based tasks can, in principle, be run on paper, but are more commonly administered via computers (see Bassett et al. 2005 for more on paper-and-pencil religiosity IATs). One factor that might determine which paradigm is most appropriate is therefore the extent to which it is possible or desirable to run a paper-and-pencil measure rather than a computer-based measure. It may not, for example, be possible to run computer-based measures in certain situations outside the research laboratory (e.g., during fieldwork): if so, a researcher might have to use a "low-tech" indirect measure or a paper-and-pencil IAT instead. Practical considerations aside, we recommend that the choice of measurement technique be primarily dictated by one's theoretical interests, as discussed above.

Indirect Measures and the Contemporary Social Scientific Study of Religion

The best scientific tools help us not only to answer our current questions but also to ask those questions in better ways and even to provoke us to ask *new* questions. At the beginning of this chapter, we introduced indirect and implicit measures as means by which to solve longstanding measurement problems. Very quickly, however, we saw how methodological advances in implicit *measures* opened up new avenues of research into implicit—that is, automatic—*cognitions* and *processes*. We have already learned the lesson of the multidimensionality of religiosity from methodological advances in self-report measures, and the new tools covered in this chapter extend this multidimensionality in a different direction, toward exploring aspects of religiosity that may be *unconscious*, for example, and even seemingly at odds with explicitly held attitudes. Indeed, these new methods have already begun to bear theoretical and empirical fruit: as it has done in other social scientific domains, the notion of implicit cognitions now features prominently in developmental and evolutionary theories of religion (e.g., Atran 2002; Boyer 2001; Kelemen 2004; Tremlin 2006; Uhlmann, Poehlman, and Bargh 2008). Therefore, insofar as social scientists are interested in the correlates, causes, and consequences of religiosity, we should welcome indirect and implicit measures into our arsenal of measurement techniques, and celebrate the new opportunities they afford us to explore this most intriguing of human phenomena.

Glossary

AUTOMATICITY: In cognition, this refers to the influence of external stimuli on a person's psychological processes without his or her knowledge or awareness of such influence. Automaticity can refer to any one or more of the following features: conscious awareness, intentionality, controllability, and efficiency.

CONTROLLABLE/UNCONTROLLABLE: Refers to the extent to which an individual is motivated and able to counteract a particular cognitive process.

FIXATION CROSS: A symbol (typically a cross) presented on the screen, usually in the center, where the stimulus is expected to be presented.

IMPLICIT MEASURES: Measures to which responses are unconscious, unintentional, uncontrollable, and/or resource efficient.

INDIRECT MEASURES: Measures that do not rely on participants' self-assessment but involve inferring participants' mental states and traits from some other behavior or response.

IMPLICIT ASSOCIATION TASK: This task evaluates the relative strength of two related pairs of associations (e.g., "Coke is good, Pepsi is bad" and "Coke is bad, Pepsi is good") by comparing the response latencies of each pair of associations.

INTENTIONAL/UNINTENTIONAL: Intentionality refers to the extent to which the individual has control over the instigation of cognitive processes.

LEXICAL DECISION TASK: A task in which participants are asked to judge whether a string of letters is a word or a nonword. Both speed and accuracy of judgment are considered.

MASK (PRIMING): A symbol (typically ######) presented before and/or after a word-based prime that diminishes the visibility of primes.

PRIME: *Verb:* temporary and unobtrusive activation of one or more mentally represented concepts. *Noun:* the stimulus that is expected to activate a mentally represented concept. For example, words like "church" and "Jesus" might be primes for the concept of "Christianity."

PROPERTY VERIFICATION TASK: A task that requires participants to categorize stimuli on the basis of some property or attribute of the target objects to which the stimuli refer.

RESOURCE EFFICIENCY: Refers to the degree of mental resources that are required in the cognitive process. Automatic processing typically requires low mental resources.

RESPONSE LATENCY: A measurement of the time interval (typically in milliseconds) between presentation of some stimulus and an individual's response. The timing is typically measured using a computer. The speed is treated as an indicator of the strength of association between representations.

SEQUENTIAL PRIMING: A simple choice reaction time task that is preceded by presentation of primes. We describe two types of sequential priming tasks: (1) semantic priming, which is based on the observation that a response to a target is faster when it is preceded by a semantically related prime, and (2) evaluative priming, which is based on the observation that a response to a target is faster when it is preceded by stimuli with congruent valence.

SIMPLE CHOICE REACTION TIME TASK: A task in which participants are asked to categorize stimuli into one of two options as quickly and accurately as they can.

SUBLIMINAL PRIMING: Presentation of priming stimuli below an individual's threshold of conscious awareness.

SUPRALIMINAL PRIMING: Presentation of priming stimuli just above an individual's threshold of conscious awareness, such that the individual is aware of the stimulus being presented without knowing what the stimulus is.

TARGET (OBJECT): The mentally represented concept that is the object of investigation.

REFERENCES

Allport, G. W., & Ross, J. M. (1967). Personal religious orientation and prejudice. *Journal of Personality and Social Psychology, 5*, 432–43.

Atran, S. (2002). *In gods we trust: The evolutionary landscape of religion*. Oxford, UK: Oxford University Press.

Bargh, J. A. (1994). The four horsemen of automaticity: Awareness, intention, efficiency, and control in social cognition. In R. Wyer & T. Srull (eds.), *Handbook of Social Cognition* (pp. 1–40). New York: Erlbaum.

Bargh, J. A., & Chartrand, T. L. (1999). The unbearable automaticity of being. *American Psychologist, 54*, 462–79.

Barrett, J. L. (1998). Cognitive constraints on Hindu concepts of the divine. *Journal for the Scientific Study of Religion, 37*, 608–19.

Barrett, J. L. (1999). Theological correctness: Cognitive constraint and the study of religion. *Method & Theory in the Study of Religion, 11*, 325–39.

Barrett, J. L., & Keil, F. C. (1996). Conceptualizing a nonnatural entity: Anthropomorphism in God concepts. *Cognitive Psychology, 31*, 219–47.

Bassett, R. L., Smith, A., Thrower, J., Tindall, M., Barclay, J., Tiuch, K., . . . & Monroe, J. (2005). One effort to measure implicit attitudes toward spirituality and religion. *Journal of Psychology & Christianity, 24*, 210–18.

Bluemke, M., & Friese, M. (2008). Reliability and validity of the Single-Target IAT (ST-IAT): Assessing automatic affect towards multiple attitude objects. *European Journal of Social Psychology, 38*, 977–97.

Bosson, J. K., Swann, W. B., Jr., & Pennebaker, J. W. (2000). Stalking the perfect measure of implicit self-esteem: The blind men and the elephant revisited? *Journal of Personality and Social Psychology, 79*, 631–43.

Boyer, P. (2001). *Religion explained: The evolutionary origins of religious thought*. New York: Basic Books.

Brenner, P. S. (2011). Identity importance and the overreporting of religious service attendance: Multiple imputation of religious attendance using the American Time Use Study and the General Social Survey. *Journal for the Scientific Study of Religion, 50*, 103–15.

Cameron, C. D., Brown-Iannuzzi, J. L., & Payne, B. K. (2012). Sequential priming measures of implicit social cognition: A meta-analysis of associations with behavior and explicit attitudes. *Personality and Social Psychology Review, 16*, 330–50.

Chaiken, S., & Trope, Y., eds. (1999). *Dual-process theories in social psychology.* New York: Guilford Press.

Chen, S., & Chaiken, S. (1999). The heuristic-systematic model in its broader context. In S. Chaiken & Y. Trope (eds.), *Dual-process theories in social and cognitive psychology* (pp. 73–96). New York: Guilford Press.

Cohen, A. B., Shariff, A. F., & Hill, P. C. (2008). The accessibility of religious beliefs. *Journal of Research in Personality, 42*, 1408–17.

Degner, J. (2009). On the (un-)controllability of affective priming: Strategic manipulation is feasible but can possibly be prevented. *Cognition and Emotion, 23*, 327–54.

De Houwer, J., & Moors, A. (2012). How to define and examine implicit processes? In R. Proctor & J. Capaldi (eds.), *Implicit and explicit processes in the psychology of science* (pp. 183–98). New York: Oxford University Press.

De Houwer, J., Teige-Mocigemba, S., Spruyt, A., & Moors, A. (2009). Implicit measures: A normative analysis and review. *Psychological Bulletin, 135*, 347–68.

Dijksterhuis, A., & Nordgren, L. (2006). A theory of unconscious thought. *Perspectives on Psychological Science*, 1, 95–109.

Dovidio, J. F., Kawakami, K., & Gaertner, S. L. (2002). Implicit and explicit prejudice and interracial interaction. *Journal of Personality and Social Psychology*, 82, 62–68.

Dovidio, J. F., Kawakami, K., Johnson, C., Johnson, B., & Howard, A. (1997). On the nature of prejudice: Automatic and controlled processes. *Journal of Experimental Social Psychology, 33*, 510–40.

Egloff, B., & Schmukle, S. C. (2002). Predictive validity of an implicit association test for assessing anxiety. *Journal of Personality and Social Psychology*, 83, 1441–55.

Fazio, R. H. (2001). On the automatic activation of associated evaluations: An overview. *Cognition & Emotion, 15*, 115–41.

Fazio, R. H., & Olson, M. A. (2003). Implicit measures in social cognition research: Their meaning and uses. *Annual Review of Psychology, 54*, 297–327.

Fazio, R. H., Sanbonmatsu, D. M., Powell, M. C., & Kardes, F. R. (1986). On the automatic activation of attitudes. *Journal of Personality and Social Psychology*, 50, 229–38.

Fiedler, K., & Bluemke, M. (2005). Faking the IAT: Aided and unaided response control on the Implicit Association Tests. *Basic and Applied Social Psychology, 27*, 307–16.

Gawronski, B., & Bodenhausen, G. V. (2006). Associative and propositional processes in evaluation: An integrative review of implicit and explicit attitude change. *Psychological Bulletin, 132*, 692–731.

Gawronski, B., & De Houwer, J. (2014). Implicit measures in social and personality psychology. In H. T. Reis & C. M. Judd (eds.), *Handbook of research methods in social and personality psychology*, 2nd ed. (pp. 283–310). New York: Cambridge University Press.

Gawronski, B., & Strack, F. (2004). On the propositional nature of cognitive consistency: Dissonance changes explicit, but not implicit attitudes. *Journal of Experimental Social Psychology, 40*, 535–42.

Gibson, N. J. S. (2006). *The experimental investigation of religious cognition*. Unpublished doctoral dissertation, University of Cambridge, Cambridge, England.

Gillings, V., & Joseph, S. (1996). Religiosity and social desirability: Impression management and self-deceptive positivity. *Personality and Individual Differences, 21*, 1047–50.

Gorsuch, R. L. (1984). Measurement: The boon and bane of investigating religion. *American Psychologist, 39*, 228–36.

Greenwald, A. G., & Farnham, S. D. (2000). Using the Implicit Association Test to measure self-esteem and self-concept. *Journal of Personality and Social Psychology, 79*, 1022–38.

Greenwald, A. G., McGhee, D. E., & Schwartz, J. L. K. (1998). Measuring individual differences in implicit cognition: The Implicit Association Test. *Journal of Personality and Social Psychology, 74*, 1464–80.

Greenwald, A. G., Nosek, B. A., & Banaji, M. R. (2003). Understanding and using the implicit association test: I. An improved scoring algorithm. *Journal of Personality and Social Psychology, 85*, 197–216.

Greenwald, A. G., Poehlman, T. A., Uhlmann, E., & Banaji, M. R. (2009). Understanding and using the Implicit Association Test: III. Meta-analysis of predictive validity. *Journal of Personality and Social Psychology, 97*, 17–41.

Greenwald, A. G., Smith, C. T., Sriram, N., Bar-Anan, Y., & Nosek, B. A. (2009). Implicit race attitudes predicted vote in the 2008 U.S. presidential election. *Analyses of Social Issues and Public Policy, 9*, 241–53.

Hadaway, C. K., & Marler, P. L. (2005). How many Americans attend worship each week? An alternative approach to measurement. *Journal for the Scientific Study of Religion, 44*, 307–22.

Hill, P. C., & Hood, R. W., Jr. (1999). *Measures of religiosity*. Birmingham, AL: Religious Education Press.

Hofmann, W., Gawronski, B., Gschwendner, T., Le, H., & Schmitt, M. (2005). A meta-analysis on the correlation between the Implicit Association Test and explicit self-report measures. *Personality and Social Psychology Bulletin, 31*, 1369–85.

Järnefelt, E., Canfield, C., & Kelemen, D. (2015). The divided mind of a disbeliever: Intuitive beliefs about nature as purposefully created among different groups of nonreligious adults. *Cognition, 140*, 72–88.

Jong, J., Halberstadt, J., & Bluemke, M. (2012). Foxhole atheism, revisited: The effects of mortality salience on explicit and implicit religious belief. *Journal of Experimental Social Psychology, 48*, 983–89.

Karpinski, A., & Steinman, R. B. (2006). The single-category Implicit Association Test as a measure of implicit social cognition. *Journal of Personality and Social Psychology, 91*, 16–32.

Kelemen, D. (2004). Are children "intuitive theists"? Reasoning about purpose and design in nature. *Psychological Science, 15*, 295–301.

Keren, G., & Schul, Y. (2009). Two is not always better than one: A critical evaluation of two-system theories. *Perspectives on Psychological Science, 4*, 533–50.

Klauer, K. C., & Teige-Mocigemba, S. (2007). Controllability and resource dependence in automatic evaluation. *Journal of Experimental Social Psychology, 43*, 648–55.

LaBouff, J. P., Rowatt, W. C., Johnson, M. K., Thedford, M., & Tsang, J. (2010). Development and initial validation of an implicit measure of religiousness-spirituality. *Journal for the Scientific Study of Religion, 49*, 439–55.

Leak, G. K., & Fish, S. (1989). Religious orientation, impression management, and self-deception: Toward a clarification of the link between religiosity and social desirability. *Journal for the Scientific Study of Religion, 28*, 355–59.

Lemmer, G., Gollwitzer, M., & Banse, R. (2015). On the psychometric properties of the aggressiveness-IAT for children and adolescents. *Aggressive Behavior, 41*, 84–95.

Livingstone, R. W., & Brewer, M. B. (2002). What are we really priming? Cue-based versus category-based processing of facial stimuli. *Journal of Personality and Social Psychology, 82*, 5–18.

Maison, D., Greenwald, A. G., & Bruin, R. H. (2004). Predictive validity of the Implicit Association Test in studies of brands, consumer attitudes, and behavior. *Journal of Consumer Psychology, 14*, 405–15.

Meyer, D. E., & Schvaneveldt, R. W. (1971). Facilitation in recognizing pairs of words: Evidence of a dependence between retrieval operations. *Journal of Experimental Psychology, 90*, 227–34.

Moors, A., Spruyt A., & De Houwer, J. (2010). In search of a measure that qualifies as implicit: Recommendations based on a decompositional view of automaticity. In B. Gawronski & K. B. Payne (eds.), *Handbook of implicit social cognition: Measurement, theory, and application* (pp. 19–37). New York: Guilford Press.

Murray, H. A. (1943). *Thematic apperception test manual.* Cambridge, MA: Harvard University Press.

Norenzayan, A., & Hansen, I. G. (2006). Belief in supernatural agents in the face of death. *Personality and Social Psychology Bulletin, 32*, 174–87.

Nosek, B. A. (2007). Implicit-explicit relations. *Current Directions in Psychological Science, 16*, 65–69.

Nosek, B. A., & Banaji, M. R. (2001). The go/no-go association task. *Social Cognition, 19*, 625–66.

Olson, M. A., & Fazio, R. H. (2003). Relations between implicit measures of prejudice: What are we measuring? *Psychological Science, 14*, 636–39.

Orne, M. T., & Whitehouse, W. G. (2000). Demand characteristics. In A. E. Kazdin (ed.), *Encyclopedia of psychology* (pp. 469–70). Oxford: Oxford University Press.

Ostafin, B. D., & Palfai, T. P. (2006). Compelled to consume: the Implicit Association Test and automatic alcohol motivation. *Psychology of Addictive Behaviors, 20,* 322–27.

Penke, L., Eichstaedt, J,. & Asendorpf, J. B. (2006). Single-attribute Implicit Association Test (SA-IAT) for the assessment of unipolar constructs. *Experimental Psychology,* 53, 283–91.

Perugini, M. (2005). Predictive models of implicit and explicit attitudes. *British Journal of Social Psychology,* 44, 29–45.

Röhner, J., Schröder-Abé, M., & Schütz, A. (2013). What do fakers actually do to fake the IAT? An investigation of faking strategies under different faking conditions. *Journal of Research in Personality,* 47, 330–38.

Rorschach, H. (1927). *Rorschach Test: Psychodiagnostic plates.* Cambridge, MA: Hogrefe.

Rudman, L. A., Greenwald, A. G., Mellott, D. S., & Schwartz, J. L. (1999). Measuring the automatic components of prejudice: Flexibility and generality of the Implicit Association Test. *Social Cognition, 17,* 437–65.

Rydell, R. J., McConnell, A. R., Mackie, D. M., & Strain, L. M. (2006). Of two minds: Forming and changing valence-inconsistent implicit and explicit attitudes. *Psychological Science, 17,* 954–58.

Saucier, D. A., & Miller, C. T. (2003). The persuasiveness of racial arguments as a subtle measure of racism. *Personality and Social Psychology Bulletin, 29,* 1303–15.

Sedikides, C., & Gebauer, J. E. (2010). Religiosity as self-enhancement: A meta-analysis of the relation between socially desirable responding and religiosity. *Personality and Social Psychology Review, 14,* 17–36.

Shariff, A. F., Cohen, A. B., & Norenzayan, A. (2008). The devil's advocate: Secular arguments diminish both implicit and explicit religious belief. *Journal of Cognition and Culture, 8,* 417–23.

Sharp, C. A., Rentfrow, P. J., & Gibson, N. J. S. (2015). One God but three concepts: Complexity in Christians' representations of God. *Psychology of Religion and Spirituality.* Advance online publication. dx.doi.org.

Sherman, J. W., Gawronski, B., & Trope, Y. (eds). (2014). *Dual process theories of the social mind.* New York: Guilford Press.

Steffens, M. C. (2004). Is the Implicit Association Test immune to faking? *Experimental Psychology, 51,* 165–79.

Teige-Mocigemba, S., & Klauer, K. C. (2008). "Automatic" evaluation? Strategic effects on affective priming. *Journal of Experimental Social Psychology,* 44, 1414–17.

Tremlin, T. (2006). *Minds and gods: The cognitive foundations of religion.* Oxford, UK: Oxford University Press.

Trimble, D. E. (1997). The Religious Orientation Scale: Review and meta-analysis of social desirability effects. *Educational and Psychological Measurement,* 57, 970–86.

Uhlmann, E. L., Poehlman, T. A., & Bargh, J. A. (2008). Implicit theism. In R. M. Sorrentino & S. Yamaguchi (eds.), *Handbook of Motivation and Cognition across Cultures* (pp. 71–94). Oxford, UK: Elsevier.

Vargas, P., von Hippel, W., & Petty, R. E. (2004). Using "partially structured" attitude measures to enhance the attitude-behavior relationship. *Personality and Social Psychology Bulletin, 30*, 197–211.

Wenger, J. L. (2004). The automatic activation of religious concepts: Implications for religious orientations. *International Journal for the Psychology of Religion, 14*, 109–23.

Wentura, D., & Degner, J. (2010). A practical guide to sequential priming and related tasks. In B. Gawronski & B. K. Payne (eds.), *Handbook of implicit social cognition: Measurement, theory, and applications* (pp. 95–116). New York: Guilford Press.

Wigboldus, D. H. J., Holland, R., & van Knippenberg, A. (2006). *Single target implicit associations*. Unpublished manuscript, Radboud University, Nijmegen, The Netherlands.

Wittenbrink, B., Judd, C. M., & Park, B. (1997). Evidence for racial prejudice at the implicit level and its relationship with questionnaire measures. *Journal of Personality and Social Psychology, 72*, 262–74.

Wittenbrink, B., & Schwarz, N. (2007). Introduction. In B. Wittenbrink & N. Schwarz (eds.), *Implicit measures of attitudes* (pp. 1–13). New York: Guilford Press.

Yarborough, C. A. (2009). *Depression and the emotional experience of God*. Unpublished doctoral dissertation, Regent University, Virginia Beach, VA.

Zahl, B. P. (2013). *A social cognitive investigation of anger toward God*. Unpublished doctoral dissertation, University of Cambridge, UK.

4.

Assessing Measures of Religion and Secularity with Crowdsourced Data from Amazon's Mechanical Turk

JOSEPH O. BAKER, JONATHAN P. HILL, AND NATHANIEL D. PORTER

Introduction

Crowdsourcing Platforms as Data Pools

Time and expense are perhaps the two biggest challenges in evaluating existing measures and developing new metrics. Measuring social characteristics of a population such as religion typically involves expensive surveys undertaken by professional survey firms or academic centers. Months pass between conception and completion. This inevitably results in a conservative tendency to replicate existing measures, even if researchers think improvements could and should be made. The cost of development and innovation is simply too high.

The purpose of this chapter is to highlight the promises and pitfalls of using the crowdsourcing platform Amazon Mechanical Turk (MTurk) as an experimental "sandbox" for developing new measures. Although MTurk is in no way a replacement for properly fielded, nationally representative surveys (Mullinix et al. 2015; Weinberg, Freese, and McElhattan 2014), the platform offers inexpensive and time-efficient opportunities for running survey experiments on diverse samples (Casler, Bickel, and Hackett 2013). The ease of constructing randomized split-ballot experiments allows for cost-effective and time-efficient testing of question wording, ordering, tone, anchoring, coverage, and frame of reference. Collecting data is relatively straightforward with the help of survey software and some basic recruitment techniques. The "turnaround" from idea to analysis can be a matter of days or weeks and the cost is more affordable than for other convenience samples.

Although there is great promise, there are also several distinct challenges. Perhaps the most substantial is the pool of MTurk "workers" themselves. They are, on average, substantially less religious than the general public (Lewis et al. 2015) and differ from the population in other important ways. There are also other logistical challenges related to recruitment that may not be immediately apparent. Workers self-select, so the way surveys are presented in the marketplace of tasks can substantially alter the composition of the sample (Chandler and Kepeler 2013). Workers also regularly make use of online message boards, so cross-talk can become a problem in some instances. There are also "types" of workers—including the experienced and the unreliable—that may bias results, depending on the instrument. Issues of attentiveness and of repeat survey takers also present distinct challenges when using MTurk as a sampling pool (Goodman, Cryder, and Cheema 2013). Similar services, such as Prolific, may provide greater control over worker skills and characteristics, but MTurk remains the largest and most established marketplace for this type of work, with a growing number of studies confirming its value (Buhrmester, Kwang, and Gosling 2011; Hauser and Schwarz 2015; Weinberg et al. 2014).

To illustrate how MTurk can facilitate developing measures of religion, the second part of this chapter shows the results of a basic survey experiment measuring religious affiliation, demonstrating how question format can influence the percentage of respondents classified as religiously affiliated or nonaffiliated. In addition to these assessments of potential measurement effects for a central measure in the study of religion, we also used MTurk data to pilot novel measures of the rationales people may give for being either religiously affiliated or nonaffiliated. These new metrics provide a window into the rhetorical justifications individuals offer for being religiously affiliated or not, as well as whether there are differences in patterns of rationales across religious traditions or types of secularity (e.g., atheism vs. agnosticism). We conclude by outlining the opportunities and limitations of crowdsourcing data for exploring issues of measurement, as well as for preliminary inquiries into substantive topics.

A Brief Overview of Amazon Mechanical Turk

Mechanical Turk is designed to "crowdsource" tasks that require human intelligence, as opposed to artificial intelligence (Paolacci, Chandler, and Ipeirotis 2010; Mason and Suri 2012). Despite rapid technological advances, computers are still unable to perform certain simple tasks—such as identifying or categorizing objects, summarizing content, or transcribing audio—with the accuracy of humans. MTurk is designed to provide a temporary workforce for simple tasks that require human intelligence. Users create accounts, linked to their Amazon.com user accounts, and either generate tasks to complete (requesters) or complete tasks (workers). The system is anonymous, although every user has a unique identifier and requesters can restrict who is eligible to work on a task according to past performance, prescreening tests, and country of origin.

Social and behavioral scientists quickly realized that MTurk provided a useful platform for recruiting convenience samples for surveys and online experiments (Buhrmester, Kwang, and Gosling 2011; Paolacci and Chandler 2014; Rand 2012). Since 2008, social research using MTurk has increased exponentially. Figure 4.1 shows the results of a Google Scholar search on the exact phrase "Amazon Mechnical Turk" by year (excluding patents and case law).[1] Although it is unlikely that all of these articles are using MTurk samples, the most-cited articles nearly all focus on using MTurk samples for social and behavioral science research.

Why did MTurk rapidly become a primary site for online convenience sampling? Two reasons are worth considering. First, the cost per recruit is substantially less than for other methods (according to one study [Antoun et al. 2015], it is about one-sixth the cost of Google Adwords and one-fifteenth the cost of Facebook), and it is relatively easy to generate large samples within short time frames. For the short survey we use in this chapter, we paid recruits fifty cents for five to ten minutes of work and generated an N of 2641 in a time span of five days. We do not know of another pool of recruits that could be tapped with similar cost and efficiency.

Second, although convenience samples are not nationally representative, MTurk samples fare comparatively well in measures of diversity (Berinsky, Huber, and Lenz 2012; Casler et al. 2013). They are

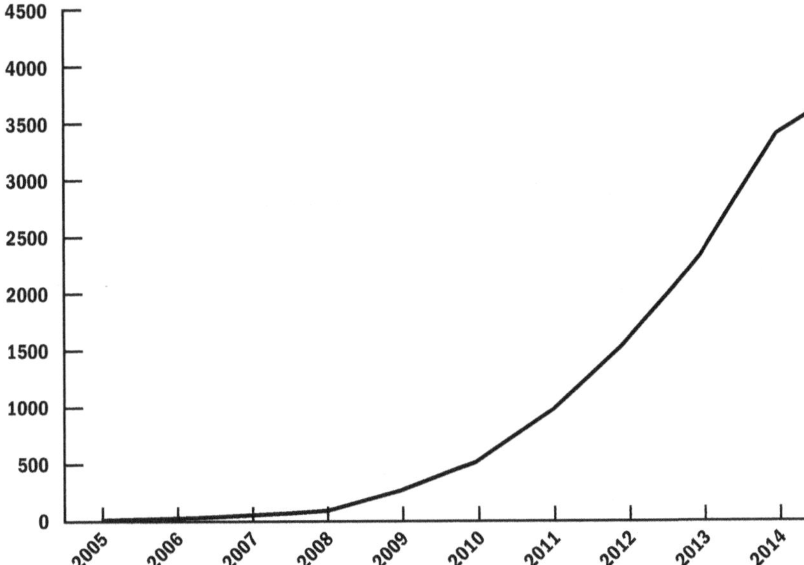

Figure 4.1. Number of Scholarly Articles Containing the Phrase "Amazon Mechanical Turk," 2005–2015. Source: Google Scholar.

considerably more diverse than the undergraduate convenience samples that have supplied the vast bulk of research subjects in the past (Behrend et al. 2011; Buhrmester et al. 2011). Still, they are not a representative cross-section of the public. On average, MTurk survey participants are younger, more educated, less wealthy, more politically liberal, and more likely to be female than the general U.S. population (Berinsky et al. 2012; Paolacci and Chandler 2014; Shapiro, Chandler, and Mueller 2013). Perhaps most importantly for the purposes of this chapter, they are considerably less religious than the general public (Lewis et al. 2015). We deal with this issue at more length in the challenges section below.

Recommended Use in Survey Design

Although the use of MTurk samples has become commonplace in fields such as psychology and economics, sociologists have not joined in. One recent study (Stewart et al. 2015) finds over five hundred psychological articles that make mention of MTurk (half of them since 2014). A similar search of a sociological index finds only nineteen such articles (Shank 2015). The lack of interest among sociologists is almost certainly due to a focus on external validity (inference to a population) as opposed to internal validity (isolating a treatment effect through experimental design). We wholeheartedly agree that if the goal is to estimate population parameters, then MTurk samples should *not* be used. Even properly weighting a convenience sample using known characteristics does not achieve representativeness because the joint distribution of these characteristics may not match the population. Moreover, treatment effects may be conditioned on unknown, or unaccounted for, characteristics of the population (Mullinix et al. 2015). If highly religious people respond differently to the treatment, then a convenience sample that does not properly account for this will mischaracterize effect sizes. In short, if one wants to describe population parameters, there are no shortcuts to proper population-based sampling.

However, if one wants to *develop* new measures to be used in population-based samples, MTurk proves very useful. We do not doubt that most social scientists constructing surveys for population-based samples do so with careful consideration and feedback from colleagues. Sometimes a short pretest is administered to check for obvious errors or problems. Still, most researchers do not systematically test the measures they construct. Split-ballot randomized experiments in survey design are an effective method of establishing the causal influence of question wording, ordering, and other factors related to context on the validity and reliability of the responses given (Fowler 2004; Schuman and Presser 1981). In such a design, respondents are randomly selected to receive near-identical surveys, with some fraction of the respondents receiving one or more experimental conditions that alter the wording, prompting, or ordering of survey items, while the control group receives an unaltered survey. While this is occasionally relied upon, it has traditionally been considered expensive and time consuming to implement during the development phase (Groves et al. 2011). Crowdsourcing in general, and MTurk in particular, changes this.

Application

Research Questions

To demonstrate the potential uses of MTurk for studying religion and secularity, we used the platform to address three research questions, making use of both a randomized split-ballot design and the fielding of novel metrics.

Our first research question involves the potential measurement effects of using different questions to classify respondents as religiously affiliated or not. Great debate accompanies changes in the composition of religious markets, and considerable discussion surrounds what proportion of particular populations should be counted as religious. Both of these concerns are evident in social scientific discourse about the rapid increase over the past thirty years in the proportion of Americans who report no religious affiliation (see Chaves 2011; Hout and Fischer 2002, 2014; Putnam and Campbell 2010). In understanding and evaluating such changes, a primary concern becomes assessing how measurement can influence frequency distribution outcomes on religious affiliation questions (cf. Dougherty, Johnson, and Polson 2007; Smith and Kim 2007). For instance, using a two-question strategy that allows individuals to be nontheist *and* religiously affiliated, rather than forcing nontheists to also claim no religious affiliation, results in higher estimates of secularity, at least if affiliated nontheists are still counted as secular (see Baker and Smith 2015:21–23).

Three primary possibilities that have been suggested—but not tested—as potentially consequential aspects of measurement influencing resulting estimates of religious affiliation are (1) the wording of the question posing religious affiliation as a "preference" or an identification with a "religious family"; (2) whether the question itself makes it clear that "no religion" or "none" is an option; and (3) the other available answer options provided, as well as the order in which they are presented. We used a randomized split-ballot design to assess these potential sources of measurement effects with a crowdsourced sample.

Our second research question addresses reasons people give for being religiously affiliated. We are interested not in people's levels of religiosity, but rather the justifications people find compelling regarding *why* they are religious or secular. Psychologists of religion have long addressed issues of religious motivation, most notably with the development and empirical assessment of concepts of "intrinsic" and "extrinsic" religiosity, which are intended to assess two different clusters of rationales for participating in religion (Allport 1966; Allport and Ross 1967). These concepts are much debated and have been measured in a variety of ways. Perhaps more importantly, it has been suggested that the dimensions essentially measure "good" and "bad" forms of religiosity by isolating utilitarian engagements with religion as "extrinsic" religiosity, through the use of questions such as, "Although I am religious, I don't let it affect my daily life" (Kirkpatrick and Hood 1990; on the measurement of these concepts, see Gorsuch and Venable 1983; Koenig and Büssing 2010). Revised subscales have been proposed to distinguish "social" extrinsic motivations, such as friendships, from selfish extrinsic motivations (see Gorsuch and McPherson 1989). Our question battery is similar to previous measures of intrinsic and social extrinsic religiosity, but we designed our questions on the basis of sociological rather than psychological theories of religious participation (e.g., Stark and Finke 2000). Specifically, we designed questions about motivations rooted in childhood socialization, influence of one's family, trust in religious leaders and organizations, and politics, along with rationales referencing personal religious experiences.

Our third research question turns MTurk's weaknesses as a sampling pool for religion into a strength by examining an exploratory substantive question in the literature on secular identities. There has been far less research on the rationales individuals may give for being nonreligious, although there have been efforts to expand the intrinsic/extrinsic concept so that secular individuals can be meaningfully included in measurement batteries (Maltby and Lewis 1996); however, to fully assess rationales for secularity with minimal nonresponse or measurement error, alternative measures are needed (Zwingmann, Klein, and Büssing 2011). Accordingly, we piloted distinct rationale measures for secularity. These measures mirror those for religious rationales where applicable by focusing on socialization, social networks, distrust in organized religion, and politics, as well as some of the factors outlined in secularization theories as leading to secularity, such as pluralism undermining confidence in exclusive truth, science undermining religion, and concerns of theodicy (see Berger 1967). Beyond general patterns of responses for rationales about being religiously nonaffiliated, we also sought to examine differences in responses by type of secularity, using a recently developed typology that divides seculars into atheists, agnostics, and nonaffiliated (theistic) believers, as prior research indicates potential differences in worldview patterns across these groups (Baker 2012; Baker and Smith 2009, 2015). Collecting new data allows us to empirically address novel topics of ongoing research on secularities, such as the degree to which "science vs. religion" narratives and opposition to the political involvement of religions are more or less salient among different types of secularists.

Data Collection and Measures

To address our research questions, we collected data through the Center for Social Research at Calvin College using Amazon's MTurk platform. Over a five-day span, we paid workers within the MTurk system fifty cents each to complete a "Human Intelligence Task" that would take them between five and ten minutes. Respondents were given a religious affiliation question to begin, with a multipronged split-ballot survey design that randomly rotated four different question wordings and four different orders of answer options. Respondents who answered that they affiliated with any type of religion were given a series of statements and asked to rate how well each "reason" described why they were affiliated with their religion. Those who answered the affiliation question with "none" were asked to evaluate how well each item in a battery of reasons described why they had no religious affiliation.

For the affiliation question, we rotated the following four question wordings randomly: (1) "With what religious family do you identify?" (2) "With what religious family do you identify, if any?" (3) What is your religious preference?" and (4) "What is your religious preference, if any?" For answers, we rotated options that placed "none" (1) after "Protestant," "Catholic," and "Jewish"; (2) as the first answer option; and (3) as the last answer option (out of a maximum of ten options). Besides Protestant, Catholic, and Jewish, the other answer options provided included "Christian (neither Protestant nor Catholic)," Buddhism, Hinduism, "Other Eastern Religion," "Orthodox Christian," "Native American," and "Other." We also rotated in and out an answer option for "Inter-/nondenominational," which was included in some answer sets and not in others. This allows us to compare whether the wording of religious "family" vs. "preference" or the inclusion of an "if any" modifier affects resulting frequency distributions, as well as whether the placement of the "none" category or the inclusion of inter- or nondenominational options influence distribution outcomes.

Next, we created a battery of rationales people might give for being religious affiliated. We asked respondents to rate the importance of each item in a battery of rationales on a five-point scale ranging from "not at all important" to "extremely important." The rationales provided for religious affiliation were the following: "I was raised religious," "Religion is important to who I am," "I enjoy learning and thinking about religious teachings," "I have had positive interactions with religious people," "I trust religious leaders and organizations to improve the world," "My religion helps explain what science cannot," "My religion is the best or only way to salvation," "I identify politically with members of my religion," "My religion provides good moral rules to live by," "My religion helps me feel better about myself and the world," "I feel close to God," "Personal religious experience(s)," "Witnessing a miraculous event(s)," "My prayers have been answered," "Most of my family is religious," and "Most of my friends are religious."

For the questions about why people choose not to affiliate with a religious tradition, we again used a five-point answer scale from "not at all important" to "extremely important." The following reasons for nonaffiliation were provided: "I was raised secular," "I am not interested in religion," "Inequities and injustices in the world," "I have had negative interactions with religious people," "I do not trust religious leaders or organizations," "Modern science undermines religious claims," "There are many religions, so just one can't be right," "I don't believe supernatural religious teachings," "Religions hurt people by trying to control politics or governments," "Religions have too many rules," "Religions are too dogmatic," "I don't know anything about religion," and "Personal suffering in my life."

Our survey also included standard measures of religious service attendance, private prayer, and theistic belief, which were all modeled on the same questions from the General Social Survey. Demographic information collected on the respondents included age, race, gender, and education level.

Findings

Measuring Religious (Non)Affiliation

Figure 4.2 shows the results of our split-ballot experiments assessing differences in distributional outcomes in nonaffiliation based on differences in question wording and answer choices. Respondents were slightly more likely to select "none" with the "preference" question wording (41.8%) as compared to the "religious family" wording (39.4%). The "if any" modifier added to the end of a question made a substantial difference in outcomes (43.5% compared to 37.6% nonaffiliated). Regarding the answer options provided, having the "inter-/nondenominational" category resulted in slightly fewer respondents who selected none (39.3%) compared to when it was not provided (42%). Overall, it appears that phrasing affiliation questions as a matter of identification rather than preference and offering a non- or interdenominational category

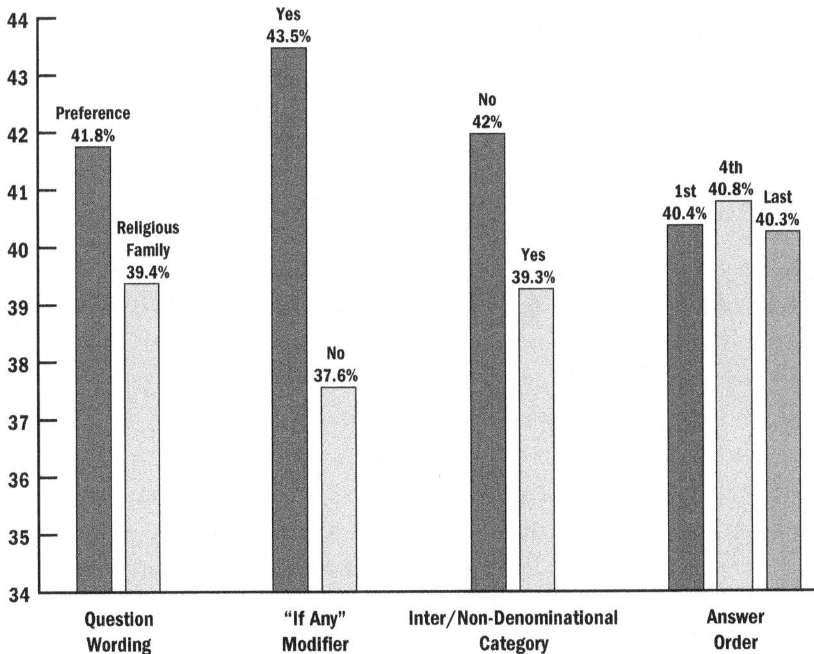

Figure 4.2. Percentage of Religious Nonaffiliates in Split-Ballot Measurement Experiment. Source: MTurk Religious and Secular Rationales Survey.

slightly reduce the proportion of respondents classified as nonaffiliated, while providing an "if any" qualifier is a methodological decision that significantly alters the outcome distributions for the proportions of respondents classified as religiously affiliated and nonaffiliated. The order in which the answer option of "none" was presented, first (40.4%), fourth (40.8%), or last (40.3%), made little difference in the proportion classified as nonaffiliated in our split-ballot experiment; however, more extreme alterations, such as providing forty answer options before "no religion" while also not using an "if any" modifier in the question, might still influence outcomes (see the appendix).

With regard to our first research question, it is clear that some decisions about question wording can consequentially influence the distributional outcomes for religious affiliation and nonaffiliation. The most important of these is whether the question itself makes it clear that nonaffiliation is an option, as evidenced by the higher proportion nonaffiliated when the question is phrased as a "preference" and especially when an "if any" modifier is included. Thus, researchers should be aware of how particular question wordings influence outcomes if they are interested in estimating population parameters. In this way we are able to use the results from our nonparametric, crowdsourced sample to inform survey practices in general, including parametric samples.

Justifications for Religious Affiliation

We now turn to assessments of our novel measures of rationales for being religiously affiliated. Here we are interested in two aspects of respondents' justifications for being religious: (1) the relative salience and popularity of each of the metrics; and (2) patterns of responses by religious tradition and sociodemographics *after controlling for religiosity.* On the first count, we want to assess the potential for using our new metrics in future studies. On the second count, we are interested in neutralizing the effects of religiosity on the probability of selecting a potential metric in order to ensure that the rationale metrics are not acting as proxies for religiosity. In other words, we are *not* interested in developing (yet another) measure of religiosity, but rather in examining patterns of religious justifications independent of religiosity. People who are more religious will tend to select more of the rationale items since we did not limit the number a respondent could affirm, but by statistically controlling for religiosity in a multivariate context, we can evaluate the unique effects of religious tradition and sociodemographic characteristics on the salience of particular rationales. This allows us to use the ease of data collection from an MTurk sample to make both methodological (salience of different rationales) and analytical (sociological patterns of rationales net of religiosity) contributions to the literature on religious motivations.

Table 4.1 shows the percentage of respondents overall and within each religious tradition category that selected each of the rationales for being

Table 4.1. Percentage Choosing Religious Rationales as "Very" or "Extremely" Important by Religious Tradition

	All affiliated respondents	Protestant	Catholic	"Christian"	Jewish	Buddhist	Other religions
Internal rationales							
Important part of identity	43.5	55.1	33.3	52.0	38.0	34.3	29.4
Enjoy learning religion	42.7	47.2	32.8	51.4	29.6	49.3	36.1
Religion beyond science	32.7	39.4	25.0	44.4	18.3	31.3	16.0
Exclusive salvation	37.1	51.3	25.0	54.1	21.1	10.4	13.4
Moral rules	64.9	71.1	59.2	74.5	50.7	61.2	50.8
Feel better b/c of religion	50.0	54.8	47.2	55.8	28.2	46.3	43.3
Feel close to God	53.0	64.4	50.6	65.3	32.4	26.9	29.4
Religious experiences	46.5	55.1	35.8	56.0	28.2	46.3	36.6
Witnessing miracles	22.9	19.5	17.8	34.1	11.3	16.4	18.5
Answered prayers	37.2	44.9	30.8	46.7	18.3	26.9	25.2

Table 4.1 (*cont.*)

External rationales							
Raised religious	42.3	47.8	55.3	44.6	32.4	14.9	20.6
Interactions with rel. people	42.0	47.5	38.9	50.3	26.8	35.8	28.6
Trust religious orgs.	24.9	28.6	27.8	26.5	12.7	20.9	16.8
Political identification	17.9	17.5	16.1	23.8	15.5	17.9	10.1
Family is religious	37.3	44.3	43.6	41.5	21.1	16.4	19.7
Friends are religious	20.3	26.2	19.2	23.4	16.9	9.0	11.8
Religiosity							
Attendance (1–10, mean)	4.22	5.24	4.08	4.70	3.59	2.57	2.66
Private prayer (1–6, mean)	3.45	3.97	3.11	3.96	2.55	2.82	2.68
Percent theist	85.6	95.6	85.0	92.5	57.8	65.8	72.3
N	1554	343	360	475	71	67	238

Source: MTurk Religious and Secular Rationales Survey.

religiously affiliated as "very" or "extremely" important. The most common rationale was, "My religion provides good moral rules to live by" (64.9%), which was the most common in every religious tradition. The second most common justification was, "I feel close to God" (53%). The top six rationales chosen reflect intrinsic motivation for affiliating, and include (in addition to the above) "my religion helps me feel better about myself and the world" (50%), "personal religious experiences" (46.5%), "my religion is important to who I am" (43.5%), and "I enjoy learning and thinking about religious teaching" (42.7%). Both the high number of average rationales given and the specific ones ranked highest suggest that those who are religiously affiliated tend toward a view of religion as tightly interwoven throughout the fabric of their lives, rather than isolated to specific times or purposes.

Being raised religious (42.3%) and having positive interactions with religious people (42.0%) were the most commonly selected external rationales for being religiously affiliated. The rationales cited least frequently were "most of my friends are religious" (20.3%) and "I identify politically with members of my religion" (17.9%), two of only four questions about the connection between religion and social networks (Everton 2015). Given the importance of social capital in studies of religion and prosocial behavior (e.g., Putnam and Campbell 2010), this suggests that the religiously affiliated either underestimate the role of relationships in religious affiliation or conceive of those ties primarily in terms of the other aspects of religion (such as morality and learning) that they enable.

Regarding patterns by religious tradition, Protestants and those in the nonspecific Christian category selected each of the rationales at higher rates than members of other traditions, with the exception that Catholics were more likely to select being raised religious as an important reason for being affiliated. Catholics also cited more trust in religious organizations and the importance of family members' religion as important slightly more often compared to the generic Christian category. However, these bivariate results must be interpreted with caution. Because we allowed respondents to select all of the rationales that applied to them, rather than a rank-order or limited-selection system, the higher rates for Protestants and the general Christian category may simply reflect higher rates of religiosity overall, as can be seen with the higher rates of religious service participation, private prayer, and theistic belief in these categories. In order to assess the extent to which respondents selected certain rationales independent of general religiosity, we conducted regression models for each of the rationale outcomes while controlling for frequency of religious service attendance, frequency of private prayer, and theistic nonbelief. This allows us to see if particular justifications for religious affiliation are more salient among different traditions, net of differential rates of religiosity by religious tradition in the sample. We also controlled for basic sociodemographics of race/ethnicity, gender, age, and education level.

Table 4.2 shows OLS regression models predicting the internal religious rationales, with Protestants as the comparison category to Catholics, "Christians," Jews, Buddhists, and a catch-all category for other

Table 4.2. OLS Regressions of Internal Rationales for Religious Affiliation

Variables	Identity	Learning	Science	Salvation	Moral rules	Feel better	Close to God	Religious Exp.	Miracles	Prayers
Catholic[a]	-.081	-.057	-.155†	-.393***	.042	.104	-.008	-.072	.093	.058
"Christian"[a]	-.021	.079	.163*	.198*	.227**	.079	.090	.016	.308***	.075
Jewish[a]	.238*	.195	-.020	-.485**	-.013	-.045	-.014	.106	.054	-.104
Buddhist[a]	.247*	.661***	.261	-.639***	.318*	.473**	-.393**	.527***	.371*	-.069
Other religion[a]	-.002	.333***	-.238*	-.813***	-.181†	.157†	-.276**	.013	.042	-.154
Black[b]	.004	.220**	.140	.085	.007	.110	.021	.122	.480***	.317***
Latino[b]	-.135	-.002	-.182	-.126	-.197†	-.214*	-.117	-.111	.126	-.084
Female	-.014	.006	.079	-.067	-.044	.059	.016	.138*	.046	.066
Age	-.002	-.001	.004	-.004	.001	-.001	.003	.001	-.005†	.000
Education	-.012	-.004	-.061**	-.052*	-.008	-.037†	-.038*	-.036†	-.052*	-.027
Atheist	-.419**	-.652***	-.537**	-.450*	-.949***	-.786***	-1.25***	-.707***	-.620**	-.599**
Agnostic	-.537***	-.333***	-.679***	-.661***	-.520***	-.752***	-1.09***	-.682***	-.591***	-.753***
Attendance	.129***	.109***	.096***	.135***	.064***	.083***	.076***	.084***	.053***	.060***
Prayer	.291***	.237***	.240***	.236***	.157***	.216***	.338***	.317***	.216***	.363***
Model stats										
Constant	-.252	-.065	-.210	.217	1.342	.601	-.182	-.374	-.176	-.908
N	1522	1522	1522	1522	1522	1522	1522	1522	1522	1522
Adjusted R-squared	.485	.354	.333	.432	.237	.300	.525	.393	.230	.433

*** P≤.001 ** P≤ .01 * P≤.05 †≤.1

Source: MTurk Religious and Secular Rationales Survey.

a: Reference category is Protestant

b: Reference category is white

religious traditions. Noticeably, there are few differences between Protestants and Catholics in the models, with the exception that Catholics are significantly less likely to select exclusive salvation and that "religion answers what science cannot." Indeed, all traditions other than the generic Christian category were significantly less likely to choose exclusive salvation as a reason for being affiliated as compared to Protestants. In contrast, respondents in the generic Christian category were more likely to select exclusive salvation and witnessing miracles than other Protestants, indicating that the general Christian label is being selected largely by theologically conservative, and often Pentecostal, Protestants.

Jewish and Buddhist respondents were more likely to say they are religious because it is an important part of their identity. Interestingly, after controlling for religiosity, Buddhists were more likely than Protestants to say that they are religiously affiliated because of religion's good moral rules, because religion makes them feel better about the world and themselves, because of a religious experience, and because they have witnessed miracles. In contrast, Buddhists were less likely to select feeling close to God as a reason for being religious. Further analyses (available on request) showed that theistic Buddhists differed little from nontheistic Buddhists in their selection of rationales, something not found for the other traditions. This suggests that explorations of nontheism in Buddhist traditions may be fruitful as a comparison point for more theistic-oriented religious traditions (see Smith and Froese 2008). Finally, both Buddhists and those in "other" religious traditions reported that they enjoyed learning about religion at significantly higher rates than Protestants did.

There were also some interesting patterns for the external religious rationales, as shown in table 4.3. Catholic respondents were significantly more likely than Protestants to report that being raised religious and trust in religious organizations were important reasons for being religiously affiliated. Interestingly, Jewish, Buddhist, and "other religion" respondents were all less likely than Protestants to report that being raised religious and having a religious family were important reasons for affiliation. There is also a noticeable pattern by race, such that African Americans were more likely than whites to say that being raised religious, political alignment with other religious believers, and the religiosity of family and friends were important reasons for being religiously affiliated.

Table 4.3. OLS Regressions of External Rationales for Religious Affiliation

Variables	Raised Religious	Religious People	Trust Rel. Orgs.	Politics	Family	Friends
Catholic[a]	.298***	.078	.182*	.095	.148	-.015
"Christian"[a]	-.109	.173*	-.015	.115	-.110	-.063
Jewish[a]	-.367*	.034	-.217	.176	-.611***	-.196
Buddhist[a]	-.883***	.253†	.107	.257	-.717***	-.292†
Other religion[a]	-.823***	-.108	-.229*	-.070	-.742***	-.304**
Black[b]	.365***	.066	.141	.235*	.418***	.360***
Latino[b]	-.071	-.166	-.148	-.217†	.115	-.055
Female	-.004	-.081	-.041	-.140	-.081	-.058
Age	-.005*	.004†	.004†	-.002	-.015***	-.003
Education	.035	.004	-.048*	-.040†	.001	-.016
Atheist	-.555*	-.855***	-.543**	-.192	-.488*	-.255
Agnostic	-.200†	-.369***	-.407***	-.223*	-.265*	-.288**
Attendance	.048***	.123***	.116***	.086***	.086***	.114***
Prayer	.020	.087***	.094***	.098***	.048*	.082***
Model stats						
Constant	1.940	.877	.634	.392	1.910	.592
N	1522	1522	1522	1522	1522	1522
Adjusted R-squared	.152	.252	.223	.113	.178	.183

*** P≤.001 ** P≤ .01 * P≤.05 †≤.1
Source: MTurk Religious and Secular Rationales Survey.
a: Reference category is Protestant.
b: Reference category is white.

Overall, our pilot measures of rationales for religious affiliation lead us to two conclusions. First, further analyses of these or similar measures with more representative samples and in relation to a wider range of covariates is warranted. All of the measures of religious rationales piloted produced enough variation in responses to be useful survey measures. Further, reliability analyses showed that the internal (Cronbach's $\alpha = .932$) and external motivation batteries (Cronbach's $\alpha = .835$) can effectively be used as additive indices with high internal reliability, pointing to the potential of the measures. In particular, future research should examine the predictors of different rationales, as well as how variance on the rationales influence related outcomes. Some specific research questions in relation to the predictors of different rationales include how the composition of social networks, strictness of one's religious group, personality traits, and religious socialization influence responses to these items. In terms of examining related outcomes, linking differing rationales to political and moral attitudes, as well as religious volunteering and giving, offers potentially fruitful paths of further inquiry.

Second, our current analyses produced some interesting patterns highlighting the influence of religious and cultural context on the resulting sociological patterning of religious rationales. In particular, members of minority religions in an area (e.g., Buddhists and Jews in our sample of Americans) are more likely to think of religious affiliation as an essential part of social identity. Minority religious affiliation necessarily sets individuals apart from their cultural context, and is in turn more likely to be perceived as integral to social identity. Regarding sociodemographic patterns, our analyses point toward continued differences in societal and communal pressure on black Americans to be involved with organized religion. While the centrality of religion to African American communities is well documented (Lincoln and Mamiya 1990), empirical evidence of higher levels of perceived external pressure to be religious is novel. Where previous research assumes but does not test social pressures as a causal mechanism of higher religiosity among African Americans (see Ellison and Sherkat 1995:1430), our analyses provide empirical evidence of higher levels of perceived external pressure to be religious among African Americans. With all of these findings, replication with more representative samples is needed to verify the external validity of the patterns we have identified.

Justifications for Religious Nonaffiliation

As we noted in outlining our research questions, quantitative examinations of the reasons people may give for being nonreligious are virtually nonexistent (but see Silver et al. 2014). For this reason we were interested in the basic descriptive patterns of responses to our nonreligious rationale questions. MTurk is uniquely suited to addressing questions in the study of secularities because of the lower average levels of religiosity among MTurk workers (Lewis et al. 2015). This makes generating a dataset with enough secular respondents to have adequate statistical power relatively easy.

Beyond general patterns, we used an additional question about theism in our MTurk dataset to classify nonreligious respondents as atheists, agnostics, or theists, as recent research indicates important differences across these categories for secular belief systems (Baker and Smith 2015). The question asked, "Which of the following comes closest to your personal beliefs about God?" Two answer options were "I am an atheist" and "I don't know if God exists and there is no way to find out." Respondents selecting these options were classified as atheists and agnostics, respectively. Those who answered the affiliation question with "none" while answering the God question with some form of theism were classified as nonaffiliated believers. We then used the categories to evaluate whether different types of rationales were more or less common among particular expressions of secularity in order to make a substantive contribution to the empirical research on secularities. Table 4.4 shows the results of these analyses, providing the overall percentage of

Table 4.4. Contingency Tables for Secular Rationales for Different Types of Secularists (% within Column Category)

Rationale	Total	Atheist	Agnostic	Nonaffiliated Believer
Science undermines religion***	71.3	85.9	66.3	42.3
Religion and politics***	59.8	67.2	54.3	48.7
Distrust religious orgs.	59.1	59.4	58.9	59.2
Disinterested in religion***	55.1	62.2	52.4	41.3
Religion too dogmatic*	45.4	44.6	48.5	41.8
"All refute all"	44.0	40.7	45.6	49.8
Religious people	37.4	38.2	33.7	41.3
Global injustice	35.5	36.6	35.0	36.5
Religions have too many rules	29.6	27.6	31.4	31.2
Raised secular	12.3	11.7	12.2	14.3
Personal suffering	9.1	6.6	10.7	13.2
Ignorant about religion**	4.1	2.9	4.1	5.3

*** $P \leq .001$ ** $P \leq .01$ * $P \leq .05$ (Chi-square tests)
Source: MTurk Religious and Secular Rationales Survey.

the nonaffiliated that said a rationale described a reason they are not affiliated "very" or "extremely well," as well as the percentages for atheists, agnostics, and nonaffiliated believers separately.

The most popular rationale selected was "science undermines religion" (71.3%), but there is considerable variation in affirmations of this sentiment across the different categories of secularity, with atheists (85.8%) much more likely to select this option compared to agnostics (66.3%) or nonaffiliated believers (42.3%). A similar pattern is evident for the idea that religion is harmful via its influence on politics and government, a rationale affirmed by atheists (67.2%) at a higher rate than agnostics (54.3%) or nonaffiliated believers (48.7%). The same pattern occurs for respondents reporting that they are uninterested in religion, with atheists the highest (62.2%), followed by agnostics (52.4%) and nonaffiliated believers (41.3%). Overall it seems that atheists are more likely to accept "religion vs. science" narratives than other types of seculars (also see Baker 2012), as well as being more likely to reference political reasons for their secularity (see Smith 2013). Meanwhile, agnostics were slightly more likely to say religions are too dogmatic (48.5%) compared to atheists (44.6%) and nonaffiliated believers (41.8%).

In contrast to the gradation across secular categories for the previous questions, all types of secular respondents reported a similar level of distrust in organized religion as a reason for being nonaffiliated (59%). Differences across the secular categories were also nonsignificant for the idea that "all refute all" in regards to religion, having experienced negative interactions with religious people, matters of personal or global suffering, the idea that religions have too many rules, or being raised secular. The rationale of "not knowing" about religion was not affirmed at a high rate by any type of respondent, although nonaffiliated believers had slightly higher levels of selecting this option compared to agnostics and atheists.

There were also some notable sociodemographic patterns to answers to some of the nonaffiliation rationale questions. Women were more likely to report negative encounters with religious people, religion having too many rules, personal suffering, and global injustice as reasons for being secular. Reflective of how social class shapes exposure to suffering (see Froese 2016), highly educated respondents were less likely to choose personal suffering as a rationale for being secular. Whites and older people were less likely to say they did not "know anything about religion." White respondents were also more likely to respond positively to the religion vs. science theme. Older and African American nonaffiliates were more likely to distrust religious leaders and organizations. Younger respondents were more likely to say religions have too many rules and to affirm science vs. religion narratives.

On the whole, these measures of rationales for being religiously nonaffiliated are helpful in understanding the reasons why different types of people are secular, and in showing which types of rationales are more or less popular among various types of nonaffiliated individuals. In particular, we find evidence that the "science vs. religion" narrative is much more concentrated among atheism than other types of secularity, especially nonaffiliated belief. A similar, but less drastic, pattern is evident for concern about the influence of religion on politics. These findings are informative, but also pose new questions. How do particular types of rationales cluster into broader worldviews? Do nonaffiliates who select particular types of rationales also tend to have distinctive profiles with regard to political and moral attitudes? Do antireligious rationales correlate with prejudice toward religious people? This pilot survey provides a foundation on which to generate better and more nuanced questions addressing why people choose to be religiously affiliated, or not (also see Vargas 2012; Zuckerman 2011; Zuckerman, Galen, and Pasquale 2016).

Discussion

We have shown how MTurk can be used as a relatively inexpensive and efficient convenience sample to develop and refine survey measures, as well as assess exploratory substantive research questions on some topics. For our first research question about measurement effects in survey questions about religious affiliation, the MTurk data demonstrate some of the consequences of changing question wording and ordering. In short, we find that including the modifier "if any" on the religious affiliation prompt has a moderate influence over the proportion of nonaffiliates. On the other hand, the ordering of "none" in the response set and phrasing the question as preference or identity have little influence over the proportion of nonaffiliates. This information does not directly answer the question of what we *should* do with affiliation measures in population-based surveys, but it does provide information for making more informed decisions about measurement, as well as debate surrounding different proportions of samples classified as nonreligious using different measures.

Regarding our second question about developing new measures of rationales for being religious, MTurk allowed us to analyze new measures at a level of detail that would be impossible with a small pilot test. This helps partially prevent the all-too-common experience of wishing one had worded a survey measure differently or realizing that some key measurement needed in the analysis has been overlooked entirely. These types of realizations often arrive during the analysis phase of research, when it is too late to do anything about them. MTurk samples partially remedy this by allowing rapid pilot tests to be fielded and refined with moderate or large samples, without incurring high costs. On our final research question, MTurk workers provided an easily accessible pool of secular Americans for examining potential differences in the belief systems and rationales of atheists, agnostics, and nonaffiliated believers.

Going forward, we recommend that survey developers consider planning for and funding a phase of survey development that includes an experimental component. This is especially important in an area such as religion because of the diversity of experiences, beliefs, and identities that fall under this umbrella, and the lack of a common vocabulary widely accessible to all to describe these experiences, beliefs, and identities. More rigorous testing is needed both to develop new measures and to refine frequently used instruments. Questions that are robust to minor changes in wording or ordering should boost confidence in their general use. Questions that are sensitive to minor changes should invite further scrutiny.

There is one other important reason for using MTurk samples as part of survey development moving forward: these studies help to better identify the strengths and weaknesses of using MTurk. It could be that we find that the analyses of our religious or nonreligious rationales do not perform similarly in a population-based sample. Knowing this, and identifying where the differences are, is important information for researchers interested in the development of new measures and instruments. We recommend proceeding cautiously. Although we see great promise in using crowdsourced convenience sampling, we also recognize that this is essentially uncharted territory for the purposes we are suggesting in this chapter. In this cautious spirit, we conclude with some of the potential pitfalls that researchers should consider as they use MTurk to run survey experiments.

Challenges for Crowdsourced Surveys

As we have already alluded to, perhaps the most important challenge for those who want to use MTurk to develop measurement on religion is the secular nature of the sample (Lewis et al. 2015; Mullinix et al. 2015). At the very least, this should serve as a simple reminder that religion data collected on MTurk cannot be used to infer anything about religion in the general public at a descriptive level. This also means that any initial power analysis to determine sample size should take into account the secular nature of the sample. Larger samples or screening techniques will be necessary if substantial numbers of religious individuals are required. The more serious concern is whether the religious individuals captured in an MTurk sample are "typical" of religious individuals in the general public on other measures. Research on political attitudes seems to suggest they are (Lewis et al. 2015), but more work is clearly needed here.

It is also worth considering how the initial request for participants (referred to as a Human Intelligence Task, or HIT) might influence who decides to self-select into the sample. Workers choose the HIT from among thousands available to them. One of the problems with the academic literature that describes the demographic breakdown of MTurk workers is that it fails to account for how sample composition will vary from collection to collection based on the description of the task (Paolacci and Chandler 2014). Researchers should be cognizant of who might be overrepresented or underrepresented based on the appeal of task description. Again, when it comes to research on religion, a description that makes it clear that they will be subject to repeated questions about religion or spirituality may skew the sample.

Many workers frequent online message boards, such as Turkopticon and subreddits on MTurk. Here they openly discuss various HITs and the requesters who offer them (Chandler, Mueller, and Paolacci 2013; Schmidt 2015). Some amount of cross-talk is inevitable. For the most part, this is not a serious concern for split-ballot survey experiments because the manipulation will not be as clear as it is in traditional psychological experiments. Still, if experimental primes or treatments risk being "discovered" through online cross-talk, researchers should do their best to mask these facets of the survey design.

Online message boards are also places where one's reputation as a requester will be determined. It may initially be tempting to exclude payment from workers who are suspected to be inattentive or who otherwise fail some metric of participant quality, but this can quickly ruin a requester's reputation. The literature suggests that it is much better to give bonuses for quality respondents based on these measures than to exclude payment (Paolacci and Chandler 2014). Timely payment (typically daily) is also important in developing a good requester reputation.

Research suggests that there are two types of workers who may undermine the quality of the data collected. On the one hand, there are those who are experienced MTurk workers and have taken hundreds of academic surveys (Chandler et al. 2013; Deetlefs, Chylinski, and Ortmann 2015; Paolacci and Chandler 2014; Rouse 2015). The concern here is that they may be "wise" to the various experimental treatments or may have filled out a commonly used psychometric scale multiple times. Again, this is less of a concern for split-ballot survey experiments because the experimental design should not be as obvious or common. The other type of worker is more cause for concern. These workers are unreliable and intentionally trying to optimize their compensation by quickly and carelessly completing surveys, or using automated programs or "bots" to complete tasks on their behalf. Both of these groups add "noise" to the data and cause a downward bias in effect size (Deetlefs et al. 2015).

Our recommendation is to identify and eliminate the unreliable MTurk workers using several techniques. First, consider only opening the task to experienced workers who consistently complete tasks well (95% or higher approved task rate and one thousand or more completed tasks are commonly used). This may be the most effective way of controlling the quality of the data collected (Peer, Vosgerau, and Acquisti 2013). Second, include attentiveness checks that can only be answered correctly if someone is reading the survey carefully. Including a question or two with only one obviously right answer will normally suffice. Although several standard attentiveness checks are available (e.g., Qualtrics includes some), we recommend developing your own. Experienced workers will be practiced at identifying commonly used checks (Rouse 2015). Last, consider including a forced minimum time for initial survey instructions (Deetlefs et al. 2015). Unreliable workers should be dissuaded from participating in a survey that does not allow them to bypass instructions.

Conclusion

As our current application shows, the possibilities for using crowdsourced platforms to address both methodological and exploratory substantive topics on a relatively small budget are considerable. In a cost-efficient and timely manner, we were able to demonstrate how question wording affects outcomes for religious affiliation, pilot novel measures of rationales for being religiously affiliated or nonaffiliated, and provide some preliminary substantive findings about the sociological patterns of rationales for being both religious and nonreligious. It is important to reiterate that we do *not* consider the use of MTurk or any other convenience sample as a replacement for properly fielded, representative surveys. Rather, we recommend that sociologists use MTurk as a platform to help refine existing measures and experiment with new ones. In assessing measures of religion, we also believe it is important to highlight the relatively irreligious nature of the MTurk sample. Larger samples may be necessary to generate the power needed to test survey effects on religion measures. With these caveats in mind, we recommend that social scientists make greater use of crowdsourcing to improve the measurement of religion.

Appendix: Measuring Religious Affiliation and Secularities in Three National Surveys

To investigate measurement issues beyond those addressed by our crowdsourced experiment, we analyzed the results of surveys with different questions taken from the same broad sampling frame (noninstitutionalized American adults) and time period to see how methodological strategies may influence the outcome distributions for the proportion of people classified as secular or religious. To do this we compared the 2006–2008 General Social Survey (GSS), 2007 Pew Religious Landscape

Survey (RLS), and 2007 Baylor Religion Survey (BRS), which each had (different) questions that can be used to classify people into three mutually exclusive types of secularity: atheism, agnosticism, and nonaffiliated (theistic) belief (see Baker and Smith 2009, 2015).[2]

The GSS asks respondents, "What is your religious preference?" with answer choices of "Protestant, Catholic, Jewish, some other religion, or no religion," then a separate question about belief in God that offers "I don't believe in God" and "I don't know whether there is a God and there's no way to find out" as answer options. This allows for the categorization of nontheists based on disbelief rather than identification with the terms "atheist" or "agnostic," which may be problematic because of their pejorative cultural connotations (see Edgell, Gerteis, and Hartmann 2007; Gervais, Shariff, and Norenzayan 2011). In contrast, the Pew RLS asks respondents, "What is your present religion, if any? Are you Protestant, Roman Catholic, Mormon, Orthodox such as Greek or Russian Orthodox, Jewish, Muslim, Buddhist, Hindu, atheist, agnostic, something else, or nothing in particular?" This effectively prevents respondents from thinking they can be both nontheist and religiously affiliated. It also forces respondents to both understand and identify with the labels of "atheist" or "agnostic" in order to be classified as nontheist; however, there was also a yes/no theism question asked later in the survey that can be used to classify respondents who said "nothing in particular," then said "yes" to theism as nonaffiliated believers.[3] Finally, the BRS asks respondents, "With what religious family do you most closely identify?" Forty options, including a write-in category, are offered, with "no religion" at the bottom. A separate question, similar to the one offered on the GSS, is asked about theism, with "I am an atheist" and "I don't know and there is no way to find out" as specific answer options. This forces identification with the term "atheist" but mirrors the agnostic response option of the GSS.

Both the GSS and the BRS end up with more atheists and agnostics than the RLS. In particular, there seems to low recognition of and identification with the term "agnostic" compared to the proportion of Americans who are agnostic in their beliefs about God, which helps explain the lower population estimate provided by self-identification in the Pew RLS (2.4%) compared to the GSS (4.6%) and BRS (6%). The higher levels of nontheism in the BRS coupled with a much lower level of nonaffiliated believers (4.8%) compared to the GSS (11.1%) and RLS (10.5%) indicate that the measurement strategy for affiliation on the BRS shifts a considerable number of "liminal nones" into affiliation (see Lim, MacGregor, and Putnam 2010).[4] The two-question method of the GSS that does not force respondents to self-identify as atheist or agnostic produces the highest overall estimate of secularity in the United States (18.2%), followed by the single-question method of the RLS (16.2%), then the affiliation-maximizing question of the BRS (15%).[5] Overall, it is clear that different measurement strategies about issues such as question wording, answer options, and whether nontheism and religious affiliation are mutually exclusive can consequentially influence resulting estimates for population parameters for both religious affiliation and specific types of secularity.

Table A.1. Distribution of Secularities Using Three National Datasets

Category	2006–2008 GSS	2007 Pew RLS	2007 BRS
Atheist	2.5	1.6	4.2
Question(s) used	Which statement expresses your belief about God?	What is your present religion, if any?	Which statement comes closest to your personal beliefs about God?
Response(s)	I don't believe in God	Atheist	I am an atheist
Agnostic	4.6	2.4	6.0
Question(s) used	Which statement expresses your belief about God?	What is your present religion, if any?	Which statement comes closest to your personal beliefs about God?
Response(s)	I don't know whether there is a God and there is no way to find out	Agnostic	I don't know and there is no way to find out
Nonaffiliated believer	11.1	10.5	4.8
Question(s) used	What is your religious preference? + Which statement expresses your belief about God?	What is your present religion, if any? + Do you believe in God or a universal spirit?	With what religion do you most closely identify? + Which statement comes closest to your personal beliefs about God?
Response(s)	None + Belief in God	Nothing in particular + Belief in God	No religion + Belief in God

NOTES

1 Using the less restrictive search phrase "Mechanical Turk" increases the number of articles in recent years by approximately 70–90%. Neither search was case sensitive.

2 Each of these samples is intended to be nationally representative of noninstitutionalized American adults; however, they do use different collection modes: face-to-face interviews (GSS), telephone interviews (Pew), and mixed mode, with an initial call to respondents who are then mailed the questionnaire (BRS). It is possible that differences between the resulting outcomes are due to survey mode, but the sociodemographics of the surveys are quite similar (tabled comparisons available on request). One exception, and a possible source of the difference in proportions nontheist, would be the higher percentage of white respondents to the BRS (84.7%) compared to the GSS (73.9%) and Pew RLS (79.6%). On patterns of race and nontheism in the United States, see Baker and Smith (2015:117–23).

3 Only 1.6% of respondents to the Pew RLS selected "atheist" as their religious identity, while 4.8% said they did not believe in God or a "universal spirit," further evidence that (dis)belief questions about theism produce more "atheists" than self-identification. Independent samples t-tests between self-identified atheists and those who said they disbelieve in God while not self-identifying as "atheist" show that self-identified atheists were more politically liberal, younger, whiter, and more likely to live in the West. Self-identified atheists were also much less likely to be married and more likely to be cohabitating or never married, and also less likely to have children. Self-identified atheists also attended religious services and prayed less than atheists classified using disbelief. Results available upon request from first author.

4 This can also be seen in the percentage of respondents who could be classified as "culturally religious"—meaning religiously affiliated, theistic believers who rarely, if ever, attend religious services or pray privately. On the BRS, 10.6% of respondents were culturally religious, compared to 8% in the 2006–2008 GSS and 4.6% on the RLS (see Baker and Smith 2015).

5 For the total percentage secular, we also included respondents to the Pew RLS who said "nothing" for affiliation, then "no" to the God question. Analyses showed that respondents who said "nothing in particular," then "no" to the theism question were more similar to atheists than nonaffiliated believers, which effectively doubles the size of the "atheist" category (3.2%) when these respondents are counted as atheists.

REFERENCES

Allport, Gordon W. 1966. "The Religious Context of Prejudice." *Journal for the Scientific Study of Religion* 5(3): 447–57.

Allport, Gordon W., and J. Michael Ross. 1967. "Personal Religious Orientation and Prejudice." *Journal of Personality and Social Psychology* 5(4): 432–33.

Antoun, Christopher, Chan Zhang, Frederick G. Conrad, and Michael F. Schober. 2015. "Comparisons of Online Recruitment Strategies for Convenience Samples: Craigslist, Google AdWords, Facebook, and Amazon Mechanical Turk." *Field Methods* 28(3). doi: 1525822X15603149.

Baker, Joseph O. 2012. "Perceptions of Science and American Secularism." *Sociological Perspectives* 55(1): 167–88.

Baker, Joseph O., and Buster G. Smith. 2009. "None Too Simple: Exploring Issues of Religious Nonbelief and Nonbelonging in the United States." *Journal for the Scientific Study of Religion* 48(4): 719–33.

Baker, Joseph O., and Buster G. Smith. 2015. *American Secularism: Cultural Contours of Nonreligious Belief Systems*. New York: NYU Press.

Behrand, Tara S., David J. Sharek, Adam W. Meade, and Eric N. Wiebe. 2011. "The Viability of Crowdsourcing for Survey Research." *Behavior Research Methods* 43(3): 800–813.

Berger, Peter L. 1967. *The Sacred Canopy: Elements of a Sociological Theory of Religion*. New York: Anchor Books.

Berinsky, Adam J., Gregory A. Huber, and Gabriel S. Lenz. 2012. "Evaluating Online Labor Markets for Experimental Research: Amazon.com's Mechanical Turk." *Political Analysis* 20(3): 351–68.

Buhrmester, Michael, Tracy Kwang, and Samuel D. Gosling. 2011. "Amazon's Mechanical Turk: A New Source of Inexpensive, yet High-Quality, Data?" *Perspectives on Psychological Science* 6(1): 3–5.

Casler, Krista, Lydia Bickel, and Elizabeth Hackett. 2013. "Separate but Equal? A Comparison of Participants and Data Gathered via Amazon's MTurk, Social Media, and Face-to-Face Behavioral Testing." *Computers in Human Behavior* 29(6): 2156–60.

Chandler, Dana, and Adam Kepelner. 2013. "Breaking Monotony with Meaning: Motivation in Crowdsourcing Markets." *Journal of Economic Behavior and Organization* 90: 123–33.

Chandler, Jesse, Pam Mueller, and Gabriele Paolacci. 2013. "Nonnaïveté among Amazon Mechanical Turk Workers: Consequences and Solutions for Behavioral Researchers." *Behavior Research Methods* 46(1): 112–30.

Chaves, Mark. 2011. *American Religion: Contemporary Trends*. Princeton, NJ: Princeton University Press.

Deetlefs, Jeanette, Mathew Chylinski, and Andreas Ortmann. 2015. *MTurk "Unscrubbed": Exploring the Good, the "Super," and the Unreliable on Amazon's Mechanical Turk*. Rochester, NY: Social Science Research Network. Retrieved January 21, 2016, papers.ssrn.com.

Dougherty, Kevin D., Byron R. Johnson, and Edward C. Polson. 2007. "Recovering the Lost: Remeasuring U.S. Religious Affiliation." *Journal for the Scientific Study of Religion* 46(4): 483–99.

Edgell, Penny, Joseph Gerteis, and Douglas Hartmann. 2007. "Atheists as 'Other': Cultural Boundaries and Cultural Membership in the United States." *American Sociological Review* 71(2): 211–34.

Ellison, Christopher G., and Darren E. Sherkat. 1995. "The 'Semi-Involuntary' Institution Revisited: Regional Variations in Church Participation among Black Americans." *Social Forces* 73(4): 1415–37.

Everton, Sean F. 2015. "Networks and Religion: Ties That Bind, Loose, Build Up, and Tear Down." *Journal of Social Structure* 16(10): 1–34.

Fowler, Floyd J. 2004. "The Case for More Split-Sample Experiments in Developing Survey Instruments." Pp. 173–88 in *Methods for Testing and Evaluating Survey Questionnaires*, ed. Stanley Presser, Mick P. Couper, Judith T. Lessler, Elizabeth Martin, Jean Martin, Jennifer M. Rothgeb, and Eleanor Singer. New York: Wiley.

Froese, Paul. 2016. *On Purpose: How We Create the Meaning of Life*. New York: Oxford University Press.

Gervais, Will M., Azim F. Shariff, and Ara Norenzayan. 2011. "Do You Believe in Atheists? Distrust Is Central to Anti-Atheist Prejudice." *Journal of Personality and Social Psychology* 101(6): 1189–1206.

Goodman, Joseph K., Cynthia E. Cryder, and Amar Cheema. 2013. "Data Collection in a Flat World: The Strengths and Weaknesses of Mechanical Turk Samples." *Journal of Behavioral Decision Making* 26(3): 213–24.

Gorsuch, Richard L., and Susan E. McPherson. 1989. "Intrinsic/Extrinsic Measurement: I/E-Revised and Single-Item Scales." *Journal for the Scientific Study of Religion* 28(3): 348–54.

Gorsuch, Richard L., and G. Daniel Veneable. 1983. "Development of an 'Age Universal' I-E Scale." *Journal for the Scientific Study of Religion* 22(2): 181–87.

Groves, Robert M., Floyd J. Fowler Jr., Mick P. Couper, James M. Lepkowski, Eleanor Singer, and Roger Tourangeau. 2011. *Survey Methodology*, 2nd ed. New York: Wiley.

Hauser, David J., and Norbert Schwarz. 2015. "Attentive Turkers: MTurk Participants Perform Better on Online Attention Checks Than Do Subject Pool Participants." *Behavior Research Methods* 48(1): 400–407. doi: 10.3758/s13428-015-0578-z.

Hout, Michael, and Claude S. Fischer. 2002. "Why More Americans Have No Religious Preference: Politics and Generations." *American Sociological Review* 67(2): 165–90.

Hout, Michael, and Claude S. Fischer. 2014. "Explaining Why More Americans Have No Religious Preference: Political Backlash and Generational Succession, 1987–2012." *Sociological Science* 1: 423–47.

Kirkpatrick, Lee A., and Ralph W. Hood Jr. 1990. "Intrinsic-Extrinsic Religious Orientation: The Boon or Bane of Contemporary Psychology of Religion?" *Journal for the Scientific Study of Religion* 29(4): 442–62.

Koenig, Harold G., and Arndt Büssing. 2010. "The Duke University Religion Index (DUREL): A Five-Item Measure for Use in Epidemological Studies." *Religions* 1(1): 75–85.

Lewis, Andrew R., Paul A. Djupe, Stephen T. Mockabee, and Joshua Su-Ya Wu. 2015. "The (Non)Religion of Mechanical Turk Workers." *Journal for the Scientific Study of Religion* 54(2): 419–28.

Lim, Chaeyoon, Carol A. MacGregor, and Robert D. Putnam. 2010. "Secular and Liminal: Discovering Heterogeneity among Religious Nones." *Journal for the Scientific Study of Religion* 49(4): 596–618.

Lincoln, C. Eric, and Lawrence H. Mamiya. 1990. *The Black Church in the African American Experience*. Durham, NC: Duke University Press.

Maltby, John, and Christopher A. Lewis. 1996. "Measuring Intrinsic and Extrinsic Orientation toward Religion: Amendments for Its Use among Religious and Non-Religious Samples." *Personality and Individual Differences* 21(6): 937–46.

Mason, Winter, and Siddharth Suri. 2012. "Conducting Behavioral Research on Amazon's Mechanical Turk." *Behavioral Research Methods* 44(1): 1–23.

Mullinix, Kevin J., Thomas J. Leeper, James N. Druckman, and Jeremy Freese. 2015. "The Generalizability of Survey Experiments." *Journal of Experimental Political Science* 2(2): 109–38.

Paolacci, Gabriele, and Jesse Chandler. 2014. "Inside the Turk: Understanding Mechanical Turk as a Participant Pool." *Current Directions in Psychological Science* 23(3): 184–88.

Paolacci, Gabriele, Jesse Chandler, and Panagiotis G. Ipeirotis. 2010. "Running Experiments on Amazon Mechanical Turk." *Judgment and Decision Making* 5(4): 411–19.

Peer, Eyal, Joachim Vosgerau, and Alessandro Acquisti. 2013. "Reputation as a Sufficient Condition for Data Quality on Amazon Mechanical Turk." *Behavior Research Methods* 46(4): 1023–31.

Putnam, Robert D., and David E. Campbell. 2010. *American Grace: How Religion Divides and Unites Us*. New York: Simon & Schuster.

Rand, David G. 2012. "The Promise of Mechanical Turk: How Online Labor Markets Can Help Theorists Run Behavioral Experiments." *Journal of Theoretical Biology* 299: 172–79.

Rouse, Steven V. 2015. "A Reliability Analysis of Mechanical Turk Data." *Computers in Human Behavior* 43: 304–7.

Schmidt, Gordon B. 2015. "Fifty Days an MTurk Worker: The Social and Motivational Context for Amazon Mechanical Turk Workers." *Industrial and Organizational Psychology* 8(2): 165–71.

Schuman, Howard, and Stanley Presser. 1981. *Questions and Answers in Attitude Surveys: Experiments on Question Form, Wording, and Context*. New York: Academic Press.

Shank, Daniel B. 2015. "Using Crowdsourcing Websites for Sociological Research: The Case of Amazon Mechanical Turk." *American Sociologist* 47(1): 47–55. doi: 10.1007/s12108-015-9266-9.

Shapiro, Danielle N., Jesse Chandler, and Pam A. Mueller. 2013. "Using Mechanical Turk to Study Clinical Populations." *Clinical Psychological Science* 1(2): 213–20. doi: 10.1177/2167702612469015.

Silver, Christopher F., Thomas J. Coleman III, Ralph W. Hood, and Jenny M. Holcombe. 2014. "The Six Types of Unbelief: A Qualitative and Quantitative Study of Type and Narrative." *Mental Health, Religion & Culture* 17(10): 990–1001.

Smith, Buster G., and Paul Froese. 2008. "The Sociology of Buddhism: Theoretical Implications of Current Scholarship." *Interdisciplinary Journal of Research on Religion* 4(2): 1–24.

Smith, Jesse M. 2013. "Creating a Godless Community: The Collective Identity Work of Contemporary American Atheists." *Journal for the Scientific Study of Religion* 52(1): 80–99.

Smith, Tom W., and Seokho Kim. 2007. "Counting Religious Nones and Other Religious Measurement Issues: A Comparison of the Baylor Religion Survey and General Social Survey." *GSS Methodological Report* no. 110.

Stark, Rodney, and Roger Finke. 2000. *Acts of Faith: Explaining the Human Side of Religion*. Berkeley: University of California Press.

Stewart, Neil, Christoph Ungemach, Adam J. L. Harris, Daniel M. Bartels, Ben R. Newell, Gabriele Paolacci, and Jesse Chandler. 2015. "The Average Laboratory Samples a Population of 7,300 Amazon Mechanical Turk Workers." *Judgment and Decision Making* 10(5): 479–91.

Vargas, Nicholas. 2012. "Retrospective Accounts of Religious Disaffiliation in the United States: Stressors, Skepticism, and Political Factors." *Sociology of Religion* 73(2): 200–223.

Weinberg, Jill D., Jeremy Freese, and David McElhattan. 2014. "Comparing Data Characteristics and Results of an Online Factorial Survey between a Population-Based and a Crowdsource-Recruited Sample." *Sociological Science* 1: 292–310.

Zuckerman, Phil. 2011. *Faith No More: Why People Reject Religion*. New York: Oxford University Press.

Zuckerman, Phil, Luke W. Galen, and Frank L. Pasquale. 2016. *The Nonreligious: Understanding Secular People and Societies*. New York: Oxford University Press.

Zwingmann, Christian, Constantin Klein, and Arndt Büssing. 2011. "Measuring Religiosity/Spirituality: Theoretical Differentiations and Categorization of Instruments." *Religions* 2(3): 345–57.

5.

Evaluating Survey Measures Using the ARDA's Measurement Wizard

CHRISTOPHER D. BADER AND ROGER FINKE

One of the most basic questions asked when one is writing or utilizing survey items is, does it measure what we think it is measuring? Answering this question is deceptively difficult, even for seemingly simple questions. The essential first step in evaluating survey measures is to learn from the past by comparing and systematically evaluating past measurement attempts. The problem, of course, is that even the most informed scholar, journalist, or policymaker can never be familiar with the hundreds of surveys conducted on religion, much less have a copy of all the survey instruments and the results for each survey item. Put simply, properly assessing survey measures requires a vast amount of information and a manageable method for assessing it.

This chapter introduces a new resource for exploring and evaluating the survey items used in previous surveys, the Measurement Wizard, which allows for quick comparisons of survey items measuring the same concept. This resource offers a customized metadata archive that gives immediate access to thousands of questions from hundreds of surveys and provides an online tool for finding, comparing, and evaluating survey items. The majority of the chapter is devoted to exploring a few examples of what we have found using this new metadatabase and software tool and demonstrating how even subtle shifts in question wording, response categories, or survey design can result in major changes in outcomes. Using the Measurement Wizard tool (and others), we can learn from past surveys to design better measures for the future.

www.theARDA.com: A Survey of Surveys

The Association of Religion Data Archives (ARDA) is an Internet resource that went online in 1998 with the mission of providing free access to quality data on religion.[1] Each year the ARDA disseminates more than sixty thousand data files free of charge. The ARDA has grown from a humble offering of thirty-three data files in 1998 to more than one thousand in 2017, with approximately 94% of these files consisting of survey data.

But the ARDA is more than an archive of data; it also is an archive of survey methodologies and measures.[2] For each survey in the ARDA's holdings, we archive the complete survey instrument, including the full wording of every question and response category, the complete instructions provided to respondents, and detailed information about methodology (e.g., the sample type, survey frame, collection years, geographic scope, and survey modes). The end result is that the ARDA has developed into a massive metadatabase of *attempts to measure religious concepts*. The surveys in the ARDA's archive have utilized a diverse array of question wordings and response categories. Comparing questions across surveys and over time offers a window into how differences in question wording and response categories influence the stories we tell about religion and even how popular notions of religion change over time.

One way of comparing survey questions would be to use the ARDA's general search engine to explore the archive's hundreds of surveys, thousands of survey questions on religion, and nearly three hundred thousand other survey items, but even carefully filtered searches and precisely tailored keywords can deliver an overwhelming amount of information, with many of the results being of little interest. For example, a search for the keyword "God" returns 5,995 questions/variables[3] relating to everything from belief in God to God's perceived characteristics and personality to affiliation with groups such as the Assemblies of God.

To avoid such information overload and hopefully reduce barriers to comparisons across surveys, we engaged in a massive metadata project utilizing the entire ARDA collection. With the support of the John Templeton Foundation, we identified 165 of the most important religion-related concepts and topics that social scientists try to measure. These include attempts to measure key indicators of religiosity (e.g., religious service attendance, affiliation, and salience of religion), key religious beliefs (e.g., belief in God and textual literalism), and items that are not direct measures of religion but are considered key correlates (e.g., attitudes about matters of sexuality, political activities and views).[4]

Then came the difficult part . . . we identified, or coded, every survey question in the ARDA's database of nearly one thousand surveys that represented an attempt to measure any of these 165 concepts or topics. As a result of this extensive project, the once overwhelming database of survey questions has now been assigned codes and organized into meaningful groups and subgroups.[5] Coding survey questions by concept revealed the rarity and simplicity of some religion measures. For example, questions about reincarnation are seldom included on U.S. surveys of religion, and the eighteen examples available in the ARDA exhibit little variation in their wording and response categories. Other concepts proved so complex in the variety of different ways that researchers have attempted to measure them that we organized the survey questions into subcategories within concepts, allowing us to compare the results of different measurement strategies. The concept "view of the Bible," for example, includes all attempts to ask respondents their opinion about the nature of the Bible. The ARDA research team discovered 141 different questions that addressed this concept, and these items were further organized into nine subcategories ranging from variations of a common question that asks respondents to rate the Bible on a scale ranging from the literal word of God to a book of fables and stories to questions asking about the reality of specific miracles recorded in the Bible.

It is our hope that this customized database will be used by ourselves and others to improve measures of religion. To facilitate wider access, we developed an online tool called the Measurement Wizard (www.theARDA.com) that allows users, regardless of their database skills, to view all of the measures tied to a specific concept and to easily access the related metadata and numerical data needed to compare and evaluate these measures. Before we offer specific examples of how it can be used to evaluate survey items, however, we first give a brief introduction to the software tool.

The Measurement Wizard

After opening the Measurement Wizard and selecting one of the 165 concepts listed, users are presented with three options for exploring the survey items used to measure a concept (see the tabs in figure 5.1): a list of "All Questions" used, a list all questions organized "By Category," or a list of "Custom Comparisons" that is generated by selecting specific criteria. The "All Questions" option provides the simplest view and simply presents all the questions tagged as measures of a concept in a long list. Figure 5.1 provides an example of this listing for thirty-nine survey questions used to measure the concept "Human Origins (e.g., God or Evolution), Beliefs about."

When the "[More]" link is clicked next to any of the measures, the response categories and frequencies are shown, and options for further analysis or saving the measure to a "questionbank" appear (see figure 5.1). Moreover, users can hold their mouse over the name of the survey to see basic details on its methodology in a hovering box, or click on the name of the survey for more complete details. Clicking on the variable name "HUMNEVOL" takes one to the complete codebook for the survey,

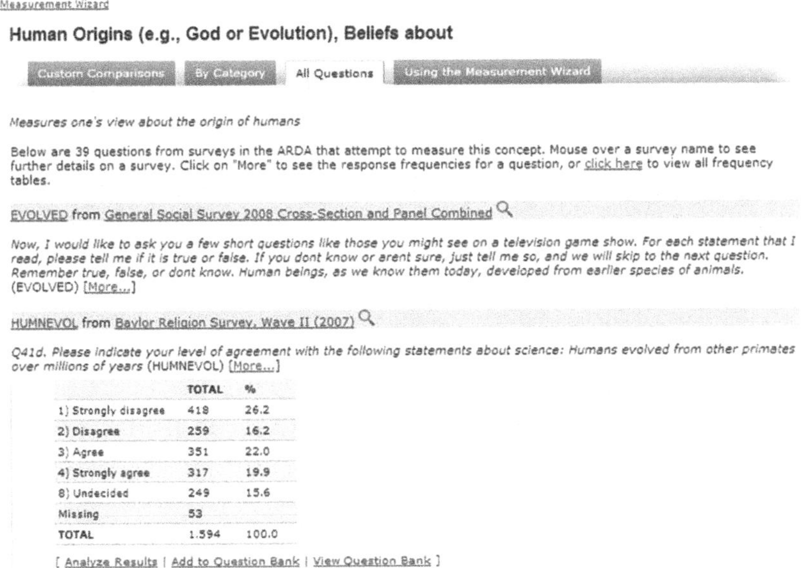

Measurement Wizard

Human Origins (e.g., God or Evolution), Beliefs about

Custom Comparisons | By Category | All Questions | Using the Measurement Wizard

Measures one's view about the origin of humans

Below are 39 questions from surveys in the ARDA that attempt to measure this concept. Mouse over a survey name to see further details on a survey. Click on "More" to see the response frequencies for a question, or click here to view all frequency tables.

EVOLVED from General Social Survey 2008 Cross-Section and Panel Combined

Now, I would like to ask you a few short questions like those you might see on a television game show. For each statement that I read, please tell me if it is true or false. If you dont know or arent sure, just tell me so, and we will skip to the next question. Remember true, false, or dont know. Human beings, as we know them today, developed from earlier species of animals. (EVOLVED) [More...]

HUMNEVOL from Baylor Religion Survey, Wave II (2007)

Q41d. Please indicate your level of agreement with the following statements about science: Humans evolved from other primates over millions of years (HUMNEVOL) [More...]

	TOTAL	%
1) Strongly disagree	418	26.2
2) Disagree	259	16.2
3) Agree	351	22.0
4) Strongly agree	317	19.9
8) Undecided	249	15.6
Missing	53	
TOTAL	1.594	100.0

[Analyze Results | Add to Question Bank | View Question Bank]

Figure 5.1. The ARDA's Measurement Wizard: All Questions.

provides more information on the collection, and gives the option of downloading the survey in a variety of different formats, such as SPSS, Excel, and Stata.

The second option for listing a concept's measures (i.e., "By Category") organizes the list into categories that measure different dimensions of the concept or simply represent different measurement approaches. Figure 5.2 provides an example of this list for the "Human Origins" concept. The Measurement Wizard team noted that questions about human origins tended to fall into six distinct groupings. Some specifically reference Darwin or Darwin's theory of evolution when asking about human origins; we categorized these as "Darwinian Theory." Some questions have simply asked the respondent if God created life on Earth (God Created?) while other ask if the respondent agrees that humans evolved from earlier forms of life (Life Evolved?). Others posit a middle ground by asking the respondent if he/she believes that God guided evolution in some way (God Directed Evolution?). On rarer occasions, the respondent has been asked his or her opinion regarding how *scientists* feel about evolution (Scientific Attitudes).

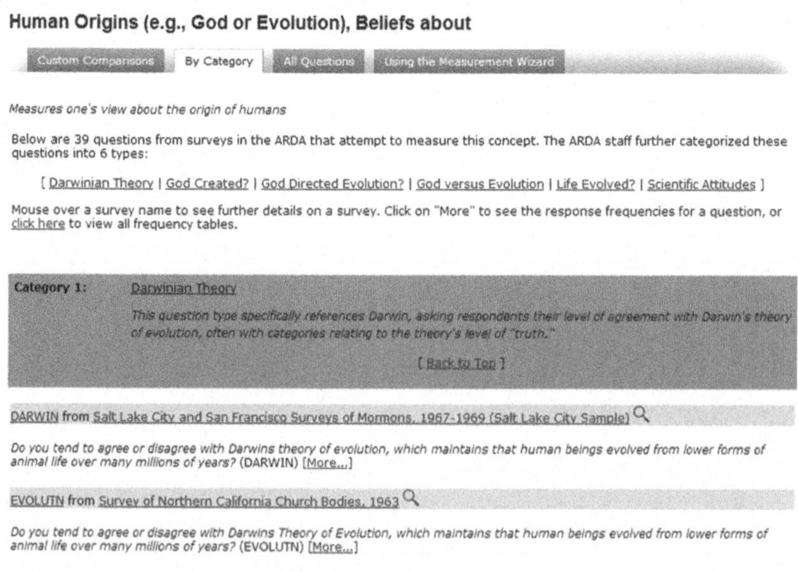

Figure 5.2. The ARDA's Measurement Wizard: By Category.

But by far the most common approach (to which we will return shortly) is to ask users to pick from a series of options regarding the possible origins of human life (God versus Evolution).

Links at the top of the "By Category" tab list each of the subcategories we identified. Clicking on them quickly jumps to all questions in that subcategory and provides a description of it. These categorizations may help the user to sort through concepts that have had many different kinds of related questions, but may also be entirely ignored, as desired.

The final option within the Measurement Wizard, "Custom Comparisons," is perhaps the most useful tool for comparing and evaluating previous measures. This option (see figure 5.3) allows users to assess measures with the same ease as a person shopping for electronics on a website, such as Amazon. On the left-hand side of the screen, users are presented with a list of criteria for selecting surveys, including the aforementioned subcategories, survey year, geographic scope (U.S. samples, regional samples, etc.), survey frame (adults, youth, etc.), sample type (random, nonrandom), and survey mode (in-person, telephone, Internet, etc.). As users select options, running totals indicate how many

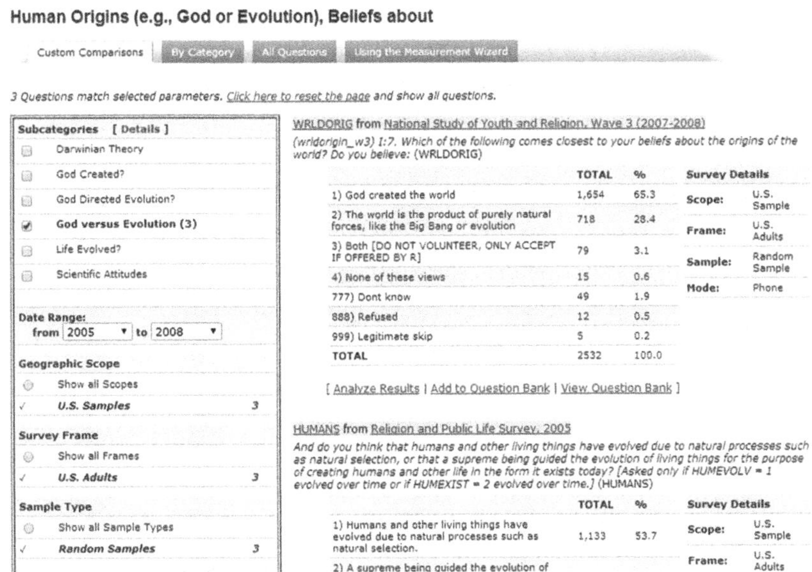

Figure 5.3. The ARDA's Measurement Wizard: Custom Comparisons.

measures fall under a combination of choices. In the example above, we chose to view only those questions that had been categorized as "God versus Evolution." This left us with eleven questions. We chose to focus on questions asked of U.S. samples, which reduced the pool to six questions. Once we had further limited ourselves to phone surveys and data collected in 2000 or later, we were left with three questions.

"Custom Comparisons" is especially useful for reducing long lists to a manageable number of comparisons. For example, the commonly used measure "Abortion, Attitude about" includes an overwhelming 440 questions. But this tool allows researchers to limit their comparison to questions asking about specific topics related to abortion, such as legality (thirty-three) or whether it should be allowed if the baby will have a "serious defect" (forty-two).

By offering instant access to more than eleven thousand survey measures of the most commonly studied religion concepts, the Measurement Wizard opens up new options for evaluating and comparing past measures. The remainder of the chapter is devoted to offering examples of what we have found using this tool. We begin by returning to the issue of human origins.

Human Origins: Finding the Missing Link (or Other Options)

One of the most basic guidelines for asking survey questions is that the response categories should be mutually exclusive and exhaustive. In other words, each respondent should have one, but only one, response that he or she can and wants to choose. A lack of appropriate response categories will result in respondents not having an option that accurately represents their views, while overlapping response categories result in respondents wanting to choose two or more responses. A second guideline is that each survey item should ask one, but only one, question at a time.[6] For example, you do not want to ask if respondents support freedom of speech and freedom of religion for all, because they might support one freedom and not the other. These guidelines are basic, but in practice, they aren't simple. Indeed, as we reviewed the questions on human origins with the Measurement Wizard, we found that they have been remarkably difficult to achieve.

Table 5.1. Explanations for Human Origins, Based on Two National Surveys

	Religion and Public Life Survey, 2005	General Social Survey, 2004
Man has not evolved	42.0%	41.3%
Man has evolved	25.7%	11.5%
God guided the evolutionary process	18.1%	40.6%
Don't know	14.1%	6.5%
TOTAL	100%	100%

Note: The full wording for General Social Survey question was, "After I read off three statements, please tell me which one comes closest to your views about the origin and development of man. (1) God created man pretty much in his present form at one time within the last 10,000 years. (2) Man has developed over millions of years from less advanced forms of life. God had no part in this process. (3) Man has developed over millions of years from less advanced forms of life, but God guided this process, including man's creation." We combined those respondents who said they "don't know" or "can't choose" or who provided no answer. The percentages for the Religion and Public Life Survey are based on responses to multiple questions. In figure 5.4, we provide details on this process and the full wording of each question involved.

There exists an abundance of survey questions on human origins, but there is little consensus on how this issue should be asked, and the results often seem contradictory. Table 5.1 summarizes the results from two highly regarded national surveys. First, let us highlight the consensus. Both surveys found that a little over 40% of the population believes that humans have *not* evolved over time, a finding that is supported by many of the other surveys we reviewed. As we move down the table, however, the remaining results of the two surveys tell very different stories.

The percentage of respondents reporting that God is involved in the evolutionary process is more than twice as high for the General Social Survey (GSS) as for the Religion and Public Life Survey (RPLS), 40.6% compared to 18.1%. God helps to explain human origins for 82% of the GSS respondents, but only 60% of those in the RPLS. Moreover, if we restrict our attention only to those accepting evolution, 78% of the GSS respondents report that God guides the process compared to 38% in the RPLS. So what is happening? The two surveys are both trusted national surveys, they are conducted only one year apart, and they are in complete agreement on the percentage believing humans have not evolved. To uncover this mystery, we return to the precise measure used in the RPLS, as well as a series of related questions.

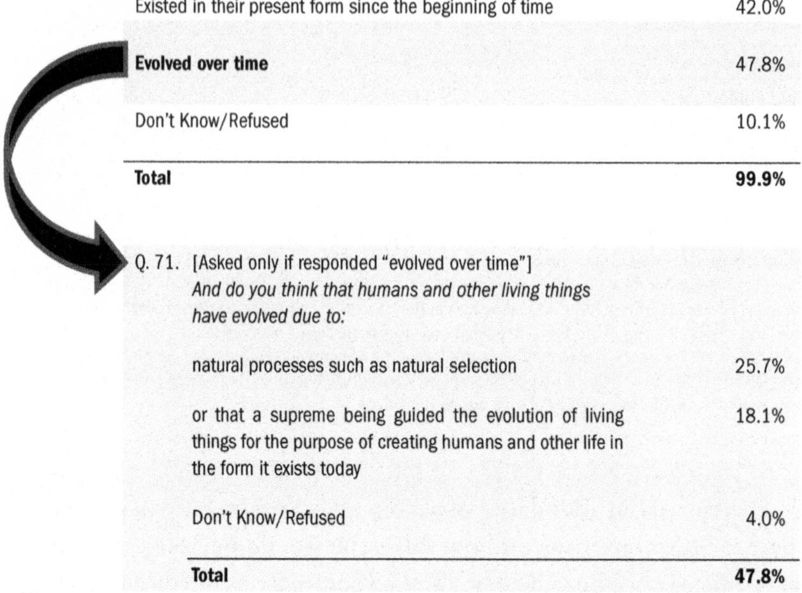

Q. 70. *Some people think that humans and other living things have evolved over time. Others think that humans and other living things have existed in their present form since the beginning of time. Which of these comes closest to your view?'*

Existed in their present form since the beginning of time	42.0%
Evolved over time	47.8%
Don't Know/Refused	10.1%
Total	**99.9%**

Q. 71. [Asked only if responded "evolved over time"] *And do you think that humans and other living things have evolved due to:*

natural processes such as natural selection	25.7%
or that a supreme being guided the evolution of living things for the purpose of creating humans and other life in the form it exists today	18.1%
Don't Know/Refused	4.0%
Total	**47.8%**

Figure 5.4. Question Set on Human Origins from the Religion and Public Life Survey, 2005.

The RPLS survey asks about human origins in two parts, while the GSS uses a single question, as shown in figure 5.4. In the RPLS, respondents are first asked if they think that "humans . . . have evolved over time" or if they think that humans "have existed in their present form since the beginning of time." The responses to this initial question were that 48% agreed that humans have evolved and 42% stated that humans have remained in their present form since the "beginning of time." For those who agreed that humans evolved, a follow-up question asked whether this evolution was due to "natural processes" or whether a "supreme being guided the evolution." Note the higher percentage of respondents who said they "don't know" in the RFLP. Ten percent of respondents cannot answer after the first question, and another 4% are unable to provide a response after the follow-up question. In sum, the percentage of "don't knows" is over twice as high in the RFLP as in the GSS.

The higher percentage of "don't knows" in the RFLP raises concerns about whether respondents felt capable of answering given the response options offered: were response options mutually exclusive and exhaustive? The responses state that evolution was either due to "natural processes" or a "supreme being" that guided the process. According to the many questions we reviewed on human origins, respondents often do not view these choices as mutually exclusive, as is seen in the larger percentage of individuals who take a middle-ground God-guided-evolution position when given the opportunity to do so.[7] We found forcing a choice between God or evolution to be common in surveys. Indeed, some survey questions specifically asked respondents to choose between Darwinian evolution and a biblical account of creation. No doubt the surveys were attempting to find levels of support for hot-button political issues, but in an attempt to find out how many were on each side, the survey questions failed to capture the actual, often moderate positions of the respondents.

A little over 40% of Americans consistently deny evolution and believe that God created the world in its current form. Another 12–20% are willing to exclude God from having anything to do with human origins; but the views of the remaining respondents (over 40%) can present very different outcomes and be used to tell very different stories depending on the questions asked and the responses given. Unfortunately, responses to some of our most frequently used measures of religion (often serving as standard controls in our models) are equally sensitive to slight differences in question format and answer choices, as we found when using the Measurement Wizard to explore patterns in responses to questions regarding the importance of religion and the nature of the Bible.

On the Importance of Religion (and How We Ask about It)

"How important is religion in your life?" This brief question, or a similar variation, is one of the most frequently asked survey questions about religion. How much importance an individual gives to religion is a question that can be easily understood by respondents and has proven a powerful predictor of religious and nonreligious outcomes in research analyses (Leege 1995). Yet, even a simple question that has received extensive research attention can offer misleading outcomes.

Using the Measurement Wizard, we compared 132 survey questions that ask about the importance a person places upon religion. These questions differ widely in the options they provide respondents. Survey researchers have long debated the inclusion of so-called middle categories when asking about the intensity of attitudes or beliefs (Schaeffer and Presser 2003). Some argue for providing only polar opinions (such as "religious" and "not religious"), forcing respondents to make a choice when they might otherwise avoid doing so. Some survey researchers are also concerned that having a middle alternative makes it easier for people to be noncommittal, rather than simply admitting that they do not know how they feel about an issue (Schuman and Presser 1996; Converse and Press 1986). Others, however, argue strongly against "artificially forcing a person to take a leaning they do not have" (Bradburn, Sudman, and Wansik 2004:141) and believe that for many issues middle categories can provide important information about less passionate respondents.[8] The importance of these categories is clearly evident with this basic question on religious importance.

In 2000, the American National Election Study asked respondents to choose between religion as being "important" or "not important." The 2002 Religion and Public Life Survey asked a similar question, but allowed respondents to assign a moderate level of importance to religion, allowing them to choose between "very important," "fairly important," and "not very important." By the 2008 Religion and Public Life Survey, respondents were able to choose from *four* options: "very important," "somewhat important," "not too important," and "not at all important." All of these surveys were bested by the Lilly Survey of Attitudes and Social Networks' (1999–2000) five options, which allowed respondents to declare religion as "not," "slightly," "moderately," "very," or even "*extremely*" important.[9]

A comparison of the frequency distributions for these four questions illustrates the consequences of adding more response options (see table 5.2). Despite the fact that these surveys asked similar questions and all involved random national samples of Americans within

Table 5.2. How Important Is Religion? Comparing Responses from Four Surveys

	Lilly 00 5 options	RPLS 08 4 options	RPLS 06 3 options	ANES 04 2 options
Extremely Important	29.9%			
Very Important	28.4%	58.3%	60.1%	
Important*	22.5%	26.8%	24.2%	76.8%
Slightly Important	8.3%			
Not Important	9.8%	7.3%	15.2%	22.4%
Not at all Important		6.5%		
Don't Know/refused	.8%	1.0%	.5%	
N =	2,561	2.905	2,003	1,212

ANES: American National Election Studies
RLPS: Religion and Public Life Survey The exact wording for the 2006 "Not Important" category was "Not very important." The exact wording for the 2008 "Not Important" category was "Not too important."
Lilly: Lilly Survey of Attitudes and Social Networks
*The specific wording for this category varied. It was "Important" for the ANES, "fairly important" for the RPLS 06, "somewhat important" for the RPLS 08, and "moderately important" for the Lilly Survey of Attitudes and Social Networks.

a span of ten years (1999–2008), the percentage of respondents selecting "not important" or "not at all important" dropped from 22.4 to 9.8 as the number of response categories increased. In part, this can be explained by the number of categories offering religion as being important. Only one of the five Lilly Survey responses gave an option of "not important." But even when the response categories were evenly distributed between important and not important, as with the 2008 Religion and Public Life survey, the increase in categories resulted in fewer selecting the "not important" response.

The distributions shown in table 5.2 would only partially support the expectations of many survey experts. Typically, when surveys have more response categories, there is a tendency for respondents to be pulled toward the middle and away from both extremes (Schuman and Presser 1996:177).[10] Although the extreme categories did get smaller as the number of categories increased, the highest level of religious importance continued to be the most frequently selected category. A more even distribution was achieved as more response categories were given at the higher end. Regardless of the responses offered, however, the distribution remained skewed, with far more respondents viewing religion as important in their life.

Reviewing survey measures on religious importance offers a similar lesson to what we found with regard to human origins: survey questions and designs that do not allow respondents to indicate *moderate* interest in religion or middle-ground positions on religious issues will miss much of American religiosity. The comparisons made possible with the Measurement Wizard allow us to see that a substantial portion of the U.S. population assigns at least some importance to religion, but they do not assign maximum importance to religion. In other words, the more chances we give Americans to choose religion as part of their life, without selecting it as the most important or only important aspect, the more variation we uncover in their interest in religion.

Views of Sacred Texts: Literal, Inspired, or Otherwise

Another topic frequently addressed on surveys is the respondent's view of the Bible or sacred texts. The relative authority that individuals give to a sacred text on matters of morality and knowledge is critical to understanding the stance that a religious community assumes relative to other social institutions, such as politics (Felson and Kindell 2007; Guth et al. 1995; McDaniel and Ellison 2008), science (Baker 2013; Ellison and Musick 1995), and education (Darnell and Sherkat 1997; Sherkat and Darnell 1999; Stroope 2011). In the past twenty years, "literalist" stances on sacred texts have come to occupy a central place in both theoretical (Bartkowski 1996; Hood, Hill, and Williamson 2005) and empirical studies of traditionalist religion (Hempel and Bartkowski 2008). Despite wide recognition of textual literalism as a powerful concept, at present no consensus exists regarding how the concept should be defined. The result is wide variation in how the concept is measured and equally wide variation in the outcomes received.

Our review of the ARDA found 141 measures and nine subcategories for the more general concept "views of the Bible." Many important comparisons could be made on these measures, including the gradual shift to asking about sacred texts rather than the Bible, but we want to offer three examples of how the response options often shaped the answers.

Over the last forty years, two of the most heavily used and highly regarded U.S. surveys have been the General Social Survey (GSS) and the American National Election Survey (ANES). Yet, between 1983 and 1990, the ANES consistently reported approximately 10% more of the American population as being "literalist" compared to the GSS. Once again, our comparisons revealed how the response options shaped outcomes. The ANES gave four options: (1) The Bible is God's word and all it says is true; (2) The Bible was written by men inspired by God but it contains some human errors; (3) The Bible is a good book because it was written by wise men, but God had nothing to do with it; and (4) The Bible was written by men who lived so long ago that it is worth very little today. Notice that only the first option allowed for the Bible to be without human error. By contrast, the GSS gave only three responses, but the first two responses both view the Bible as the "word of God": (1) the actual Word of God and to be taken literally, word for word; (2) the Word of God but not everything in it should be taken literally, word for word; and (3) an ancient book of fables, legends, history, and moral precepts recorded by men.

To confirm that the differences were due to wording, the 1984, 1985, and 1987 GSS asked both questions. The original ANES version of the question produced an average estimate of 46.1% of Americans being literalists, while the newer version produced an average of 38.6% literalists. This pattern was further confirmed by similar results from the 1990 ANES and by a series of "Middletown" surveys conducted from 1978 to 2000 (see Lynd and Lynd 1929, 1937; Hoover 1990).

Like the previous example offered on "importance of religion," the changes in response categories changed the outcomes received. For the literalist measures, however, the change in response categories also changed the definition of the concept being measured. GSS respondents could report believing in the Bible as the "Word of God" without being defined as literalists. For the GSS, a literalist was someone who agreed that the Bible was "the actual Word of God and to be taken literally, word for word."

The questions on sacred texts also illustrate how two-part questions can change the responses. In 2006 and 2007 the Pew Research Center's Religion and Public Life surveys asked a single question about the Bible that provided the answer options literalist, inspired but must be interpreted, and not divinely inspired. For the 2008, 2009, and 2010 surveys, however, Pew switched to a two-question format that first asked respondents whether the holy text in their particular tradition was "the word of God" or "a book written by men and not the word of God." Those who responded that a sacred text was the word of God were asked a follow-up about whether the sacred text should be "taken literally, word-for-word" or not. Interestingly, the proportion of the sample who would be classified as literalists was basically the same between the different question formats, but there were substantial differences in the sizes of the other categories.

In table 5.3, we compare the results of the one-question sacred-text question included on the Religion and Public Life Survey, 2007, with the two-question version included only a year later in 2008. The two-question version resulted in fewer respondents selecting the middle category (Word of God, but not literal; 29% compared to 44%) because they had to first answer that the sacred text was the word of God, then answer that they were not literalists. Absent the initial option of a middle category, more respondents selected "not the word of God" (25%) compared to the single-question format (16%). Nearly twice as many respondents had to be classified as "don't know" or "other" using the two-question format (11%) compared to the single-question version (6%). Figure 5.5 provides further detail on how we estimated the final percentages for the two-question sequence.

Table 5.3. Views of the Bible: Two Different Approaches from the Religion and Public Life Survey

The Bible is . . .	Religion and Public Life Survey, 2007 [One Question]	Religion and Public Life Survey, 2008 [Two Questions]
Word of God, Literal	34.1	32.7
Word of God, Not Literal	43.7	28.7
Written by Men	16.0	25.5
Other	2.6	4.7
Don't Know/Refused	3.7	6.5
Total	100.1	98.1*

* Approximately 1.9% of respondents are lost between the first and second question in this two-question sequence.

Q. 165. *Which comes closest to your view?*

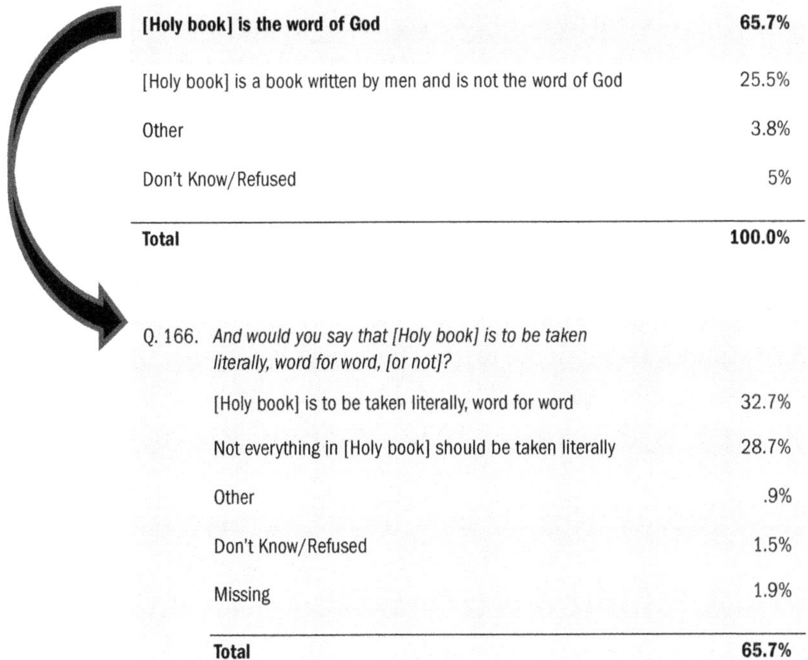

[Holy book] is the word of God	**65.7%**
[Holy book] is a book written by men and is not the word of God	25.5%
Other	3.8%
Don't Know/Refused	5%
Total	**100.0%**

Q. 166. *And would you say that [Holy book] is to be taken literally, word for word, [or not]?*

[Holy book] is to be taken literally, word for word	32.7%
Not everything in [Holy book] should be taken literally	28.7%
Other	.9%
Don't Know/Refused	1.5%
Missing	1.9%
Total	**65.7%**

Figure 5.5. Question Set on Views of the Bible from the Religion and Public Life Survey, 2008.

While both questions appear to have produced similar categories of literalists, there is more measurement error in the two-question version, as evinced by the higher proportion of "don't know" responses and the significant reduction of the middle category. Literalists likely select the most authoritative option available (Jelen 1989), thus producing similar results with one- or two-question strategies; however, the other categories are potentially compromised by using the two-question format. Using only the two-question format, we would conclude that there are more literalists than interpretists, but results from other surveys and from previous Religion and Public Life polls suggest that the inverse is the case.

A final example shows that the literalist category itself may be affected by the other response options offered. Instead of providing the three response options popularized by the GSS, the Baylor Religion

Surveys provided four response options: (1) literalism; (2) divinely inspired but requires interpretation; (3) contains human errors; and (4) a book of history and legends. The availability of multiple middle categories produced fewer literalists in the 2007 BRS (22%) compared to the 2008 GSS (32%). This subtle change produces significant differences in the composition of the literalist category. For example, 74% of literalists in the BRS think of themselves as politically conservative, compared to only 47% of the literalists in the GSS sample. As with questions about human origins, both the wayt a question about one's stance toward a sacred text is asked and the response options provided strongly influence the resulting distributions and composition of the categories of interest. This is not surprising, as questions about human origins, evolution, and hermeneutic views of sacred texts address complex concepts. But even seemingly "simple" questions require closer inspection. Consider one of most tried and trusted measures of religion: the importance of religion in the lives of respondents.

Knowing God: What Are My Choices?

When asking about complex behaviors, attitudes, or beliefs, for which religion certainly qualifies, survey researchers recommend using multiple approaches (Converse and Presser 1986). However, survey experts are equally concerned about asking so-called double-barreled questions in which two distinct opinions or options are bound together into a single question. The clearest questions ask for "only one answer on only one dimension" (Bradman, Sudman, and Wansik 2004:325). Yet, as the next example will show, when one is asking questions about God or many other religion topics, it is difficult to know when a survey question is measuring only "one" dimension.

Sociologist and Catholic priest Andrew Greeley was a pioneer in recognizing the potential importance of conceptions of God in explaining religious and nonreligious attitudes. He viewed individual beliefs about God's disposition as the primary component of one's personal, religious narrative and a key aspect of the "story" that guides our lives. The manner in which individuals construct that religious narrative, Greeley argued, should have a significant impact upon both religious and nonreligious behaviors and attitudes: "The central religious symbol is God. One's 'picture' of God is in fact, a metaphorical narrative of God's relationship with the world and the self as part of that world" (Greeley 1995:124).

Through a series of interviews, Greeley found that individuals often expressed images of God in comparison to earthly relationships and by referencing human characteristics. He constructed a series of God-image items and financially supported their inclusion on the 1983 GSS (Hertel and Donahue 1995). These items ask respondents to locate their conception of God between contrasting adjectives on a scale ranging from 1 to 7. Specifically, Greeley contrasted more maternal, gracious, or friendly adjectives with terms that suggested a God with a more authoritarian nature. One question asked respondents whether God is more like a "mother" (1) or "father" (7). Others asked respondents to choose between God as a master/spouse, judge/lover, or friend/king. Using these items Greeley indeed found images of God to be significantly related to a number of beliefs and attitudes (Greeley 1988, 1989, 1991, 1993). The Greeley items opened up an expansive research agenda regarding how conceptions of God impact nonreligious beliefs and behaviors and subsequently appeared on the 1991, 1998, and 2008 GSS.

More recently, Paul Froese and Christopher Bader (Bader and Froese 2005; Froese and Bader 2007, 2008, 2010) built upon Greeley's work, examining the role of images of God in predicting a variety of moral and political attitudes and behaviors. Although the two strains of research complement one another, they reveal a simple but key difference in survey methodology. Greeley's items required choosing between two characteristics—it was impossible for a respondent to indicate a strong preference for God as both a "friend" and a "king," for example. Consequently, the Greeley item is an indicator of the extent to which a person *prefers* one version of God to another.

Using the Measurement Wizard, we can easily locate items that ask about God's characteristics that use Greeley's "two-adjective" approach and/or a single-adjective approach. Selecting the "God, Image of" concept in the Measurement Wizard displays 170 questions—perhaps overwhelming at first. But surveys have taken a wide variety of approaches to asking about images of God, which have been coded into subcategories. For example, some simply ask if God answers prayers. Others focus upon God's level of engagement with the world, God's anger, the extent to which God imposes rules upon us, or a number of other approaches. By using the "Custom Comparisons" feature we can select two subcategories that represent our inquiry: "two-adjective" and "single-adjective." Doing so reduces our list of questions to a more manageable fifty-one items (see figure 5.6).

Viewing this subset of items is immediately revealing—two major surveys have taken two different approaches to measuring images of God. The General Social Survey has tended toward a two-adjective approach; the Baylor Religion Survey has asked about a single adjective at a time. For example, BRS respondents were asked how well the term "kingly" describes God's nature. A different question asked how well the term "friendly" describes God, as opposed to the General Social Survey, in which respondents choose between "friend" and 'king."

Figure 5.7 presents frequencies for FRNDKING from the 2008 GSS. The highest percentage of respondents (28%) are clustered in the middle of the scale, indicating that many respondents do not view "friend" and "king" as either/or propositions. The BRS items allow us to split respondents into four groups: those who believe that *neither* term is a good descriptor for God, those who believe that God is "kingly" but not

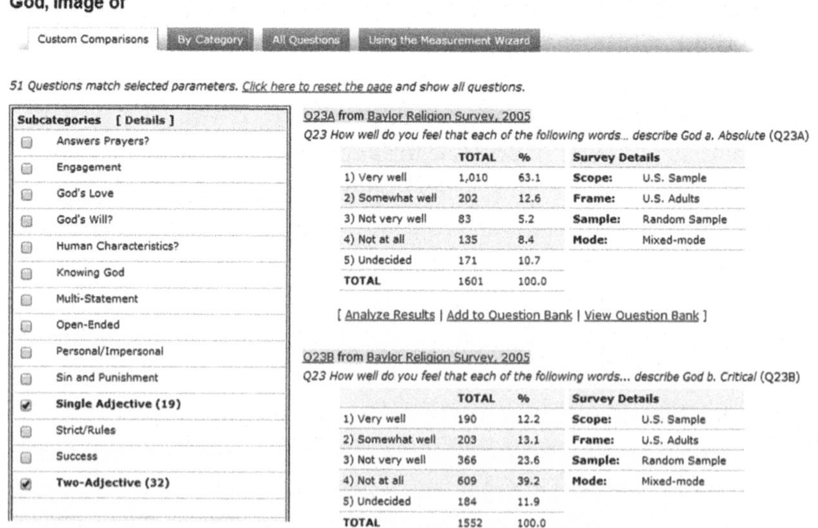

God, Image of

Custom Comparisons | By Category | All Questions | Using the Measurement Wizard

51 Questions match selected parameters. Click here to reset the page and show all questions.

Subcategories [Details]
☐ Answers Prayers?
☐ Engagement
☐ God's Love
☐ God's Will?
☐ Human Characteristics?
☐ Knowing God
☐ Multi-Statement
☐ Open-Ended
☐ Personal/Impersonal
☐ Sin and Punishment
☑ **Single Adjective (19)**
☐ Strict/Rules
☐ Success
☑ **Two-Adjective (32)**

Q23A from Baylor Religion Survey, 2005

Q23 How well do you feel that each of the following words... describe God a. Absolute (Q23A)

	TOTAL	%	Survey Details	
1) Very well	1,010	63.1	**Scope:**	U.S. Sample
2) Somewhat well	202	12.6	**Frame:**	U.S. Adults
3) Not very well	83	5.2	**Sample:**	Random Sample
4) Not at all	135	8.4	**Mode:**	Mixed-mode
5) Undecided	171	10.7		
TOTAL	1601	100.0		

[Analyze Results | Add to Question Bank | View Question Bank]

Q23B from Baylor Religion Survey, 2005

Q23 How well do you feel that each of the following words... describe God b. Critical (Q23B)

	TOTAL	%	Survey Details	
1) Very well	190	12.2	**Scope:**	U.S. Sample
2) Somewhat well	203	13.1	**Frame:**	U.S. Adults
3) Not very well	366	23.6	**Sample:**	Random Sample
4) Not at all	609	39.2	**Mode:**	Mixed-mode
5) Undecided	184	11.9		
TOTAL	1552	100.0		

Figure 5.6. Images of God in the Measurement Wizard.

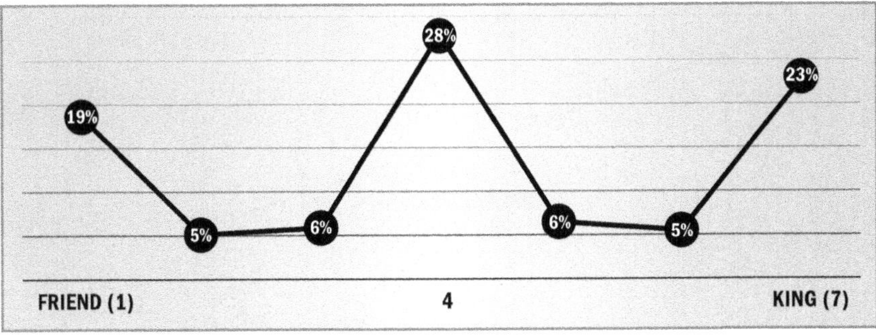

Figure 5.7. God as Friend OR King.
FRNDKING from the General Social Survey, 2008: "Here are sets of contrasting images. On a scale of 1–7 where would you place your images of God between the two contrasting images? This set of contrasting images shows friend at 1 on the scale and king at 7. If you imagine God as a friend, you would place yourself at 1. If you imagine God as a king, you would place yourself at 7. If you imagine God as somewhere between friend and king, you would place yourself at 2, 3, 4, 5, or 6."
Note: The General Social Survey, 2008, includes both a cross-section of respondents and a panel. The God questions reproduced in this chapter were administered to the panel, consisting of 1,536 respondents who had also been interviewed in 2006.

"friendly," those who believe that God is "friendly" but not "kingly," and, finally, those who believe that God is both "friendly" and "kingly."[11] Nearly 60% of BRS respondents simultaneously believe that both "friendly" and "kingly" describe God. The BRS includes a set of questions about abortion similar to the GSS. Using an additive index in which higher values equate to more permissive attitudes about abortion makes it immediately apparent that the *combination* of God descriptors held by the individual is a stronger predictor of moral attitudes (see figure 5.8).[12]

These differing approaches to measuring conceptions of God impact the conclusions we draw from analyses. People who believe that God is neither friendly nor kingly hold the most permissive abortion attitudes, while those who imagine God as both a friend and a king hold the most restrictive abortion attitudes. These four combinations are indicative of four distinctive theologies. Those who refuse both terms may view God as beyond human characteristics and emotions such as judgment. Those who view God as only friendly probably conceive of a being that only interacts with the world in positive ways—a being that simply loves

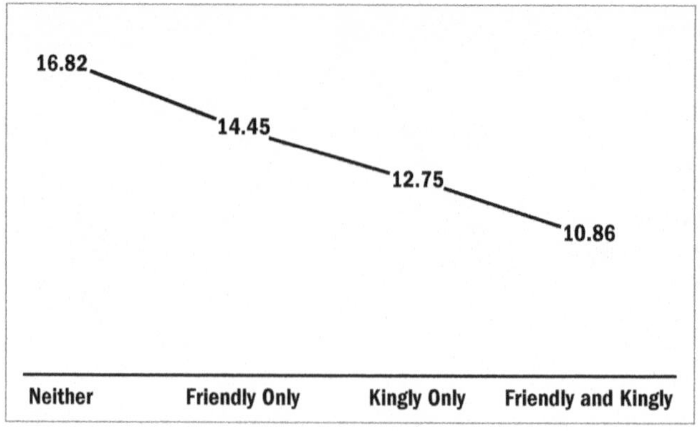

Figure 5.8. Analysis of Variance: Attitudes about Abortion by God as "Friendly" and/or "Kingly" (Baylor Religion Survey Wave 1, 2005). $F = 22.58$; $p<.000$.

too much to ever become angry, the Benevolent God described by Froese and Bader (2010). Someone who imagines God as only a king may perceive an unapproachable being that rules from a distance. A person who ascribes both friendly and kingly characteristics to God is perhaps imagining God in very humanlike terms, as someone who is watching over people as a friend, but unafraid to call out bad behavior.

The comparisons shown in the Measurement Wizard helped to identify areas where we are forcing unnecessary choices upon respondents or making assumptions about what aspects of theology are complementary or "opposites." Understanding these forced choices and underlying assumptions is especially important as we ask survey questions across religions and cultures.

Multi-Item Measures

The examples provided above demonstrate how the Measurement Wizard can facilitate the comparison of survey questions. However, many of our religion measures are strongest when combined into scales and indices (Hill and Hood 1999; see Hill and Pargament in this volume). Clearly our scales and indices will be improved with greater attention to the individual items of which they are composed, but we also need tools that will facilitate the direct comparison of the indices themselves.

To this end, we have spent the last several years developing an extension of the Measurement Wizard—Wizard Scales. As of this writing, the feature provides detailed information on 126 different indices and scales ranging from religion measures, such as conceptions of God, religious beliefs, and religiosity to measures related to religion, such as political attitudes, civic engagement, trust, and tolerance.

Clicking on a topic will provide a list of all of the related scales we have identified. Clicking on an individual scale/index in this list will provide detailed information on that scale/index. For example, under Conceptions of God there are entries for "God's Judgement." Clicking on the first option, "God's Judgement (Froese/Bader), 2005," produces a wealth of information (see figure 5.9).

At the top of each entry, users will find a link to the data file(s) where the scale/index is located. From this link, users can view detailed methodological information about the study, a full codebook, and options for downloading the study in a variety of different formats. In cases where the index/scale was introduced or explained in a particular publication, its citation is provided. The main information provided on this page is a detailed breakdown of both how to create the scale/index and all of the items contained within it. Any general instructions are at the top of the

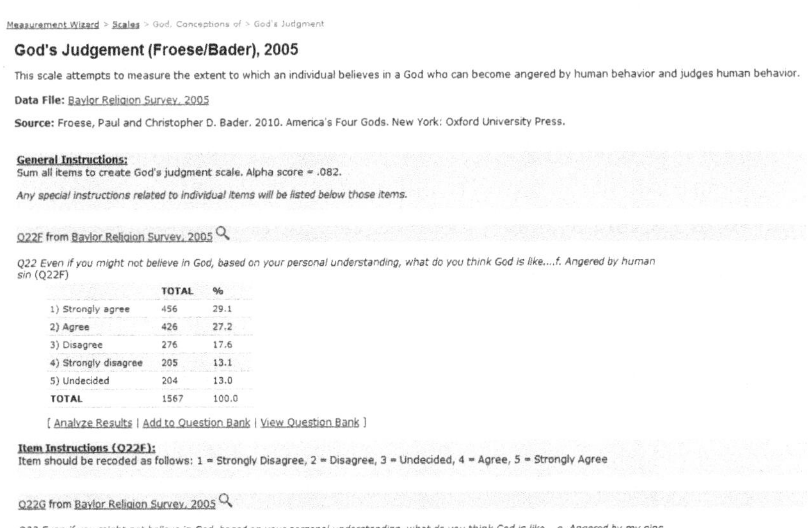

Measurement Wizard > Scales > God, Conceptions of > God's Judgment

God's Judgement (Froese/Bader), 2005

This scale attempts to measure the extent to which an individual believes in a God who can become angered by human behavior and judges human behavior.

Data File: Baylor Religion Survey, 2005

Source: Froese, Paul and Christopher D. Bader. 2010. America's Four Gods. New York: Oxford University Press.

General Instructions:
Sum all items to create God's judgment scale. Alpha score = .082.

Any special instructions related to individual items will be listed below those items.

Q22F from Baylor Religion Survey, 2005

Q22 Even if you might not believe in God, based on your personal understanding, what do you think God is like....f. Angered by human sin (Q22F)

	TOTAL	%
1) Strongly agree	456	29.1
2) Agree	426	27.2
3) Disagree	276	17.6
4) Strongly disagree	205	13.1
5) Undecided	204	13.0
TOTAL	1567	100.0

[Analyze Results | Add to Question Bank | View Question Bank]

Item Instructions (Q22F):
Item should be recoded as follows: 1 = Strongly Disagree, 2 = Disagree, 3 = Undecided, 4 = Agree, 5 = Strongly Agree

Q22G from Baylor Religion Survey, 2005

Q22 Even if you might not believe in God, based on your personal understanding, what do you think God is like....g. Angered by my sins

Figure 5.9. Example of the Wizard Scale Feature in the Measurement Wizard.

page. In the case of "God's Judgement," this scale is the simple sum of all of the included items, which if created properly should generate an Alpha score of .82.

Complete frequencies are provided for the individual items, along with links for quickly performing cross-tab analyses by basic demographics ("Analyze Results") and links for adding the item to a personal question bank. In many cases, survey questions will require recoding before being combined into a scale. When this is the case, the specific instructions for each item will be provided below the individual items. In the example above, the user should reorder categories for question Q22F from the Baylor Religion Survey such that Undecided is in the middle, rather than the last category.

The Wizard Scales tool is in its infancy, and we hope that the research community will provide us with feedback regarding how to improve its function. However, it is our hope that the ability to view and compare scales and indices will further encourage the improvement of our measures of religion.

Conclusion

Are we measuring what we think we are measuring? To answer this question, we used the ARDA's massive metadatabase of survey measures, and the Measurement Wizard, to compare and evaluate past survey questions. The answer: even subtle changes to wording altered the findings received and the stories told. Further, the population of interest also determines the relative effectiveness and utility of a given measure.

A comparison of the results of differing survey designs, varying question wordings, and available response categories need not be focused upon finding "correct" or "incorrect" approaches. Sometimes there are clear downsides to certain strategies, but there is much value in the comparison itself, and differing response patterns between approaches can tell important stories about religion. Responses given to even a short and seemingly simple question on "How important is religion in your life?" can vary widely depending on the response categories given. When participants were asked about Darwinian evolution as the best explanation for human origins, responses varied substantially depending on how the question was asked. If God was clearly excluded from this evolutionary process, support for the explanation dropped sharply. Questions on both human origins and images of God illustrated how the actual beliefs of respondents can be masked when they are forced to choose between options when they might support or disagree with both. We found that even when two responses seem to survey designers to be incompatible or on opposite ends of a continuum, they might be viewed as compatible or even complementary to respondents. Likewise, the middle categories in questions about textual literalism substantially influence the resulting distributions and composition of the resulting categories of interest.

Developing survey measures of religion is deceptively difficult, and researchers would benefit from carefully examining past attempts in detail. It is our hope that the Measurement Wizard will become a useful tool for more effectively evaluating past measures and for designing improved measures for the future.

NOTES

1 The acronym ARDA (www.theARDA.com) initially was for the American Religion Data Archive and was funded by the Lilly Endowment, Inc. The ARDA is now funded by the Lilly Endowment, Inc., the John Templeton Foundation, Pennsylvania State University, and Chapman University. It has a significant collection of international data and has multiple features for educators, journalists, and congregations, as well as researchers.

2 For a more complete review of the ARDA's resources, see Finke, Bader, and Whitehead 2012 or Finke and Bader 2011. Or, visit theARDA.com.

3 As of this writing.

4 A complete list of concepts is available on the website (www.theARDA.com).

5 In essence, we conducted qualitative content analyses of the survey questions contained within the ARDA's metadatabase. To ensure thorough coverage and intercoder reliability, multiple researchers searched for and coded the concepts.

6 This is commonly referred to as avoiding a double-barreled question.

7 Even on the RPLS, when respondents were later asked, "How certain are you about how life developed on Earth?" 59% of those who rejected evolution were "very certain" compared with only 32% of those who reported agreeing that humans evolved over time. Although young earth creationists and strict materialists are clear about their beliefs (see Baker 2012), for many of the remaining respondents the answer is not as simple as choosing between God and evolution.

8 While Bradburn, Sudman, and Wansik (2004) argue for providing middle options in questions, they *also* warn against "scale-point proliferation," or adding so many

categories as to "annoy or confuse the respondent because of the hairsplitting they entail" (p. 331).

9 All surveys mentioned are available for viewing, online analysis, and download at theARDA.com. Variables mentioned include RELIG IMP from the American National Election Studies, 2000; IMPTREL from the Religion and Public Life Survey, 2002; RELIMP from the Religion and Public Life Survey, 2008; and FAITHIMP from the 1999–2000 Lilly Survey of Attitudes and Social Networks.

10 Schuman and Presser (1996) note three major effects of the inclusion of a middle position: (a) the percentage of "don't know" responses increases; (b) the growth of the middle position comes almost entirely from a decline in the polar positions; (c) the decline in the polar positions tends to occur proportionately—in other words, respondents tend to be pulled from the polar positions equally.

11 We categorized an individual as accepting a descriptor for God if he or she said it described God "somewhat well" or "very well" and as rejecting a descriptor if he or she was "undecided" or believed that the term described God "not very well" or "not at all."

12 The Baylor Religion Survey asks respondents, "How do you feel about abortion under the following circumstances?" The survey asks about five circumstances, including the possibility of the child having a serious defect, the woman's health being in danger, the pregnancy being the result of rape, the woman not being able to afford the child; and the woman not wanting more children. Possible responses include "Not wrong at all," "Only wrong sometimes," "Almost always wrong," and "Always wrong." The final additive scale has an Alpha score of .91.

REFERENCES

Bader, Christopher, and Paul Froese. 2005. "Images of God: The Effect of Personal Theologies on Moral Attitudes, Political Affiliation, and Religious Behavior." *Interdisciplinary Journal of Research on Religion* 1(11).

Baker, Joseph O. 2012. "Public Perceptions of Incompatibility between 'Science and Religion.'" *Public Understanding of Science* 21(3): 340–53.

Baker, Joseph O. 2013. "Acceptance of Evolution and Support for Teaching Creationism in Public Schools: The Conditional Impact of Educational Attainment." *Journal for the Scientific Study of Religion* 52(1): 216–28.

Bartkowski, John P. 1996. "Beyond Biblical Literalism and Inerrancy: Conservative Protestants and the Hermeneutic Interpretation of Scripture." *Sociology of Religion* 57(3): 259–72.

Bradburn, Norman, Seymour Sudman, and Brian Wansik. 2004. *Asking Questions*. San Francisco: Jossey-Bass.

Converse, Jean M., and Stanley Presser. 1986. *Survey Questions: Handcrafting the Standardized Questionnaire*. Thousand Oaks, CA: Sage.

Darnell, Alfred, and Darren E. Sherkat. 1997. "The Impact of Protestant Fundamentalism on Educational Attainment." *American Sociological Review* 62(2): 306–15.

Ellison, Christopher G., and Marc A. Musick. 1995. "Conservative Protestantism and Public Opinion toward Science." *Review of Religious Research* 36(3): 245–62.

Felson, Jacob, and Heather Kindell. 2007. "The Elusive Link between Conservative Protestantism and Conservative Economics." *Social Science Research* 36(2): 673–87.

Finke, Roger, Christopher D. Bader, and Andrew Whitehead. 2012. "Innovations in the Development and Use of Social Science Data Archives." *Leadership in Science and Technology: A Reference Handbook*, edited by William Sims Bainbridge. Thousand Oaks, CA: Sage.

Finke, Roger, and Christopher D. Bader. 2011. "Data and Directions for Research in the Economics of Religion." *The Oxford Handbook of the Economics of Religion*, edited by Rachel McCleary. New York: Oxford University Press.

Froese, Paul, and Christopher D. Bader. 2007. "God in America: Why Theology Is Not Simply the Concern of Philosophers." *Journal for the Scientific Study of Religion* 46(4): 465–82.

Froese, Paul, and Christopher D. Bader. 2008. "Unraveling Religious Worldviews: The Relationship between Images of God and Political Ideology in a Cross-Cultural Analysis." *Sociological Quarterly* 49(4): 689–718.

Froese, Paul, and Christopher D. Bader. 2010. *America's Four Gods: What We Say about God and What That Says about Us*. New York: Oxford University Press.

Greeley, Andrew M. 1988. "Evidence That a Maternal Image of God Correlates with Liberal Politics." *Sociology and Social Research* 72: 150–54.

Greeley, Andrew M. 1989. *Religious Change in America*. Cambridge, MA: Harvard University Press.

Greeley, Andrew M. 1991. "Religion and Attitudes towards AIDS Policy." *Sociology and Social Research* 75: 126–32.

Greeley, Andrew M. 1993. "Religion and Attitudes toward the Environment." *Journal for the Scientific Study of Religion* 32: 19–28.

Greeley, Andrew M. 1995. *Religion as Poetry*. New Brunswick, NJ: Transaction.

Guth, James L., John C. Green, Lyman A. Kellstedt, and Corwin E. Smidt. 1995. "Faith and the Environment: Religious Beliefs and Attitudes on Environmental Policy." *American Journal of Political Science* 39(2): 364–82.

Hempel, Lynn M., and John Bartkowski. 2008. "Scripture, Sin, and Salvation: Theological Conservatism Reconsidered." *Social Forces* 86(4): 1647–74.

Hertel, Bradley R., and Michael J. Donahue. 1995. "Parental Influences on God Images among Children: Testing Durkheim's Metaphoric Parallelism." *Journal for the Scientific Study of Religion* 34: 186–99.

Hill, Peter, and Ralph W. Hood, eds. 1999. *Measures of Religiosity*. Birmingham, AL: Religious Education Press.

Hood, Ralph W. Jr., Peter C. Hill, and W. Paul Williamson. 2005. *The Psychology of Religious Fundamentalism*. New York: Guilford.

Hoover, Dwight W. 1990. *Middletown Revisited*. Ball State Monographs, no. 34. Available at libx.bsu.edu. Retrieved April 5, 2013.

Jelen, Ted G. 1989. "Biblical Literalism and Inerrancy: Does the Difference Make a Difference?" *Sociological Analysis* 49(4): 421–29.

Leege, David C. 1995. "Religiosity Measures on the National Election Studies: A Guide to Their Use in Voting Studies, Part I." In *NES Conference on Values and Predispositions*. Tempe, AZ.

Lynd, Robert S., and Helen M. Lynd. 1929. *Middletown: A Study in Contemporary American Culture*. New York: Harcourt, Brace.

Lynd, Robert S., and Helen M. Lynd. 1937. *Middletown in Transition: A Study in Cultural Conflicts*. New York: Harcourt, Brace.

McDaniel, Eric L, and Christopher G. Ellison. 2008. "God's Party? Race, Religion, and Partisanship over Time." *Political Research Quarterly* 61(2): 180–91.

Schaeffer, Nora Cate, and Stanley Presser. 2003. "The Science of Asking Questions." *Annual Review of Sociology* 29: 65–88.

Schuman, Howard, and Stanley Presser. 1996. *Questions and Answers in Attitude Surveys*. Thousand Oaks, CA: Sage.

Sherkat, Darren E., and Alfred Darnell. 1999. "The Effect of Parents' Fundamentalism on Children's Educational Attainment: Examining Differences by Gender and Children's Fundamentalism." *Journal for the Scientific Study of Religion* 38(1): 23–35.

Spilka, Bernard, Philip Armatus, and June Nussbaum. 1964. "The Concept of God: A Factor-Analytic Approach." *Review of Religious Research* 6: 28–35.

Stroope, Samuel. 2011. "Education and Religion: Individual, Congregational, and Cross-Level Interaction Effects on Biblical Literalism." *Social Science Research* 40(6): 1478–93.

6.

Using the Total Survey Error Paradigm to Improve Cross-National Research on Religion

TOM W. SMITH

Introduction

Durkheim (1938:139) noted in 1895 that "comparative sociology is not a particular branch of sociology; it is sociology itself, in so far as it ceases to be purely descriptive and aspires to account for facts."[1] Of course, this also applies to other social sciences. Genov (1991:1) has observed that "contemporary sociology stands and falls with its own internationalization. . . . The internationalization of sociology is the unfinished agenda of the sociological classics. It is the task of contemporary and future sociologists." For political science, Brady (2000:48) has noted that cross-national research has "produced theoretical insight about political participation, the role of values in economic growth and political action, and many other topics." In economics, a cross-national approach has become imperative as globalization has restructured economies (Freeman 2006, 2007; Bardhan and Kroll 2003).

As the Working Group on the Outlook for Comparative International Social Science Research (Luce, Smelser, and Gerstein 1989:549) has noted, "A range of research previously conceived as 'domestic' . . . clearly needs to be reconceptualized in light of recent comparative/international findings." Fortunately, the social sciences are increasingly recognizing the value of cross-national research. At the Social Science Research Council's (SSRC) meeting on Fostering International Collaboration in the Social Sciences, Ian Diamond, head of the Economic and Social Research Council (UK), indicated that "social science is a global undertaking and . . . has been increasingly so for years," and David Lightfoot of the National Science Foundation noted that a "major reason for international collaboration is similar to that for interdisciplinary research, it is one of the most productive ways of making new and innovative connections" and that "none of the social sciences is essentially national in character" (SSRC 2006).

Thus cross-national research not only has great promise but is an absolute necessity if we are to understand contemporary human societies in general and the role of religion in particular. To be useful, comparative survey research needs to meet high scientific standards of reliability and validity and achieve functional equivalence across surveys. This is challenging because comparative survey research is a large-scale and complex endeavor that must be well designed and well executed to minimize error and maximize equivalence. This goal can be notably advanced by the application of the total survey error (TSE) paradigm to cross-national survey research.

First, this chapter briefly introduces TSE and explains how it can be used to identify and address survey errors, including the challenge of functional equivalence in cross-national surveys. Second, the chapter addresses many of the practical challenges that different languages, structures, and cultures pose in conducting cross-national survey research, giving extensive attention to question wording. Drawing on TSE and illustrating with many examples, this section reviews how comparison errors can be minimized and comparative reliability and validity can be maximized. The final section is devoted to addressing the challenges faced when studying religion cross-nationally. Building on the previous section, and using numerous examples, this section discusses how comparison errors and other errors identified by TSE can be reduced for religion measures.

The Concept of Total Survey Error

Total survey error (TSE) is the sum of all the myriad of ways in which survey measurement can go wrong (Smith 2005). Put another way, TSE is "the difference between its actual (true) value for the full target population and the value estimated from the survey," as Lessler (1984:405) noted. The concept of TSE has a long lineage stretching back at least to Deming (1944), although the term itself seems to have been first used by Brown (1967) to describe what is now known as TSE. It is noteworthy that every major description of TSE—from Deming (1944) through Hansen, Hurwitz, and Madow (1953), Kish (1965), Brown (1967), Anderson, Kasper, and Frankel (1979), Groves (1989), Smith (1996, 2005, 2011), Biemer and Lyberg (2003), and Alwin (2007) to Pennell et al. (2014)—has produced a different taxonomy. Moreover, as Deming (1944:359) noted about his seminal classification of errors in surveys, "the thirteen factors referred to are not always distinguishable and there are other ways of classifying them."

What attempts to categorize survey errors generally have in common are (1) distinguishing two types of error—(a) variance or variable error, which is random and has no expected impact on mean values, and (b) bias or systematic error, which is directional and alters mean estimates—and (2) classifying error into branching categories in which major categories are subsequently subdivided until presumably all notable survey-error components are separately delineated. TSE combines the two components of (1) and accomplishes (2). The various TSE descriptions vary mainly in how detailed the depiction of errors is and in the exact description and placement of certain errors within the overall classification schema. In general, TSE classifications have become more detailed over time, and general categories of error have been more closely tied to specific, operational components of a survey (e.g., sample frame, interviewer, questionnaire, data processing). Figure 6.1 illustrates one model of TSE. It has two error flows (variable in dashes and systematic in solid lines) from each error source. It has thirty-five components (the right-most boxes in each path).[2] However, this model does not delineate all possible subcategories of error components. For example, the box "Medium" could be subdivided in various ways (Smith 2011, 2012).

TSE Interactions

Interactions are a key component of TSE, but have been largely neglected in the TSE literature (Groves 2005; Smith 2005, 2008). TSE discussions have largely focused on each component separately and in turn. This wrongly contributes to the idea that the errors occur independently of one another. Nothing is further from the truth. There are usually close connections and interactions among the different error components.

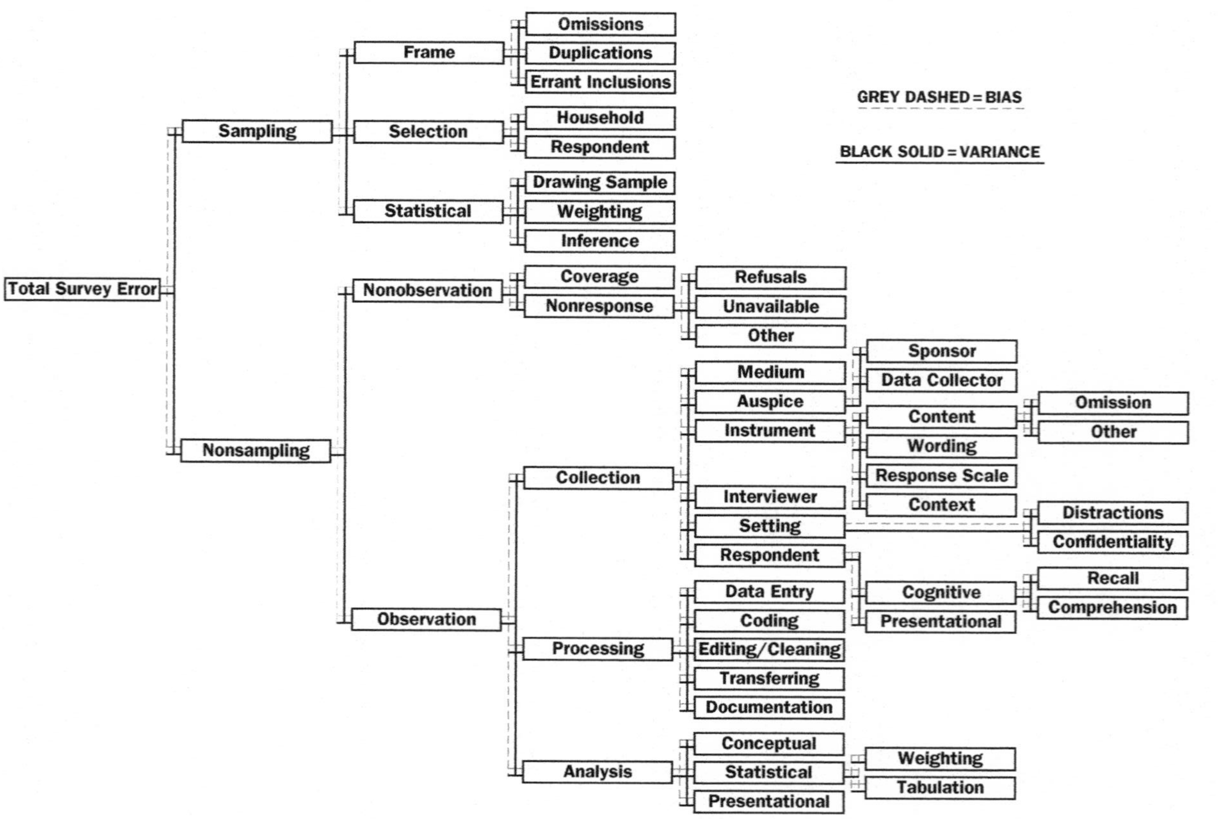

Figure 6.1. Total Survey Error.

For example, poorly trained interviewers will make more mistakes in the administration and recording of questions and also tend to have a lower response rate, thus creating a link between measurement error and nonresponse bias (Smith 2011).

TSE and Multiple Surveys

Traditionally, TSE was used to describe the error structure of a single survey. But much of survey research involves the use of two or more surveys. Fortunately, TSE can be easily adapted to apply to and improve such multisurvey research (Smith 2011).

For comparative studies that are the focus here, TSE has multiple valuable uses. First, it can act as a blueprint for designing studies. As a study is planned, each error component can be considered in order to minimize each source of error. Using the TSE framework can ensure that all countries follow the same guidelines and deal with the same issues. This improves both the data quality and its comparability. Second, it can be a guide for evaluating error that actually occurred once the surveys have been conducted. One can go through each component and assess the level and similarity of the error structures. This can be done both as part of the immediate evaluation of just-collected primary data or employed well after the data collection as part of secondary analysis. Third, TSE can set a methodological research agenda for studying error structures in comparative surveys and for designing experiments and other research to understand and reduce TSE. Fourth, it extends beyond examining the separate components of error and provides a framework for the combining of the individual error components into their overall sum. Understanding the specific sources of errors and the magnitude and direction of error is essential for improving surveys and reducing TSE, but understanding the TSE in existing surveys is necessary for optimizing their analysis. Unfortunately, it is not possible to quantitatively measure and combine the various error components into a single overall number. Finally, by considering error as an interaction across surveys, it establishes the basis for a statistical model for handling error across surveys. As figure 6.2 illustrates, each component is measured in each survey (as shown by the stacked boxes), and across each component there is a potential interaction in the error structures.

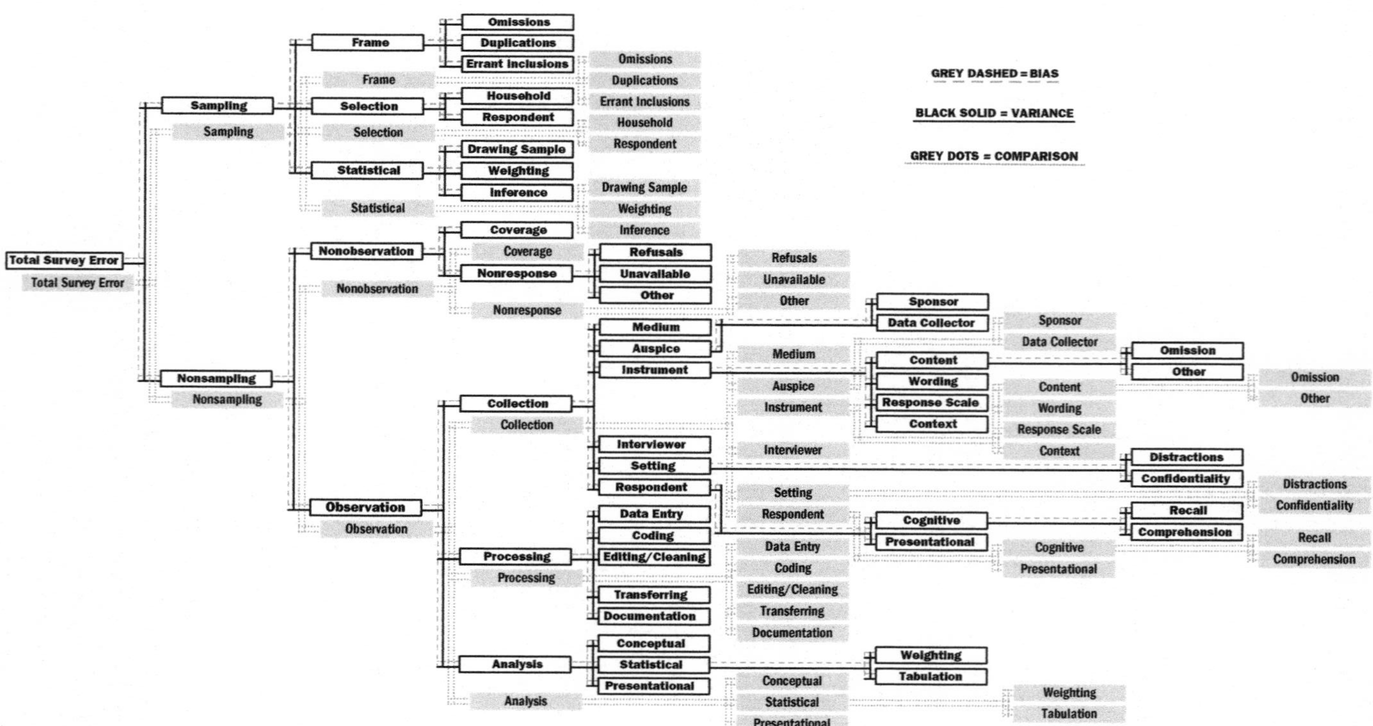

Figure 6.2. Total Survey Error: Comparison Error.

TSE Comparison Error in Cross-National Surveys

The interaction of errors across surveys leads to what Weisberg (2005) refers to as "equivalence problems" or "comparability effects," or what has been referred to as "comparison error" (Smith 2011). Comparison error occurs both for each component and in the aggregate across all components. For example, errors due to mistranslations are comparison errors that are interactions between the question-wording components of each study. The TSE paradigm indicates that one needs to consider all of the many components of comparison error across surveys, including both the individual comparison errors from each component and the cumulative comparison error across all components.

TSE can both identify error in individual surveys and minimize comparison error across surveys. The latter goal will often mean that "comparability may drive design" (Harkness et al. 2010). For example, TSE can be used first to improve country-specific questions and then further to optimize questions comparatively and thus minimize comparison error (Braun and Harkness 2001). Consider a fourfold table in which questions are either "good" (e.g., reliable, valid, clear) or "poor" and either "well translated" or "poorly translated." To write better initial questions, there are many well-established strictures and guidelines that can and should be applied, such as Gricean maxims of conversation (Grice 1989), the Tourangeau and Rasinski (Tourangeau, Rips, and Rasinski 2000) model of the response process to survey questions, and standard item-development techniques such as general and cognitive pretesting (Fitzgerald et al. 2011; Miller et al. 2011; Willis 2015).

Comparison error is especially likely in studies involving a large number of countries and societies that are very different from one another (e.g., varying greatly on languages, structures, cultures). The inclusion of more countries means a larger number of components (e.g., research teams, field staffs, translations) that must be planned and coordinated. The larger number also means that the goal of achieving functional equivalence across all countries is harder since more bilateral comparisons must be optimized and steps to make two countries more similar will often draw one or both of the countries away from still other societies. Of course, figure 6.2 illustrates only the simplest of cross-national situations: bilateral surveys. The stacked boxes would increase to equal the number of surveys employed (i.e., the number of countries covered). The number of comparison errors expands even more. With two surveys there is one comparison per box. For ten surveys there would be forty-five bilateral comparisons per box. Multiply by the thirty-five boxes and there are 1,575 bilateral comparisons. If interactions are considered, the number of comparisons becomes enormous. Likewise, the greater the dissimilarities across countries in language, structure, and culture, the more challenging it is to develop equally relevant, reliable, and valid items.

The aim of minimizing error in general and comparison error in particular in both the study design and its execution does not mean that procedures need to be identical. Similar results can be achieved through different means. For example, having 100 percent valid interviews is the goal of almost all surveys. This can be achieved through various interviewer recruitment and training strategies and through various case-verification procedures, including validation recontacts with respondents, having supervisors observe interviews in the field or monitor telephone interviews, embedding special validation questions in surveys, utilizing computer audio-recorded interviewing, checking time stamps, using GPS tracking, and detecting faked data with analytical methods. While the validation procedures utilized often vary notably across organizations and surveys, this variation is not problematic to the extent that the same outcome of eliminating faked interviews is achieved.[3] But if some techniques are less effective than others, then comparison error will occur in part because of these differences.

However, one does not want to permit legitimate, even necessary, variation to become unnecessary and often harmful deviance. Sometimes the cross-national differences are due to the application of usual, customary practices; these may be neither locally optimal nor best to further comparability. A balance is needed between the undesirable poles of rigid standardization and disruptive, uncoordinated variation.

If the study-design features are equivalent and procedures are successfully implemented, one might expect component errors to be similar and thus for TSE to be on a par across surveys. While this is often a plausible expectation, it cannot be taken as guaranteed. True variation can interact with measurement error to create comparison error (Andreenkova 2015; Jeveline 1999). The sensitivity of topics and questions often varies across societies (Frank and Sabarre 2015). For example, asking about drinking alcohol is not an especially sensitive topic in most European societies, but would be so in conservative Muslim countries. As a result, social-desirability bias concerning alcohol consumption (and other religious and social taboos) would likely be much greater in the latter than in the former.

Components of TSE and Comparison Error

TSE emphasizes that many components of error must be considered and that total error must be assessed. Likewise, comparison error must be examined across all of the components and its total impact evaluated. Many components of TSE have been shown to be important in establishing (or, conversely, in undermining) functional equivalence in cross-national survey research (Jowell et al. 2007). For example, studies have shown that undercoverage and sample bias have distorted international student testing scores (Carnoy and Rothstein 2013; Loveless 2014; Medrich and Griffith 1992). Other studies have shown the impact of differences in mode (Skjaak and Harkness 2002; Skjaak, Harkness, and Smith 2000); interviewer recruitment, training, and supervision (Smith 2007a); variations in hard-to-survey populations (Smith 2014), and nonresponse rates (Billiet and Matsuo 2011; Stoop 2012).

Comparison error involving question wording is probably the single largest challenge in cross-national survey research, involving straightforward translation issues and the even more complex issues involving structural and cultural factors. For that reason, it has been the main focus of methodological research in cross-national survey research literature, and other error components have often been neglected.

Obtaining Functional Equivalence and Similarity in Comparative Surveys

Two or more surveys in two or more countries by their very nature cannot be identical. The target populations always differ, and differences relating both to conducting the surveys (e.g., sample frames, field staffs, interview training, survey climate) and to the societies in general (language, structure, culture) are complex and substantial. Typically, the object has been to maximize comparability or functional equivalence. What this means, however, is often unclear. Johnson (1998) identified fifty-two different types of "equivalence" in cross-national survey research and did not search for the uses of alternative terms such as "comparability." Johnson describes functional equivalence as falling under the general category of interpretive equivalence, which he characterizes as involving "equivalence of meaning" and elaborates that functional equivalence is "universal in a qualitative, although not quantitative, sense." Johnson (1998:6) further describes "concordance of meaning" as central to the concept of functional equivalence. At the item level, it indicates that across surveys, questions would be understood in a similar manner and would both operate as a similar stimulus and capture answers with similar response options.

As used here, "functional equivalence" indicates the goal of striving to achieve as close a similarity as is practical across comparative surveys at the item, scale, and survey levels. It first considers functional equivalence at the item level across matched pairs of questions, then at the scale level across batteries of items, and finally at the survey level across all aspects and components of the studies. Item-level equivalence is obviously essential for comparison between single measures. Single items are usually used for most demographics and many behaviors. While there are very limited possibilities for testing functional equivalence quantitatively by comparing single items since their distributions are a function of a varying and undetectable degree of substantive variation and measurement error, one can examine relationships with other variables to see if the items are performing as expected.

Item-level, functional equivalence is also a good foundation for building functionally equivalent scales. Most attitudinal analysis depends on the use of multi-item scales, and these are needed even more in cross-national research than they are in monocultural research. The extra complexity and intersurvey variability of cross-national studies typically requires more measures and elaborate designs. Smith (1989) has indicated as a rule of thumb that one needs three times as many indicators in a cross-national survey to measure a scale or construct as reliably and validly as in a single society.

But even if item- and scale-level functional equivalence is achieved, that does not mean that the surveys and their various measures will necessarily be functionally equivalent. As TSE stresses, one needs to assess all of the components and determine that functional equivalence is obtained across components and collectively. For example, if one sample undercovers certain subgroups (e.g., religious minorities) or if in one survey nonresponse bias underrepresents other segments, then even well-constructed measures will not produce functionally equivalent measurement across surveys.

In cross-national survey research, the individual surveys need to be well designed and well executed and designed to minimize comparison error, and applying the TSE perspective greatly facilitates these goals. From the design and execution perspective, the goal is to have surveys designed with similar features (e.g., target population, content, interviewer training) and carried out to a similar (and hopefully high) level of attainment. That is, they need to be designed to do the same thing, and those intentions need to be achieved. Similar designs and procedures alone are not enough to achieve comparability. The level of error is a function both of the totality of comparative survey design features and the degree to which the protocols are realized. TSE is a product of the outcomes or results of the survey and not just its ideal design intentions. Realization will depend on diligence and supervision in general and specific quality-control procedures in particular. The proof of survey data quality is in the execution of the protocols and the confirmation of the quality of the collected data.

Challenges of Cross-National Survey Research

There are challenges associated with doing comparative surveys related both to the conducting of surveys and to their specific substantive content (Smith 2010). In terms of conducting comparative surveys, there are numerous factors contributing to the possibility of comparison error. These special concerns of cross-national survey research need to be fully taken into consideration and integrated using the TSE approach. First, cross-national surveys are almost always collected by different organizations and field staffs, and house effects are to be expected. Second, national laws on privacy regulation and when and how surveys may be conducted also hinder comparability. As World Association for Public Opinion Research (WAPOR) has documented in recent decades, governments sometimes restrict the content of surveys, and when pre-election surveys may be conducted and/or released (Chung 2012; Smith 2004). Third, there is notable variation in established business practices such as in how interviewers are recruited, trained, supervised, compensated, etc. (Jowell et al. 2007). Finally, there are large differences in the survey climate across societies (Smith 2007a). Interviews are much easier to obtain in some countries than in others, leading frequently to large typical differences in response rates (Couper and de Leeuw 2002). In these and others ways, differences in the conducting of surveys can often lead to comparison error.

Language

Besides the cross-national differences related to the conducting of surveys, there are many other societal differences related to the substance or content of the survey. Countries can be thought of as varying on several key dimensions: language, structure, and culture. Whenever more than one language is used within a nation or when different languages are used across nations, translation and adaptation of questions need to be carried out. Questions in two or more languages need to convey the same meaning, have similar connotations, and be expressed in the same manner (e.g., language level; common vs. technical/expert usage, formal vs. informal; use of dialects; Smith 2007b). Whenever this challenging task is not successfully executed, comparison error emerges for question wording.

Survey questions have two parts: the question-asking part, where the substance of the item is posed, and the response-recording part, when answers are recorded. The substantive part of the question or stimulus needs to convey the same meaning in all languages. To have a high degree of comparability or equivalence, one first wants to ensure that the key concept words and, of course, the question as a whole have the same meaning (i.e., that respondents in different societies being interviewed in different languages assign the same meaning to the words and phrases in the question and that the objects, actions, and modifiers are closely equivalent in what people think about across surveys)—for example, that the concept of "spirituality" in English closely matches the meaning and context of translated terms in other languages. As Braun and

Harkness (2005:96) have noted, to achieve this goal one needs to keep in mind that "statements, questions, and other utterances have what is generally called semantic meaning; that is, meaning(s) language users regularly associate with the words and the arrangement of words present in any given utterance. They also have pragmatic meaning; that is, meaning which is determined by the interdependence of what is said with the context in which it is said."

Questions also need to convey the same connotations. Merriam-Webster's online dictionary defines "connotation" as "an idea or quality that a word makes you think about in addition to its meaning" and as "the suggesting of a meaning by a word apart from the thing it explicitly names or describes," and Dictionary.com defines it as "the associated or secondary meaning of a word or expression in addition to its explicit or primary meaning." Unless the connotations are similar across translations, the overall meaning of items will not be similar. For example, "home" often implies a lot more than just one's residence, often indicating a place of warmth and family ties (e.g., "home is where the heart is"). While the terms "address," "residence," "house," "dwelling," and "home" all might be used in questions about where one lives, they would often convey very different contexts. Similarly, there are various terms for a nonreligious person, such as "free thinker," "secularist," "unbeliever," "nonbeliever," "infidel," "kafir," "paynim," "agnostic," and "atheist," which convey different ways of not being religious, general or religion-specific references, and a range of neutral to negative connotations. Additionally, the variations and nuances that exist in one language will typically not match those existing in other languages.

Finally, questions need to be similar on a range of other linguistic traits such as the use of informal vs. formal language, technical or expert vs. common terms vs. slang, and standard pronunciation and terms vs. dialects and regional variations. The language register and vocabulary will depend on such matters as the target population (e.g., general population vs. technocrats or professional employees) and general language rules and practices (e.g., the familiar vs. formal /"*tu*" vs. "*vous*" distinction in French, or whether "God" is capitalized and what the word's implication is across languages).

The response options or answer-recording component is the second part of a survey question. There are many different types of response options, such as open ended vs. closed, closed with few vs. many categories, verbal vs. numerical options, and magnitude-measurement scales vs. fixed-response scales, among others. Smith et al. (2005) discuss the different possibilities and their suitability for cross-national research. Besides having different measurement features, response options have different error structures. For cross-national studies, one wants response options that minimize both intranational measurement error and international comparison error. To minimize comparison error, one first wants the response options to have similar familiarity or at least the same ability to follow the response options across countries. For example, one study tried to use a response scale in which rungs on a ladder denoted response options, but found that this was not understood in some countries. The researchers instead developed a scale that had steps ascending to the top of a mountain, which was understood in all societies (Gallup 1976). Similarly, the ratio-level, magnitude measurement scales have some superior statistical properties, but are unusable in societies with high innumeracy.

Second, the specific response options need to have the same strength and the same interval between response options. For example, a five-point Likert scale using "Strongly Agree," "Agree," "Neither Agree nor Disagree," "Disagree," and "Strongly Disagree" would want versions in other languages to have their categories represent the same points on the "Totally Agree" to "Totally Disagree" continuum as the English points did. Smith et al. (2005) conducted experiments in the United States, Germany, and Japan that show, first, how the strength of response options can be calibrated and the interval between them measured, and, second, how the comparability of the response options across countries/languages can be assessed and adjusted as needed.[4]

To minimize comparison error in wordings, one first needs to utilize a rigorous and comprehensive procedure for item development, testing, and translation. The best approach for achieving this is the TRAPD model (Translation, Review, Adjudication, Pretesting, and Documentation) (Harkness et al. 2010; Willis 2015). Besides applying rigorous translation procedures as illustrated by the TRAPD approach, a series of quantitative steps can and should be taken at both the developmental stage and as part of post-hoc assessment to test and improve translation and therefore minimize wording comparison error (Smith 2007b, 2009a, 2013b).

Structure

Next, there are structural differences between countries. "Structural" refers to formal differences in the organization of society, in aspects such as laws and institutions. Examples would include the structure or organization of the government and political system such as centralized vs. decentralized, the selection and status of the head of state vs. head of government, parliamentary vs. nonparliamentary electoral systems, democratic vs. nondemocratic governments; and the existence and nature of various governmental policies and programs (e.g., the legal status of religion and laws governing "freedom of religion"). These structural differences often make it difficult to ask the "same" question across countries. For example, a question about the head of state would be about the hereditary monarch in Great Britain, the hereditary emir in Qatar, popularly elected presidents in Germany and the United States, and a Federal Council chosen by the Federal Legislature in Switzerland. In Great Britain and Germany, the powers of the head of state are limited; in the United States, the elected president is both head of state and head of government; in Qatar, the emir's power is comprehensive. Thus, a question about head of state refers to those chosen in very different ways with very different powers across countries.

Differences in governmental laws and policies also need to be understood and carefully considered when one is designing comparative questions. For example, countries vary on the legal status of religions, with some having a state religion and others not explicitly recognizing any religion. Questions about the role of religion in society need to take into consideration the legal status of religion and the specific legal status of specific religions. In another example, asking about financial contributions to religion is complicated by the existence of religious taxes in some countries. While mandatory taxes would in most cases not be reported in a question about voluntary, personal giving, the situation is often less clear. In Germany, Protestants, Catholics, and Jews are subject to a governmental religion tax that applies to their respective religions. But Germans can legally avoid the tax if they disavow their religious adherence. Thus, in a sense, those who pay the tax are doing so voluntarily. A comparative study of religious giving needs to decide how to count taxes and to design questions that clearly include or exclude them as the study intends. If items fail to take the structural differences into consideration, then comparison error related to question wording and/or analysis will occur.

Culture

Finally, there are cultural differences across countries. Of course, "culture" is an encompassing enough term that it could easily subsume both language and structure as subparts of culture. Here, it is taken to cover aspects of society outside of language and structure. Countries vary in a myriad of ways. This creates various challenges for comparative survey research. First, some aspects of society may be important in some countries, but virtually nonexistent in others. For example, elective plastic/cosmetic surgery is very popular in Brazil and a way to improve both personal happiness and social position, but is rare in many other countries. Godparents are crucial family members in many societies and do not exist in many others.

Second, cultural traits are often described as either "emic," referring to those that are culture specific or close to being societally unique, or "etic," which describes aspects seen as universal that are "understood in a consistent manner across cultures and national boundaries (i.e., to the extent that they have interpretive equivalence)" (Johnson 1998:11). Some concepts are so emic that they are even hard to formulate in other languages for other cultures. For example "*giri*" is an indigenous Japanese concept having to do with social interaction, duty, and obligation that at least one researcher, Ruth Benedict (1946:133), described as follows: "There is no possible English equivalent and of all the strange categories of moral obligation which anthropologists find in the culture of the world, it is one of the most curious." Similarly, the American concept of "hard work" is readily understood in the United States as a chief means by which individuals can advance and improve their lot in life. In other countries the concept is not as clear and pervasive and has been misunderstood to mean "work that is difficult to do" or that people can advance by taking on difficult work, perhaps because there is higher pay for such tasks.[5]

Researchers are often drawn towards the etic or universal rather than the emic or particularistic since they see it as impossible to compare what is unique and does not exist across countries. But that can be a mistake. If one only examines the etic and ignores the emic, one both creates cross-national images of societies that are more homogenous than they actually are and generates a more superficial portrait of each individual society.

Studying Religion across Nations and Religions

Keeping in mind the prior discussion of minimizing comparison error in general and of dealing with the complexities created by differences in language, structure, and culture and by the etic-emic continuum in particular, we now consider approaches to studying religion across nations. Major approaches include the following: (1) using only general, decentered items with no religion-specific questions, (2) employing only religion- and/or country-specific items focusing on the important beliefs, behaviors, and structures of specific religions, (3) asking about the same religious behaviors and beliefs across all countries/religions despite the fact that many of these may be of low relevance and/or hard to understand in languages, countries, and religions with little exposure to them, and (4) incorporating both some general behavior and belief items in all countries plus some country/religion-specific questions asked only in some countries or of followers of particular religions. Examples and assessment of these various approaches are presented next.

There are several possible approaches to designing a cross-national, comparative survey—the universal or etic approach, the religion-specific or emic approach, and blends or combinations of the universal/etic and particularistic/emic approaches. The universal/etic approach develops general measures of religion designed to be asked in all countries and to pertain to members of any or no religions. This approach is illustrated by a seven-item Index of Religiosity developed by Miller, Cotter, and Inglehart (2015) covering eighty-six countries (and all major world religions) in the European and World Values Surveys (EVS/WVS).

1. For each of the following, indicate how important it is in your life.
    a. Religion: Is it very important, rather important, not very important, or not at all important?

2. Here is a list of qualities that children can be encouraged to learn at home. Which, if any, do you consider to be especially important? Please choose up to five!
   a. Religious faith
3. I am going to name a number of organizations. For each one, could you tell me how much confidence you have in them: is it a great deal of confidence, quite a lot of confidence, not much confidence, or none at all?
   a. Churches/Religious leaders: [Use the latter in non-Christian countries]
4. Independently of whether you attend religious services or not, would you say that you are:
   a. a religious person, not a religious person, an atheist?
5. Apart from weddings and funerals, about how often do you attend religious services these days?
   a. [Show card with responses from "More than once a week" to "Never, practically never"]
6. Apart from weddings and funerals, how often do you pray?
   a. [Show card with response from "Several times a day" to "Never, practically never"]
7. How important is God in your life? Please use this scale to indicate. 10 means "very important" and 1 means "not at all important."
   a. [Card with 1–10 scale is shown]

The scale has a general, universal orientation, but does drift into specific religious behavior and belief. The first three items are part of general batteries that address many aspects of life without any focus on religion and broach the topic in only the most general of terms ("Religion," "Religious faith," "Churches/Religious leaders"). The fourth item focuses only on religion, but is still very general ("Religious person" . . . "Atheist"). The fifth and sixth items mention religious behaviors that are common in many, but not all religions. The last item is about the importance of a specific religious belief. It is relevant to the main monotheistic religions, but does not fit well with polytheistic and pantheistic religions.

The Gallup World Poll (GWP) follows a similar approach. Its global core items on religion used to consist of the following four items (Gallup 2008):[6]

1. In this country, do you have confidence in each of the following or not? How about religious organizations (churches, mosques, temples, etc.)?
2. Could you tell me what your religion is?
3. Is religion an important part of your daily life?
4. Have you attended a place of worship or religious service within the past 7 days?

As in the EVS/WVS, the Gallup World Poll has a general item on confidence in institutions that includes religious organizations, asks about people's religious affiliation (as does EVS/WVS, but it is not part of the index of religiosity listed above), includes a general measure on the importance of religion, and, like the EVS/WVS, covers one religious behavior. The Gallup World Poll tries to make its items applicable to all religions and all countries by both using very general measures and using some inclusive terms. Religious organizations are illustrated by mentions of churches (Christianity), mosques (Islam), temples (Buddhism, Hinduism, et al.), and etc. (other religious place). Its behavioral measure of involvement covers attending religious services (especially relevant for Christians, Muslims, and Jews) and places of worship (tapping more into Buddhism, Hinduism, etc.). But the seven-day time span is more appropriate to the former than to the latter.

The religion-specific or emic approach would design in-depth surveys to measure religion in each covered country. Given that many countries have large majorities identifying with a particular religion, the surveys would cover the behaviors, beliefs, and structures associated with the main religion(s). Comparatively, one would apply this same approach in each country. One would then compare how religion functioned across societies. No major, cross-national survey program (e.g., EVS/WVS, European Social Survey [ESS], GWP, International Social Survey Program [ISSP], Latinobarometer) applies this approach, for two main reasons. First, all of these studies are general topic surveys and do not focus on religion or any other single topic. Second, even comparative studies that do focus on religion avoid this approach since it maximizes measurement differences across countries/religions, and this greatly hinders comparisons.

An approach used by the ISSP 2008 round on Religion III was to expand beyond its previous Western and Christian-centric orientation by adding behaviors and beliefs reflecting Eastern religions. The added behaviors were asked of all respondents in all countries. They covered visiting holy sites ("How often do you visit a holy place for religious reasons such as going to [shrine/temple/church/mosque]? Please do *not* count attending regular religious services at your usual place of worship, if you have one.") and having a religious shrine or object in the home ("For religious reasons do you have in your home a shrine, altar, or a religious object on display such as a [country-specific list: icon, retablos, mezuzah, menorah, or crucifix]?"). In addition to focusing on religious behaviors that were more common among several Eastern religions than such measures as attending religious services and being a member of a religious organization or congregation, these items were also made more accommodating by allowing references to places and objects that were meaningful to particular countries and religions. Of course, this later step does deviate from the usual survey-research practice of question-wording standardization. These items worked well in both being meaningful measures cross-nationally and showing more religious behaviors in East Asia than more Western, Christian-centric measures did.

The ISSP also added three items about non-Western religious beliefs on nirvana, reincarnation, and ancestor worship ("Do you believe in . . . E. Reincarnation—being reborn in this world again and again; F. Nirvana; G. The supernatural powers of deceased ancestors"). The ancestor-worship item worked well, showing high levels in East Asia (Japan, Korea, Taiwan) and South Africa and much lower levels almost everywhere else and low levels of "Don't Know" and "No Answer" responses in most countries. The item on nirvana was high in East Asia and low in almost all other countries. Nirvana did have high "Don't Know/No Answer" responses, averaging 29 percent globally. This high level was both expected and meaningful since it mostly indicated that people were simply unfamiliar with the term and concept of nirvana. Using reincarnation was more problematic. It showed unexpectedly high levels in many countries, often equaling or exceeding those of East Asia. In Turkey, where a global high of 89 percent believed in "reincarnation," it was mistranslated both by the omission of the follow-up phrase and by the use of Turkish words that actually referred to resurrection. In Latin American countries (Chile, Mexico, Uruguay, Venezuela) and among Spanish speakers in the United States) the item was translated appropriately, but had belief levels of 33–45 percent. While it is possible that belief in reincarnation is much greater than anticipated in Latin America and among American Hispanics, it is plausible that many people misunderstood it to refer either to resurrection or to being born-again Christians, even though the wording clearly mentioned something other than these two more familiar concepts. Similarly, among Jews in Israel there was an appropriate translation, but a suspiciously high level of endorsement of reincarnation (54 percent). The Israeli researchers reached the similar conclusion that many Israeli Jews confused reincarnation with resurrection. (For other analysis on how reincarnation is understood in European surveys, see Siegers 2013.)

The Sub-Saharan Africa Religion Survey (2010) illustrates a blended approach. It covers nineteen countries that are predominantly Christian, Muslim, or mixed. First, the survey asks everyone some identical questions about both of these world religions as well as a few questions about "ancestral, tribal, animist, or other traditional African religions." Second, it also has numerous identical questions about various religious beliefs (e.g., about God, miracles, reincarnation) and activities. Third, it has a series of parallel but religion-specific questions asked of just Christians or Muslims (e.g., "Aside from weddings and funeral [sic], how often do you attend religious services?" and "On average, how often do you attend the mosque or Islamic center for *salah* and *jum'ah* prayer?"). Fourth, it has parallel questions asking Christians and Muslims about the other faith (e.g., "How comfortable would you be if a child of yours someday married a Christian/Muslim? Would you be very comfortable, somewhat comfortable, not too comfortable, or not at all comfortable?"). Finally, it asks some nonparallel questions to either Christians ("Which, if any, of the following do you believe in? That Jesus will return to earth in your lifetime?") or Muslims ("And is taking a pilgrimage to Mecca very important to you, somewhat important, not too important, or not at all important?"). This multifaceted approach produces comparative data across these countries and these two religions. But globally, religion is not a dichotomy, and adopting this approach for Christians, Muslims, Jews, Buddhists, Hindus, Taoists, etc., would be extremely difficult.

Several examples will illustrate the challenges of covering specific religious behaviors and beliefs clearly, reliably, and consistently in cross-national surveys. Praying is a religious behavior that is difficult to measure across religions, cultures, and languages. First, there is the issue of distinguishing prayer from meditation. Praying is by definition a religious act and meditating may or may not be. The religiousness of meditation varies across religions (usually it is religious in Buddhism and is not in Christianity) and across individuals (e.g., meditation to seek spiritual insight or oneness with God vs. to lower blood pressure). Second, what counts as praying varies. There are public, collective praying aloud during some religious services, private, personal praying, saying the rosary, saying grace at meals, lighting candles, prayer wheels, prayer flags, mezuzah, tefillin, etc. A comparative question on praying needs to carefully consider what counts as praying across religions and then ensure that the defined behavior is being captured consistently across religions and languages. Finally, an item about the frequency of prayer needs to be suitable across religions. The standard ISSP measure provides a pretty full and detailed range ("Never"/"Less than once a year"/"About one or twice a year"/"Several times a year"/"About once a month"/"2–3 times a month"/"Nearly every week/"Every week"/"Several times a week"/"Once a day"/"Several times a day")—but even this does not fully capture Islam's injunction of five specified daily prayers.

Questions about "god" are also difficult to measure comparatively. For example, does one start off with a nonreligious or nonsectarian term like "supreme being" or use the "name" of "god" in particular languages? The latter is problematic since the term for "god" in many languages is the name of the "god" in a particular religion. Using a nonreligious/sectarian term may cause problems if the term is not widely and consistently understood by people and/or if it does not closely align with what is covered by the name-of-god term.

Asking about belief in "god" often presents a range of possible choices. Two examples will illustrate some of the cross-national and conceptual challenges. The Religious and Moral Pluralism (RAMP) survey asked,

WHICH OF THESE STATEMENTS COMES NEAREST TO YOUR OWN BELIEF?
I believe in a God with whom I can have a personal relationship.
I believe in an impersonal spirit or life force.
I don't believe in any God, spirit, or life force.
I believe that God is something within each person, rather than something out there.
I really don't know what to believe.

The ISSP in 2008 (Smith 2013a) asked,

PLEASE INDICATE WHICH STATEMENT BELOW COMES CLOSEST TO EXPRESSING WHAT YOU BELIEVE ABOUT GOD.
I don't believe in God.
I don't know whether there is a God and I don't believe there is any way to find out.
I don't believe in a personal God, but I do believe in a Higher Power of some kind.
I find myself believing in God some of the time, but not at others.
While I have doubts, I feel that I do believe in God.
I know God really exists and I have no doubts about it.
Don't know.

IPSOS Global @dvisory survey in 2011 asked,

WHICH OF THE FOLLOWING BEST DESCRIBES YOUR PERSONAL BELIEFS ABOUT YOUR GOD OR SUPREME BEING?
I definitely believe in God or a Supreme Being.
I definitely believe in many Gods or Supreme Beings.
Sometimes I believe, but sometimes I don't believe in God/Gods or Supreme Being/Beings.
I'm not sure if I believe in God/Gods/Supreme Being/Beings.
I don't believe in God/Gods/Supreme Being/Beings.

None of these questions are well suited for pantheism. The first two do not cover polytheism. The IPSOS item does address polytheism, but the formulation is rather jumbled. Each uses the term "God," which presents some challenges for translations into other languages, especially when non-Christian religions dominate in countries using those languages. Each offers alternatives terms (ISSP, "Higher Power"; RAMP, "Impersonal spirit or life force"; IPSOS, "Supreme Being/Beings") either as a linguistic alternate for "God" or as a substantive alternative to "God." RAMP and ISSP distinguish between a personal god and a "Higher Power" or an "impersonal spirit or life force," while IPSOS does not.

Translating these variable terminologies into other languages is difficult since the distinctions between the concepts are often imprecise in English and would be even more difficult to duplicate in languages/cultures with fundamentally different ideas about the existence and nature of a supreme being. Heelas and Houtman (2009) found that even within the eleven Christian and European countries that RAMP covered, the response option that "God is something within each person, rather than something out there" was not understood consistently across surveys and may have been poorly translated in some cases.

Many other important theological concepts are often difficult to convey across languages, even among adherents to the religion that uses the concept and especially across religions. The Catholic concept of transubstantiation during the sacrament of the Eucharist is especially complex. Jesuit missionaries had to modify or delete this concept to avoid it being misunderstood as cannibalism (Harvey 2003). Similarly, the Christian concept of the trinity is difficult to convey and to be correctly understood as monotheistic rather than polytheistic. Similarly, the nature of god varies across the various denominations of Hinduism from monotheism to pantheism.

A final example concerns how religious affiliation is both collected and analyzed (Kim et al. 2009). Pew (2012, 2014) calculated an index of religious diversity in countries around the world. This was based on the distribution within each country of "eight major world religions" ("Buddhism, Christianity, folk or traditional religions, Hinduism, Islam, Judaism, other religions considered as a group, and the religiously unaffiliated"). From a comparative perspective, one issue that comes up is how these eight "religions" were selected. Another is that they do not count any divisions within these major blocks, such as Catholic and Protestant Christians, Shia and Sunni Muslims, and ultra-Orthodox and Reform Jews. This greatly underestimates diversity and division within many countries. For example, Iraq is listed as 99 percent Muslim with one of the world's lowest religious diversity scores (0.2), and the diversity/division/conflict between Shia and Sunni is invisible. Comparative studies of religions need to capture crucial intrareligious subdivisions (e.g., Protestant denominations in Christianity, Shia, Sunni, and other variants in Islam, and Judaic traditions like Orthodox, Conservative, and Reform and perhaps even cultural/secular/ethnic Jews) and then decide when using these subdivisions is essential in analysis, such as perhaps for better understanding "religious diversity" or when separating evangelical and mainline Protestants in examining American elections.

Conclusion

Cross-national survey research is a complex endeavor involving many components and notable organizational and methodological challenges. Utilizing the TSE approach can notably facilitate this process and help to reduce error in general and comparison error in particular. But applying TSE to cross-national survey research is not just a matter of having comparative surveys follow the TSE paradigm. TSE also needs to be adaptive and responsive to the particular errors that are more frequent and greater in magnitude in comparative survey research. There is mutual synergy when TSE is combined with standard cross-national survey concerns about achieving functional equivalence (Uskul and Oyserman 2006).

One of the largest challenges is keeping track of all of the components of TSE, how they can be individually and collectively minimized, and how comparison error can be reduced. On the one hand, this is too complex a goal for researchers to merely think in general terms of seeking functional equivalence, as comparative survey research has traditionally done. On the other hand, focusing on TSE and comparison error without close attention to the greatest sources of error in cross-national survey research fails to take advantage of what is known about optimizing comparative, functional equivalence.

While doing cross-national survey research well is always a complex task, it is especially challenging in the study of comparative religion

(Smith 2009a). In the case of religion, particular attention needs to be focused on how comparable questions can be asked in different languages, about different religions, and in different nations and cultures. While optimizing translations is always of major importance, achieving comparability across religions is particularly difficult because of the cultural and structural differences across countries related to the nature, role, and practice of religion.

The secondary analysts face the same challenges that the primary researchers do, but of course have no control over how studies are designed and surveys conducted. Yet they too can benefit from following the TSE paradigm and assessing whether functional equivalence has been achieved in the studies they plan on analyzing. They need to know the datasets they plan to utilize and to understand them not just from an analyst's perspective (e.g., knowing variable names and the response categories) but also from a data user's perspective. As data users, they need to assess all of the components of TSE and to evaluate whether comparison error has been minimized to an acceptable level to permit scientifically reliable and valid comparative research. To do this they need enough methodological competency to evaluate the datasets, and there has to be detailed documentation of the survey design and methods to permit such an assessment. That is, researchers need not only substantive expertise on a topic (e.g., comparative religious beliefs) but also methodological training about the collected data (e.g., cross-national surveys). If the cross-national data are deemed to be problematic, the secondary analyst may be able to improve comparability through a series of techniques such as post-harmonization of the target populations, weighting to adjust for undercoverage and/or non–response bias, recoding items to be more equivalent, and restricting analysis to only the most comparable items.[7] If the comparison error is too great and none of the adjustment techniques can adequately alleviate the problem (e.g., a mistranslation of items across surveys), then the intended research needs to be abandoned or changed. Fortunately, there are a number of well done cross-national surveys with religious content that most researchers would find appropriate for meaningful comparative analysis. But every researcher needs to make that judgment regarding the specific analysis he or she plans to do.

NOTES

1 Parts adapted from Tom W. Smith, "Improving Cross-National/Cultural Comparability Using the Total Survey Error Paradigm," paper presented to the Second International Conference on Survey Methods in Multinational, Multiregional, and Multicultural Contexts (3MC 2016), Chicago, July 2016.

2 For a discussion of many of the specific components of TSE see Alwin 2007; Pennell et al. 2014; and Smith 2005, 2011.

3 Kish (1994) makes a similar observation about probability samples using different sample frames but still representing equivalent target populations.

4 For another approach to standardizing measurement across cross-national surveys using vignettes, see King et al. 2004.

5 For a related approach, see the differences in comparative research of Asking the Same Questions, Asking the Same Questions by Decentering, Asking Different Questions, and Combination Approaches (Harkness et al. 2010).

6 Currently, they have dropped the first and last of these four (Pugliese 2015).

7 For information on data harmonization, weighting, and other methodological aspects of cross-national research, see the Cross-Cultural Survey Guidelines (ccsg.isr.umich.edu).

REFERENCES

Alwin, Duane. 2007. *Margins of Error: A Study of Reliability in Survey Measurement.* New York: Wiley.

Anderson, Ronald, Judith Kasper, and Martin R. Frankel. 1979. *Total Survey Error: Applications to Improve Health Surveys.* San Francisco: Jossey-Bass.

Andreenkova, Anna. 2015. "Measuring Acquiescence in Different Cultures: Results of Experiments with Translation and Scale Types." Paper presented to Comparative Survey Design and Implementation, London, March.

Bardhan, Ashok, and Cynthia Kroll. 2003. "The New Wave of Outsourcing." Fisher Center for Real Estate & Urban Economics Working Paper. University of California–Berkeley.

Benedict, Ruth. 1946. *The Chrysanthemum and the Sword: Patterns of Japanese Culture.* Boston: Houghton Mifflin.

Biemer, Paul P., and Lars E. Lyberg. 2003. *Introduction to Survey Quality.* New York: Wiley.

Billiet, Jaak, and Hideko Matsuo. 2011. "Dealing with Nonresponse Bias in ESS: Reflections on the Opportunities of Random Sample." Unpublished report, Catholic University Leuven.

Brady, Henry E. 2000. "Contributions of Survey Research to Political Science," *PS*, 33, 47–57.

Braun, Michael, and Janet A. Harkness. 2005. "Text and Context: Challenges to Comparability in Survey Questions," in *Methodological Aspects in Cross-National Research*, edited by Juergen H. P. Hoffmeyer-Zlotnik and Janet A. Harkness. Mannheim, Germany: ZUMA.

Brown, R. V. 1967. "Evaluation of Total Survey Error." *Statistician*, 17, 335–56.

Carnoy, Martin, and Richard Rothstein. 2013. "What Do International Tests Really Show about U.S. Student Performance?" *Economic Policy Institute* report, Jan. 28.

Chung, Robert. 2012. *The Freedom to Publish Public Opinion Results: A World Wide Update of 2012*. Lincoln, NE: WAPOR.

Couper, Mick P., and Edith D. de Leeuw. 2002. "Nonresponse in Cross-Cultural and Cross-National Surveys," in *Using Surveys across Cultures and Nations*, edited by J.A. Harkness, F. J. R. van de Vijver, and P. P. Mohler. New York: Wiley, 157–77.

Deming, W. Edwards. 1944. "On Errors in Surveys." *American Sociological Review*, 9, 359–69.

Durkheim, Emile. 1938. *The Rules of Sociological Method*. Glencoe, IL: Free Press.

Fitzgerald, Rory, et al. 2011. "Identifying Sources of Error in Cross-National Questionnaires: Application of an Error Source Typology to Cognitive Interview Data." *Journal of Official Statistics*, 27, 1–32.

Frank, Stacey, and Nina Sabarre. 2015. "Questionnaire Design for Cross-Cultural Survey Research." American Association for Public Opinion Research Webinar, March 3.

Freeman, Richard. 2006. "What Does the Growth of Higher Education Overseas Mean for the US?" Paper presented to Allied Social Sciences Association, Boston.

Freeman, Richard. 2007. "Is a Great Labor Shortage Coming?" in *Reshaping Workforce Policies for a Changing Economy*, edited by H. Holzer and D. Nightingale. Washington, DC: Urban Institute.

Gallup, George H. 1976. "Human Needs and Satisfactions: A Global Survey." *Public Opinion Quarterly*, 40, 459–67.

Gallup Inc. 2008. *World Poll Questions*. https://media.gallup.com.

Genov, Nikolai. 1991. "Internationalization of Sociology: The Unfinished Agenda." *Current Sociology*, 39, 1–20.

Grice, Paul. 1989. *Studies in the Way of Words*. Cambridge, MA: Harvard University Press.

Groves, Robert M. 1989. *Survey Errors and Survey Costs*. New York: Wiley.

Groves, Robert M. 2005. "Total Survey Error: Past, Present, and Future." Paper presented to the International Total Survey Error Workshop, Washington, DC, March.

Hansen, Morris H., William N. Hurwitz, and William G. Madow. 1953. *Sample Survey Methods and Theory*. New York: Wiley.

Harkness, Janet A., Michael Braun, et al. 2010. "Comparative Survey Methodology," in *Multinational, Multicultural, and Multiregional Survey Methods*, edited by Janet A. Harkness et al. New York: Wiley.

Harkness, Janet A., Ana Villar, and Brad Edwards. 2010. "Translation, Adaption, and Design," in *Multinational, Multicultural, and Multiregional Survey Methods*, edited by Janet A. Harkness et al. New York: Wiley.

Harvey, Elizabeth D. 2003. *Sensible Flesh: On Touch in Early Modern Culture*. Philadelphia: University of Pennsylvania Press.

Heelas, Paul, and Dick Houtman. 2009. "RAMP Findings and Making Sense of the 'God within Each Person, Rather Than out There.'" *Journal of Contemporary Religion*, 24, 83–98.

Jeveline, Debra. 1999. "Response Effects in Polite Cultures: A Test of Acquiescence in Kazakhstan." *Public Opinion Quarterly*, 63, 1–28.

Johnson, Timothy P. 1998. "Approaches to Equivalence in Cross-Cultural and Cross-National Survey Research." *ZUMA-Nachrichten-Spezial*, 3, 1–40.

Jowell, Roger, et al., eds. 2007. *Measuring Attitudes Cross-Nationally: Lessons from the European Social Survey*. London: Sage.

Kim, Jibum, Jaesok Son, Yongmo Lee, and Tom W. Smith. 2009. "Trends of Religious Identification in Korea: Changes and Continuities." *Journal for the Scientific Study of Religion*, 48, 789–93.

King, Gary, Christopher J. T. Murray, Joshu A. Salomon, and Ajay Tandon. 2004. "Enhancing the Validity and Cross-Cultural Comparability of Measurement in Survey Research." *American Political Science Review*, 98, 191–207.

Kish, Leslie. 1965. *Survey Sampling*. New York: Wiley.

Kish, Leslie. 1994. "Multipopulation Survey Designs: Five Types with Seven Shared Aspects." *International Statistical Review*, 62, 167–86.

Lessler, Judith. 1984. "Measurement Error in Surveys," in *Surveying Subjective Phenomena*, edited by Charles F. Turner and Elizabeth Martin. New York: Russell Sage.

Loveless, Tom. 2014. "How Well Are American Students Learning? With Sections on the PISA-Shanghai Controversy, Homework, and the Common Core," in *The 2014 Brown Center Report on American Education*, Brown Center of Education Policy.

Luce, R. Duncan, Neil Smelser, and Dean R. Gerstein, eds. 1989. *Leading Edges in Social and Behavioral Science*. New York: Russell Sage.

Medrich, Elliot, and Jeanne E. Griffith. 1992. "International Mathematics and Science Assessment: What Have We Learned?" *NCES Research and Development Report* 92-011. National Center for Education Statistics.

Miller, Jon D., Anna G. Cotter, and Ronald Inglehart. 2015. "The Origins of Religiosity: A Cross-National Analysis Using the European and World Values Surveys." Paper presented to the World Association for Public Opinion Research, Buenos Aires.

Miller, K., et al. 2011. "Design and Analysis of Cognitive Interviews for Comparative Multinational Testing." *Field Methods*, 23, 379–96.

Mohler, Peter, and Timothy P. Johnson. 2010. "Equivalence, Comparability, and Methodological Progress," in *Multinational, Multicultural, and Multiregional Survey Methods*, edited by Janet A. Harkness et al. New York: Wiley.

Pennell, Beth-Ellen, Lars Lyberg, Peter Mohler, Kristen Cibelli Hibben, and Gelaye Worku. 2014. "A Total Survey Error Perspective on Comparative Surveys." University of Michigan: Institute for Social Research, Survey Research Center. October.

Pew Research Center. 2012. *The Global Religious Landscape: A Report on the Size and Distribution of the World's Major Religious Groups as of 2010*. December.

Pew Research Center. 2014. *Global Religious Diversity: Half of the Most Religiously Diverse Countries Are in the Asia-Pacific Region*. April.

Pugliese, Anita. 2015. Gallup Organization, personal communication, November 20.

Siegers, Pascal. 2013. "Reincarnation Revisited: Question Format and the Distribution of Belief in Reincarnation in Survey Research." *Survey Methods: Insights from the Field*, 4(4), 1–11.

Skjåk, Knut Kalgraff, and Janet Harkness. 2002. "Data Collection Methods," in *Cross-Cultural Survey Methods*, edited by Fons J. R. Van de Vijver and Peter Ph. Mohler. New York: Wiley.

Skjåk, Knut Kalgraff, Janet Harkness, and Tom W. Smith. 2000. "Findings from a Seven-Country Modes Experiment." Paper presented to the American Association for Public Opinion Research, Portland, OR.

Smith, Tom W. 1989. "The Ups and Downs of Cross-National Survey Research." GSS Cross-National Report No. 8. Chicago: NORC, December, 1988. *IASSIST Quarterly* 12 (Winter): 18–24.

Smith, Tom W. 1996. "Total Survey Error: The Art and Science of Survey Design." Inaugural Address of the Howard Beers Lecture Series, University of Kentucky.

Smith, Tom W. 2004. "Freedom to Conduct Public Opinion Polls around the World." *International Journal of Public Opinion Research*, 16, 215–23.

Smith, Tom W. 2005. "Total Survey Error," in *Encyclopedia of Social Measurement*, edited by Kimberly Kempf-Leonard. New York: Academic Press.

Smith, Tom W. 2007a. "Integrating Translation into Cross-National Research." Paper presented to the Midwest Association for Public Opinion Research, Chicago.

Smith, Tom W. 2007b. "Survey Non-Response Procedures in Cross-National Perspective: The 2005 ISSP Non-Response Survey." *Survey Research Methods*, 1, 45–54.

Smith, Tom W. 2008. "Applying the Total Survey Error Paradigm to Cross-National Research." Paper presented to the Conference on Logic and Methodology in Sociology of Research Committee 33, International Sociological Association, September, Naples, Italy.

Smith, Tom W. 2009a. "Religious Change around the World." Report prepared for the John Templeton Foundation. Extracted version published as GSS Cross-National Report No. 30.

Smith, Tom W. 2009b. "A Translation Experiment on the 2008 General Social Survey." Paper presented to the International Workshop on Comparative Survey Design and Implementation, Ann Arbor, Michigan.

Smith, Tom W. 2010. "Surveying across Nations and Cultures," in *Handbook of Survey Research*, 2nd ed., edited by Peter V. Marsden and James D. Wright. Bingley, UK: Emerald.

Smith, Tom W. 2011. "Refining the Total Survey-Error Perspective." *International Journal of Public Opinion Research*, 23, 464–84.

Smith, Tom W. 2012. "Total Survey Error in Comparative Perspective." Plenary paper presented to the RC33 8th International Conference on Social Science Methodology, Sydney, Australia.

Smith, Tom W. 2013a. "Beliefs about God across Time and Countries," in *ISSP Data Report: Religious Attitudes and Religious Change*, edited by Insa Bechert and Markus Quandt. Koeln, Germany: GESIS.

Smith, Tom W. 2013b. "An Evaluation of Spanish Questions on the 2006 and 2008 General Social Surveys," in *Surveying Ethnic Minorities and Immigrant Populations: Methodological Challenges and Research Strategies*, edited by Joan Font and Monica Mendez. Amsterdam: IMISCOE-Amsterdam University Press.

Smith, Tom W. 2014. "Surveying Hard-to-Survey Populations in Comparative Perspective," in *Hard-to-Survey Populations*, edited by Roger Tourangeau et al. Cambridge: Cambridge University Press.

Smith, Tom W., Peter Mohler, Janet Harkness, and Noriko Onodera. 2005. "Methods for Assessing and Calibrating Response Scales across Countries and Languages." *Comparative Sociology*, 4, 365–415.

SSRC. 2006. "Fostering International Collaboration in the Social Sciences: Proposed Strategies for the Future," Report of the Social Science Research Council.

Stoop, Ineke. 2012. "Nonresponse in Comparative Studies Enhancing Response Rates and Minimising Nonresponse Bias." Paper presented to the European Conference on Quality in Official Statistics, Athens, Greece.

Sub-Saharan Africa Religion Survey. 2010. Codebook, Association of Religion Data Archives, Pennsylvania State University.

Tourangeau, Roger, Lance Rips, and Kenneth Rasinski. 2000. *The Psychology of Survey Response*. Cambridge: Cambridge University Press.

Uskul, Ayse K., and Daphna Oyserman. 2006. "Question Comprehension and Response: Implications of Individualism and Collectivism." *Research on Managing Groups and Teams: National Culture and Groups*, 9, 177–206.

Weisberg, Herbert F. 2005. *The Total Survey Error Approach: A Guide to the New Science of Survey Research*. Chicago: University of Chicago Press.

Willis, Gordon B. 2015. "The Practice of Cross-Cultural Cognitive Interviewing." *Public Opinion Quarterly*, 79, 359–95.

Wright, Benjamin D., and Geoffery N. Masters. 1982. *Rating Scale Analysis*. Chicago: MESA.

SECTION II

Beyond Surveys

7.

From Documents to Data

CHRISTOPHER P. SCHEITLE

Several chapters in this book explore generating measures from different types of content, whether that content consists of product reviews on Amazon.com or digitized books in Google's database. This chapter is similar in that it is focused on generating measures from types of content. However, the focus here is less on generating measures created from keyword searches or other types of computer-assisted measure generation and more on traditional coding of content found in types of documents. One might call this more "old school." This does not mean that the web does not play an important role. As I will show, the increasing presence of all types of documents online means that even more traditional content analyses of documents will often begin on the web. In fact, the web is making access to historical and contemporary documents of all sorts easier.

Documents offer unique ways to examine religion's role in society. In some cases the documents being examined represent units of analysis that are rarely examined in our usual individual- or congregation-focused surveys. In other cases, documents offer ways to generate measures of phenomena that surveys simply have not yet included or cannot include because the phenomena are historical in nature. On a more practical note, generating measures from documents, while often labor intensive, tends to be relatively inexpensive, which makes this method a potentially attractive option for graduate students. Finally, although I imagine some might disagree, I would also argue that exploring documents is simply fun and rewarding. While it can be fun and rewarding to develop a survey instrument, if that instrument is handed off to a survey firm for the actual data collection, then we do not get to see and interact with our research subjects. This is not the case when we are looking through and exploring documents.

Content analysis is often idiosyncratic. The measures, methods, and challenges found within a content-analysis project will be shaped by the type of content being analyzed. Issues like the representativeness of the content source and the reliability of the content coding should obviously always be considered. I will discuss some of these issues in the context of the examples I discuss in this chapter, but my primary goal is to more generally illustrate and hopefully inspire more use of this method in the social scientific study of religion. I offer a discussion of three types of documents along with a case study for each type that draws from my own research. The chapter ends with some discussion of other potential sources of religion-related measures from documents.

Government Documents

In our lives as employees, patients, business owners, nonprofit leaders, students, and citizens, we often bemoan having to fill out form after form before we can accomplish what seemed at first like an easy task. For social scientists, though, bureaucracies' tendency to create paperwork presents an opportunity to generate measures from that paperwork. This is true even when one is studying religion.

It is common knowledge among social scientists who study religion, although more surprising to others, that the federal government does not collect much data on religion. Still, it is often assumed that there must at least be some registry where all congregations are counted. This registry is often hypothesized to exist with the Internal Revenue Service (IRS), since it is thought that congregations must, say, apply for tax exemption. Congregations, however, have a special and somewhat confusing status with the IRS that does not require them to officially gain tax-exempt recognition (Scheitle 2010; Scheitle, Dollhopf, and McCarthy 2016). This means that when a reporter or other individual asks us how many congregations exist in the United States, a state, or a city, we are forced to provide ranges or estimates with disclaimers.

These sorts of roadblocks might make many swear off government documents as a potential source of data in the study of religion. This would be a hasty decision, though, as there are possibilities vis-à-vis government documents for the study of religion. I illustrate one such possibility from my own work in detail here, and at the end of the chapter I provide some other ideas for sources of measures.

The case study I illustrate here involves tax return documents for religious nonprofits. As noted above, religious congregations are not required to file the same applications and annual returns with the IRS required of most other nonprofit organizations, or more formally, 501(c)(3) public charities.[1] However, religious nonprofits that are not congregations *are* required to apply for tax exemption and file annual reports with the IRS.[2] This means that religious nonprofits that are not a congregation or denomination do apply for tax exemption and file annual reports with the IRS.[3] This became important for my own research when I realized that such religious nonprofits had been pointed to by both social scientists and church leaders as having greater significance in the American Christian religious market.

In his book *The Restructuring of American Religion*, Robert Wuthnow (1988) devoted a chapter to what he called "special purpose groups." He noted that "literally scores of such organizations have emerged in American religion since World War II. . . . Their causes range from nuclear arms control to liturgical renewal, from gender equality to cult surveillance, from healing ministries to evangelism" (100–101). Writing almost exactly twenty years later, the sociologist D. Michael Lindsay (2007) observed that evangelical Christianity's "center of gravity today is not found at the level of the local congregation. Instead, evangelical business leaders, working with entrepreneurial ministers, have organized the movement around a constellation of parachurch organizations" (194). This label, "parachurch organization," is the one that is often used among writers within the Christian community to describe these special-purpose, noncongregational organizations (White 1983; Willmer, Schmidt, and Smith 1998).

Although social scientists had written about the apparent growth in numbers and influence of such parachurch organizations, and individuals like Lindsay (2007) had collected some extensive interview and observational data, there really had not been much, if any, systematic quantitative analysis of these organizations. The primary obstacle appeared to be simply that no one had any way to produce data on these organizations. When I looked at the types of organizations being pointed to, though, it became clear that many of them were 501(c)(3) public charities. This meant that most of them would probably be registered with and, depending on the amount of revenue they generate, filing tax returns with the IRS. The question then becomes, how can I access those documents? This is where the growing availability of documents on the web comes into play.

It turns out that there are multiple websites where a person can search for and access digital copies of nonprofits' tax returns, called 990s, for free. These websites include foundationcenter.org and www.guidestar.org. Much of a 990 form is financial information, such as total revenue, total expenses, breakdowns of different types of revenue and expenses, and so forth. If one were just interested in this financial information, then one could acquire a database of many financial variables for nonprofit organizations from the National Center for Charitable Statistics. A finances-only file, though, would not contain many of the rich measures that could be produced from such a document.

I utilized several criteria in determining which organizations' documents I would extract measures from. I chose to focus on Christian organizations because the overwhelming amount of discussion on parachurch organizations was in a Christian context, although one could conceivably think of Muslim parachurch organizations. I also chose to focus on larger organizations, as defined by revenue, and by whether the organization was working on a national and/or international scale, as defined by having activities in multiple states and/or nations. This was due to both practical and theoretical interests. On the theoretical side, I wanted my focus to be on organizations that were making the largest impact in the religious market, and being larger in size and having a wider geographic footprint seemed like a proxy for potential influence and audience. If one were interested in understanding organizational founding or entrepreneurship, this would not be the focus one would take. On the practical side, at the time of my project those nonprofits with gross receipts less than twenty-five thousand dollars did not need to file any annual return, while those with gross receipts between twenty-five and one hundred thousand dollars were required to file a shorter financial statement called a 990-EZ. This highlights the point that when examining documents, the researcher should be aware of any gaps in coverage between the documents available and the phenomena being examined. Having set some criteria, I utilized several sources to identify organizations, including IRS files acquired from the National Center for Charitable Statistics, websites like MinistryWatch.com, and membership organizations like the Evangelical Council for Financial Accountability (see Scheitle 2010 for more information if interested).

What does a 990 form actually look like? Figure 7.1 shows the top half of the first page of the 2013 990 form for the Fellowship of Christian Cowboys.

This first section of the 990 document contains information such as the following:

Organization's name and address (Box C);
Whether the organization is disbanding, just starting, changing names, or recently moved (Box A);
Where the organization is legally domiciled (i.e., incorporated) (Box M);
Current mailing address (Box C);
When the organization was formed (Box L);
Whether the organization has a website (Box J);
Whether the organization represents an umbrella of subordinate "chapters" (Box H(a)).

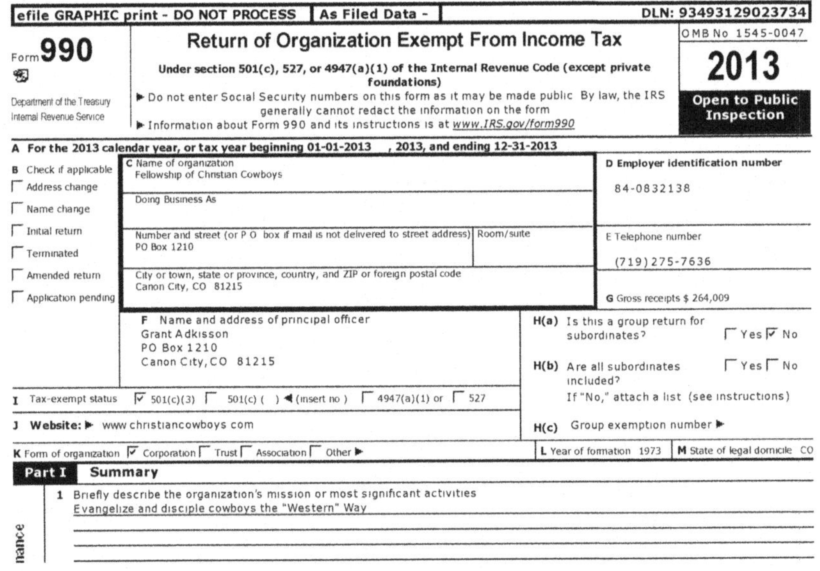

efile GRAPHIC print - DO NOT PROCESS | As Filed Data - | DLN: 93493129023734

Form 990
Department of the Treasury
Internal Revenue Service

Return of Organization Exempt From Income Tax
Under section 501(c), 527, or 4947(a)(1) of the Internal Revenue Code (except private foundations)
▶ Do not enter Social Security numbers on this form as it may be made public By law, the IRS generally cannot redact the information on the form
▶ Information about Form 990 and its instructions is at www.IRS.gov/form990

OMB No 1545-0047
2013
Open to Public Inspection

A For the 2013 calendar year, or tax year beginning 01-01-2013 , 2013, and ending 12-31-2013

B Check if applicable
☐ Address change
☐ Name change
☐ Initial return
☐ Terminated
☐ Amended return
☐ Application pending

C Name of organization
Fellowship of Christian Cowboys
Doing Business As
Number and street (or P O box if mail is not delivered to street address) | Room/suite
PO Box 1210
City or town, state or province, country, and ZIP or foreign postal code
Canon City, CO 81215

D Employer identification number
84-0832138
E Telephone number
(719) 275-7636
G Gross receipts $ 264,009

F Name and address of principal officer
Grant Adkisson
PO Box 1210
Canon City, CO 81215

H(a) Is this a group return for subordinates? ☐ Yes ☑ No
H(b) Are all subordinates included? ☐ Yes ☐ No
If "No," attach a list (see instructions)
H(c) Group exemption number ▶

I Tax-exempt status ☑ 501(c)(3) ☐ 501(c) ( ) ◀ (insert no) ☐ 4947(a)(1) or ☐ 527

J Website: ▶ www christiancowboys com

K Form of organization ☑ Corporation ☐ Trust ☐ Association ☐ Other ▶
L Year of formation 1973
M State of legal domicile CO

Part I Summary
1 Briefly describe the organization's mission or most significant activities
Evangelize and disciple cowboys the "Western" Way

nance

Figure 7.1. Top Half of Page 1 of 990 Form.

At first glance, much of this information might appear as though it is only background information, or the organizational equivalent of demographics. But even this type of seemingly simple information could represent unique measures given the right research question or theoretical literature. As an example, in one piece of research I was interested in what shapes leadership compensation in these organizations. Why do two organizations with similar revenue pay their executive directors differently? There are a variety of theoretical concepts that could factor into leadership compensation, such as differences in norms across subsectors of the nonprofit population of organizations. One concept that I was interested in assessing, though, was the power of the leader within the organization. How might a leader's power be measured, though? Obviously, if we want to explain leadership compensation, then we cannot use leadership compensation as our measure of power. It might be possible to generate measures by surveying organizations regarding their decision-making processes and structure, but I was faced with trying to come up with a measure using only the 990 document itself.

As I was collecting data from the 990s from a variety of organizations, I noticed that a sizable proportion of the organizations appeared to be named after individuals (e.g., John Doe Ministries). It occurred to me that if an organization is named after a leader, then that leader is likely to wield a significant amount of power. After all, without John Doe, John Doe Ministries might lose its primary product or at least its legitimacy. I created a measure based on organizations' names representing whether it appeared to be a person's name and whether that person was listed as the primary leader on the 990 form (CEO, executive director, etc.). It turns out that my hypothesis was correct. Even when accounting for differences in revenue, organizational activities, and other factors, "leader-named" organizations have higher leadership compensation levels (see Scheitle 2009b). Of course, this was a fairly blunt measure and does not by any means represent all of the potential gradations and subconcepts involved with leader power. It does, though, show how what might seem like throw-away background information like organizational names can lead to useful measures of social concepts.

If we continue examining the 990 document, we will discover other potential measures. On the second page, for instance, is a section where the organization must describe its overall mission and its specific major activities. Figure 7.2 shows an excerpt of this section for the Fellowship of Christian Cowboys. Unlike the background information shown on figure 7.1's 990 excerpt, it probably does not take much imagination to see the richness of potential measures in figure 7.2's information. First, one could code the appearance of specific key words, such as "Jesus," "God," "Christ," "Christian," and so forth. Such word counts could represent not only the religious affiliation of the organization but also its extent of religious expression. In my own work, I used such a measure to compare the nature and extent of religious expression in 990s for religious nonprofits that receive any government funding compared to those that do not (Scheitle 2009a). There are also potential measures of target audience or constituencies, in this case, "cowboys" and "young people." We also learn that this organization has chapters, which could be a potentially useful measure of organizational structure. Similarly, we might learn from this section whether the organization's activities are primarily within one state or region in the United States, or whether the organization's activities are spread across the nation and even internationally (and what nations).

Finally, we obviously learn about the activities of the organization from this content, which would probably be key in subdividing the

Form 990 (2013) Page **2**

Part III **Statement of Program Service Accomplishments**
Check if Schedule O contains a response or note to any line in this Part III . . . . ☑

1 Briefly describe the organization's mission
Our purpose is to present, to cowboys and all whom they influence, the Good News of Jesus Christ and the adventure of receiving Him as Savior and Lord Our vision is to bring cowboys and all those who enjoy the western lifestyle together and to support them in impacting their communities for the Kingdom of God

4a (Code) (Expenses $ 86,033 including grants of $ 0) (Revenue $ 3,611)
The Line Rider - monthly e-publication Our magazine is encouragement to our members, spurring them on to live the Christian life by interjecting Bible study's with everyday life stories The E-Line Rider is distributed to over 800 families monthly A smaller web version is also available online

4b (Code) (Expenses $ 29,301 including grants of $ 21,734) (Revenue $ 8,893)
Cowboy Church Services Because of the lifestyle of the competing rodeo cowboy, many are not able to attend a home church Therefore it was the desire of the founding fathers of FCC that church would be brought to the arena FCC sponsors many church services throughout the US Some of those include the National Little Britches Rodeo Finals, Wrangler National Finals Rodeo, Denver Western Stock Show, Houston Livestock and Rodeo, Cheyenne Frontier Days, National High School Finals Rodeo, and National Jr High School Finals Rodeo, as well as many smaller community events

4c (Code) (Expenses $ 22,790 including grants of $ 4,382) (Revenue $ 24,834)
Rodeo Bible Camps Are a unique blend of biblical teaching and rodeo instruction The FCC is dedicated to providing an atmosphere for young people to develop their people skills, rodeo skills and life skills RBC's were designed to create a generation of young people who will be committed to Jesus Christ and reaching their peers for Christ We have 17 chapters that host RBC's with approximately 1250 young people attending

(Code) (Expenses $ 5,411 including grants of $ 0) (Revenue $ 0)
Chapters Groups of individuals throughout the U S influencing their communities for Christ The National Office of FCC provides discipleship, ministry, bible study materials to all of our chapters, growing them spiritually and helping them to develop strategies to impact their communities with the gospel of Jesus Christ We have 30 active chapters through out the United States

Figure 7.2. Excerpt from 990 Form of Fellowship of Christian Cowboys.

population of organizations. In the case shown here we might code "publications," "camps," "preaching/worship services," and "chapter support" as particular activities. It might also be useful to create a measure for an organization's primary activity or overall mission. This might be one of the specific activities determined by, say, total expenses. Or, this might be based on some more holistic coding of the organization's mission statement. In the case of figure 7.2, we might determine that this organization is primarily in a networking or fellowship category.

For my own project, I ended up creating over two hundred variables describing almost two thousand of the largest Christian parachurch organizations based in the United States (if interested, the reader can view and download the codebook and data at the Association of Religion Data Archives: www.theARDA.com). This was accomplished with only a couple thousand dollars to support an undergraduate research assistant's help, and while that assistance was extremely helpful in making the data collection faster, it was by no means necessary. Could I have sent a survey to the same organizations asking some of the same questions? Sure, but not only would that have probably cost more money; the response rate would have been significantly lower (after all, I effectively had a 100 percent response rate from the documents).

Newspapers and Other Traditional Mass Media

Pointing to newspapers, magazines, or other traditional forms of media as a source of data might seem misguided given their steadily declining circulation and economics (Barthel 2015). Depending on the research question, this might indeed be a significant problem. For instance, given advertising's shift to social media and other venues, it is probably not particularly fruitful to view content in newspapers as a way to generate measures of advertising trends and patterns. However, there are questions for which newspapers could still prove valuable. Newspapers still cover news events, and in this area they serve as potential sources of measures for those events and the coverage of those events. In fact, social movement scholars have long utilized newspapers to generate measures of movement activity and coverage (e.g., McAdam and Su 2002; Earl, Soule, and McCarthy 2003; Martin, McCarthy, and McPhail 2009),[4] and in doing so they have also built a subliterature examining the mechanics and potential biases of newspaper-based measures (Smith, McCarthy, McPhail, and Augustyn 2001; Earl, Martin, McCarthy, and Soule 2004; McCarthy, Titarenko, McPhail, Rafail, and Augustyn 2008). A recent paper by Beyerlein, Soule, and Martin (2015) used these newspaper-generated measures to examine whether religion-sponsored protest events tend to be policed differently than secular protests. Although one can read in more detail the different measures that social movement scholars have generated from newspaper articles, it is worth brainstorming here in relation to one example article. Consider this Associated Press article from December 12, 2015:

> RICHARDSON, Texas—About 20 people, half of them armed with rifles, rallied outside a suburban Dallas mosque against Islamist violence and Syrian refugee resettlement.
>
> The demonstration organized by the Bureau of American-Islamic Relations drew a counter-demonstration by about 50 people. An Associated Press photographer reported that while there were frequent discussions between both sides, they were peaceful and intervention by the dozen police officers wasn't needed.
>
> The protesting group included members of the "Three Percenters" who consider themselves patriots protecting the homeland from Muslims. They previously organized armed protests outside a mosque in Irving, another Dallas suburb.
>
> Hundreds participated in a "United Against Racism and Hate" rally at Fair Park in Dallas. The demonstrators marched a few blocks to the Martin Luther King Jr. Community Center to protest anti-Islamic activities and rhetoric.

What measures could we produce from such an article? We could begin with the location of the protest, both in terms of being in Richardson, Texas, and in terms of being held at a mosque. Each of these could represent a distinct measure, the first being the city of the protest and the second being the protest's setting (potential measure values of congregation, school, a park, city hall, and so forth). The former could be useful for the purposes of linking the newspaper measures to community-level measures, such as the demographics of the community. We also could create a measure for the number of protesters (twenty), whether there was a counterprotest (yes), and the size of the counterprotest (fifty). We could also code whether there was a police presence (yes) and its size (twelve). There are other measures to be created here, but these serve as some quick and obvious examples.

Newspaper articles about protests and demonstrations are not the only subject in which researchers interested in religion-related phenomena might be interested. I turn to providing a case study of how newspaper-generated measures have been useful in some of my own work.

In the later years of graduate school I began noticing articles or short news entries in the newspaper involving crimes against religious congregations. Most of these appeared to be fairly standard street crimes—vandalism, burglary, and so forth—although there were stories of crimes that were confirmed or suspected to be motivated by racial, immigrant, or religious biases. I took note of these newspaper items and began to mull over the issue of criminal victimization of congregations. This struck me as an interesting and potentially important phenomenon for which I had not seen much research.

A few years later I decided that I wanted to research the victimization of congregations more seriously. My first instinct was to look for measures in some of the national surveys of congregations that had been conducted, such as the National Congregations Study (Chaves, Anderson, and Eagle 2014) or the U.S. Congregational Life Survey (Woolever, Wulff, Bruce, and Smith-Williams 2001; Woolever, Bruce, Kopacz, and Smith-Williams 2009). Unfortunately, these did not contain any measures of victimization. The closest measures were questions in the National Congregations Study asking about which issues the congregation had demonstrated or lobbied public officials about, for which "crime, drugs, community safety" was one possible response. This clearly did not get at victimization experiences. It became clear that I was not going to just download some quick measure of congregational victimization across some national sample. Such a measure would likely need to come from a new survey of congregations, which would likely require some grant funding. I worked with a colleague to apply for and acquire funding from the National Science Foundation for such a survey, but before we got to that point I wanted to find a way to create measures of congregational victimization, even if they were exploratory or preliminary (after all, there was no guarantee at the time that grant funding would come through). I ended up turning to the very source that first motivated me to pursue this research interest: newspapers.

I knew from the beginning that there are some obvious problems with relying on measures generated from newspaper reports of crime. First, a crime will only appear in a newspaper if it becomes public knowledge. This possibility is likely to increase with the severity of the crime and according to whether or not the victim reports it to the police and/or media. Second, even if a crime is reported to the media and/or police, it might be more likely to receive newspaper coverage if it is unusual in some way (Sorenson, Peterson Manz, and Berk 1998). Unfortunately, it is difficult (i.e., impossible) to assess the biases in newspaper reports without some external comparison measure, so all I could do was be aware of such weaknesses. In the face of no other measures, newspaper reports offered at least an initial source of exploratory measures.

The first decision to be made concerned which newspaper database I would utilize in identifying newspaper reports of crimes against religious congregations. This was accomplished by trying out a few databases with test searches to compare the amount of and overlap in results. It turned out that a database called NewsBank produced the most comprehensive results (note: databases' availability and coverage obviously change over time, so this may have changed since then). After choosing a database, I had to make a decision about the time period I would examine and whether and how I would sample within that time period. I decided to focus on crimes that occurred in 2012, which was the most recent complete year at the time of my data collection. I first considered randomly sampling days within 2012 to conduct searches for reports, but I found that this led to unevenness across the year (e.g., five days selected in one month, one day selected in another month). I ended up doing a systematic selection of every tenth day in 2012 from a randomly selected starting date.

After I selected a sample of dates in the defined time period, it was then necessary to locate specific articles from those dates—that is, to find the documents that would serve as the source of my measures. Research assistants and I would search for predefined combinations of terms, such as "mosque AND vandalism." In total there were forty-four search combinations for each date. The search results would be examined and any articles that appeared related in some way to a crime on congregational property in the United States would be saved. This first pass at collecting articles included cases that were unclear or questionable in nature. Indeed, content analyses almost always include such borderline cases that researchers must make a decision about including or excluding. As an example, one article identified in the search process discussed the death of a woman in the parking lot of a church in Texas after a van "went out of control." Upon further examination, though, there was no mention of foul play or other sign that the authorities or anyone else viewed this as a crime, so this case was eventually excluded. A different article from North Carolina discussed a man who was killed by a vehicle while cutting the lawn of a congregation's property. In this case, though, the driver was charged with reckless driving and causing a death by motor vehicle. This case was included in the final sample of articles since it appeared to have more signs of criminal behavior. My interest was in measuring any type of criminal behavior that touches the life and operations of a congregation, but a narrower or different goal might have made different decisions about such borderline cases. It was also necessary to identify and sort out newspaper reports covering the same crime (e.g., a follow-up article).

With the sample of articles selected and cleaned, it was then time to generate some measures by coding the articles' content. One initial measure was simply the length of the article. It was fairly clear that the crime reports came in two general formats. The first format consisted of one- or two-line crime reports, usually in a type of police blotter format. The second format consisted of more full-length newspaper articles. Such a basic measure could be of interest in ascertaining how different crimes are treated in newspaper coverage. For instance, full newspaper articles represented about 60 percent of our cases overall, but almost 90 percent of our cases involving arsons were full newspaper articles. This makes sense given that arsons might be seen as more article-worthy than a minor vandalism incident.

Let us examine a sample article to brainstorm some of the other measures that could be coded:

Church vandalized
Times, The (North Little Rock, AR) - Thursday, December 6, 2012
Author: Greg Rayburn Editor

The Pulaski County Sheriff's Office currently is investigating the case of a North Little Rock church that sustained about $8,000 worth of damage after someone had drawn graffiti on the building. Officer Wesley Tyra of the Sheriff's Office was told by Pastor James Hayes of Mount Pilgrim Baptist Church, 26622 Highway 365 North, North Little Rock, the vandalism was done to several locations on the outside of the building. The report was taken at 8:45 P.M. on Dec. 3.

"Hayes proceeded to point out to me multiple locations amongst the church's exterior where an unknown party had spray-painted white supremacist markings in white paint all over the north side of the church building," reported Tyra. "I observed that the paintings were done in an area that is not visible from the roadway (Highway 365 North)." As Hayes reviewed the spray paint markings he noted that the markings were of several different images. "The letters 'KKK' and a swastika symbol were painted on the building. I also found the symbol referred to as "Lighting Bolts" along with what is referred to as the 'Stormfront Cross'," Tyra reported.

An exhaustive canvass of the area was conducted in an attempt to locate any items of evidence of value such as discarded spray paint cans etc. "This canvass was met with negative results. I contacted Sgt. Jones in reference to this incident as well and briefed him as to the details of the incident," stated the report. "Pastor Hayes stated that he could not report any problems within the church's primarily black congregation that would lead him to a possible reason for this activity."

Across the street from Mount Pilgrim Baptist Church is Palarm Liquor Store where Tyra made contact with two store cashiers. "They were asked if they had seen any suspicious behavior or activity across the street during their workday at the liquor store," said Tyra. "Both told me that they had not. I was made aware of a camera attached to the business that gave a fairly direct view of the church across the street."

> The $8,000 in damage would be the cost of repainting the exterior and repairing windows.

First, we would want to create a measure for the type of crime(s) the case contains. In this case, we would probably code the case as a vandalism incident. Next, we would want a measure of the religious tradition of the victim congregation. Broadly speaking, we can code that the victim was a Christian congregation. In many cases this is the most we can code, as the newspaper report might only state that "a church was vandalized," especially if the report were of the blotter format. In this particular article, though, we also learn that the victim is a "primarily black congregation." We also learn that the vandalism included hate symbols such as a swastika, KKK letters, and the "Stormfront Cross." It would be useful to have a measure indicating whether the crime involves such signs and symbols and whether the article mentions that the police are treating it as a formal hate crime. It could also be noteworthy that the article mentions a liquor store across the street. Such a measure might be used as a sign of potential crime attractors. Other potentially useful measures include the date of the crime (which is often different from that of the article), any estimates of financial damage, and whether the vandalism occurred on the interior and/or exterior of the congregation.

In the data that I collected for 2012, there were 624 crime incidents identified in the newspaper articles (see Scheitle 2016). Since this was based on a 10 percent sample of days, this would project to about six thousand for the entire year. The incidents were actually fairly proportional across religious traditions to the distribution of religious congregations in the United States. Ninety-three percent of the coded incidents involved Christian congregations, 2.7 percent involved Muslim congregations, 1.8 percent involved Jewish congregations, with the remaining incidents involving Mormon, Buddhist, Hindu, Sikh, Unitarian-Universalist, and Unity congregations. The most common crimes were thefts or burglaries (65 percent), vandalisms (23 percent), and arsons (6 percent). Arsons and vandalisms, though, were disproportionately concentrated among the Jewish, Muslim, other non-Christian victims. This suggested that there are differences in the types of crimes experienced by congregations of different traditions. We also found that the incidents involving Muslim congregations disproportionately occurred in the month when Ramadan took place. All of these findings must be put into context with the potential biases and problems with newspaper-generated measures. But in the face of no measures, newspapers provided a source of at least some initial exploratory measures of crimes involving religious congregations.

Web Pages and "Documents"

Although we do not always think of websites as "documents" in the same way we might a government form or newspaper article, a website is in many ways just a collection of individual documents. There are, however, some unique challenges with this particular type of content relative to the other examples explored above. First, websites are often more dynamic. If an organization files a tax form or a newspaper publishes an article, that document is generally stable into the future. With a website, though, one could find content drastically changed from one day to the next. Identifying the boundaries of a website can be difficult as well. In one of my earliest research projects I analyzed links found on the websites of religious congregations (Scheitle 2005), and establishing how far or deep into a website I would look for links was one issue that had to be determined.

Websites can offer some content, though, that can be more easily bounded and tends to be more stable. Organizational mission statements, for example, are often clearly defined and, while subject to change, do not tend to do so frequently. As above, I offer one illustration from my work.

How religious denominations and congregations view and address actual or potential sexual-minority participants is an interesting social and organizational issue, and some research has examined this issue through interviews with congregational leaders (Olson and Cadge 2002; Cadge, Olson, and Wildeman 2008; Cadge and Wildeman 2008). At one point I became aware that several Protestant denominations had established formal or informal programs through which congregations could adopt a specific label or designation that was meant to publicly state the congregation's openness to welcoming sexual minorities as participants. In the United Church of Christ (UCC), for example, this is called the Open and Affirming designation. Congregations in the UCC could adopt this Open and Affirming label after going through a process of internal discussion and voting.

An element of the UCC's program that interested me was that in adopting this Open and Affirming (ONA) label a congregation was required to write a statement or "covenant" stating its ONA philosophy or stance. From some exploratory research, I noticed that these statements were not uniform in length or content, even though by requirement the statement had to assert that the congregation welcomed individuals of all "sexual orientations, gender identities and gender expressions" into the full life and ministry of the congregation ("Covenants" 2015). I immediately began to wonder about the sources and nature of variations in these statements.

The UCC's website offers a directory of ONA congregations, which was obviously a good start since it represented the full population I was interested in. A request to the ONA program gave me access to the date of ONA adoption for all of the ONA congregations, which I thought could be a useful measure even if I did not fully know exactly at the time how I would use this variable. The next step was to generate measures from the actual ONA statements. My colleagues and I began to locate as many websites for the UCC congregations in the ONA directory as we could find (see Scheitle, Merino, and Moore 2010). We were able to locate a website for 532 of the 586 ONA congregations that existed at the time (about 91 percent). Of those, we were able to find some statement concerning the welcoming of sexual minorities for 408 congregations (70 percent of all the ONA congregations and 77 percent of those for which we found websites). Note that the absence of a statement is itself a potential measure.

Let us look at two example statements to consider the measures that we might generate. The first is from the Community Church of Washington, D.C., and the second is from the Tehachapi Community Church in Tehachapi, California ("Covenants" 2015).

> Example #1: We seek to be an expression of God's Love in the world. We are an inclusive and diverse church; a place of unconditional love that inspires all individuals in our community, regardless of race, culture, age, gender identity, gender expression, sexual orientation, ability, and socio-economic status. Partnering with the Holy Spirit and the community, we

are committed to fighting and eradicating social ills that oppress God's children, preventing them from experiencing a fulfilled life. Following the example of our Savior Jesus Christ, we declare ourselves to be an Open and Affirming Church.

Example #2: We are people on a continuing journey within the mystery of God, seeking justice in our neighborhood and world, relying on the presence of Christ's Spirit to show us when and where we are to serve. We, Tehachapi Community Congregational Church, United Church of Christ, seek to reflect these values as the sacred community. The justice we seek is by its very nature a universal concept, embracing and welcoming all people. We recognize that the LGBT (lesbian, gay, bisexual, and transgender) community has been the target of discrimination and judgment and we consciously choose to renounce any discrimination and judgment, by declaring ourselves an open and affirming (ONA) church, embracing justice and welcoming all people, including people of diverse sexual and gender orientation, into the full communion of our church and our friendship.

A few differences can be seen between these two examples. In the first, for instance, sexual and gender minorities are specified along with other statuses, such as race, age, ability, and social class. The second example only discusses sexual and gender minorities. We could, therefore, generate a measure indicating whether the statement focuses exclusively on sexual and gender minorities. Another measure could indicate whether, among those like the first example, sexual and gender minorities are mentioned first among the statuses specified. Measures could also be created for the length of the statement, whether the statement cites scripture, the religious keywords used, and how it is presented on the website. Regarding the latter, measures might indicate whether the statement is on the primary homepage of the congregation, for instance, or whether it is presented as a full formal statement (e.g., with adoption date) or just as a summary statement.

In the publication that resulted from this research (Scheitle, Merino, and Moore 2010), we found that early adopters of the ONA designation appeared to publicize their status more explicitly (as measured by whether a statement was found on the website) and to focus more clearly on the sexual- and gender-minority component of the ONA program (as measured by whether the statement focused only on these statuses or whether it gave more prominence to these statuses if discussing others). Such findings correspond to other research on the diffusion and institutionalization of organizational programs.

Brainstorming Other Possibilities

I presented three case studies from my own work using various types of documents to generate religion-related measures, but I have seen other document-based research or databases that have sparked ideas for research on religion. I describe some of these below in case they might be of interest for a reader to pursue in his or her own research.

The case study above highlighted the tax filings of religious 501(c)(3)s, but these are not the only potential source of measures from government documents. When Grim and Finke (2006, 2007, 2010) were interested in examining the factors that predict variations in nations' regulation of religion and the consequences of those regulations, they were faced with a lack of measures. One of the first places one might think to look would be to national constitutions or formal laws. Grim and Finke note, though, that such measures would often lack validity given the fact that such constitutional and legal decrees do not always translate into the reality on the ground (i.e., they are often ignored, even by the government). They ended up turning to a type of government document in the form of annual International Religious Freedom Reports issued by the U.S. State Department. Such a report is issued annually for each nation and can be used to provide measures of the formal laws, informal practices, and tensions surrounding religious regulation and freedom (see Grim and Finke 2006 for a detailed discussion of their data collection).

Interestingly, the United States is not represented in the Religious Freedom Reports utilized by Grim and Finke, but tensions surrounding the regulation and restriction of religion are not absent from the United States. As just one example, many religious minorities face regulatory obstacles when trying to acquire permits or zoning changes (Treene 2015). There could be opportunities for studying historical and contemporary conflicts surrounding such issues through government documents. Municipalities are increasingly making permits, documents related to rezoning requests, and other government processes public on their websites. As an example, consider the website for Lee County, Florida, which has a population over 650,000.[5] The county government's website allows one to search for zoning cases being debated from 1964 through the present. I did a simple search for the word "church" and was provided 741 cases. A quick glance at these shows that the number of unique congregations represented are fewer, as there are often multiple entries for a particular congregation. Exploring the cases is fascinating and presents a wide range of quantitative and qualitative data. The first entry is from 1964. A congregation named St. Hilary's Episcopal Church was applying for part of its land to be rezoned so the congregation could then sell that part to a business. The website provides digitized documents concerning this request, including the permit application, the original cover letter from the congregation's lawyer, handwritten notes of objection by neighbors of the congregation, a flyer distributed by a neighborhood association objecting to the rezoning request, a signed petition by multiple neighborhood organizations against the rezoning, a notice for a public hearing, a list of property owners neighboring the church, a letter by the church's contractor and member pleading its case in response to the opposition (stating that the real opposition is due to two neighborhood grocery stores "fear[ing] future competition"), and the decision and reasoning by the zoning board (all voted "aye"). Court documents, such as written decisions from state and federal court cases, are also often freely available through the web. One illustration of using such documents to generate religion-related measures comes from an article by Wybraniec and Finke (2001). The authors examined the text of over two thousand court decisions to assess how the treatment of religious groups by courts varies across time and the tradition of the group.

The United States Patent and Trademark Office (USTPO) has searchable databases for both patents (invention-related) and trademarks (word/phrase/symbol-related) that might also be put to use. The U.S. Copyright Office offers a similar type of database covering music, film, and written works. A search found a variety of religion-related games in the patent database. For instance, patent 7,458,581 describes a board game called "Stairway to Heaven." The patent abstract describes it as such:

> The invention is a Christian board game that teaches biblical principles. The Christian board game comprises a board game, dice, angel playing pieces, jewel crown, chance cards, guide cards, and jewel cards. By rolling the dice, the angel playing pieces follow the path designated on the board game and taking up a chance card, guide card, or jewel card when instructed. When a player lands on a jewel card spot, and answers the question correctly, a jewel is given to said player. The object of the game is to be the first player to ascend the stairway to heaven and have collected seven jewels to fill up his or her jewel crown.

The patent database provides information on the inventor and his or her location, the filing date, references to previous related patents, a more detailed description of the game's layout and rules, and images related to the game.

The trademark database might be even richer for research on religion. A search for "Jesus" finds over six thousand records, although some of these are found because the applicant's name is Jesus. One that is more explicitly connected to religion is trademark number 86474659. The entry for this mark notes that it is associated with the production of "Hooded sweatshirts; Long-sleeved shirts; T-shirts." The entry provides the applicant's name (Love Influencing the Earth LLC, based in Nevada), the filing date, whether the trademark is live or dead, codes related to the elements of the trademark, and a description of the trademark ("The mark consists of the words 'Jesus Geek' in a stylized format, displayed over a design of eyeglasses.").

There are other potential opportunities for generating religion-related measures from government documents, although some might require being granted access by relevant authorities. As an example, the social movement scholars McCarthy, McPhail, and Smith (1996) were granted access to archives containing permit applications for planned protests or demonstrations by the National Park Service, the U.S. Capitol Police, and the Washington, D.C., Metropolitan Police Department. From these applications they were able to generate measures for the type of protests, the location and duration of the protest, the planned activities (i.e., marches, picketing), the size of the protests, the sponsor(s) of the protest, and whether there are expected counterdemonstrations. They note that some of these applications noted religion-related demonstrations, such as planned demonstrations for "spreading the gospel," "evangelizing," and religious group applications to protest or advocate for legislation or other political agendas. Whether or not one is interested in religion-related demonstration events, such examples reinforce the reality that there are potentially rich sources of measures just waiting to be generated from documents if a researcher is enterprising.

The second case study presented above focused on using contemporary newspapers to generate measures of crimes taking place on the property of religious congregations. There are other possibilities for generating quantitative and qualitative data on religion from newspapers, magazines, and other media. I personally enjoy just browsing through historical newspaper databases. The Library of Congress's *Chronicling America* website offers a wide variety of freely accessibly digitized historical U.S. newspapers from the nineteenth and early twentieth century. Subscription-based databases offered by Readex and ProQuest offer even wider coverage. The possibilities for examining historical presentations of religion and religious groups in media are vast. In my own work I have used these historical newspapers to generate measures of tract and Bible societies in the United States. For instance, a search for "tract society" in the ProQuest database returns an 1852 report of the New York City Tract Society that appeared in the *New-York Daily Times*, which would become the *New York Times*. The report includes information on the leaders of the organization, the annual budget and expenses, number of missionaries supported, number of tracts and Bibles distributed, and other activities of the organization. The use of religion in historical obituaries, marriage and birth announcements, and other defined sections of newspapers could be interesting areas to explore and from which to generate measures.

Finally, the last case study considered webpages as a source of measures, with the specific example of congregational statements of being open and affirming to sexual and gender minorities. As with the other categories of documents explored in this chapter, there are many other possibilities for analyzing website documents. I often run into these possibilities through chance. For instance, a recent issue of *National Geographic* focused on how the Virgin Mary is viewed and treated across the world (Orth 2015). Within the issue was a timeline documenting various apparitions, images, miracles, and other phenomena linked to

Mary. The social scientist in me immediately began to think about the possibilities for generating measures from such data. The footnote to the chart stated that the data were from www.MiracleHunter.com. I went to the website, which claims to be "the best resource for miracles on the web." The site contains a database of reported miracles organized by category (e.g., apparition, stigmata, etc.). Information concerning each miracle is offered, such as the time, location, details concerning content and nature of the miracle, how many witnesses there were and who they were, whether the miracle was investigated and/or approved by Catholic Church officials, and so forth. One could imagine social science research examining the predictors of perceived miracle locations and timing, how local culture or history shapes the content of miracles, and the social and historical factors that shape whether a miracle is officially approved. Obviously, some initial research would need to be done to assess the website itself, but this is just an illustration that there are many resources out there that could be of interest in the social scientific study of religion.

Concluding Thoughts

The examples and discussion above implicitly highlight some of the benefits of looking to documents as a potential source of measures of religion-related phenomena, but let us make some of these benefits more explicit. First, documents provide a way to access historical events, groups, or behaviors that were not captured by surveys or that occurred before the advent of surveys. Want to collect measures of nineteenth-century Bible and tract societies? Well, such societies' annual reports, newspaper articles, and other documents generated by or discussing those societies are probably the only option for creating measures.

Beyond historical phenomena, documents might allow one to study current events that are beyond the current scope of survey research. Want to collect measures of international religious freedom? Even the best multinational surveys only cover a fraction of all nations (and often the very nations that are not covered are the ones a researcher might be most interested in for this particular question). Documents like the U.S. State Department's annual reports for all nations might be the only option (Grim and Finke 2006). There are cases in which even when a researcher could utilize survey data, using documents instead or as a supplemental source of measures could provide many advantages. For instance, in the case presented above concerning parachurch organizations, it would be possible to send a survey to such organizations. However, the response rate would probably be fairly low. Annual reports filed with the IRS provide ways to generate measures for 100 percent of the targeted organizations. Sure, such reports might not include every measure one might include in one's survey, but if one is primarily interested in organizational types of measures, then such forms are abundantly rich. For some topics, such as finances, required financial reports might provide more valid and reliable measures than survey questions. In the case study above using newspapers to examine crimes taking place at religious congregations, a survey of congregations would undoubtedly be preferable. However, since surveys of congregation had not asked about this topic, newspaper articles at least provided an initial way to generate exploratory measure of the phenomena.

There are some practical advantages to using documents in research on religion, too. Although doing so is often labor intensive, generating measures from documents is usually inexpensive. This is something to consider for younger researchers and students who might want to collect original data but for whom major grant funding is unlikely.

None of this is to say that document-derived measures can replace or are equivalent to survey-derived measures. As the illustrations above highlight, documents can be great for certain research questions, particularly concerning historical topics and/or religious organizations and movements, which surveys rarely target. Documents probably will not be as useful for understanding the religious behaviors and beliefs of individuals (although, one could easily imagine research utilizing social media, diaries, yearbooks, or other more personal documents). Hopefully, this chapter, and the complementary chapters in this volume, will inspire others to consider this type of research in the social scientific study of religion.

NOTES

1 This exemption also includes integrated auxiliaries of a church and associations of churches (i.e., denominations).

2 This occasionally raises some tricky questions about the line between a noncongregational religious nonprofit and a congregation, and the IRS and some reli-

gious organizations have struggled with these questions in the past (see Scheitle 2010 for more discussion of this).

3 There are some variations in these annual reporting requirements based on the revenue of the organization, though.

4 If the reader is interested in these data, I would recommend visiting the website for the Dynamics of Collection Action project, where one can access detailed documentation and request access to the data. The website is currently located at web.stanford.edu.

5 "Lee County, Southwest Florida." Accessed November 30, 2016, www.leegov.com.

REFERENCES

Barthel, Michael. 2015. "Newspapers: Fact Sheet." *Pew Research Center: Journalism & Media* Accessed November 30, 2016, www.journalism.org.

Beyerlein, Kraig, Sarah A. Soule, and Nancy Martin. 2015. "Prayers, Protest, and Police: How Religion Influences Police Presence at Collective Action Events in the United States, 1960–1995." *American Sociological Review* 80(6): 1250–71.

Cadge, Wendy, Laura R. Olson, and Christopher Wildeman. 2008. "How Denominational Resources Influence Debate about Homosexuality in Mainline Protestant Congregations." *Sociology of Religion* 69(2): 187–207.

Cadge, Wendy, and Christopher Wildeman. 2008. "Facilitators and Advocates: How Mainline Protestant Clergy Respond to Homosexuality." *Sociological Perspectives* 51(3): 587–603.

Chaves, Mark, Shawna L. Anderson, and Alison Eagle. 2014. *National Congregations Study*. Cumulative data file and codebook. Durham, NC: Duke University, Department of Sociology. Accessed at www.theARDA.com.

"Covenants." 2015. *Open and Affirming Coalition*. United Church of Christ. Accessed at openandaffirming.org.

Earl, Jennifer, Andrew Martin, John D. McCarthy, and Sarah A. Soule. 2004. "The Use of Newspaper Data in the Study of Collective Action." *Annual Review of Sociology* 30: 65–80.

Earl, Jennifer, Sarah A. Soule, and John D. McCarthy. 2003. "Protest under Fire? Explaining the Policing of Protest." *American Sociological Review* 68(4): 581–606.

Grim, Brian J., and Roger Finke. 2006. "International Religion Indexes: Government Regulation, Government Favoritism, and Social Regulation of Religion." *Interdisciplinary Journal of Research on Religion* 2: Article 1. Accessed November 30, 2016, www.religjournal.com.

Grim, Brian J., and Roger Finke. 2007. "Religious Persecution in Cross-National Context: Clashing Civilizations or Regulated Religious Economies?" *American Sociological Review* 72(4): 633–58

Grim, Brian J., and Roger Finke. 2010. *The Price of Freedom Denied: Religious Persecution and Conflict in the Twenty-first Century*. New York: Cambridge University Press.

Lindsay, D. Michael. 2007. *Faith in the Halls of Power: How Evangelicals Joined the American Elite*. New York: Oxford University Press.

Martin, Andrew W., John D. McCarthy, and Clark McPhail. 2009. "Why Targets Matter: Toward a More Inclusive Model of Collective Violence." *American Sociological Review* 74(5): 821–41.

McAdam, Doug, and Yang Su. 2002. "The War at Home: Antiwar Protests and Congressional Voting, 1965-1973." *American Sociological Review* 67: 696–721.

McCarthy, John D., Clark McPhail, and Jackie Smith. 1996. "Images of Protest: Dimensions of Selection Bias in Media Coverage of Washington." *American Sociological Review* 61(3): 478–99.

McCarthy, John, Larissa Tatarenko, Clark McPhail, Patrick Rafail, and Boguslaw Augustyn. 2008. "Assessing Stability in the Patterns of Selection Bias in Newspaper Coverage of Protest during the Transition from Communism in Belarus." *Mobilization* 13(2): 127–46.

Olson, Laura R., and Wendy Cadge. 2002. "Talking about Homosexuality: The Views of Mainline Protestant Clergy." *Journal for the Scientific Study of Religion* 41(1): 153–67.

Olson, Laura R., and Christopher Wildeman. 2008. "Facilitators and Advocates: How Mainline Protestant Clergy Respond to Homosexuality." *Sociological Perspectives* 51(3): 587–603.

Orth, Maureeen. 2015. "How the Virgin Mary Became the World's Most Powerful Woman." *National Geographic*, December. Accessed at ngm.nationalgeographic.com.

Scheitle, Christopher P. 2005. "The Social and Symbolic Boundaries of Congregations: An Analysis of Website Links." *Interdisciplinary Journal of Research on Religion* 1(1): 1–21.

Scheitle, Christopher P. 2009a. "Identity and Government Funding in Christian Nonprofits." *Social Science Quarterly* 90(4): 816–33.

Scheitle, Christopher P. 2009b. "Leadership Compensation in Christian Nonprofits." *Sociology of Religion* 70(4): 384–408.

Scheitle, Christopher P. 2010. *Beyond the Congregation: The World of Christian Nonprofits*. New York: Oxford University Press.

Scheitle, Christopher P. 2016. "Crimes Occurring at Places of Worship: An Analysis of 2012 Newspaper Reports." *International Review of Victimology* 22(1): 65–74.

Scheitle, Christopher P., Erica J. Dollhopf, and John D. McCarthy. 2016. "Exploring Religious Congregations' Registration with the IRS." *Nonprofit and Voluntary Sector Quarterly* 45(2): 397–408.

Scheitle, Christopher P., Stephen M. Merino, and Andrew Moore. 2010. "On the Varying Meaning of 'Open and Affirming.'" *Journal of Homosexuality* 57(10): 1223–36.

Smith, Jackie, John D. McCarthy, Clark McPhail, and Boguslaw Augustyn. 2001. "From Protest to Agenda Building: Description Bias in Media Coverage of Protest Events in Washington D.C." *Social Forces* 79(4): 1397–1423.

Sorenson, Susan B., Julie G. Peterson Manz, and Richard Berk. 1998. "News Media Coverage and the Epidemiology of Homicide." *American Journal of Public Health* 88: 1510–14.

Treene, Eric W. 2015. "Understanding the Impact of the Religious Land Use and Institutionalized Persons Act." *Public Lawyer* 23(1): 3–7.

White, Jerry. 1983. *The Church and Parachurch: An Uneasy Marriage*. Portland, OR: Multnomah Press.

Willmer, Wesley K., J. David Schmidt, and Martyn Smith. 1998. *The Prospering Parachurch: Enlarging the Boundaries of God's Kingdom*. San Francisco: Jossey-Bass.

Woolever, Cynthia, Deborah Bruce, Joelle Kopacz, and Ida Smith-Williams. 2009. *U.S. Congregational Life Survey, Wave* 2. Data file and codebook. Accessed at ww.theARDA.com

Woolever, Cynthia, Keith Wulff, Deborah Bruce, and Ida Smith-Williams. 2001. *U.S. Congregational Life Survey*. Data file and codebook. Accessed at ww.theARDA.com

Wuthnow, Robert. 1988. *The Restructuring of American Religion: Society and Faith since World War II*. Princeton, NJ: Princeton University Press.

Wybraniec, John, and Roger Finke 2001. "Religious Regulation and the Courts: The Judiciary's Changing Role in Protecting Minority Religions from Majoritarian Rule." *Journal for the Scientific Study of Religion* 40(3): 427–44.

8.

Historical Research

Oneida Online

WILLIAM SIMS BAINBRIDGE

This chapter will use a very well-known religious group of the nineteenth century to illustrate many of the ways historical data can be assembled, and many of the problems faced in using online sources to develop a coherent and theory-relevant picture of the past.[1]

Originally emerging in New England, the Oneida community was established in upstate New York in 1848, under the leadership of John Humphrey Noyes, a religious leader who believed he had achieved perfection and knew how to lead others to that goal. So much has been written about Oneida, and so much information has been assembled in a small number of paper archives, that it might not be cost-effective to undertake a major research project on this particular group in the way described here. Yet the very fact that we can anchor online data in a well-developed corpus of information about Oneida allows us to explore with efficiency and clarity the possibilities for studying historical religious phenomena that are far less well understood. Of necessity, this chapter will often emphasize tiny details of research methodology, to alert the reader to problems and their possible solutions, but it also will consider how the data relate to larger theoretical issues.

Oneida was a religious utopian community, so right away we can see that developing online methods to study it may contribute to future research on religious organizations, social innovations, and communities more generally. The newest information technologies support innovation in historical research, especially if conducted from a social scientific perspective that seeks deeper understanding of how different social processes interweave to form communities. For example, we still benefit from reading the now-historical field research on "Middletown"

(Muncie, Indiana), performed in the 1920s and 1930s, but now the original pages of the U.S. Census for that town are available online up through 1940 (Lynd and Lynd 1929, 1937). Research on the census records of religious communities began in the early 1980s, but was limited to a dozen archives around the country where microfilms were stored, while today anyone may access such data from anywhere, online. We can only imagine what other kinds of quantitative data can be extracted from Internet-based archives and used to test hypotheses. There have been rather few quantitative studies of utopian communities, although one supported the hypothesis that religion adds strength to social experiments (Stephan and Stephan 1973; Kanter 1972).

A criticism of traditional history is that it consists of heroic tales of kings, kingdoms, and battles, ignoring the daily lives of ordinary people. In the case of religious movements, the tendency has been to focus on a single charismatic leader and the group as a whole, ignoring much of what came between, and indeed assuming that a mystical concept like *charisma* could assume scientific status (Weber 1978 [1922]; Berger 1963; Shils 1965; Stark 1965; Roth 1975; Olin 1980). That means that a host of other factors have been downplayed, notably the diverse roles of influential members other than the designated leader, and their network of connections to other movements and aspects of the wider socioeconomic system. In the case of Oneida, the traditional histories provide some hints, but the current wealth of online data about the lives of individual Americans and families in the second half of the nineteenth century allows us to trace myriads of connections between movements, as people migrated from one to another, and see with ever greater clarity the connections between religious organizations and specific secular institutions of the society.

Indeed, Oneida was an early example of the increasingly difficult problem of defining the boundaries of religion. Worship services were really not significant in the community, and the emphasis on achieving perfection in this life seemed to suggest that members were becoming the worldly equivalent of angels, thus draining some of the significance away from the supernatural dimensions of Christian faith. It is perhaps too simplistic to say that it was a movement that sought to give the intellect dominance over the emotions, yet it was among the most intellectual religious movements of its day, as evidenced by its library and extensive publications. Many of its practices foreshadowed the secular Communist movements of later years, yet it was deeply embedded in the wider capitalist marketplace. Thus, examining its connections to other innovative cultural phenomena, whether through economic exchange or the transfer of members in and out of Oneida, can address social scientific questions about the meaning and possible contradictions of "religious community."

What are the various roles, functional or dysfunctional, played by participants in religious movements? To what extent are "charismatic leaders" mere figureheads for a collective effort, versus really dominating followers? Can social movements and community experiments of all kinds be conceptualized as assemblies of components, as an automaker places one or another kind of engine or driver's seat inside a chassis, of which some of the options are religious and others secular? What are the dynamics of groups that combine to form a community, such as nuclear families, networks of friends devoted to particular recreational activities, and activist dissident factions? Must we understand religious movements as reflections of historically limited conditions in the surrounding world, for example, seeing the many communal experiments of nineteenth-century America as merely outliers on the cultural distribution of new communities then being established across the continent? How can we develop and test abstract theories about the human desire to achieve spiritual transcendence, from the brute facts recorded in the extensive historical record? Moving beyond the boundaries of one particular community, what historical variant of public opinion research can we use to learn about the beliefs and values of the wider society of bygone eras?

The recent development and availability of a host of Internet tools, archives, websites, and blogs allow us to answer a surprising number of questions about even groups as relatively obscure as Oneida.

Cults, Sects, and Controversy

Sociologists of religion are well aware of the controversy surrounding novel cult movements and strict sects/schismatic groups. Such "deviant" groups are frequently the target of negative claims about their founders, beliefs, and practices. Sometimes these claims are true, and sometimes they are simply inflammatory rhetoric designed to outrage the community against a threatening group. Often the truth, such as it is, lies in between. One great benefit of online tools is that they can help us explore the claims made about religious groups using creative sources of data.

For example, Oneida was not a schismatic movement, but emerged afresh as John Humphrey Noyes developed his own Perfectionist beliefs regarding the possibility of transcending sin and recruited individuals and families to his nascent movement. Thus, it might be called a cult, rather than a sect (Stark and Bainbridge 1979). Oneida proved a controversial group early in its career, with claims that Noyes used the group as an instrument for the gratification of his own selfish desires. In particular, Noyes gained control over people and economic resources, and began sexually exploiting young girls.

An angry 1879 letter from Professor John Mears, D.D., the most influential opponent of Oneida, published in the *New York Tribune*, available through the commercial online digital library Newspapers.com, outlines these charges. Mears called Oneida "an organized system of concubinage" disguised in religious terminology: "Abolishing marriage, they have put in its place customs and practices which cannot be described for vileness, and which are the more shocking from the saintly phrases with which they are concealed and recommended" (Mears 1879:2). In the year that Mears published his letter, and in response to an anti-Oneida crusade Mears organized among clergy and public officials, Noyes fled to Canada, presumably rather than face formal charges of statutory rape.

A number of online resources allow us to examine the extent of Oneida's problem with underage sex. In her book on Oneida, sociologist Maren Lockwood Carden cites an 1884 medical study by Ely van de Warker that is currently available for free in Google Books (van de Warker 1884). Carden judges that the study was reasonably accurate, despite the nonrandom nature of the Oneida women studied, and it reports that the median age at which Noyes or his closest associates introduced them to sexual relations was thirteen, with a range from ten to eighteen (Carden 1969:100).

Another source, an unofficial but rather fascinating website, Salmon Creek Genealogy & Publishing, copyright 2014 by Laura Wayland-Smith Hatch, offers a simple but effective kinship tree, apparently of all Oneida members.[2] I cannot vouch for all its data, but it cites extensive sources and has matched other datasets when I have compared them for most (but not all) individual cases. Table 8.1 presents data from this online genealogy database for Oneida, listing thirteen children of John Humphrey Noyes, each of whom had a different adult mother, only the first of whom was married to him.

Frankly, this table did not take long to assemble, requiring pasting into a spreadsheet data from two webpages for each line, one for the child and one for the mother, some editing and age calculations, then pasting of the result into the word processor. Among the editing required was removal of a pregnancy of Mary L. Bolles, which resulted in a stillbirth for which a date and baby name were not given. Also, Victor Cragin Noyes had a twin sister who was stillborn, but given the ironic name Victoria, since death had triumphed in her case. In two senses, Victor seems to have taken after his father. First, he suffered from episodic mental illness that once caused him to be placed in a mental hospital, but later he was able to contribute useful work to the community. Second, members of the community occasionally imputed innate

Table 8.1. Parents' Ages for the Children of John Humphrey Noyes

Child's name	Mother's name	Birth Year	Father's Age	Mother's Age
Dr. Theodore Richard Noyes	Harriet Ann Holton Noyes	1841	29	33
Victor Cragin Noyes	Mary Elizabeth Johnson	1847	36	36
Constance Bradley Noyes	Sarah Ann Summers	1849	38	22
Jessie Catherine Baker Hatch	Catherine E. Hobart	1858	46	43
John Humphrey Noyes	Charlotte Miller Leonard	1869	58	23
Pierrepont Burt Noyes	Harriet Maria Worden	1870	58	30
Holton Van Velzer Noyes	Mary Elizabeth Van Velzer	1871	59	23
Gertrude Hayes Noyes	Harriet Noyes Olds	1871	60	22
Irene Campbell Newhouse	Arabella Campbell Woolworth	1873	61	23
Godrey Barron Noyes	Maria Fanny Barron	1873	61	31
Dorothy Hendee Noyes Barron	Beulah Foster Hendee	1876	64	29
Miriam Trowbridge Noyes	Helen Campbell Miller	1877	65	30
George Langstaff Noyes	Leonora Hatch	1879	67	20

selfishness to him, under the theory that in his mother's womb he may have stolen life from his sister.

The table shows that the youngest woman who gave birth to a child by John Humphrey Noyes was twenty, not thirteen. This does not absolve him of the sins for which Mears accused him, but it does show how quantitative analysis of historical data can be illuminating. We also see that in his late fifties, Noyes increased his rate of personal propagation, and we may well wonder how the demographics of Oneida were changing more generally, an issue we shall examine later.

Virtual Field Research

Charismatic-influence theories of religious movements focus upon the special gifts of key religious figures that provide them with the ability to attract and dominate other people. But is it really true that each and every religious movement, or the Oneida community in particular, was simply the product of a charismatic individual? One alternative is the theory that so-called charismatic leaders express feelings that the followers already have (Friedland 1964). Perhaps members of the Oneida community were not really followers, but partners in creation of the movement, perhaps some of them playing crucial leadership roles of their own. Rank-and-file members of any movement may exhibit a range of motivations and perform a diversity of functions. Observational field research inside contemporary religious movements can address such questions directly, but now the historical archives allow us to achieve something quite comparable in historical research.

In both cultural anthropology and sociology, interviews and ethnographic field research undertaken by an individual scientist are standard methodologies, yet they would seem impossible in historical studies, because time machines really do not exist to take us back to earlier eras. However, as professional biographers could tell us, following the life course of one or more specific individuals can be the historical equivalent. Here I will do this with four individual members of Oneida: Charles Guiteau (1841–1882), Pierrepont Noyes (1870–1959), Sewell Newhouse (1806–1888), and James Towner (1823–1913). They briefly illustrate different theoretical points and increasing levels of research difficulty, suggesting a large number of online routes to data relevant for historical studies of people who participated in religious movements.

Charles Guiteau

Guiteau has his own Wikipedia page, so one would think that Internet-based research on him could stop there. He is best known for having assassinated President James A. Garfield in 1881, and for dying by hanging for this offense the following year. Wikipedia devotes a paragraph to his connections with Oneida, which he joined in 1860:

> Despite the "group marriage" aspects of that sect, he was generally rejected during his five years there, and was nicknamed "Charles Gitout." He left the community twice. After leaving, he went to Hoboken, New Jersey, and attempted to start a newspaper based on the Oneida religion called *The Daily Theocrat*. This failed and he returned to Oneida, only to leave again and file lawsuits against the community's founder, John Humphrey Noyes. Guiteau's father, embarrassed, wrote letters in support of Noyes, who had considered Guiteau irresponsible and insane.

The Wikipedia article cites books for these facts, but the one by Hayes and Hayes dates from the year of the hanging, and is unlikely to be in the local library. It now can be downloaded from Google Books (Hayes and Hayes 1882).

Wikipedia briefly mentions a book Guiteau wrote, *The Truth*, saying it was "almost entirely plagiarized from the work of John Humphrey Noyes," but does not link to a copy. It also may be downloaded from Google Books, and then compared with the main source that Guiteau presumably plagiarized, that huge 1847 collection of early essays by John Humphrey Noyes titled *The Berean* (Guiteau 1879; Noyes 1847). Another source, which Guiteau was likely to have possessed, was the 1867 edition of the *Hand-book of the Oneida Community*, which currently can be purchased through Google Books but not, like the earlier examples, downloaded for free. However, the full text is freely available from the website of Syracuse University Library, along with other Oneida documents and a catalog of all the materials from the community physically preserved at this campus not far from Oneida.[3] The ideas in *The Truth* were clearly derived from the teachings of Noyes, but "plagiarized" generally means verbatim copying. Guiteau's writing style is less erudite, and entering many phrases from *The Truth* into Google did not turn up any of the publications by Noyes, a reasonable empirical test of plagiarism under its narrow definition.

Clearly, the Internet can help students, scholars, and scientists find many kinds of ordinary information about well-known historical religious movements, notably published books and archive collections held at public institutions. But what else? Googling "Charles Julius Guiteau site:newspapers.com" in late January 2015 got 15,800 hits, and all the highly rated ones were newspaper articles about his execution. Newspapers.com requires a subscription for full use, as does the related Ancestry.com employed extensively later in this chapter. Searching within Newspapers.com, and setting the date range at 1850–1880 to exclude stories about the assassination, turned up just 244 articles mentioning "Charles Guiteau," but many of them were not about Charles Julius Guiteau, but for example Harry C. Guiteau, following an algorithm that assumed "C" could stand for Charles. The first hit for Charles Guiteau is a *New York Times* article dated October 11, 1880, in which he is merely one of many people listed as having left calling cards at a hotel where former president Grant was staying.[4] This was many months before Garfield's assassination, but it is worth noting that the brief article about Grant's visit was immediately to the left of one that headlined Garfield honoring Grant, on the newspaper's front page, so the juxtaposition may have contributed to Guiteau's decision to assassinate the president, or the calling card was an early symptom of his plan to do so.

Ancestry.com is a commercial service giving subscribers access to extensive historical records where the names of large numbers of people may be found. Entering "Charles Julius Guiteau" in the search engine for the U.S. Census, setting the preference so that an exact match is not required, does indeed find Guiteau at age nine in the 1850 census, but with the last name spelled differently. The original manuscripts of the census were all handwritten in that period, by enumerators who visited each home, asking a representative of the household to provide the information. Back in 1840, only the name of head of household was written down, but starting with 1850, one row of the census form was devoted to each person. Thus, the census taker may have heard a name incorrectly, or the handwriting may be messy. In this case, it looks like the name is spelled this way: "Charles J. Gurtteare." How do we know this is the right person?

Citing four sources, Guiteau's Wikipedia page says, "Guiteau was born in Freeport, Illinois, the fourth of six children of Jane August (née Howe) and Luther Wilson Guiteau, whose family was of French Huguenot ancestry. He moved with his family to Ulao, Wisconsin (now Grafton, Wisconsin), in 1850 and lived there until 1855, when his mother died. Soon after, Guiteau and his father moved back to Freeport."[5] Charles is listed in the 1850 census as one of three people on adjacent rows of the form with the same last name, indeed written out only for the first: L. W. Gurtteare (age forty male, birthplace New York), Francis M. (age fourteen female, birthplace Michigan), and Charles J. (age nine male, birthplace Illinois). The page covers forty-two residents of Grafton, Wisconsin, and the Guiteaus are three of seven residents in household 1428, headed by John Howe (age sixty-five male, birthplace New York). Household 1429 also contained people named Howe, but the two households are written on different pages of the original records, and there can be uncertainty whether they really lived in different dwellings, or were separated merely by the page break.

Where is his mother? The Wikipedia article says quite clearly that she died in 1855, so she should have been listed in the same household, unless perhaps she was on extended travel. However, the first of the references from the Wikipedia page is to the catalog page of the Charles Guiteau Collection of documents at Georgetown University, which says something quite different: "Charles Julius Guiteau was born on September 8, 1841, in Freeport, Illinois, the fourth of six children of Luther Wilson Guiteau and Jane Howe. The latter died when Charles was quite young, on September 25, 1848."[6] This is a warning that Wikipedia articles may contain errors, and of course anyone doing an extensive study of Guiteau would consult a great variety of sources. Here we use him as a very preliminary example of the kinds of online searches that today would help organize such scholarship, and in the future may be the sole data collection methodology if all historical documents are eventually posted online.

Evidence of the relevance of Guiteau for religion is a rather fine article by D. Jamez Terry (2011), "The 'Assassination-Instrument' of God:

Religious Interpretations of the Garfield Assassination," which notes not only the connection to Oneida's radical faith but also the problematic nature of the insanity defense that failed to save Guiteau from hanging, in part because such a defense seemed antireligious (Terry 2011). The relevance to Internet research is that the journal that published this article was *Cult/ure: The Graduate Journal of Harvard Divinity School*, a student-run online journal that enables graduate students to advance toward academic careers.

The early book about Guiteau by Hayes and Hayes begins with extensive quotations from his own autobiography, provided through interviews documented by a shorthand writer while Guiteau was in prison, including this information about his father:

> About thirty years ago, he became interested in the publications of John H. Noyes, who is the founder of the Oneida Community, and was under his influence more or less during that entire period. I used to hear him talk about the Community a great deal in his family and I became interested in it, in that way, in my early boyhood. (Hayes and Hayes 1882:22)

This identifies Guiteau as one of the common cases in which recruitment to a cult is accomplished through a social relationship to someone who is already connected to it. But Guiteau's full story reminds us that many of the people attracted to any reasonably successful cult are not really suitable to become members, and are likely either to drop out quickly or be rejected.

Pierrepont Noyes

One might think also that there is little more to learn about Pierrepont Noyes, one of the children of John Humphrey Noyes, because he became a leader of the corporation that followed the commune, and in 1937 published an autobiography about his childhood at Oneida, appropriately titled *My Father's House*. I had originally read a university library's copy, but for this project I purchased one online from Amazon.com, which despite the low price turned out to be number 368 of 500 copies autographed by the author. Electronic copies of books consist of pure information, but an autographed hard copy may have some of the quality of a sacred relic, suggesting one of the more spiritual ways in which Internet-based information differs from more traditional forms. Among the most impressive sections of this autobiography is a description of an intentionally set fire that destroyed the barn very near the Mansion House, killing about two dozen horses. The arsonist was caught, and Pierrepont reported this fact without naming the man: "He was a young man in his early thirties, who, having been brought to the Community when a child and reared in its isolation, was suddenly flung, like the rest of us, into a world he knew little about" (Noyes 1937:212).

The fire took place soon after John Humphrey Noyes had fled to Canada, and Oneida was in the process of abandoning the customs that had marked it as a utopian religious commune, so the arsonist's actions are sociologically interesting as evidence about how individuals may sometimes behave when their social surroundings are undergoing radical change. As told by Pierrepont, the story does explain that the arsonist had pretended to a local, nonmember woman that he was personally wealthy, but since the Oneida properties were held communally, this seduction subterfuge failed, and in anger he burned the barn. Unfortunately, since we were not given the man's name, we could learn little more. I tried Googling various keywords, but for example "fire" and "Oneida" produced thousands of hits, even after I added the year when I guessed the event might have taken place.

The name of the arsonist was well known within the Oneida community, and could be found on the blog by recent residents of the Mansion House, dating from 2010:

> Two of the Community young men including James Vail were involved in a fight with a drunken Irish railroad worker. Vail would later father a child with Harriet Worden, and be arrested and convicted for attempting to burn down the Mansion House and successfully destroying a horse barn, killing several horses trapped inside. The arson was said to be caused by a dispute between Vail and Community at the time of the break-up over a team of horses he claimed belonged to him and not the Community.[7]

The blog told more about the earlier fight, and carried a picture of Vail. Notice that the two sentences about the barn destruction used the words "burn" and "arson" but not "fire." I had easily located the blog when googling other Oneida-related topics, and simply read all its pages with interest, stumbling across Vail's name.

The bloggers had done a wonderful job putting up their unofficial Oneida website, but as in journalism we cannot trust any one source for any important fact. The Salmon Creek website reported that James Spencer Vail had been born in Newark, New Jersey, January 2, 1850, so this matches the statement by Pierrepont Noyes that the arsonist was in his early thirties, as the fire must have happened around 1881. The 1880 U.S. Census of Oneida says James Vail was thirty, born in New Jersey, and working in "general service." The Salmon Creek page for Vail said that in 1878 he and Harriet Worden had produced a daughter named Stella Vail Worden, a name in a form that correctly suggested that he and Harriet had not been conventionally married, but may have been operating within the complex marriage system of Oneida. The genealogy reported that Harriet had produced two other children, Ormond Noyes Burt with Abram Burt in 1863, and Pierrepont Burt Noyes with John Humphrey Noyes in 1870.

Among the most poignant moments in the autobiography of Pierrepont Noyes came just after the community had dissolved its complex marriage system, and he asked his mother whom she would marry. He reports that she replied, "Perhaps no one. Your father is already married; so is Ormond's father" (Noyes 1937:165). Notice that, at least as recorded for posterity, their conversation said nothing about the father of Pierrepont's half-sister, Stella, who was James Vail. In coming years, Abram Burt actually behaved like a good step-father to Pierrepont, even helping pay for his education. One obvious lesson is that people whom social scientists interview, and those who write the documents historians cite, may omit crucial but embarrassing facts, even if they do not censor to the extent of intentionally distorting what they say. More instructive for our current purposes is a point about society inside religious sects, cults, and communes. Human relations inside these highly cohesive, complex communities will often connect a child with multiple adults in ways such that analysis requires thinking outside our ordinary assumptions about family structures.

Sewell Newhouse

After Noyes fled Oneida, a protracted process of transformation began, including division of the commune's property among individual owners. The only person who totally opposed the final Plan of Division was Sewell Newhouse (Carden 1969:115). In many respects, he was the most loyal to Noyes of the men possessing power at Oneida, but his opposition may really have reflected loyalty to himself rather than to Noyes, as he was absolutely central to Oneida's economic success. It is all very well to call Oneida a commune, yet it was also a manufacturing corporation, and in late years employed about as many outside workers as community members. Agriculture contributed but was insufficient, so Oneida was economically very different from the largely agricultural communes associated with other religious movements of the period. Early on it had a printing business, later manufactured silk thread, and in its final days launched a silverware industry that still today bears the name Oneida. But its most successful business was animal trap manufacture, as it produced many thousands of metal traps in various sizes each year, following the design invented by Newhouse.

The demographic records for Sewell Newhouse look quite normal, with one wife named Eveliza and a son named Milford. All three of them are buried at the Oneida cemetery, as one may see online by entering their names into the search fields of www.findagrave.com. The first annual report of the community, published in 1849, includes brief testimonials of many members. Sewell: "Since I have been here, I have learned to be sober-minded. I have found that trifling conversation produces barrenness, and pray that I may henceforth walk soberly and meekly before God and man." Eveliza: "I can bear witness to the power of God in this Association, manifested in healing us from sickness, and in bringing hidden things to light. I have been conscious of a refining process going-on in my spirit ever since I became acquainted with this body." The report often uses the term "body" to refer to its social group—a fact that is easy to verify simply by searching the entire text for that word, which is used 113 times, either referring to the Oneida community or referring to the physical body of an individual.[8]

Even when religion is our main focus in studying a community, the nature of the research may benefit from economic data, or in a case like this, technological data. As part of its nationwide marketing program, Oneida published several editions of a book about animal trapping, ostensibly written by Newhouse but edited by Oneida, reprinted even decades after his death (Newhouse 1869). It was wide ranging, discussing strategic issues in trapping as well as a diversity of methods, but featuring the Newhouse design. The frontispiece was typically a signed engraving of Newhouse himself, and the interior included many drawings of animals, camping equipment, and Newhouse traps of various sizes but uniform design. A comprehensive 1907 book surveying steel traps devotes an entire chapter to the Oneida traps, beginning, "In or about 1823 the first Newhouse traps were made. At that early date only a few of the smaller sizes were manufactured but these have been added to until now the famous Newhouse trap is manufactured in twenty-five different sizes" (Harding 1907:50). Thus, Newhouse began making traps long before joining Noyes's group, and influenced trap manufacture long after his death. One way a researcher can study the traps themselves is simply to buy some, because at any given time a large number are for sale on eBay or online antique dealers. A company in Cleveland, Ohio, named Oneida Victor, makes several models of Newhouse traps even today.[9]

Trapping technology is part of the Oneida story, because the trap industry funded the longevity of this otherwise radical commune, but any technology that played a significant role in the lives of people may relate powerfully if indirectly to their religion. Some technologies are central to their religious mission; often the technology was printing, as was true in the case of Oneida. The online Oneida archive of Syracuse University includes an 1875 report by Harriet Noyes, wife of the leader, on the printing business, which documents the specific printing presses the community acquired, and which can all be looked up online.[10] One was a design developed by Josiah Warren, who was involved with utopian social experiments and saw inexpensive printing as a necessary tool for social change.[11]

James W. Towner

The story of James W. Towner may be the most interesting of the four for social scientists, yet more difficult to assemble, despite many connections and clues, therefore useful here as an example of challenges and opportunities. Shortly before his death, he wrote a genealogy of his family, containing some rather limited information about himself, published posthumously and currently available online (Towner 1914). He received limited formal schooling, but was a very intelligent autodidact who became a schoolteacher and Universalist minister early in adulthood, taking an active role speaking in public for abolition of slavery. Born in New York State, he married an Ohio woman with the remarkable name Cinderella Sweet, and in 1854 they moved to Iowa. He worked in the lumber business and studied law, was admitted to the Iowa bar in 1859, and was a professional attorney thereafter in Iowa, Ohio, New York, and eventually California, where he became the first judge of Orange County.

He served in the Union Army during the Civil War, until he lost his left eye at the battle of Pea Ridge in 1862. Remarkably, after recovering, he returned to battle with only his right eye to guide him. After the war, he and Cinderella lived for about eight years in the Cleveland, Ohio, area, before joining Oneida. Neither the autobiography he included in the family genealogy nor several of the biographical sketches written about him while he lived in California mentioned his years at Oneida, or his earlier support for the much more chaotic "free love" Berlin Heights community in the Cleveland area (Towner 1913; 1914). This was a dynamic series of secular communes and complex family relations that couched free love in terms of women's emancipation, and aligned itself with wider socialist movements. In an article published in the journal *Communal Societies* and currently downloadable for free from its website, Joanne E. Passet reports,

> James W. Towner became leader of the Berlin Heights communitarians who sought membership at the Oneida Community even though he had not participated in the original free love experiment. After attending the 1856 convention of socialists in Berlin Heights, he returned to Iowa but remained in contact with Free Lovers through correspondence, articles written for the *Social Revolutionist*, and occasional visits. Towner and his wife, Cinderella Sweet, lived in Berlin Heights briefly in the 1860s, but relocated to Cleveland when it became evident that association with Berlin socialists jeopardized his goal of joining the Oneida Community. (Passet 2005:100)

Towner had helped Oneida with legal matters, include the Guiteau case, then became a full-fledged member of the community as it was facing a growing list of internal problems (Crosby 1998; Fox 2010:131). Lawrence Foster, who has studied communal societies extensively, wrote in another freely available *Communal Societies* article, "Eventually, a faction challenging the old order and calling for reform coalesced around James William Towner, a capable leader who had joined Oneida along with a small group of his followers during the mid-1870s, but he too was unable to secure enough support to replace the still-present John Humphrey Noyes" (Foster 1988:13). In her book about the transformation of Oneida from a utopian community to a modern industrial corporation, Maren Lockwood Carden reported that a crucial factor in the failure of Oneida's complex marriage system was the emergence of this dissident faction:

> As he grew older, Noyes sometimes delegated the role of "first husband" to one of his several central men. Early in 1879, two of them questioned Noyes's right to decide who was to introduce young women of the Community to sexual experience. One of these men, William A. Hinds, had been at Oneida since its founding; the other, James W. Towner, had joined in 1874. It is probable that their outspoken protest was precipitated by some personal disappointment over the selection of first husbands. In any event, approximately thirty men and women joined them to form a highly aggressive party protesting Noyes's authority. (Carden 1969:99)

Carden reports that the "Townerites" and the "Noyesites" did not really differ in age or religiosity, and that other scholars had been wrong to suggest that Townerites were simply a small group already led by Towner, who had joined Oneida with him five years earlier. The escape of John Humphrey Noyes to Canada in 1879 did not cause defeat for his party, and Towner also soon left, taking with him a number of other members who moved to California and began ordinary lives. Yet that did not mean that Towner's orientation toward religion changed very much. Searching Newspapers.com turned up an obituary for Cinderella Sweet Towner in 1894 that included this revealing evidence:

> After the services the remains will be taken to Rosedale crematory, at Los Angeles, for cremation. The pall bearers are selected from the Royal

> Arch Masons, of which the judge was member. The Masonic fraternity will attend the funeral, and a number will go up to Los Angeles with the remains. The following Royal Arch Masons will act as pall bearers: Dr. M. A. Menges, Hon. H. A. Peabody, R. E. Hewett, Dr. I. D. Mills, J. S. Haywood, A. J. Wood. They will accompany the remains to the crematory. Rev. E. R. Watson of the Unity society will officiate. ("Santa Ana" 1894:3)

Googling "Royal Arch Masons," plus the names of members listed, turned up an 1894 publication of this fraternal organization, listing James Towner as a "high priest" (Caswell 1894). Membership in the Masons is not incompatible with membership in a Protestant denomination, but as the word "priest" indicated, it possessed quasi-religious qualities. Searching the online memorial website Find A Grave reveals that Cinderella was buried at Oneida, although she died in California, which suggests her remains were cremated precisely to render transport back to Oneida feasible.[12] Her Find A Grave webpage shows a picture of her tombstone, with her name on it, and a nice photo of her in life.

There is also a page indicating that James W. Towner was buried at Oneida, with a portrait of him but no picture of his tombstone.[13] However, Find A Grave also has a page for him at the Fairhaven Memorial Park in Santa Ana, California, where he died.[14] My immediate assumption was that the Oneida information was wrong, but an entry in the RootsWeb blog at Ancestry.com indicated otherwise. A blogger had visited the California cemetery and discovered that the grave was for a different James W. Towner, who had died at the age of one in 1914 and whose tombstone bears the legend, "Our Darling Baby."[15] Near the baby's tombstone is one for his father, H. Fred Towner, and the online information about Oneida genealogies shows that the baby's grave belongs to the great-grandson of the James Towner featured here.

The remarkable example of James W. Towner illustrates how, with diligence both in finding and in assessing information sources, researchers can not only assemble biographical material from a wide array of online resources but also can contribute to sociological theory of religion. Putting the point briefly in the context of this methodological chapter: *religion* is a somewhat arbitrary concept, distinguished from similar phenomena largely by convention rather than by strict logic. Both the Berlin Heights movement and the Masons were in many ways similar to Oneida, and yet neither was defined as a religious movement. For Towner, Unitarianism was comparable to Oneida; today we tend to think of it as harmless to the point of being bland, yet in its demotion of Jesus it was radical in its early days. As the biblical example of Moses reminds us, the legal profession is a secularized offspring of religion. Furthermore, both Towner and Newhouse illustrate the fact that radical religious movements like Oneida do not really consist of a single charismatic leader, John Humphrey Noyes in this case, dominating a mass of followers. The subculture-evolution model of cult formation may not exactly fit Oneida, but deserves consideration even in cases of a famous leader. Towner was not by nature a follower, and without Newhouse the Oneida community might have failed economically long before the surrender of power by its charismatic leader.

Systematic Census Data

Consideration of four individual members of the Oneida community revealed that they experienced very different social relations and contributed in very different ways to its history. Thus, we need to consider not only individuals but also their social relations with each other. Children were intentionally separated from their mothers at Oneida, as part of the general plan to dissolve biological families into a spiritual community. Yet when the community abandoned its formal social order in 1880, nuclear families immediately reemerged. We saw that clearly in the cases of Pierrepont Noyes and James Towner, and the so-called Townerites illustrated the existence of social groups within the community, while many others may have existed implicitly. One well-documented example is the group of women who shared the then-popular hobby of collectively sewing together quilts, and several websites today display the "Best Quilt," one saying, "It tells the story of women in 1873 who wanted a remembrance of the Community and its life."[16] With the sociology of the family in mind, we can approach the question of Oneida's internal structure of relationships using tools borrowed from demography.

One way to gain more context on the life of a person like Towner, who belonged to an enduring family and linked one utopian phenomenon to others, is to look him up in online archives of the historical censuses, including the 1875 census of New York State, which came soon after he joined Oneida. His lifespan was from August 18, 1823, to November 19, 1913. The 1830 and 1840 censuses did not list children's names, and 1890 records no longer exist, but table 8.2 shows him and his household or family in eight censuses. His first wife really did have the romantic name of Cinderella, but census takers often misspelled it. Their son Frederick

Table 8.2. The Towner Family in the Records of the United States Census

Name	Age	Sex	Profession	Other Data	Birthplace
1850 U.S. Census, Westfield Township, Medina County, Ohio, pages 192–193					
Samuel R. Richards	33	M	Blacksmith	$700	New York
Amy Richards	29	F			New York
Maria	8	F			Ohio
William	6	M			Ohio
George	2	M			Ohio
Daniel C. Cornwall	34	M	Farmer	$800	New York
James W. Towner	27	M	Clergyman	married in year	New York
Cindrilla	21	F		married in year	Ohio
Joseph C. Henry	38	M	Shoe maker	$350	Massachusetts
1856 Iowa State Census, Dover Township, Fayette County, page 392					
J. W. Towner	32	M	Lawyer		New York
C. A. Towner	27	F			Ohio
A. J. Towner	5	M			Ohio
F. E. Towner	0	M			Ohio
1860 U.S. Census, West Union Township, Fayette County, Iowa, page 128					
J. W. Towner	36	M	Lawyer	$1,200; $500	New York
C. S. Towner	30	F			Ohio
A. J. Towner	9	M			Ohio
F. E. Towner	4	M			Iowa
H. Sweet	38	F			Ohio
M. A. Tenny	17	F			Ohio
L. Mallory	29	F	School Teacher		Ohio
1870 U.S. Census, 10th Ward, Cleveland, Ohio, page 115					
Towner, James W.	48	M	Lawyer	$2000	New York
Towner, Cindarilla	41	F	Keeping House		Ohio
- Arthur	19	M	Work on Rail Road		Ohio

Table 8.2. (*cont.*)

1870 U.S. Census, 10th Ward, Cleveland, Ohio, page 115					
- Frederick	14	M			Iowa
- Lillian	9	F			Iowa
1875 New York State Census, 2nd Election District, Town of Lenore, Madison Co., page 43					
Jas. W. Towner	51	M	Lawyer	married	Essex Co.
Cinderilla Towner	46	F		married	Ohio
Arthur Towner	24	M			Ohio
Frederic Towner	19	M			Ohio
1880 U.S. Census, Town of Lenore, Madison Co., New York, page 53					
Towner, James W.	56	M	Lawyer	married	New York
Towner, Cinderella	51	F		married	Ohio
Turner, Arthur	29	M	Machinist	married	Iowa
Turner, Lillian	19	F	Gen Service		Ohio
1900 U.S. Census, Santa Ana Township, California, page 3					
Towner, James W.	76	M	Lawyer	head	New York
Towner, Emilie M.	67	F		wife	Massachusetts
1910 U.S. Census, Santa Ana Township, California, page 19A					
Towner, James W.	86	M	own income	head	New York
Towner, Emilie	77	F		wife	Massachusetts

died soon after the 1875 Census, so we do not see him afterward. Their daughter is missing from the 1875 Census, which might indicate she was visiting elsewhere, or simply was overlooked. After Cinderella died in 1894, James married Emilie M. Van Scotten, who shows up as his wife in 1900 and 1910.

All these data came from Ancestry.com, but initially I could not find Towner in the 1850 records using that service's search engine. However, the related site called RootsWeb had a page for him where users as well as Ancestry.com employees posted information, noting that in 1850 he and his newlywed wife lived in the same household as did Amy Richards in Ohio.[17] Searching for her revealed that the Ancestry.com indexers had misread Towner's name as Lownes, thus blocking the search. Census search engines use a variety of algorithms searching for similar names, of which the most influential is Soundex, patented way back in 1918, used by the U.S. Census indexing projects of the 1930s, incorporated as an option in Ancestry.com, and requiring that the first letter of the name be read correctly. Note that the 1880 U.S. Census itself misspelled the last names of two of Towner's children as Turner. Data like those in table 8.2 can serve as a framework for collecting other data, and RootsWeb is an example of how vast historical databases are being assembled and annotated by large numbers of people, many of whom are volunteers.

I am occasionally credited with having brought the original documents of the U.S. Census to the attention of scholars studying religious movements, particularly in the case of the Shakers, back in 1982 (Cosgel 2001). The actual story illustrates the value of good luck and having an open mind to new research possibilities, without requiring any particularly creative set of assumptions. I was a member of the faculty of the Sociology Department at the University of Washington, where demographers were doing a study that tracked men from the 1880 U.S. Census to the 1900 Census (Guest 1987; Guest, Landale, and McCann 1989). At that time, the U.S. government maintained microfilms of old censuses at a dozen locations around the country, and one of them happened to be just down the hill from our campus. My colleagues had set up a microfilm reader that could photocopy the records, and were kind enough to let me use it despite the fact that I was not a member of their research team. After leaving that university, I was able to continue the work at other locations.

In Massachusetts, the existence of state censuses in 1855 and 1865 made it possible to track individual members of that state's Shaker communities every five years from 1850 to 1870 (Bainbridge 1982, 1984). Table 8.3 illustrates one kind of longitudinal analysis for the population of the Oneida community—one that looks at the changing age distribution. The analysis covers just the main branch at Oneida, New York,

Table 8.3. Changing Age Distribution of the Oneida Community, 1850–1880

	1850	1855	1860	1865	1870	1875	1880
Age < 20	45.6%	40.4%	34.0%	23.8%	18.9%	27.4%	27.5%
Age 20–49	44.0%	44.4%	47.4%	48.1%	52.4%	43.6%	38.5%
Age 50+	10.4%	15.2%	18.7%	28.2%	28.6%	29.1%	34.0%
Total	182	171	209	206	227	237	200
Female	46.2%	47.4%	50.2%	52.9%	54.2%	53.6%	51.0%

especially leaving out the most significant other branch in Wallingford, Connecticut, because data for the years 1855, 1865, and 1875 were not available. Wikipedia implied that all members had moved to the main site before 1880: "The branches were closed in 1854 except for the Wallingford branch, which operated until devastated by a tornado in 1878."[18] However, the *Historical Dictionary of Utopianism* says, "Wallingford kept in close contact with Oneida and remained in existence until the demise of the mother community in 1881, its membership varying between 25 and 85 during the 30 years it remained a Perfectionist enclave" (Morris and Kross 2004:318). Indeed, the 1880 Connecticut census lists twenty-three members at the Wallingford community.

The most noteworthy trend in the age distribution is the huge drop in the percentage of children, from 45.6 percent in 1850 to only 18.9 percent in 1870. One way to understand Oneida's complex marriage system is as a collective birth control method, in which for example women past the childbearing ages often took responsibility for erotic interactions with young men, and men were taught a technique to avoid impregnation during intercourse. But in the mere five years from 1870 to 1875, the percentage of children hops back up to 27.4 percent. As table 8.1 shows, the reproductive activity by the leader increased in the 1870s, and the same must have happened for many followers as well.

There is something suspicious about the 1880 data. The round number of members, exactly two hundred, is not implausible, because given a large dataset some numbers will have zeroes to the right. However, each page of the 1880 census has fifty lines of data, one for each person enumerated, so the Oneida data fill exactly four pages, and loss of a page could easily have rounded the total down to two hundred. When I had worked with microfilms and original paper census manuscripts decades earlier, I had counted a total of 262 members for Oneida and Wallingford combined, but now the total seems to be only 200 + 23 = 223. To explore this discrepancy, I combined the data for 1875 and 1880 in a spreadsheet, and began linking data for individuals across the two censuses.

Once I had linked as many names across the two censuses as I confidently could, I sorted alphabetically by the 1875 data, and found that only one of the first thirty-nine names could be found in 1880. That one case was Alice M. Ackley, who married, became Alice M. Kinsley, and thus moved down in alphabetical order. Using the online membership database, I checked to see how many of the elderly 1875 members with names early in the alphabet might have died by 1880, and found that Fanny Knisley Barron died in 1878 at the age of seventy-four. Of the six people age sixty or above in 1875, fully five were still alive at the time of the 1880 census: John M. Abbott (age seventy-eight at death), Laura Ann Bishop Abbott (eighty-four), Emily Harriett Dutton Allen (ninety-one), Alvah Barron (eighty-nine), and Mary P. Beach (seventy-six). Clearly, the 1880 Census is missing the people at the beginning of the alphabet, and indeed the first page of Oneida's membership appears to be missing from this copy of the U.S. Census manuscripts. Whenever we have evidence that data are missing, we lose confidence in the results of our analysis, although the problem here may not be too serious, as it would have been if the loss were obviously correlated with one of our analytical variables, as with other Oneida censuses that listed people by age rather than in alphabetical order.

Public Opinion

It is not feasible to administer public opinion surveys in the past, and the image of a scholar climbing into a time machine holding a stack of questionnaires is ridiculous. However, some mass media of the past have been preserved, and famous religious phenomena like Oneida are familiar to at least many people today, if not the entire living population. Earlier we quoted from an angry statement by John Mears, published in the *New York Tribune* and accessed through Newspapers.com. There currently exist several such online newspaper archives, and a very different one may be better designed for many research purposes. Chronicling America, begun in 2005, is a database and companion website produced by the National Digital Newspaper Program (NDNP), a partnership between the Library of Congress (LoC) and the National Endowment for the Humanities, maintained by the LoC.[19] As of June 13, 2015, it offered clear images of 9,550,430 newspaper pages dating from 1836 to 1922, with a rather sophisticated word search system. It was possible to look for a particular combination of words in a particular year and state of the union. For example, in the year 1922, only 0.7 percent of 3,762 pages from Texas newspapers contained the word "Jewish," compared with fully 4.1 percent of 18,791 pages from newspapers published in New York State. Here we shall very briefly consider how this marvelous database can be used for systematic social science research on religion, without dealing with all the many challenges and opportunities.

Entering "John Humphrey Noyes" as the search term, with no other variables, turns up sixty-nine newspaper pages, the first of which dates from 1869. It consists of excerpts from the recently published edition of *New America* by William Hepworth Dixon, who had visited and studied several religious communes ("Dixon's New America" 1867:6; Dixon 1867). In 1875, Charles Nordhoff published a book about these communities, *Communistic Societies of the United States*, also based on visits and still widely read today (Nordhoff 1875). Rather richer in social theory was the study published by John Humphrey Noyes himself in 1870, *History of American Socialisms* (Noyes 1870). The documents he had used are preserved at his alma mater, Yale University, notably the A. J. MacDonald Collection of Utopian Materials.[20] MacDonald had planned to write a great book on American communes and had interviewed people at many of them, including Noyes, but died unexpectedly in 1854. Years later, by a miracle, Noyes discovered that MacDonald's notes still existed and employed them in writing his own scholarly survey. Thus the very first newspaper article turned up by this particular search connects periodicals to books and demonstrates that social research on religious utopian communities was well established nearly a century and a half ago.

In order to see how quantitative research can be done with the old newspaper archives, we shall briefly use much broader topics that turn up far more newspaper articles than searching terms related to the Oneida community can do. Table 8.4 shows results of two simple tabulation comparisons across two-decade periods of time for the entire nation. First, we imagine that we are beginning a historical study of the place in American culture of that parareligious phenomenon, astrology. None of the newspapers from 1836 represented in the collection contained that word, but three did in 1837. An article published by the *Caledonian* in St. Johnsbury, Vermont, referred to astrology in Chinese marriages. An article in the *Vermont Telegraph* listed astrologers among the professions heavily taxed in Burma. The *Maumee Express* in Ohio carried a joke news item, reporting, "A learned German astrologer has ascertained that the earth will be destroyed by a commet [sic] in just twenty-two million years! The astute philosopher deserves the public thanks for postponing the event to so distant a day." Naturally, one might want to invest several days reading all the early newspaper articles about astrology, but these three indicate that it was considered a foreign superstition, even worthy of ridicule. These examples also make a methodological point: the indexing system was asked to find the word "astrology" but also came up with "astrologer" and "astrologers."

As table 8.4 shows, the frequency of "astrology" and closely related words increased greatly from 1840 to 1919, but the population and newspaper publishing also increased, so researchers will need some way of norming the data. Of course, one could calculate the percent of all newspaper pages in each period containing the word, but this might not correct for shifts in the general scope of newspapers, for example, an increase in the pages devoted to obituaries, real estate sales, advertisements, and pictures. Here, we can compare the frequency of "astrology" with that of "astronomy," a word in the same general topic area but without the quasi-religious connotation. In 1840–1859 the frequency of "astrology" was only 18.8 percent of the frequency of "astronomy," but by the early decades of the twentieth century the mystical view of the heavens had gained more attention than the scientific.

Our second example shows how searching for combinations of words can be useful. Suppose we want to compare the popularity of religious music with that of secular music, a study that could fill an entire book. But some of the most common music-related words have multiple meanings, for example, "band," which can be a verb as well as a synonym for the noun "ring." A purist might say we cannot know the meaning of "band" without reading it in context, and for some studies that may be necessary. But here we can improve the situation somewhat by considering only pages that contain the word "music." We do that by searching for three pairs of words: "music" and "band," "music" and "hymn," "music" and "choir." It appears that musical bands were dropping in popularity, relative to all other kinds of music, but were mentioned on a large faction of the pages containing "music," dropping from 58.7 percent to 39.0 percent. Strikingly, the fraction of pages

Table 8.4. Examples of Word Frequency Searches in Historical Newspapers

Years	astrology	astronomy	astrology/ astronomy	music	music and band	music and hymn	music and choir
1840–1859	1265	6713	18.8%	107,590	58.7%	6.6%	5.0%
1860–1879	3212	7411	43.3%	315,285	58.4%	6.4%	6.7%
1880–1899	9792	16,179	60.5%	914,197	49.9%	5.6%	9.8%
1900–1919	18,091	14,969	120.9%	1,550,768	39.0%	4.4%	10.2%
1840–1919	32,360	45,272	71.5%	2,887,840	45.3%	5.0%	9.5%

containing "music" that also contained "choir" rose from 5.0 percent to 10.2 percent.

Quantitative research need not be limited to raw numbers, percentages, or ratios, because the possibility of searching for combinations of words allows assembly of tables suitable for correlation coefficients. For example, in the 1840–1859 data, 893 newspaper pages included all three of these words: "music," "choir," and "hymn." Of those pages having "music" but not "choir," just 6.5 percent had "hymn." Of those having both "music" and "choir," fully 20.0 percent also had "hymn."

Of course, scholars would want to read many of the newspaper articles turned up in these searches, in part to understand how they were intended to shape public opinion in the period when the Oneida community still existed, or was fresh in public memory. One way to do comparable research on today's public opinion is to begin with familiar search engines like Google, which on June 14, 2015, got about forty-two thousand hits for "John Humphrey Noyes." Depending upon the nature of the religious phenomenon under study, there may exist current opinion shapers, even for an extinct movement like Oneida. The Oneida Community Mansion House is a historical landmark, with an appealing website.[21] Connected to the museums and archives that some of the most prominent communes have become is the Communal Studies Association, which publishes the journal *Communal Societies* and proclaims these goals:

> To encourage and facilitate the preservation, restoration, and public interpretation of America's historic communal sites.
>
> To provide a forum for the study of intentional communities, past and present.
>
> To communicate to the general public the successful ideas from, and lessons learned by, communal societies.[22]

Many superficially defunct religious movements have recently experienced something like virtual revival in online communities, notably the Process Church of the Final Judgement that was very similar to Oneida but lasted roughly 1963–1975 (Bainbridge 1978). Today, while officially defunct, it is represented by numerous websites, musical bands, and three Facebook groups.[23] Not so, apparently, for the Perfectionism taught by John Humphrey Noyes. The Oneida Community Mansion House has a Facebook page, but it serves as an information source mainly about events at the museum.[24] No group is attached to it, and clicking "like" opens a "More Pages You May Like" list that is simply advertisements for small businesses of the sort tourists might visit. Whether intended as jokes or unusual research tools, three personal Facebook pages exist that were supposedly created by John Humphrey Noyes.

Conclusion

Oneida provided an excellent example of the kinds of social science research possible with online historical data, but students and professional academics alike need to keep in mind two caveats. (1) Some imagined research projects may not be feasible, for example, projects focused on one of the other religious communes of Oneida's period, because the data are too fragmentary or unreliable. (2) Some very valuable research projects may be entirely feasible, but we have not yet imagined them or discovered the practical method to accomplish them. Taken together, these two points suggest the importance of pilot studies, and the need to find the right balance between ambition and modesty in beginning a research project. An example of the first point from my own experience was the many hours I wasted comparing 1860 Census records of Baton Rouge, Louisiana, with published lists of recruits to the Confederate Army, hoping to determine the social factors shaping when men would volunteer but finding that I could not reliably match many of the names. An example of the second point was my discovery of the increasingly extensive online resources devoted to the long-defunct Process Church of the Final Judgement.

The data sources available online are constantly growing, but unevenly, especially for historical data that originated in different decades. No U.S. Census records more recent than 1940 are currently available, because of the confidentiality rules governing privacy of living people, and Chronicling America ends with newspapers published in 1922, largely because the goal for historians was to begin from the beginning, and only slowly work their way up to the present. Of course, many more recent publications are covered by copyright, and the effort to scan in all the newspapers and magazines of the entire twentieth century would be more than monumental. There is something paradoxical about the fact that a huge gap from about 1925 until 1995 exists in online historical records, given how extensive publication was during that span of seven decades, yet the explanations are obvious.

Vast amounts of recent information have naturally flooded online, since the birth of the Internet, but we cannot rely upon it all to persist. In 2004, the respected newspaper *Rocky Mountain News* published an article, both on paper and online, about a very successful animal shelter called Best Friends that had evolved over the years from the far more radical Process. But in 2009, *Rocky Mountain News* went out of business, and since then the text of the very informative article has only sometimes been available, on often unreliable websites (Kilzer 2004). In response to the 2004 article, Best Friends posted a six-part, accurate if somewhat detoxified account of its early history, titled "Before Best Friends." As of April 29, 2016, two of the installments could still be found by entering the obscure place name "Xtul" into the website's search engine. The URLs of those pages suggest what the URLs of the other four must have been, but entering them into the browser address field results in a standard page of the website, with the message "Sorry. That dated story was removed." The Internet Archive, Wayback Machine, had saved material from the Best Friends website 1,873 times, beginning December 18, 1996, but no part of that historic article was included.[25]

Linking Oneida to the frankly rather similar Process reminds us that today's religious movements quickly become historical with the passage of time. In his book *The Nature of Social Science*, sociologist George Homans argued not only that all the social sciences should unite as a single comprehensive discipline but also that history belonged among them (Homans 1967). As Erik Erikson showed in his biography of Martin Luther, the history of religion can also be approached from a psychological perspective (Erikson 1958). Thus there is nothing innovative about suggesting that the history of religious movements can be written in social scientific terms. However, the vast proliferation of historical data online, and the development of sophisticated tools like search engines, could be in the process of revolutionizing social history, in religion as in many other domains. This chapter has only hinted at the possibilities, and it can only begin to demonstrate the importance of careful assessment of information sources, which is central to the historian's craft. Yet the free or low-cost access to online historical resources offers tremendous opportunities for education of students as well as enabling professional research in the social science of religion.

NOTES

1 The views expressed in this essay do not necessarily represent the views of the National Science Foundation or the United States. [Legally required note.]

2 Salmon Creek Genealogy & Publishing, "A Genealogy of the Oneida Community," accessed January 25, 2015, www.laurahatch.com.

3 Syracuse University Library, "Hand-book of the Oneida Community 1875," accessed January 25, 2015, library.syr.edu.

4 "Gen. Grant's Day of Rest," *New York Times*, October 11, 1880, p. 1.

5 Wikipedia, "Charles J. Guiteau," accessed March 8, 2015, en.wikipedia.org.

6 Georgetown University, "Charles Guiteau Collection," accessed January 12, 2014, repository.library.georgetown.edu

7 Hayes and Hayes 1882.

8 Syracuse University Library, "The Oneida Community Collection," accessed July 25, 2015, library.syr.edu.

9 Oneida Victor Inc., Ltd., "Oneida Victor Long Spring Traps," accessed May 24, 2015, www.oneidavictor.com.

10 Syracuse University Library, "The Oneida Community Collection," accessed May 24, 2015, library.syr.edu.

11 Wikipedia, "Josiah Warren," accessed May 24, 2015, en.wikipedia.org.

12 Find a Grave, "Cinderella Sweet Towner," accessed April 19, 2015, www.findagrave.com.

13 Find a Grave, "James W. Towner," accessed April 19, 2015, www.findagrave.com.

14 Ibid.

15 Rootsweb, "TOWNER-L Archives," accessed April 19, 2015, archiver.rootsweb.ancestry.com.

16 Waltsmusings, "The Oneida Community," accessed April 28, 2016, waltsmusings.wordpress.com.

17 Rootsweb, "Bly, McKnight, Mulcahy, and Plosila Families," accessed May 25, 2015, wc.rootsweb.ancestry.com.

18 Wikipedia, "Oneida Community," accessed March 31, 2015, en.wikipedia.org.

19 Library of Congress, "Chronicling America: Historic American Newspapers," accessed June 14, 2015, chroniclingamerica.loc.gov.

20 Discover Yale Digital Content, "A. J. Macdonald Writings on American Utopian Communities, 1843–1865," accessed January 25, 2015, discover.odai.yale.edu.

21 Oneida Community Mansion House, "Our History," accessed June 14, 2015, www.oneidacommunity.org.

22 Communal Studies Association, "About," accessed June 14, 2015, www.communalstudies.org.

23 Process Church of the Final Judgment, accessed July 25, 2015, www.processchurchofthefinaljudgment.com; Sabbath Assembly, accessed July 25, 2015, sabbath-assembly.bandcamp.com; Facebook, "Process Church of the Final Judgement," accessed July 25, 2015, www.facebook.com; Facebook, "Reunion Group for the Process Church & Foundation Faith," accessed July 25, 2015, www.facebook.com.

24 Facebook, "Oneida Community Mansion House," accessed November 30, 2016, www.facebook.com.

25 Wayback Machine, bestfriends.org, accessed April 29, 2016, web.archive.org; bestfriends.org.

WORKS CITED

Bainbridge, William Sims. 1978. *Satan's Power*. Berkeley: University of California Press.

Bainbridge, William Sims. 1982. "Shaker Demographics: An Example of the Use of U.S. Census Enumeration Schedules." *Journal for the Scientific Study of Religion* 21: 352–65.

Bainbridge, William Sims. 1984. "The Decline of the Shakers: Evidence from the United States Census." *Communal Societies* 4: 19–34.

Berger, Peter. 1963. "Charisma and Religious Innovation: The Social Location of Israelite Prophecy." *American Sociological Review* 28(6): 940–50.

Carden, Maren L. 1969. *Oneida: Utopian Community to Modern Corporation*. Syracuse, NY: Syracuse University Press.

Caswell, Thomas H., ed. 1894. *Proceedings of the Grand Chapter of Royal Arch Masons of the State of California at Its Annual Convention*. San Francisco: Eastman.

Cosgel, Metin M. 2001. "The Commitment Process in a Religious Commune: The Shakers." *Journal for the Scientific Study of Religion* 40(1): 27–38.

Crosby, Thomas F. 1998. "A Rare First Edition: J. W. Towner, Orange County's Original Superior Court Judge." *Chapman Law Review* 1: 91–104.

"Dixon's New America." 1867. *New-York Tribune*, March 14, p. 6.

Dixon, William H. 1867. *New America*. Philadelphia: Lippincott.

Erikson, Erik H. 1958. *Young Man Luther: A Study in Psychoanalysis and History*. New York: Norton.

Foster, Lawrence. 1988. "The Rise and Fall of Utopia: The Oneida Community Crises of 1852 and 1879." *Communal Societies* 8: 1–17.

Fox, Russell. 2010. *The Noyes Plays: The True History of John Humphrey Noyes and the Oneida Community*. Bloomington, IN: iUniverse.

Friedland, William H. 1964. "For a Sociological Concept of Charisma." *Social Forces* 43: 18–26.

Guest, Avery. 1987. "Notes from the National Panel Study: Linkage and Migration in the Late-Nineteenth Century." *Historical Methods* 20: 63–77.

Guest, Avery M., Nancy S. Landale, and James C. McCann. 1989. "Intergenerational Occupational Mobility in the Late-19th-Century United States." *Social Forces* 68(2): 351–78.

Guiteau, Charles J. 1879. *The Truth: A Companion to the Bible*. Boston: Lothrup.

Harding, Arthur R. 1907. *Steel Traps*. Columbus, OH: Harding.
Hayes, Henry G., and Charles Joseph Hayes. 1882. *A Complete History of the Life and Trial of Charles Julius Guiteau, Assassin of President Garfield*. Philadelphia: Hubbard.
Homans, George C. 1967. *The Nature of Social Science*. New York: Harcourt, Brace, and World.
Kanter, Rosabeth M. 1972. *Commitment and Community: Communes and Utopias in Sociological Perspective*. Cambridge, MA: Harvard University Press.
Kilzer, Lou. 2004. "Friends Find Their Calling." *Rocky Mountain News*, February 28.
Lynd, Robert S., and Helen Merrell Lynd. 1929. *Middletown: A Study in Contemporary American Culture*. New York: Harcourt, Brace.
Lynd, Robert S., and Helen Merrell Lynd. 1937. *Middletown in Transition: A Study in Cultural Conflicts*. New York: Harcourt, Brace.
Mears, John. 1879. "The Oneida Community." *New York Daily Tribune*, March 24.
Morris, James M., and Andrea L. Kross. 2004. *Historical Dictionary of Utopianism*. Lanham, MD: Scarecrow Press.
Newhouse, Sewell. 1869. *The Trapper's Guide*. New York: Oakley.
Nordhoff, Charles. 1875. *The Communistic Societies of the United States*. New York: Harper.
Noyes, John H. 1847. *The Berean: A Manual for the Help of Those Who Seek the Faith of the Primitive Church*. Putney, VT: Spiritual Magazine.
Noyes, John H. 1870. *History of American Socialisms*. Philadelphia: Lippincott.
Noyes, Pierrepont. 1937. *My Father's House: An Oneida Boyhood*. New York: Farrar & Rinehart.
Olin, Spencer C., Jr. 1980. "The Oneida Community and the Instability of Charismatic Authority." *Journal of American History* 67(2): 285–300.
Passet, Joanne E. 2005. "Beyond Berlin Heights: The Free Lovers in History and Memory." *Communal Societies* 8: 91–112.
Roth, Guenther. 1975. "Socio-Historical Model and Developmental Theory: Charismatic Community, Charisma of Reason, and the Counterculture." *American Sociological Review* 40(2): 148–57.
"Santa Ana." 1894. *Los Angeles Herald*, May 21, p. 3.
Shils, Edward. 1965. "Charisma, Order, and Status." *American Sociological Review* 30(2): 199–213.
Stark, Rodney, and William Sims Bainbridge. 1979. "Of Churches, Sects, and Cults: Preliminary Concepts for a Theory of Religious Movements." *Journal for the Scientific Study of Religion* 18: 117–31.
Stark, Werner. 1965. "The Routinization of Charisma: A Consideration of Catholicism." *Sociological Analysis* 26(4): 203–11.
Stephan, Karen H., and G. Edward Stephan. 1973. "Religion and the Survival of Utopian Communities." *Journal for the Scientific Study of Religion* 12: 89–100.
Terry, D. Jamez. 2011. "The 'Assassination-Instrument' of God: Religious Interpretations of the Garfield Assassination." *Cult/ure: The Graduate Journal of Harvard Divinity School* 6, cultandculture.org.

Towner, James W. 1913. "James William Towner." *Pacific Unitarian* 22(2): 40–41.
Towner, James W. 1914. *A Genealogy of the Towner Family*. Los Angeles: Times Mirror.
van de Warker, Ely. 1884. "A Gynecological Study of the Oneida Community." *American Journal of Obstetrics and Disease of Women and Children* 17(8): 785–810.
Weber, Max. 1978 [1922]. *Economy and Society*. Berkeley: University of California Press.

9.

What Is a Religious NGO?

Conceptual and Classificatory Challenges in Research on Transnational Religion

EVELYN L. BUSH

Much has changed in the study of international relations in recent decades, particularly the actors that capture researchers' attention. A field long dominated by a focus on states now places greater emphasis on civil society organizations, many of which have been associated with major social and political transformations. Key among these are national and international nongovernmental organizations (NGOs and INGOs). Mobilizing around a plethora of social and political issues ranging from education to healthcare to human rights, INGOs have dramatically increased in numbers and relevance, especially since the end of World War II and the establishment of the United Nations (Boli and Thomas 1999:23). Boli and Thomas argued in 1999 that INGOs embody characteristics of an expanding "world culture," defined by features—individualism, bureaucracy, rationalism, commitment to science—that sociologists of religion have long associated with the concept of secularism.

An example of a well-known INGO is Oxfam International, which was founded in 1942 to "challenge the structural causes of the injustice of poverty" (Oxfam International 2017). In addition to providing humanitarian relief in response to natural disasters, Oxfam works through a variety of information campaigns designed to encourage grassroots mobilization against unfair political and economic practices that produce pockets of concentrated poverty in many parts of the world. Oxfam's website provides a statement of its beliefs, describing itself as "secular, open-minded and pluralistic. We welcome all beliefs that advance human rights" (Oxfam International 2017).

But at the same time that secular INGOs have been acting as carriers of global civil society transformations, religious actors have been quietly making inroads of their own, and also in the form of NGOs. An example would be World Vision International (WVI). Like Oxfam, WVI addresses poverty on an international scale, and is a major provider of humanitarian aid in the wake of major disasters. But unlike Oxfam, with its focus on political-economic structures, WVI addresses poverty primarily through its child sponsorship program, describing how "[e]verything we do has just one goal: the sustained well-being of children, especially the most vulnerable" (World Vision International 2017a). Most significantly, also unlike Oxfam, WVI describes itself as a Christian organization whose mission, in part, is to "[w]itness to Jesus Christ by life, deed, word, and sign that encourages [sic] people to respond to the Gospel" (World Vision International 2017b).

Like secular NGOs, religious NGOs like WVI mobilize around a plethora of issues ranging from opposition to human trafficking to encouraging debt forgiveness and providing HIV/AIDS prevention and care. Indeed, for religious and secular actors alike, the NGO has become a standard form of organization through which civil society groups organize, especially in their transnational manifestations. For those endeavoring to engage with governmental and intergovernmental institutions, whether to obtain funding from them, secure contracts to carry out their programs, or influence their policies, the NGO is the form of organization that is recognized as the legitimate vehicle for doing so. This is as true for religious as for secular organizations, as the former have also increased dramatically in numbers in recent decades (Bush 2007). Consequently, if we want to paint an accurate picture of religious presence and influence in civil society, we cannot confine our analyses to "the religious sphere." To the contrary, we need measures of religion's presence and influence across what are typically thought of as "secular" NGO sectors.

Unfortunately, attempts to collect data on religious INGOs often confront vexing challenges. Some of these challenges are rooted in unsettled analytical questions about how to define and code for key terms like "religious" and "nongovernmental"; others are technical in nature, and simply make it difficult to arrive at accurate counts of religious NGOs (RNGOs). Both types of problems will be covered in this chapter, which is organized into three sections.

The first section focuses on the challenge of identifying "religiosity" within NGOs. Drawing on my own research, I will show how the hybrid nature of religious NGOs can often result in their religious identities being overlooked or misclassified. I illustrate how the use of multiple measures of religiosity can help ameliorate these problems, offering more detail, precision, and flexibility in later analysis. Unlike other religious organizations, where a single dichotomous code of "religious" or "not religious" is used, I propose that, in the study of NGOs, more fine-grained measures are needed that allow us to understand where and to what extent religion permeates organizational goals and activities.

The second section addresses the problem of distinguishing NGOs both from other forms of religious organizations and from state-sponsored actors. This sorting process is more difficult than might first appear and requires precise coding criteria to ensure accurate measures. Arriving at valid measures of religion that capture these differences is important both for descriptive clarity and for testing some of the theoretical questions addressed with these data.

The third and final section focuses on technical problems endemic to research on international organizations using online directories and websites. For a variety of reasons, online sources often fall short of meeting the criteria for sound sampling frames and are fraught with validity and reliability issues. While the challenges are many, I will focus on a small number that I think will be most useful for researchers embarking for the first time on international NGO research.

The challenges described in this chapter emerged in the context of three separate research projects examining "religious NGOs." The first project was part of my dissertation research (Bush 2005), which focused on how secular world culture has influenced global religious mobilization, particularly at the United Nations (UN). This multimethod project included the collection and comparison of religious organizational data from two different international organizational directories, the Yearbook of International Organizations (YBIO) and an online directory of human rights organizations compiled by Human Rights Internet (HRI). The second project entailed a later effort to construct a more current and detailed data file of religious human rights NGOs (hereafter referred to as "HR project" or "HR data file") for inclusion in the

Association of Religion Data Archives (ARDA).[1] The data file was created by coding websites and directory profiles of some eight hundred religious human rights organizations listed in HRI's directory.[2] The third project, titled "Religious NGOs at the United Nations in New York and Geneva," examined how religious NGOs attempt to influence the UN and with what effects (hereafter referred to as "UN project").[3] This three-year project, funded by the Arts and Humanities Research Council (AHRC) in the United Kingdom, was also carried out using multiple methods, one of which was a survey of UN-affiliated NGOs. In contrast to the HR data file, wherein all of the NGOs (n = 640) included are "religious," the AHRC survey contains survey responses (n = 192) from both secular (n = 134) and religious (n = 58) NGOs.

A few notes on abbreviations: for brevity's sake, throughout this chapter, except where finer distinctions are analytically relevant, I will use the acronym "RNGO" (religious nongovernmental organization) rather loosely to include both religious NGOs and faith-based organizations (FBOs) which, as will be described, are not precisely the same thing. I will use "RNGO" and "NGO" to be inclusive of national and international actors, except where the distinction between national and international is germane to the issue at hand. I will use the word "directories" broadly to include a variety of informational sources, including directories, yearbooks, organizational databases used by professional associations, etc.

Identifying the "Religious" in Religious NGOs

In the study of RNGOs beyond the religious sphere, and especially internationally, it quickly becomes clear that religion is a contested category, and that there exist a variety of cognitive schema that individuals and organizations use to conceptually locate religion within societies. As a result, researchers cannot assume that potential sources of data are organized along conceptual lines that conform to their own definitions or the needs of their research. Incompatible definitions of what exactly a "religious NGO" is, and of what features of an organization are relevant to defining them as such, can be sources of error if not made explicit.

Challenge #1: Locating the "Religious" in NGOs

Unfortunately, the task of locating religious organizations beyond the religious sphere is not as straightforward a task as it might initially appear to be. Because of their hybrid structures, the determination as to whether or not a given organization is, in fact, "religious" can be difficult to make, not only for researchers but also for members of NGOs. Consider, for example, some of the responses Julia Berger (2003) received when, conducting her research on religious NGOs at the UN, she asked interview respondents, "Are you a religious NGO?"

> A representative of Jewish Women International (JWI) was unable to respond . . . commenting that the answer depends on one's definition of "religious," adding that JWI "is founded on the Jewish principles of tikkun olam" (repairing the world) and observes Jewish holidays. The distinction between "religious" and "secular" was equally challenging for the Zionist Organization of America, which sees itself as "more secular than religious but . . . Jewish." Other organizations described themselves as "non-secular" (US Servas), "a-religious" (Petits Freres) . . . "faith-based working in a secular way" (Susila Dharma International), whereas others admitted to never having contemplated the question. (Berger 2003:21)

During my own fieldwork on religious NGOs, I had similar encounters, wherein individuals I interviewed wrestled with the question of whether or not their organizations "really" were religious, and the results of the NGO survey likewise suggested that self-identification as a "religious NGO" is more complicated than one might expect. For example, our survey asked three different questions intended to capture religiosity. The first question was intended to identify what are referred to in the United States as "faith-based organizations" (FBOs). The survey asked, "Is your organization formally affiliated with any religious organization, institution, or denomination?" Thirty-two respondents answered "yes" to this question.

Second, the survey asked, "Does your NGO identify with a religious tradition?" This question cast a wider net, attempting to reach beyond organizations that are formally affiliated with religious institutions proper, to include those that identify as religious but do not have such formal ties. Forty-two respondents answered "yes" to this question. So far, there were no surprises.

But then we asked a third question: "Which of the following best characterizes your NGO?" Importantly, the response options were not mutually exclusive; respondents could choose multiple responses. The breakdown of responses (n = 192) was as described in table 9.1:

Table 9.1. Which Best Characterizes Your NGO? (N = 192)

Secular	110
Secular w/ Religious Roots	16
Religious	9
Faith-based	34
Ethnic/Cultural	12
Spiritual	14
Other	17

Surprisingly, only nine respondents chose the label "religious," and accounting for overlap between categories, only thirty-seven NGOs described themselves as either religious or faith-based or both. To clarify, even though forty-two organizations said that they identified with a religious tradition (second question), only nine of those would describe their organization as "religious." Even if we include the apparently preferable descriptor "faith-based," we still fall short of the forty-two, with only thirty-seven organizations choosing to self-designate as either "religious" or "faith-based." It is important to remember here that the options were not mutually exclusive, meaning that the outcome is not a result of forcing respondents to choose one option over another.

Rejection of the religious label has a variety of sources. For example, Jewish NGOs are sometimes hesitant to describe their organizations as "religious" because their memberships include secular Jews or those who think of Judaism more in ethnic than religious terms. Some organizations that might otherwise identify as religious have concerns about being inaccurately associated with proselytism, a practice that, according to open-ended responses to the UN survey, some NGOs consider ethically problematic for service-oriented NGOs. Some indigenous groups do not recognize a separate sphere or institution where a thing called "religion" resides, instead viewing the separation between religious and secular as a colonialist construction. These stances toward religion may conflict with definitions of religion used by researchers. For instance, indigenous "cultural rights" campaigns often focus on protecting places or practices that a given community considers sacred. From a sociological or anthropological perspective, these campaigns would be considered germane to studies of religiosity, but the organizations that mobilize around them would probably not self-identify as "religious NGOs," and may even be principally opposed to the term "religious" as a descriptor.

The implication of this ambiguity is that asking NGOs to self-identify as religious is not likely to yield reliable measures. This is true whether the information is culled through surveys, interviews, or directories. As a result, researchers are forced to choose between risking Type I or Type II errors. If we allow NGO members to define their organizations for themselves, or we categorically omit, for example, ethnic Jewish NGOs or NGOs representing indigenous peoples, we risk losing data that might be relevant to our questions. But if we uncritically include all organizations whose public performances (websites, titles, mission statements) show evidence of what we as researchers see as religiosity, we risk imposing our own meanings on organizations that might reject a religious identity for themselves, or including organizations (such as the Red Cross) that are only nominally religious.

Solutions to #1: Detailed Variables and Coding Schemes

Fortunately, these definitional problems can be addressed in the construction of data files. First, researchers can include codes not only for different religious traditions and denominations but also for forms of religion that could be considered "borderline," such as ethnic Jewish, indigenous, "spiritual," or "new age." By doing so, researchers can either include or exclude such groups according to the needs of a given analysis, allowing for both flexibility and precision. This approach also allows us to capture otherwise hidden variation that might exist between these different types of religious NGOs in terms of their relationships with other variables.

But second, researchers are not limited to relying on NGO self-reports. We can set our own criteria for what counts as "religious." But, in establishing our own criteria, we need to disaggregate into distinct variables the multiple dimensions—missions, goals, activities, membership, symbology—along which organizations may or may not be religious. Doing so allows researchers not only to choose their own thresholds for what qualifies as "religious" but to examine how different dimensions of religiosity relate to other variables of interest. While collecting the data for the HR file, I created a distinct variable for each of five indicators of religiosity:

1. Religion is mentioned in the NGO's name. While this might intuitively be the most obvious indicator of religious identity, it can actually be misleading. For example, a hypothetical organization titled the Religious Freedom Association may be comprised entirely of secularists whose goal is to keep religion out of government affairs. Conversely, the fact that World Vision International does not contain an unambiguously religious reference in its name does not negate its Christian identity and mission. As these examples suggest, the potential for both Type I and Type II error is high if we rely solely on organizations' names in making our determinations.
2. The NGO openly declares that its mission is rooted in or inspired by a religious tradition.
3. The NGO routinely engages in religious activities such as prayer, worship, religious observances, practices, or teaching, or uses explicitly religious images or references (such as scripture) on its website or directory profile.
4. The NGO's members either are, or proactively attempt to mobilize, persons of faith, whether clergy or laity, around human rights concerns. These would include organizations that were founded by clergy (priests, nuns, rabbis, monks, etc.) and portray these origins as relevant to their organizational identity.

While these first four criteria might seem relatively straightforward, they can still leave researchers in ambiguous territory. Take, for example, the Red Cross. Clearly, the organization uses overt religious imagery in its branding, and some of its founders were personally motivated by religious convictions. But it operates entirely as a secular organization in terms of its missions, goals, and activities. Should it be included in a dataset of "religious NGOs"? Another example would be Scientology. While Scientologists protect their interests using the language of "religious freedom," the group's status as a religion is legally and socially contested in some countries. Whose definition of religion should be used to decide whether or not Scientology is coded as "religious" in an NGO dataset? The definition used by the NGO itself? The opinion of a particular government? Creating distinct variables for each dimension of religiosity, ideally in addition to allowing NGOs to self-identify, allows researchers to choose among multiple criteria and to examine how these different criteria are related to other variables.

5. The organization engages in evangelism. This fifth criterion is probably the strictest for defining an organization as "religious." And in attempting to ascertain whether or not an organization "propagates the faith," we quickly encounter a new subset of questions about definition and classification. A variety of motives can underlie attempts to introduce one's religion to others, and whether or not an organization "evangelizes" can be subject to interpretation. In constructing the HR dataset, I encountered four different ways in which RNGOs generally spread their faith, and created a unique variable for each:
   - 5a. Openly Seeking New Adherents: These groups explicitly describe their missions as including the introduction of their beliefs to the uninitiated, usually with the intent of converting them. They either explicitly use words and phrases such as "evangelization" or "assistance to missionaries," or this goal is clearly implied by the use of phrases such as "introducing others to the way of the Buddha" or "bearing witness to the news of Jesus Christ."
   - 5b. Religious Education Only: These NGOs engage in religious or theological education. However, while they explicitly aim to promote greater awareness of religious doctrines, positions, beliefs, or teachings, it is not clear that they do so with an aim toward conversion. Rather, their aim seems to be more to sway opinion on particular social issues, without any obvious concern with increasing membership. For example, part of the mission of the NGO Catholics against Capital

Punishment is to "promote greater awareness of Catholic Church teachings that characterize capital punishment as unnecessary, inappropriate and unacceptable in today's world." Groups that offer academic theology courses could also be included in this category.

5c. Social Evangelism: These groups describe themselves as bringing their religions to others, but through "good works," and there is no clear evidence of attempts to seek converts through the dissemination of religious belief, materials, teachings, etc. An example would be Dorcas Aid International, which describes itself as a "Christian relief and development organisation, committed to fulfil the command Jesus Christ gave to His followers to take care of the poor and oppressed (Matt. 25:31–46). . . . We operate in partnership with local churches and Christian organizations, awakening and empowering them to share the love of Christ through practical deeds."

5d. Distribution of Religious Materials: Some NGOs are involved in the distribution of religious texts (e.g., Bibles, Korans) or religious videos, broadcasts, etc., but it is not clear whether the purpose is to seek converts, distribute materials to current believers, or build alliances. Examples would include some Christian organizations that distribute Bibles in places where Christians are persecuted. It is not always clear in these cases whether conversion is among the objectives of Bible distribution, or whether the purpose of the latter is simply to provide Bibles to already-practicing Christians who are otherwise denied access to them. This category would also include organizations like the Council on American-Islamic Relations, which distributes copies of the Quran to elected officials and policy makers. The council describes the goal of its campaign as one of familiarizing Americans with Islam in order to "protect civil liberties" and "promote mutual understanding." While the organization is concerned with familiarizing non-Muslims with Islam, there is no clear indication that conversion to Islam is among its goals.

All four of these categories describe ways in which RNGOs share their religions with others. Yet, aside from the first category, it is debatable whether each particular form of sharing constitutes evangelism. By coding them separately, individual researchers can choose which criteria to use. In addition, they can explore which forms of "religion sharing" are related to a variety of variables ranging from religious growth to social program effectiveness.

Challenge #2 Accounting for Variation in Religion-State-Society Relations

And finally, competing subjective definitions of religion are not the only sources of error when one is attempting to get accurate counts of religious actors across societies. Even if there were unanimous NGO agreement on what qualifies as "religious," variation also exists in religion's online visibility due to structural factors that vary internationally. For religious actors, operating across multiple countries requires appealing not only to multiple diverse publics with diverse collective orientations toward religion but also responding effectively to widely varying bureaucratic and legal parameters defined by states. Compare, for example, China and the United States. In China, religion is tightly regulated by government, and unregistered groups are treated with suspicion or worse. These conditions can be expected to be sources of disincentive for many NGOs to proactively and publicly identify as religious. In contrast, in the United States, religious groups are not only commonly accepted as contributors to social welfare, but government money is actually set aside (e.g., PEPFAR, faith-based initiatives) for groups that openly declare a faith-based affiliation. Here, public religious identification is incentivized.

Interacting with international variation is the fact that incentives and disincentives for overtly religious framing can vary across religions themselves, since neither governments nor publics confer legitimacy equally upon all religious groups. In extreme cases, while one or two dominant religions might be accepted, others face outright persecution. The implication is that, when one is making international and interreligious comparisons, "number of religious NGOs" or "number of [Muslim or Buddhist or Christian] NGOs" can be misleading indicators of religious sentiment, impulse, or even mobilization.

For example, during my fieldwork, I interviewed a representative of a Catholic NGO operating in the United States who described an attempt to create an interfaith alliance with a lesser-known Islamic organization. A conflict ensued over whether or not to keep the overtly Catholic name of their organization or change to an interfaith name. Serious concerns were raised about the loss of the "Catholic brand," which is familiar and relatively trusted among American donors (even those who are not Catholic). What would the implications of that name change be for the organization's ability to attract donations? This is just one example of how, even in secular democracies, incentives for overt identification as religious vary by religion in addition to varying across geographical contexts.

Solution #2

There is no easy way around international variation in the visibility of RNGOs. Potential *sources* of variation can be identified with control variables that account for country characteristics, such as *dominant religion*, *religious heterogeneity*, *repression* (of both NGOs and religious groups), *religion's constitutional status*, etc. But this approach will not do much to help us arrive at more accurate measures of religious mobilization. Thus, we need to be somewhat conservative in interpretation of findings, being clear about whether what we capture with our data is some measure of "religiosity" within given contexts or whether numbers and types of RNGOs instead tell us more about social and political contexts themselves and what they will or will not permit in terms of religious expression.

In addition to variables that capture relevant country characteristics, we can use theoretical frameworks that encourage more contextual interpretations. The religious economies model (Stark and Finke 2000), for example, assumes "religious demand" to be constant and religious "consumption" a function of options available in a given context to meet that demand. Similarly, the political process model (PPM), which is an orienting strategy used in the study of social movements (McAdam 1999), moves political contexts, rather than activists, into the foreground of analyses seeking to explain movement mobilization. These approaches can be used to interpret religious data in terms of the way political factors shape opportunities for public and political religion (for example, Smith 1996).

In summary, the study of religious NGOs invites us to rethink some of the assumptions and categories that we use to define our objects of inquiry. When we move our analyses of religion out of the "religious sphere" and into the other sectors of social life, we can no longer assume that what it means to be "religious" is self-evident, prompting us to take a multidimensional approach to data collection. What is more, when we expand our search to include international NGOs, the visibility of religion can be expected to vary internationally, regardless of how it is defined. The next section will extend the focus on political context by examining the other half of the term "religious NGO," and what it means for a religious organization to be "nongovernmental."

Identifying the "Nongovernmental" in Religious NGOs

The question of what defines an organization as "nongovernmental" is particularly important for researchers who are interested in NGOs as manifestations of politically autonomous civil societies. And in the literature on global civil society, while NGOs are treated as one indicator of an independent civil sphere, it is also recognized that NGO independence from governments is often questionable, given the extent to which NGOs are, even if not controlled by governments, often funded by them at least in part. When we add religion to the mix, not only do the same concerns about government support apply, but additional factors make assumptions about NGO independence from government even more problematic.

Challenge #3: Identifying Institutional Boundaries

To fully understand how religion complicates the government-NGO relationship, we need to first consider a prior distinction—between religious NGOs and religious institutions proper (e.g., churches, missionary societies, religious orders), the latter having been involved in international sectors such as healthcare and education since long before the arrival of the NGO as a distinct organizational form. The need to distinguish between religious institutions and religious NGOs became especially apparent in the creation of the HR data file, as the organizations listed in the HRI directory were often associated with religious institutions, and in a variety of ways. For example, a large number (n = 140) of self-identified "Catholic NGOs" had various forms of formal affiliation with the Holy See. But even for those Catholic organizations whose profiles did not mention such formal ties, the simple fact of their Catholic identity prompted consideration of the methodological and analytical implications of the way interorganizational structures vary across religious traditions. Because of the Catholic Church's hierarchical and centralized system of coordination and control, most Catholic NGOs are technically not institutionally independent from the Church. In fact, if the implications of Roman Catholic organizational structure were taken to their logical conclusion, one could argue that many of the thousands of Catholic organizations in the world would be more accurately conceptualized as one organization, the Roman Catholic Church, with thousands of branches. But even if this "count" might be technically accurate, it would not yield meaningful comparisons with NGOs that identify with other traditions.

This is not to say that NGO ties to religious institutions are unique to Catholicism. Indeed, in the United States, the very concept of "faith-based initiative" or "faith-based organization" (FBO) implies that a service or advocacy organization has a tie to a formal religious establishment. Likewise, when perusing international human rights, development, and other civil society directories, one finds that many of the "NGO" listings are actually for religious institutions proper, such as churches, councils of churches, or religious orders. In the HR data file, 310 (almost half) of the "human rights organizations" were actually religious organizations (e.g., churches, councils of churches, Catholic justice and peace commissions) or their programs. In other words, the term "religious NGO" masks considerable organizational diversity.

These distinctions are important to questions about "nongovernmental" status even in secular democracies where both religious establishments and RNGOs are legally considered nonstate, civil society actors. For example, research from our UN survey showed that religious NGOs and programs of "traditional" religious institutions differ from each other significantly along a variety of dimensions, including sources of funding and the kinds of factors that influence their agendas (Bush

2017). These kinds of factors have implications for who has voice, whose interests are served, and whose agendas are carried out through their organizations. Had we not created variables to distinguish among these different forms of religious organization, and simply lumped together all religious actors as simply "religious NGOs," we would not have been able to observe this kind of variation.

In addition, not all countries are secular democracies. Consequently, institutional religion's distance from the state cannot be assumed. In fact, not only does religion's independence from the state vary across countries, but religious traditions also vary in terms of their historical relations with the nation-state system itself. These types of variation have implications for RNGO independence and for the kinds of power that are exercised through RNGOs.

Consider, for example, International Catholic Organizations (ICOs) and their relationship to the Holy See. As described in the *Modern Catholic Dictionary*, ICOs are

> associations whose members are expert in particular areas of human concern and who witness on the international level to the Church's teachings in those fields. . . . [A]n ICO . . . must be Catholic . . . in that its pronouncements and activities are in harmony with the magisterium of the Church. The statutes of each ICO, and any substantial amendments to them, must be approved by the Holy See. Moreover, candidates for president, general secretary, and chaplains or ecclesiastical assistants require Roman approval.[4]

This control by the Holy See becomes analytically important when we take into account that, in international relations, the Holy See is not treated as a civil society actor, but as a quasi-state. Its status at the UN as Permanent Observer State confers upon it privileges, such as participation in the General Assembly, denied to other religious actors. How, if at all, does this privileged status of Catholicism influence Catholic NGOs? By creating a distinct variable for ICOs, I was able to show that formal ties to the Holy See are indeed consequential. In particular, 84.6 percent of ICOs in the HR data file have ECOSOC consultative status, a designation that allows NGOs to attempt to influence the United Nations through participation (attendance, delivery of oral and written statements, provision of expert information or advice) in UN meetings and conferences. UN access is not granted to unaffiliated religious human rights NGOs in the same proportions as it is to ICOs, with only 10.9 percent of unaffiliated RNGOs in the HR dataset having ECOSOC consultative status.

Islam at the UN presents a similar problem for interpreting RNGO data, as Islamic NGOs are often closely aligned with Organization for Islamic Cooperation (OIC), which also has UN observer status. The OIC is an intergovernmental coalition of fifty-seven majority-Muslim countries that, when working in collaboration, form a powerful voting bloc within the UN. Since many member states of the OIC do not recognize a legal separation between religion and state, the meaning of an OIC-affiliated RNGO's status as nongovernmental can be ambiguous.

At first glance, these distinctions might appear to be merely academic, but they are not. To the contrary, they are a subject of some consternation. For example, in the NGO survey, we asked the following open-ended question: "Which religious groups at the UN have the most influence when it comes to agenda setting at the UN?" The open-ended responses were telling, with several respondents suggesting that Muslim and Catholic NGOs should not be perceived as independent actors. Here are just three examples:

> "OIC is a compact political group which has been influencing the UN agenda through its supported NGOs."
>
> "Religious organizations are not independent NGOs. They are backed by the administrations of their religion, be it the Vatican or others."
>
> "[T]he religious NGOs as a whole just act through or in coalition with the Vatican and the OIC, because they are more influence [sic] than NGOs in general."

Depending upon the research question, the public or private status of these organizations may need to be problematized, and variation in "nongovernmental" statuses may need to be taken into account.

Solution #3: Detailed Coding of Interorganizational Relationships

If researchers are interested in how religious or political influence is related to organizational form, interorganizational ties, or religion-state relations, a detailed coding scheme that can capture variation on these factors is needed. In constructing the HR dataset, I created a variable (*Inst_affil*) that contained the following categories:

> 0 = no evidence of affiliation with a formal religious organization or institution. These organizations appeared to operate independently of any formal religious institutions, but were coded as "religious" according to the criteria described in the previous section (n = 256).
>
> 1 = the organization was itself a religious organization, such as a church, temple, yearly meeting (Quaker), etc., or the organization was itself a "council of churches," "conference of bishops," or other organizational structure that represents a formal alliance of church bodies or other religious equivalents (n = 83). This category could be broken down further to distinguish between individual organizations and alliances of multiple organizations.
>
> 2 = the "organization" was actually a *program* of a church, temple, synagogue, council of churches, etc. (n = 189).
>
> 3 = the organization was one of the Holy See's justice and peace commissions that were inspired by Vatican II. Typically, these commissions are led by bishops (n = 38).
>
> 4 = the organization was formally recognized by the Holy See as an International Catholic Organization (ICO) (n = 16).

Here, a cautionary note is in order. Notice that organizations coded as 1 could be (and often were) related to other organizations in the data file that were coded as 2, 3, or 4. How should these organizational pairs be counted? Say a religious institution, a church for example, has three different HR programs operating in three different regions. Is this one RNGO? Or is it four? Or is it three, meaning we only count the programs and not the organization that initiated them? The decision as to what exactly constitutes a case will vary according to the research question (e.g., How many religious institutions have developed faith-based human rights initiatives? vs. How many human rights initiatives are faith-based?). Thus, the data need to be organized to allow for this flexibility.

In my own research, in situations where both a religious organization and its HR program were listed in HRI, each record was entered into the data file as a separate case. However, in addition, I created a separate variable (*duplicate_type*) indicating that the case was either a religious organization or a human rights program that had a "counterpart" in the dataset. To allow users to precisely identify pairs (for example, to eliminate duplicates, triplicates, etc.), I also created a variable identifying the case number of the religious organization or HR program that a given case was affiliated with. This method of recording makes it possible to isolate either religious establishments or programs, or collapse them into one case, for analysis.

In addition to creating variables to distinguish and identify linkages between religious establishments and NGOs or programs, elsewhere in the data file, I also coded for ecumenical and interfaith organizations and, to capture formal relations with the international state system, I created a variable indicating whether an NGO had consultative status with the UN. Such a variable could be created for any number of international institutions that have formal mechanisms in place for consultative relations with NGOs. One could also create a variable to indicate whether an organization's headquarters are located in an OIC country or, more broadly, to indicate forms of religion-state relations in countries where NGO headquarters are located, ranging from theocracy to strict religion-state differentiation to atheistic government. The information required to create these variables could be extracted from other data sources, such as the ARDA's religion freedom data file.

Data can also be collected on sources of RNGO funding to obtain yet another measure of government support. One obstacle to collecting this data would be international variation in reporting requirements, which would reduce reliability. Of course, this obstacle can be surmounted in survey research by asking NGOs about their funding sources. In the UN survey, in addition to asking each NGO about the size of its budget, we asked the NGOs to report the proportions of funding that they derived from each of the following sources:

a. National governments
b. International institutions
c. Foundations
d. Individual private donations
e. Members of religious communities

This variable allowed us not only to observe differences between religious and secular NGOs in terms of their funding sources but also to observe how the latter are related to other variables, like organizational priorities, and the extent of their involvement with and access to diplomats at the UN.

In general, by creating variables that capture the different ways in which NGOs are associated with religious institutions, and the different ways in which both are associated with states and international institutions, we allow researchers some flexibility in terms of where they draw boundaries between state and nonstate actors, and in terms of their ability to observe differences among groups across the different categories. Of course, this approach still leaves analysts with plenty to consider, since decisions to either include or exclude particular categories of actor will result in different pictures of religious presence and influence, and require different interpretations. For example, if we count as "NGOs" organizations that are created by or closely affiliated with the Vatican or the OIC, are we obtaining a valid measure of civil society (i.e., nongovernmental) influence? A measure of religious institutional influence? Or are we actually capturing a measure of state power? And what of those RNGOs that are institutionally independent but derive considerable portions of their funding from states? Should they be treated conceptually in the same terms as resource-independent RNGOs? By coding data in ways that allow us to account for the variety of organizational forms and relationships that exist, we will at least have empirical observations to inform our judgments.

In summary, in attempts to measure the presence and influence of "religious NGOs," the question of what counts as a "nongovernmental" or otherwise independent organization is fraught with ambiguity, and even more so than with secular NGOs, since international variation in religion-state relations creates an additional reliability issue. First, religious traditions vary in terms of interorganizational structure, the implication being that many so-called NGOs are actually religious bodies that are controlled not by groups of lay believers but by formal religious institutions. This difference may or may not compromise the validity of measures, depending upon the questions motivating one's research. And second, in places where religion and state are institutionally aligned, we cannot assume that religious organizations should be counted on the civil society side of a state-society divide. Variables need to be created and/or coded in ways that account for such variation in organizational form, institutional ties, and religion-government relations.

Challenges in Conducting Web-Based Research

This final section zeroes in on some technical issues researchers can expect to confront when using online sources to collect data on international NGOs. The examples in this section are drawn from experiences using the YBIO and HRI, which are both international directories. The main advantage of using an international directory (as opposed to multiple national directories) is that data can be expected to be relatively uniform across countries, since they are collected through one centralized source that presumably seeks the same information about each organization regardless of where it is located. This would probably not be the case if one were using multiple directories compiled by mutually independent sources in different countries. Relatively speaking, then, international data collected by a centralized source are likely to be more reliable, though, as already described, that reliability may come at the cost of international validity. But despite the advantages, researchers can expect to confront several challenges.

Challenge #4 Reliance on Nonacademic Sources

Perhaps the most obvious challenge is that directories cannot be assumed to have been assembled with researchers' needs in mind. They are more likely to have been created to serve the needs of populations working in or benefiting from the sectors they provide information about, whether they focus on business, activism, recreation, or hobbies. As a result, information is likely to not be as frequently updated or as complete as data collected for research purposes, or to have been collected using sampling frames and coding rules that meet social science standards.[5] For example, information contained in the individual HRI profiles was often incomplete or outdated, and uneven from profile to profile.

Solution #4: Use Multiple Data Sources

One way to gather more complete information is to use multiple data sources. Fortunately, researchers today not only have the Internet but also, unlike as recently as fifteen years ago, it is now commonplace, indeed expected, for formal organizations to have websites. Thus, rather than relying on directories alone, researchers can go "straight to the source" for information about most organizations, without having to do costly surveys or interviews. In fact, I ended up using HRI primarily to obtain my initial list of organizations, but relied heavily on NGO websites to actually populate the code sheets.

But, as with any method or source, websites present their own data collection challenges, not least of which is the fact, despite their apparent ubiquity, that not all organizations have them. When that is the case, a decision needs to be made about what to do with those cases that one knows exist, since they are in a directory, but that do not have a web presence. On the one hand, to include them in an analysis is to introduce variation in the quantity and quality of information across cases. In terms of the quantity, cases for which information is drawn solely from a directory are likely to have data missing on a greater number of variables than would cases that have both websites and profiles. In terms of quality, individual websites are "direct" sources of information, whereas information drawn from a directory profile, having already been interpreted to fit the categories of interest to the authors of the directory, is "second hand" and therefore potentially less valid vis-à-vis the definitions and categories used by a given researcher.

But on the other hand, to exclude the organizations that were listed in a directory but do not have websites introduces Type II error through the loss of data. And the error is likely to be systematic, biased in favor of organizations that have the resources or inclination to have a web presence. This form of bias is particularly problematic when one is collecting international data, since disparities in access to resources are exacerbated. These resources might include, for example, money, literacy, foreign language skills, secretarial staff, or Internet access. And, particularly with human rights NGOs, web presence can be expected to vary depending upon features of countries' political contexts, such as states' recognition of the right to freedom of speech or levels of repression.

Paradoxically, when examining organizational fields such as human rights or religious freedom, we might conceivably find relatively fewer websites in places where mobilization is actually greater, precisely because human rights abuses and religious persecution often include the suppression of speech and political or religious organizing.

Another reason not to exclude organizations for which there is relatively limited information is that, depending upon the research question, limited information may be sufficient. Not all research requires complex multivariate analyses, and a small number of key variables, such as organizational founding dates or countries of operation, may be sufficient to yield important findings. For example, a simple trend line tracking organizational growth and decline can be created with little more than organizational founding dates. From there, a trend line (or several) can be paired with data from other sources (e.g., key historical events, country characteristics, economic indicators, health statistics) to give fuller pictures of how religious transformation is related to a variety of social factors. It makes sense, then, to keep cases for which available information is rudimentary. However, it would also be useful to create a variable that provides information about the quantity, quality, and names of data sources that are used for each case.

Challenge #5: Accounting for International Branches

A final complication arises more directly as a result of the "international" in INGOs. By definition, to be international implies that an organization has branches or operations in multiple countries. How should each INGO and its branches be conceptualized and counted? As one INGO? Or as multiple NGOs, based on the number of branches? Take, for example, Jesuit Relief Services (JRS). According to its website, JRS has offices in eleven countries. Technically, JRS is only one INGO and perhaps should be counted as such. However, if the goal is to arrive at a meaningful indicator of global religious presence, or perhaps to compare religions in terms of their size or geographical reach, the count of eleven NGOs is arguably more valid.

We also need to consider the ways in which INGO headquarters and branches tend to be dispersed. Say, for example, a researcher's concern is with capturing regional variation in religious mobilization. JRS has four offices in sub-Saharan Africa, but its international headquarters are in Europe. This structure is reflecting a broader tendency among the larger INGOs, which operate throughout the global south but have headquarters based in Europe, the United States, or Canada. If we only create cases for, and only count, INGO headquarters and fail to count their branch offices, we obtain radically distorted views of RNGO dispersal across countries and regions of the globe.

Solution #5: Create Cases and Variables for Headquarters and Branches

The most efficient solution is to create one case for each INGO in addition to three variables. The first variable simply indicates the country where each organization's headquarters are located, while a second would indicate the number of countries in which each case (INGO) has branches. A third variable, or set of variables, could offer some estimation of regional dispersal. In the HR data file, I created eight dummy variables (e.g., *br_africa*, *br_ltn_amer*) indicating whether or not each organization had branches in each of eight different regions, following the regional classification system used by the UN. Another option, which might provide more detail, would be to record the actual number of branches in each region instead, and yet another would be to create variables indicating presence/absence or numbers of branches in every individual country. By recording information on branches, researchers can choose to count INGOs as singular entities (counting each INGO and its branches as one case), or instead count each branch as a case, which arguably would provide more meaningful estimates of NGO density and dispersal.

If enough information is available, individual cases could be created for headquarters and branches. In this case, an organization like JRS would appear in the dataset as twelve distinct cases, one case being the headquarters and the remaining eleven cases being the branches. Here, we would add a variable to distinguish between headquarters and branches, and for each branch add a variable providing the case number for the headquarters in the data file that the branch is linked to. Unfortunately, information about organizational branches is often insufficient for research to benefit from this method, and I bring it up to caution against generalizing information about headquarters and applying it to branches. Say, for example, a website for a large INGO indicates that it has branches in sixty-five countries. The website is quite detailed, and provides substantial information (e.g., founding date, mission, locations of operation, numbers of employees or volunteers, financial information, activities) about the INGO *as a singular entity*. But any one of those variables might—indeed, most likely will—vary from branch to branch. For example, a branch in Nigeria might have been established in 1974 and have fifty-five employees, while a branch in Kenya was established in 1976 and has fourteen employees. Unfortunately, even basic information like this will often not be available for individual branches on organization websites. And because the information is likely to vary across branches, the cells for them cannot be populated by simply using the data for the INGO as a singular entity. To collect such data is possible, but often it will require the time and resources to contact individuals NGOs and ask for detailed information about branches, which can be quite numerous.

Lessons Learned

This chapter has illustrated that, when research moves beyond "the religious sphere" and into the NGO sector, the seemingly obvious concepts of religion and nongovernmental become difficult to define. This difficulty is due to a variety of factors. One is the hybrid nature of religious NGOs, which often provide services or use methods that we think of as "secular" at the same time that religion may serve as a source of inspiration or institutional support. Another is the international variability in religion and state relations, which prevents us from assuming that religious actors are by default nongovernmental actors. These boundary issues become challenges when we are attempting to collect and categorize international data on "religious NGOs." But the chapter has also illustrated how key concepts can be clarified through the use of multiple measures and more detailed categorization for each measure, which in turn allow for more precision and flexibility in later analyses.

In general, multiple measures work by allowing researchers to move the conceptual boundaries determining what is included or excluded in a given analysis. For example, with regard to whether or not an NGO is "religious," breaking organizations into their component parts—names, mission statements, goals, activities, affiliations, membership—allows researchers to switch between, say, strict criteria, such as presence of evangelism or formal religious affiliation, to more relaxed criteria, such as references to religious ideas as inspiration for what would otherwise be considered secular activities. Likewise, with regard to what counts as a "governmental" actor, researchers' thresholds may vary from simply receiving a grant from a secular government to being a government-sponsored NGO in a formal theocracy. By making these distinctions, we can arrive at more nuanced understandings of how religion and state, and religious and secular, interact across different contexts, as well as a more detailed understanding of religion's growth, decline, or transformation across civil society sectors.

The chapter also drew attention to how various forms of religion-state relations create reliability issues insofar as they are related to variation in the extent to which religious identities are likely to be overt and visible. One solution offered was to create variables that account for this contextual variation; another was to be conservative in the interpretation of counts of religious NGOs, acknowledging that the numbers we produce may tell us more about variation in social and political opportunities for mobilization and less about impulses or efforts toward doing religious organizing.

And finally, the development of the Internet and of normative expectations that formal organizations maintain web presences has been a game changer for researchers interested in organizational identities. Rather than being limited to information provided by directories, and needing to rely on expensive surveys or interviews to fill in the details, researchers can now turn to websites, which are rich in information about organizational missions, sources of inspiration, goals, and methods of achieving them. But they need to be interpreted with caution, bearing in mind that websites are public performances of group identities that may or may not be shared by all of their members. Furthermore, subjective agreement among researchers, NGOs, and audiences on definitions of key concepts cannot be "checked" in the same way that they can through interviews. Nonetheless, through the use of detailed variables and classification schemes that allow a diversity of definitions, many of these obstacles can be sufficiently overcome to produce relatively detailed knowledge about the myriad ways in which religious actors engage with civil societies.

NOTES

1 The Association of Religion Data Archives, "Religious Human Rights NGOs," accessed December 1, 2016, www.theARDA.com.

2 I would like to acknowledge my research assistants, Yuyu Fan and Dominique Viola, for their work in coding organizational profiles for this dataset. I would also like to thank Kacy Ellis, Robert Martin, and Katia Yurguis for their assistance with earlier efforts at collecting this data.

3 The project was funded by the Arts and Humanities Research Council, Religion and Society Programme, in the United Kingdom. In addition to myself, serving in the role of consultant, the core of the research team included two coprincipal investigators, Jeremy Carrette and Hugh Miall, and two postdoctoral research associates, Sophie-Helene Trigaud and Verena Beittinger-Lee. Julia Berger and Jeff Haynes served as external consultants.

4 Catholic Dictionary, "International Catholic Organizations (ICO)," accessed March 13, 2010, www.catholicculture.org.

5 An exception is the YBIO, which has been updated annually by the UIA since 1908.

WORKS CITED

Berger, Julia. 2003. "Religious Nongovernmental Organizations: An Exploratory Analysis." *Voluntas: International Journal of Voluntary and Non-profit Organizations* 14(1): 15–40.

Boli, John, and George Thomas. 1999. *Constructing World Culture: International Nongovernmental Organizations since 1875*. Stanford, CA: Stanford University Press.

Bush, Evelyn. 2005. *Transnational Religion and Secular Institutions: Structure and Strategy in Human Rights Advocacy*. Doctoral dissertation, Cornell University.

Bush, Evelyn. 2007. "Measuring Religion in Global Civil Society." *Social Forces* 85(4): 1645–66.

Bush, Evelyn. 2017. "Representation, Accountability, and Influence at the UN: Results from the Survey of Religious NGOs." Chapter 3 in *Religion, NGOs, and the United Nations: Visible and Invisible Actors in Power*, edited by Jeremy Carrette and Hugh Miall. London: Bloomsbury Press.

McAdam, Doug. 1999. *Political Processes and the Development of Black Insurgency, 1930–1970*, 2nd ed. Chicago: University of Chicago Press.

Oxfam International. 2017 "Our Purpose and Beliefs." Available at https://www.oxfam.org. Accessed February 28, 2016.

Smith, Christian. 1996. *Resisting Reagan: The U.S. Central American Peace Movement*. Chicago: University of Chicago Press.

Stark, Rodney, and Roger Finke. 2000. *Acts of Faith: Explaining the Human Side of Religion*. Berkeley: University of California Press.

World Vision International. 2017a. "Child Well-Being Aspirations and Outcomes." Available at http://www.wvi.org. Accessed February 28, 2016.

World Vision International. 2017b. "Mission and Values." Available at https://www.worldvision.org. Accessed February 28, 2016.

10.

Reviewing Millions of Books

Charting Cultural and Religious Trends with Google's Ngram Viewer

ROGER FINKE AND JENNIFER M. MCCLURE

Despite the importance of trend data for understanding key substantive and theoretical questions on American culture and religion, almost no such data exist.[1] Unlike economics, education, employment, crime, and other areas consistently covered by the census or other government agencies, the data collections on culture and religion have been fewer in number and less systematic. The Gallup polls, the General Social Surveys, and the National Election Studies chart a few trends over the last few decades, and church membership data have been estimated going back to 1776 (Gaustad 1976; Finke and Stark 1986; Stark and Finke 1988), but there is no source of data that offers multiple measures over the history of America.[2]

For this reason, the millions of books scanned into Google Books offer scholars a unique opportunity to quickly review trends that have been ignored by other collections. When Google Books is combined with Google's Ngram Viewer, over two billion words and phrases can be quickly searched and charted over time. Moreover, the search tool is highly sophisticated for both single- and multiple-word searches. The Ngram Viewer allows users to limit their searches by customizing them to parts of speech and inflection, or expand the searches by making them case insensitive or using wildcard characters. Including more than three million books and primarily covering the time period from 1800 to 2008, this resource offers us a unique window into the life of America for more than two hundred years.

Yet, despite the great promise of this collection, many questions remain on how it can and should be used. To what extent do the words and word combinations used in books offer accurate measures of cultural and religious changes? And even though the body of text searched is vast, do the results reflect the culture as a whole? Finally, does the pool of authors writing books and the audiences reading them vary over time as literacy and education levels increase?

The purpose of this chapter is fourfold. First, we introduce the Google Ngram Viewer and review both the promise and the potential limitations. Second, we evaluate how well the trends charted by the Ngram Viewer match known cultural and religious trends. Third, we assess how the pool of authors and readers of books has changed over time. And, fourth, we discuss how the tool can be used most effectively for future research. Charting over-time trends and generating historical data are the most obvious contributions of this new tool. Yet, we conclude that one of the most promising contributions is using the Ngram Viewer to identify and access the books being used from Google Books.

Google Books and the Ngram Viewer

In December 2004, Google announced an initiative to digitize more than fifteen million books and to make the contents available for searching. They initially partnered with the university libraries of Harvard, Oxford, Stanford, and Michigan, as well as the New York Public Library. Within a few years, however, their library partnerships increased to more than forty and now include Princeton, Cornell, Texas, Virginia, Wisconsin, and California.[3] The inclusion of Harvard and Princeton was especially crucial for the study of American religion and culture, because of their early founding dates and because they were each founded as seminaries and continue to support seminaries.

By 2010, the initiative had reached the goal of digitizing fifteen million books, and a research note in *Science* introduced the world to Google's Ngram Viewer (Michel et al. 2011a).[4] The initial Viewer, developed in 2009, relied on a collection of 5,195,769 digitized books, representing approximately 4 percent of all books ever published. The authors explained that the subset of books was selected according to the quality of scans (i.e., the optical character recognition, or OCR) and the availability of complete information on the date and place of publication. Due to problems with dating, all periodicals were excluded.[5] Google later released a 2012 version of its Viewer that was based on "more books, improved OCR, improved library and publisher metadata" and included several improvements to the Viewer software.[6]

Michel and his coauthors coined the term "culturomics" for the new data collection and analysis techniques (2011a:176). They devoted much of their research note to demonstrating how their new tools could chart changes in grammar and vocabulary over time. This included the transition from irregular to regular verbs (e.g., "burnt" to "burned") and the formation of new words as well as the words that became obsolete over time. But the authors clearly viewed the new measures as documenting more than changes in lexicon or grammar; they proposed that the Viewer allowed the social sciences and humanities a method with which "to investigate cultural trends quantitatively" (Michel et al. 2011a:176).

The authors accompanied these bold claims with a high level of transparency on where and why problems might occur. The brief seven-page *Science* article was initially published with an eighty-five-page online supplement (Michel et al. 2011b), and more documentation soon followed. Some concerns could easily be addressed.[7] For example, when presenting the trends in charts, they divide the number of matches in a given year by the total number of possible words for that year. And, to avoid sudden surges and dips from one year to the next, they do a smoothing of the data across three years or more. There were other challenges, however, that were more difficult to overcome.

Perhaps the most challenging is maintaining synonymy in the searches. Words often share the same spelling but have very different meanings, refer to different people, or are used in many different ways. Once again, the Viewer offers several options for reducing this problem. The simplest is to use multiple words rather than a single one. Rather than doing a single search for "classical," the user can do separate searches for "classical music," "classical period," and "classical conditioning." The searches also can be refined by specifying the part of speech or whether the word is capitalized. This allows the user to distinguish between "worship" as a verb or "worship" as a noun and between "Catholic" or "catholic." These and other search options allow for a continual refinement of searches, yet the challenge of maintaining synonymy remains. For example, the names of Daniel Webster, John Smith, Horace

Mann, Adam Smith, and even Abraham Lincoln are shared by many in American history.

Accurately charting cultural trends over time also poses challenges. Michel and his colleagues (2011a) note that, prior to 1800, the number of books is too small to reliably quantify, and after 2000, the method for collecting books moved beyond libraries, with publishers now submitting books for inclusion. As a result, they limited their analysis to the time period from 1800 to 2000. The earlier years of the 1800s are still more prone to error due to the reduced number of publications per year, the reduced quality of the scans, and the more limited metadata on the publications (Michel et al. 2011b). Since Ngram trends are time specific, Google has paid careful attention to accuracy of the date of publication. They omitted books that contained works from multiple years, as well as journals and periodicals, which were often dated with the first year of the publication, not the actual date of the specific piece. They also omitted books with poor optical character recognition quality and with inaccurate language metadata. These filters greatly increased the accuracy of the Google Ngram data (Michel et al. 2011b:6–8).

The most serious concerns, however, are the possible biases of the corpus that are related to the cultural topics being measured or to the variable of time. The authors acknowledge that the corpus of books is limited by the books acquired and preserved by the libraries, raising concerns that the books might not represent the larger body of books or the culture more generally. Yet another concern about the corpus, though not addressed by the authors, is about the change in authors and readers over time. As the rate of literacy increases, does this change the pool of readers and authors of the books being published over time? Were the authors and readers of books in the early nineteenth century an educated elite that failed to reflect the larger culture? As we will review below, this bias poses one of the most serious threats to interpreting cultural and religious trends in the nineteenth century.

Despite these potential limitations, especially for the earlier years of the collection, the promises of this massive new source of information remain many. Below we attempt to assess the potential of the Google Ngram Viewer for accurately charting historical trends and for future research.

Assessing the New Measurement Tool

The greatest challenge for assessing the validity of new cultural and religious trend measures is that we have few criterion measures for comparison. Hence, we first assess whether the reported trends are in agreement with well-known historical events. Do the measures accurately reflect what we know occurred? Next, we evaluate whether the new data are sensitive to subtle changes in language. In particular, we will look at how the words "Pentecostal" and "fundamentalist" (and related variations) have changed over time. Does the new tool allow us to capture more subtle shifts? In short, we want to assess the Ngram tool's ability to measure prominent as well as subtle changes in American religious history.

Documenting the Well Known

When trends are well marked by distinctive words or a series of words, the Ngram tools nicely reflect some meaningful and often important historical time periods or events. Not surprisingly, when Americans are at war with another nation, the opposing nation is mentioned more frequently in books. As shown in figure 10.1, Germany always receives substantial attention in American publications, but the interest surged during World War I and II. The mention of Japan slowly rises as Japanese immigration begins in the late nineteenth century, falls after the passage of the Immigration Act of 1924, and then peaks near the end of World War II. Vietnam is seldom mentioned prior to the 1950s, surges during the 1960s and early 1970s, and has remained relatively high since the end of the war—though never reaching the levels of Germany or Japan.

But the Ngram trends often reflect important historical changes and events even when the events are not as significant as war. The trend line for Mormons and other variants of the group's name (e.g., "Latter-day Saints," "Mormon," etc.) offers an important example. As shown in figure 10.2, the Ngram results display four clear surges in activity: the late 1830s and early 1840s, much of the 1850s, the late 1860s and early 1870s, and the late 1880s. Each of these surges reflected important controversies between the Mormon Church and the larger culture.

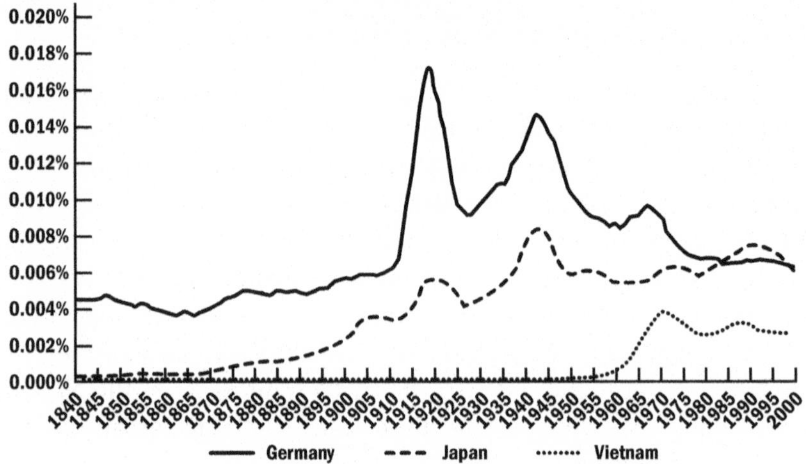

Figure 10.1. Ngram Trends for Nations, 1840–2000.
Note: This figure was made by searching "Germany, Japan, Vietnam" in the Google Ngram American English Corpus with three-year smoothing (books.google.com).

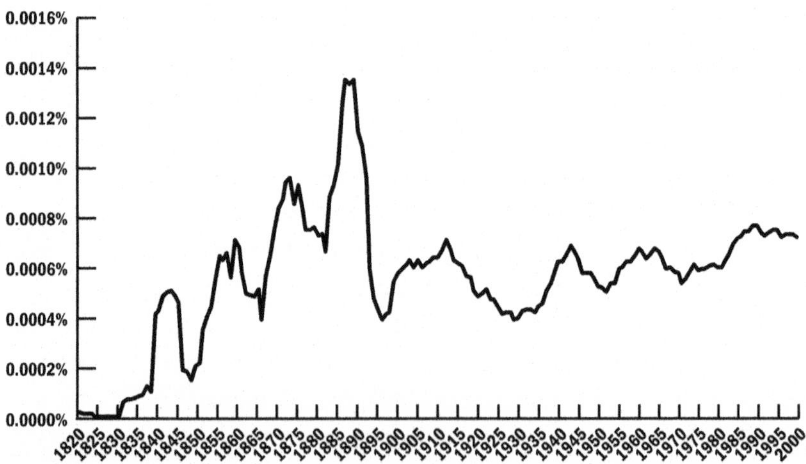

Figure 10.2. Ngram of Mormonism-Related Terms, 1820–2000.
Note: This figure was made by searching "Mormon+mormon+Mormons+mormons+latter day saints+Latter day saints+Latter Day Saints+Latter Day saints+Latter day Saints+LDS+lds" in the Google Ngrams American English Corpus with three-year smoothing (books.google.com).

Founded in the early 1830s, the Mormon Church received little attention until after 1838, when the governor of Missouri, Lilburn Boggs, issued an executive order referring to the Mormons as enemies and stating that they "must be exterminated or driven from the state if necessary, for the public peace" (Arrington and Bitton 1992:44). Shortly thereafter, seventeen Mormons were killed by an angry mob. The Mormons then moved to Nauvoo, Illinois, where their prophet, Joseph Smith, quickly became the mayor and military leader of the rapidly growing community. But after Joseph Smith and his brother Hiram were imprisoned and killed in 1844, the Mormons began their march west in 1846. Following this departure, the trend line dropped sharply. In 1852, however, when their second prophet, Brigham Young, publicly acknowledged the practice of polygamy within the church, the start of the second surge began. By 1856, the Republican presidential candidate, John C. Fremont, campaigned against the "twin relics of barbarism, slavery and polygamy," and the eventual winner, James Buchanan, removed Brigham Young as the territorial governor and sent troops to Utah, resulting in what was known as the Utah War (as quoted in Hansen 1981:144).

The trend line dropped during the years of the Civil War, but the campaign against polygamy continued once the war was over. There was a short drop during the late 1870s, perhaps due to the 1879 Supreme Court ruling upholding the Anti-Bigamy Act of 1862, but the drop was short-lived. Once the Edmunds Act of 1882 and the Edmunds-Tucker Act of 1887 were in place, polygamy was prosecuted as a felony and a pledged allegiance to antipolygamy laws was required for voting and holding office. In the late 1880s, the trend line quickly moved to the highest level in history.[8] But when the fourth Mormon prophet, Wilford Woodruff, issued a manifesto in 1890 declaring that he and the church would submit to the laws of the nation, the trend line plummeted (Hansen 1981; Arrington and Bitton 1992). Since 1890, the Mormon membership has skyrocketed from 188,263 worldwide to more than six million in the United States alone,[9] but the attention received in books remains far below the 1890 peak.

The examples just offered demonstrate that Ngram measures can reflect the cultural attention given to well-documented historical events and trends. As expected, the measures for Germany, Japan, and Vietnam all surged when America was at war with each country, demonstrating the tool's ability to capture major historical events. More impressive, however, is that Ngram measures could detect the cultural attention given to less prominent historical events involving the Mormon Church. Each of the four nineteenth-century peaks on the Mormon graph reflected prominent historical struggles between the Mormon Church and the larger culture. These examples demonstrate some of the promises, but many challenges remain.

Documenting Subtle Shifts in Meaning

Whereas the words "Mormons," "Latter-day Saints," and other variants have consistently referred to a specific religious group, other religious terms change over time. This change in meaning reduces the ability of Ngrams to provide a standardized measure for charting trends of a specific group over time, but it does help to uncover important changes in the way words are used. For example, Ngram trends help to illustrate how the commonly used words "Pentecostalism" and "fundamentalist" have changed in meaning and use over time.

Over the past few decades, Pentecostalism has been the most rapidly growing segment of Christianity. The growth has been most stunning in the global South (Jenkins 2002), but Pentecostal groups in the United States have also shown remarkable growth. The Church of God in Christ has become one of the largest, if not the largest, of the historically African American denominations, and the Assemblies of God has gone from 6,703 American members in 1916 to more than three million in 2012.[10] Most of the contemporary Pentecostals trace their heritage back to the African American holiness pastor William J. Seymour and his revivals at 312 Azusa Street in Los Angeles (Wacker 2001).[11] Beginning in 1906 the young movement placed a strong emphasis on the gifts of the Holy Spirit, including speaking in tongues and healing.

However, the movements arising from the Azusa Street revivals were not the first American religious groups to describe themselves as Pentecostals. Prior to the Azusa Street movements, the word "Pentecostal" referred to holiness movements affiliated with the Methodist Church. These groups began feuding with the Methodist hierarchy in the mid-nineteenth century, and several split from the Methodists in the late nineteenth century to form the Association of Pentecostal Churches.

This group later merged with the First Church of the Nazarene in 1907 to form the Pentecostal Church of the Nazarene. But the use of "Pentecostal" in their name was short lived. Twelve years later, they dropped the word "Pentecostal" to avoid any confusion over their ties with the new "Pentecostals" who were speaking in tongues (Melton 1991). From the 1920s forward, the word was conceded to the new Pentecostals associated with the Azusa Street revivals.

Figure 10.3 displays how the use of the word "Pentecostal" increased in the nineteenth century as the holiness movements increased in number and voiced concerns about the modernizing trends of the Methodist Church. But the most significant increases came after 1960 with the rapid growth of the new Pentecostals. Figure 10.3 also shows the rise in the use of the word "Pentecostalism" since the 1960s. Whereas "Pentecost" is in the vocabulary of all Christian groups and "Pentecostal" sometimes goes beyond those traditions referring to themselves as Pentecostals, "Pentecostalism" seems to be distinctive to the movements arising from the Azusa Street revivals. In short, the graph captures the attention given to two very different Pentecostal movements, but understanding the graph requires knowledge of American religious history.

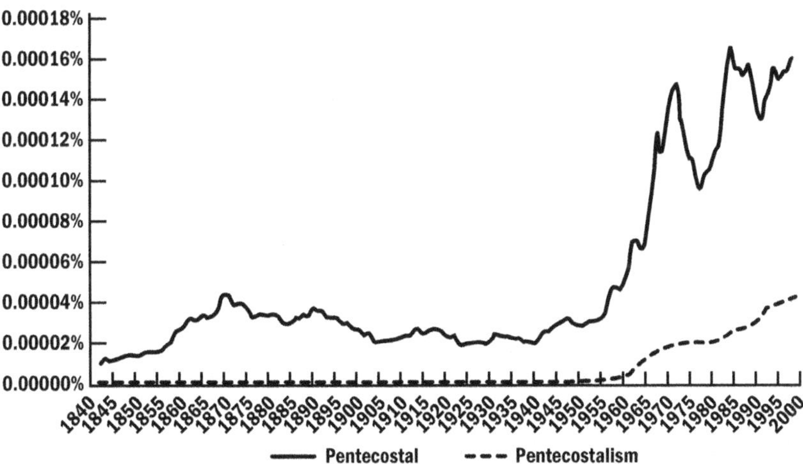

Figure 10.3. Ngram Trends for "Pentecostal" vs. "Pentecostalism," 1840–2000. Note: This figure was made by doing a case-insensitive search for "Pentecostal, Pentecostalism" in the Google Ngrams American English Corpus with three-year smoothing (books.google.com).

The word "fundamentalist" also offers an example of how both the meaning and the use of a religious word can change over time. Initially, "fundamentalist" was used to describe those who held tightly to the teachings outlined in a booklet entitled *The Fundamentals* that was published between 1910 and 1915. A Baptist editor would later coin the word "fundamentalist" in 1920 to describe those who are willing "to do battle royal for the Fundamentals" (Marsden 1980). Figure 10.4 shows that initial use of the term as a noun rises after 1920, falls in the early 1930s, and then shows a gradual increase. The use of fundamentalist as an adjective shows a similar start, first arising in the 1920s and having a similar level of use. But the trend lines begin to show a substantial separation in the 1950s. By 1970, the rate of using "fundamentalist" as an adjective was over six times higher than that of its use as a noun. By 1990, the rate was over ten times higher. This suggests that in its early usage, the word "fundamentalist" frequently referred to specific groups or people, but the word is now being used far more frequently to describe a type of group or person. Although bigrams are not shown in figure 10.4, it is also interesting to explore what words are paired

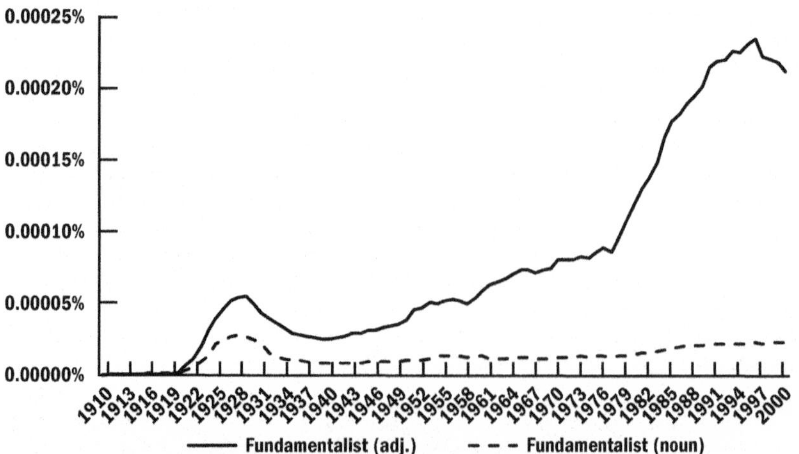

Figure 10.4. Ngram Trends for "Fundamentalist," Comparing Its Use as a Noun and an Adjective, 1910–2000.

Note: This figure was made by doing a case-insensitive search for "fundamentalist_ADJ, fundamentalist_NOUN" in the Google Ngrams American English Corpus with three-year smoothing (books.google.com).

with "fundamentalist." When used as an adjective, "fundamentalist" is most frequently paired with "Christians" since the 1980s. When "fundamentalist" is used as a noun, however, "Christian" and "Islamic" have similar rates of describing a fundamentalist.

These two examples serve to illustrate both the challenge and the opportunity of this research method. On the one hand, the challenge of synonymy is clearly evident. Words can change in both their meaning and the way they are used over time. Thus, Ngrams can sometimes fail badly at offering a standardized measure over time. On the other hand, the Ngram searches can offer important insights into how the meanings and uses of words have changed over time. "Pentecostal" (and related terms) referred to two different religious movements at two different points in time. The Ngram trend line captured both the growth of the holiness/Pentecostal movements associated with Methodism in the nineteenth century as well as the movements associated with the Azusa Street Revivals that promoted speaking in tongues and miraculous healing in the twentieth century. The Ngram tool also helped to measure how the term "Fundamentalist" (and related terms) has been used over time. Once frequently used as a noun referring to a specific group of religious believers in the 1920s and 1930s, by the close of the twentieth century it was about ten times more likely to be used as an adjective to describe a group. Although failing to offer a standardized measure over time, each of these measures helps to identify important changes in American religious history.

Assessing the Corpus of Books

Given that even the most carefully researched books rely on "only" a few hundred other publications, it is easy to be impressed with the millions of books instantly accessed by Google Ngrams. Yet, even the most basic text on research methods warns that a large data collection does not ensure a representative collection. To what extent does the corpus of books reflect the interests of a broad cross-section of the society or only a select stratum? One of the most frequently mentioned concerns is whether the corpus represents the books actually being read. Since each book is given equal weight, the measure fails to account for the number of books actually published and read for that year. Moreover, because the books are primarily drawn from major university libraries, questions could be raised about the books being selected.

For religion and culture, however, one of the most significant biases might occur from the changes in the authors and readers of books over time. To what extent do the books represent the interests of the entire population or the interests of cultural and educated elites? As late as 1870, when the Department of Education offered its first statistical report, only 2 percent were high school graduates (Bureau of the Census 1975), and 20 percent of the population was estimated to be illiterate, compared to 0.6 percent in 1979 (Carter et al. 2015). The rate of literacy was obviously even lower as we move to the early years of the nineteenth century. How did this change in the potential pool of authors and readers change the ability of the books to serve as a measure of culture and religion? This potential bias raises at least two significant measurement concerns for the study of religion. First, to the extent that a bias is closely related to the variable of time, it will reduce the measure's ability to accurately chart religious trends over time. Second, if the bias is related to a topic being studied, it will distort the perceived relationships religion holds with other topics of interest.

Below we review the distinctive problems this sampling concern poses for religion in the nineteenth century. We will first chart a couple of Ngram trends on religion, and then we offer an assessment on how these trends are distorted by the changing pool of authors and readers.

Reviewing the Trends

When Michel and his colleagues reviewed trends on the mention of God in books, they noted that "God is not dead but needs a new publicist" (2011a:182). Given the results shown in figure 10.5, it is hard to challenge their conclusions. The trend line shows a continual drop from 1840 until about 1920, when it begins to plateau and eventually shows a modest rise at the end of the twentieth century.[12]

Moreover, this trend is not limited to a single religious term. When we limit our search to terms more specific to Christianity and limit our attention to the latter half of the nineteenth century, a similar pattern is displayed. As shown in figure 10.6, the mention of "Jesus" shows a similar decline throughout the nineteenth century and continues to decline

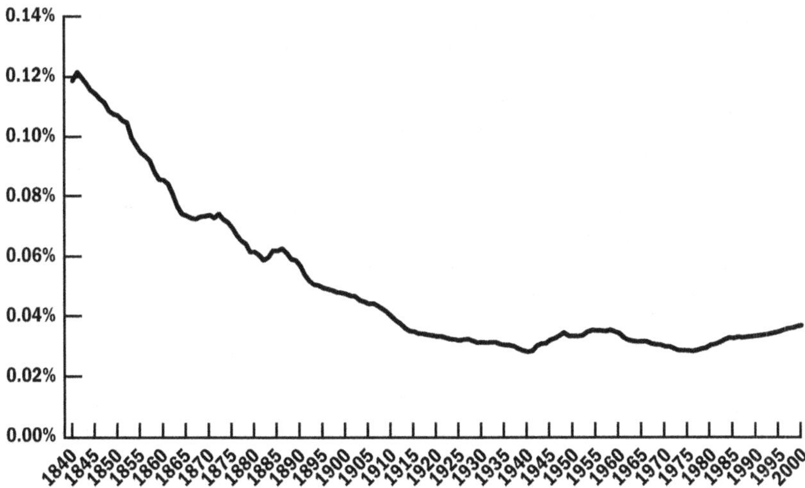

Figure 10.5. Ngram Trend for "God," 1840–2000.
Note: This figure was made by searching for "God+god" in the Google Ngrams American English Corpus with three-year smoothing (books.google.com).

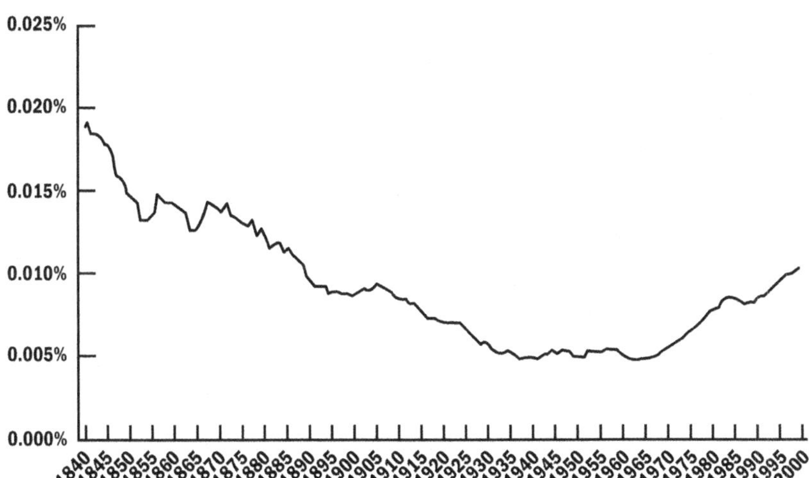

Figure 10.6. Ngram Trend for "Jesus," 1840–2000.
Note: This figure was made by doing a case-insensitive search for "Jesus" in the Google Ngrams American English Corpus with three-year smoothing (books.google.com).

until the 1930s. Although the trend line for "Jesus" does rebound after the 1970s, it never approaches the high rates shown earlier. Both God and Jesus seem to need a new publicist.

What is initially perplexing, however, is that atheism needs a new publicist as well. Like the trends shown for God and Jesus, the trend line for atheism shows a substantial drop in the latter half of the nineteenth century. As shown in figure 10.7, atheism shows modest rebounds in the 1930s and 1960s, but the trend line ends the twentieth century at one of the lowest levels for the entire 160-year span. So what is happening?

Rather than attributing these changes to a declining interest in God, Jesus, or atheism, we suggest that the change can be attributed to the close relationship religion held with higher education in early America. Throughout much of the nineteenth century, early American colleges were largely staffed by clergy, financially supported by religious denominations, and frequently established to help train clergy. As a result, the concerns and conversations of the highly educated clergy played a prominent role in determining both what was written and what was read in early America.

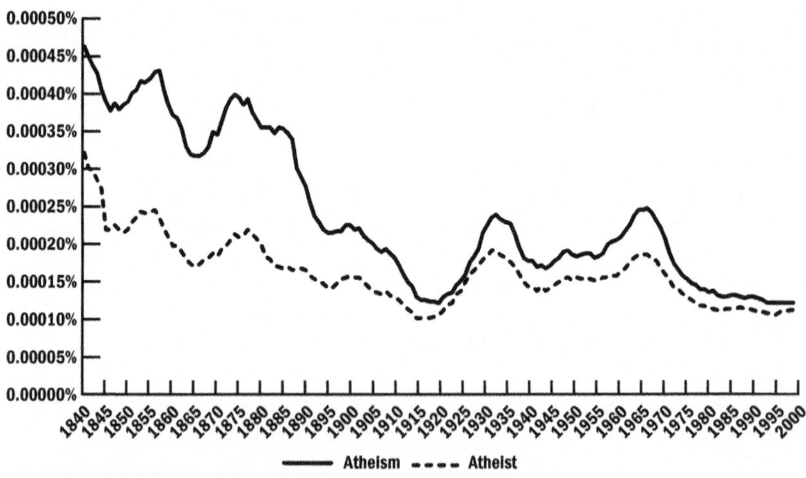

Figure 10.7. Ngram Trends for "Atheism" and "Atheist," 1840–2000.
Note: This figure was made by doing a case-insensitive search for "Atheism, Atheist" in the Google Ngrams American English Corpus with three-year smoothing (books.google.com).

A Shifting Pool of Authors and Readers

Prior to the Civil War, the development of colleges in America was dominated by religious denominations. Colin B. Burke's (1982) detailed data collection on *American Collegiate Populations* found that from 1810 to 1860, 82 to 86 percent of college students were enrolled in colleges supported by religious denominations. One of the most obvious reasons for this dominance is that the religious groups were one of the few reliable sources of financial support for higher education (Ringenberg 1984; Marsden 1994; Burtchaell 1998; Thelin 2011). Burke explains that even the state colleges relied heavily on endowments "because no college before the Civil War was tied to a fixed and adequate tax base" (Burke 1982:44).

But the tie between religion and higher education in early America went far beyond financial arrangements. The faculty of these early institutions was dominated by clergy (Ringenberg 1984; Marsden 1994; Burtchaell 1998). In part, this was the case because many of these institutions were initially founded to train clergy for the ministry, but it also was the result of clergy being far more educated than the general population. The three dominant colonial religions, Congregationalists, Presbyterians, and Episcopalians, all expected their clergy to have seminary educations at a time when literacy was low for the population as a whole (Finke and Stark 2005). The influence of the clergy and religion was even felt at the state schools. Historian William C. Ringenberg (1984:81) reports that "state universities almost invariably required students to attend chapel services and Sunday religious exercises. In many cases these requirements continued through the end of the century."

The Morrill Act of 1862, however, signaled a dramatic shift in higher education, both in the source of support and in the training offered. The initial act provided for the development and support of land-grant colleges, and this support continued to expand over the years that followed. But the act also specified the type of education that should be provided. Although allowing for scientific and classical studies, the act required a focus on agriculture, the mechanic arts, and training that would "promote the liberal and practical education of the industrial classes in the several pursuits and professions in life."[13]

Changes also were evident in higher education at the private schools during the final decades of the nineteenth century. One of the most significant changes for our measures was the waning influence of the clergy. This decline was clearly evident in the governing boards, faculty, and administrators of the prominent Ivy League schools. The practice of college presidents being clergy ended at Harvard in 1869, at Yale in 1899, and at Princeton in 1902 (with the appointment of Woodrow Wilson). But this decline went far beyond the Ivy League. A study of governing boards at fifteen private colleges found that clergy representation dropped from 39 percent in 1860 to 23 percent in 1900 and to 7 percent by 1930 (Ringenberg 1984:127).

The training being provided at the private schools was beginning to change as well. Whereas many of these schools were founded for the training of clergy, the percentage of students training for the ministry was dropping. Using data from Burke's collection, figure 10.8 charts the percentage of higher education enrollments that are in theological schools (1982:216). The combination of increasing numbers entering higher education (Burke 1982) and of the most rapidly growing American denominations not requiring seminary training for their clergy (Finke and Stark 2005) resulted in a sharp decline. As might be

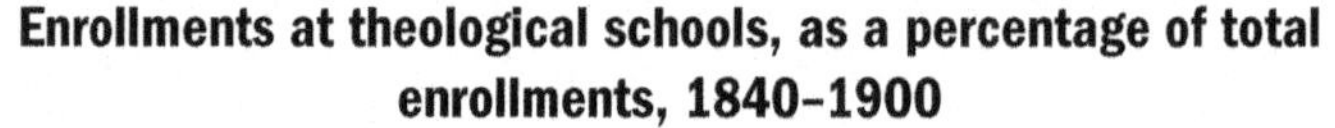

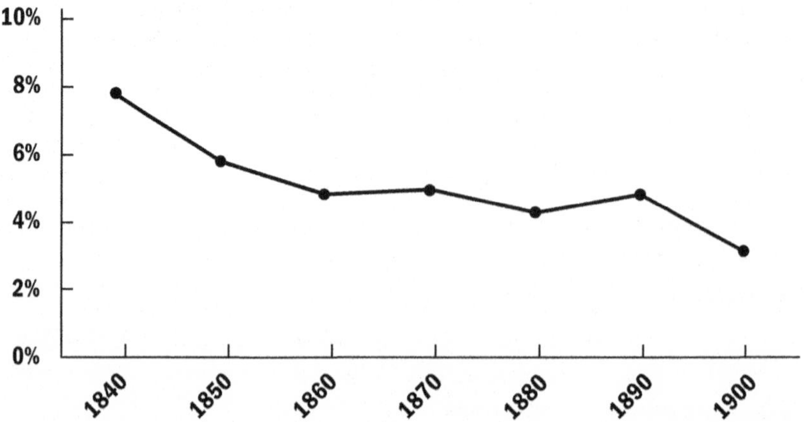

Figure 10.8. Trends in Theological Enrollments, 1840–1900. Source: Burke 1982:216.

expected, the 1840–1900 trend line for percentage enrolled in theological schools looks remarkably similar to the Ngram Viewer rates for references to God, Jesus, and atheism, holding correlations of 0.82, 0.55, and 0.62 respectively.

Even this brief review and limited data help to identify an important limitation for using the Ngram viewer to chart religious trends. Google's expansive collection offers an accurate picture of what was published, but the books fail to accurately represent the population as a whole during most of the nineteenth century. Because of the clergy's high level of education and the prominent role they and their denominations played in the higher education of early America, the corpus of books held in these college libraries included many volumes touching on religion. Referring to the late eighteenth century, Ringenberg (1984:49) noted that because "clergymen donated most of the volumes, the libraries emphasized theology." The literary societies of the early nineteenth century would soon expand the collections, yet religion remained an area of focus.[14]

But the lack of representativeness also raises concerns about the books of early America accurately representing the religious interests and concerns of all Americans. Just as many secular interests of the culture might have been underrepresented by the books being published, many religious groups might also be ignored. To what extent are the Baptists, early Methodists, and others not relying on a highly educated clergy (Finke and Stark 2005) underrepresented in the corpus of books? Even though religious topics are overrepresented in the early corpus of books, the religious authors and readers primarily came from only a few denominations. The clergy of select denominations remained highly influential in what was read and written in much of the nineteenth century.

Prospects for Future Research

Many of the sampling concerns just raised, as well as the measurement issues discussed earlier, are not distinctive to the Google Ngram Viewer and the corpus of books it draws on. Like the Ngram Viewer, historians often rely on a subset of written sources. They have long debated how their accounts are limited by the sources available, with more recent accounts attempting to draw on new sources and methods for studying religion (Taves 2011). Likewise, the problem of synonymy is not limited to the measures used by the Ngram Viewer. Social scientists and historians struggle to understand how meanings might vary over time and across cultures. For survey research, and especially cross-cultural survey research, synonymy remains one of the greatest measurement challenges (see Smith 2017).

So, can the Ngram Viewer be used for research? We propose that the Ngrams Viewer can and should be used. Building on the examples just reviewed, we offer an assessment on the potential pitfalls and promises of this research tool. We suggest that the Ngram Viewer should be complemented with other research methods and propose that the Google book collection offers a readily available resource for understanding and interpreting the Ngram Viewer results.

Breadth of Coverage

As just reviewed, scholars need to be aware of the overrepresentation of religious topics in the books of the nineteenth century. Because of the close relationship higher education and literacy held with religious groups and the highly educated clergy, both the authors and the readers of early American books were more likely to address religious topics. This produces misleading trend lines over time during the nineteenth century and underrepresents the interests of secular groups and the upstart religious sects and churches during this time period. Given our preliminary assessment, however, this bias in the corpus is sharply reduced by the end of the nineteenth century.

Despite these concerns, however, the Ngram Viewer's impressive breadth of coverage offers great research promise for developing new measures and new insights. The size of the collection is the most impressive. Whereas many historical accounts are limited by a small set of written sources that are often confined by region, religion, or time period (e.g., newspapers, journals, magazines, diaries, etc.), the Ngram Viewer includes 3.4 million books covering diverse geographic areas, topics, and time periods of American history. But it is the diversity of the sources of books included in the corpus that is the most important.

This diversity ensures that if a view was published, it will most likely be included.

The benefit of drawing on a diverse set of sources, rather than a single collection or small group of sources, can be illustrated if we return to the Mormon example discussed earlier. Using the recently developed Chronicle tool for searching *New York Times* news coverage throughout its history (chronicle.nytlabs.com), figure 10.9 charts the coverage given to Mormons.[15] Unlike the Ngram Viewer trend line, which accurately reflected multiple significant conflicts in Mormon history, the *New York Times* coverage shows a single sharp spike in the late 1850s that overshadows all other time periods. Thirty-five out of one thousand articles included the mention of "Mormon," "Mormons," "Latter-day Saints," or "LDS" in 1858, but the rate was only eight in one thousand in 1870 and dropped to three in one thousand in the late 1880s, when the federal government was seizing church assets and Mormon polygamists were being arrested following the passage of the Edmunds and the Edmunds-Tucker Acts (Hansen 1981:144–45). The *New York Times* coverage points to an important and newsworthy time in the 1850s, but other significant events are almost completely missing.

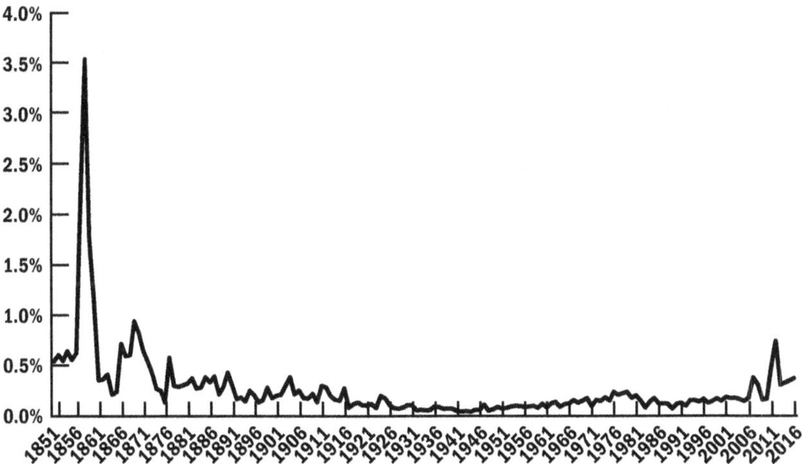

Figure 10.9 Use of Mormonism-Related Terms in the *New York Times*, 1851–2016.
Note: This figure was made by combining the results for "Mormon," "Mormons," "LDS," and "Latter-day Saints" on chronicle.nytlabs.com.

Even a highly respected news source cannot come close to matching the coverage or diversity of the Google book collection.[16] Because the breadth of the collection searched by Ngrams is so vast, it is less influenced by the distinctive interests of any single source. The views of a single editor or author or the interests of a select region or religion are less likely to fully shape the story told. Size alone does not ensure a representative description of the entire culture, but the vast size of the Google book collection does ensure that the publications held in libraries are represented.

Refining the Measures

When scholars use the Ngram Viewer for research, the greatest challenge remains synonymy. Finding Ngram searches that identify a distinctive religious feature, person, event, or group poses a major challenge when they are constructing religion measures. As a result, virtually all Ngram searches will require some refinement for improving the measures. As readily acknowledged by Michel and his colleagues (2011b:34), words often share the same spelling but have very different meanings. Some words hold multiple meanings regardless of the time period, and others change meaning or refer to a different person or group at different points in time. The Pentecostal and fundamentalist examples illustrated how meaning changes can sometimes offer important insights into religious changes. When attempting to construct standardized measures over time, however, we want the meanings and the measures to remain consistent.

There is no easy or single solution for addressing the challenge of synonymy, but there are several ways the measures can and should be refined. First, as with any research design, clearly defining the concept being measured is essential. What is included in the definition, and what is excluded? This might seem obvious, but it is an essential first step for refining the searches that follow. Moreover, this step helps in assessing whether the concept can and should be measured with the Ngram Viewer.

A second method for refining the measures is effectively using the power of the Ngram Viewer. Although it is fun and somewhat addictive to do quick searches in the Ngram Viewer, generating precise measures typically requires a more careful use of the parameters available. The Viewer currently offers the following options for refining searches: wildcard search, inflection search, case insensitive search, part-of-speech tags, and Ngram compositions.[17] As noted earlier, our use of part-of-speech tags helped us to better understand how the use of the word "fundamentalist" changed over time, and our use of a 2-gram (or bigram) allowed us to understand how the word was used differently when describing Christians and Muslims. In short, refining the measures requires a knowledge and understanding of the Ngram Viewer.

Refining the measures and improving their precision also requires knowledge of American religion. This knowledge improves the definitions offered, as well as the terms and parameters used for conducting searches. As with any research project, the Ngram searches are an iterative process. Some searches fail to offer a distinctive Ngram, or the meaning is unclear until additional searches are conducted. Holding knowledge of American religious history places both the search and the results of the search within the larger historical context. For example, the findings shown in figure 10.3 on nineteenth-century Pentecostals are meaningful if the researcher knows that early Methodist holiness movements referred to themselves as Pentecostals. Without this knowledge, however, the results are confusing and meaningless.

Generating Quantitative Measures

Perhaps the most obvious use of the Ngram Viewer for future research is to develop quantitative measures of religion and culture. All of the data points shown in the Ngram Viewer graphs can be saved to a data file and merged with other measures over time for analysis. In an effort to democratize access to these trend data, we created a dataset with more than four hundred Ngram variables and twenty historical trend variables for dissemination through theARDA.com.[18] The Ngram variables include both data for specific religious terms and composite data, where scales are created out of similar words (e.g., Atheist scale = atheist + Atheist + atheism + Atheism). The historical component of the dataset was drawn from many sources, the most common being the *Historical Statistics of the United States* (Carter et al. 2015). It contains a few of the measures collected by the census, including total population, GDP, median age, sex ratios, and immigration. When available, it also includes measures on education and clergy training, such as the general levels of education, private institutions of higher education, and seminaries. See the appendix to this chapter for a list of all of our historical variables and their source.

By combining existing historical data sources with the Ngram measures, we are hoping to stimulate new lines of research. Yet, we offer the new measures with important precautions. First, the data file offers some simple Ngram and bigram searches, but for most research projects the measures will need to be refined. Our goal was to simply offer initial measures for some common religion concepts or terms. Second, as with many trend data files, measures included in the file are often highly correlated, with numerous correlations above 0.9 or below -0.9. This high level of multicollinearity should be taken into account when selecting the models and analysis used with data.

The most important precaution, however, is that researchers should seek additional information for understanding what the measures mean. For example, is increased attention due to fame or infamy? As noted earlier, an in-depth knowledge of American religion will help a researcher to understand many of the measures, yet more information is often needed. Below we review how the Ngram Viewer and the Google book collection offer access to the primary sources used in the searches and how this can reveal more about the measures given.

Exploring the Primary Sources

Although charting trends over time and generating historical data are the most obvious contributions of the Ngram Viewer, using the tool to discover the sources underlying the data is perhaps the most promising. As we review below, the Ngram searches identify the books mentioning the topics of interest, and Google Books often gives researchers immediate access to these primary sources. This allows researchers to understand how the word is used and to better assign meaning to the Ngram measures. Moreover, gaining access to the sources in a digital format allows additional searches across the books of interest. Rather than being limited to a single measure on whether the word or phrase was mentioned, researchers can review the context of how it is used, allowing for additional coding and more measures.

The nineteenth century trend line on Mormons in figure 10.2 offers one of many examples where more information would be useful. Knowing that Mormons are receiving more mentions in published books tells us nothing about who was writing these books or what was being said. Were they apologetic accounts written by Mormons, attacks on Mormons from the antipolygamy movements, or something completely different? Answering these questions requires researchers to return to the books being searched.

Fortunately, the Ngram Viewer offers a complete bibliography of every book containing the Ngram(s) being searched. When the results are presented for the Ngram "Mormons," for example, links at the bottom of the page allow the researcher to review a bibliography for each of the time periods listed. For the "Mormons" search, researchers can link to the full citations of 300 books published between 1820 and 1857, 270 books published between 1858 and 1883, 221 books published between 1884 and 1890, and so on. When attempting to understand and interpret the findings for a select historical period, the researcher can quickly review citations for the actual sources.

But the Ngram Viewer offers much more than a full bibliography. For many of the books cited, a single click takes the user to an e-book copy of the book or document. At the top of the document a small tool bar lists the number of times the Ngram is used in the book and allows the reader to easily jump from one mention of the word to another. Moreover, the researcher can quickly do searches for additional words of interest and once again can jump from one use of the word to another. As a result, detailed coding and reviews of the documents are greatly simplified for the e-books. For example, a quick search can answer the question about whether the books mentioning Mormons also mentioned polygamy. If so, how often was it mentioned and did the author support the practice?

Unfortunately, not every book cited is available as an e-book. For our example on the Ngram "Mormons," about 40 percent of the books from 1820–1890 were available from a link in Google Ngram. Yet, even this level of coverage greatly reduces the work needed to find and review the primary sources. Moreover, the complete bibliography allows researchers to request additional books to secure more complete and representative coverage. Google Books and Google's Ngram Viewer offer new options for sampling sources, reviewing the text, and coding the documents. But even if the review of the source materials is less systematic and complete, it can assist researchers in understanding the data generated.

Social scientists have long acknowledged that no single research design is the "right" choice for all research projects. Experimental designs offer advantages in isolating the independent variable and assigning causal ordering, surveys allow researchers to generalize findings to a larger population of interest, and field research allows for more in-depth interviewing and observations in a natural setting. In most cases, however, a mixed-methods approach offers a far more complete understanding than any single method can provide (Axinn and Pearce 2006). The Ngram Viewer and Google Books offer unique resources and opportunities for mixing research methods. While the Ngram Viewer can offer broad historical trends and rich quantitative data, the Google book collection allows for a more in-depth look at the context and meaning of measures, as well as providing opportunities for coding additional quantitative measures.

Conclusions

The study of religion and culture more generally is handicapped by a lack of measures that can document changes over time. Google's Ngram Viewer, and the "culturomics" proposed by its developers, offers one option for filling this void. This paper has introduced and assessed the Ngram Viewer and the 3.4 million books it reviews for America.

We find that although the problem of synonymy in the searches remains a significant problem, the tool has great promise for future research. The Ngram Viewer was able to chart significant historical events in the history of the Mormon Church and captured subtle changes in meaning for the use of the words "fundamentalist" and "Pentecostal" over time. The Mormon example illustrated how the Ngram Viewer could provide a standardized measure for some Ngrams, and the "fundamentalist" and "Pentecostal" examples helped to demonstrate how search parameters could help to capture changes in meaning over time. We propose that, when knowledge of American religion is combined with a careful use of the Ngram Viewer search parameters, the synonymy of the searches is often improved, and the subtle changes are more effectively detected.

We also conclude that the corpus of books has limitations not acknowledged by the developers. Whereas the corpus reflects the books placed in college libraries, the books fail to represent the entire culture, especially when literacy is low and books are not readily accessible. This conclusion is especially important for religion measures. Because of the close tie between select religions and higher education in early America, the books secured in college libraries failed to fully represent the entire culture. Secular interests, as well as those of the rapidly growing upstart religions, are not fully represented.

Finally, we propose that the use of mixed methods will greatly improve our understanding of the measures generated. Whereas most of our attention focused on the Ngram Viewer's quick production of quantitative measures over time, the tool also provides full citations for the primary sources used and often offers ready access to the sources in Google Books. Together they clarify the meaning of the measures being used, and they provide a more complete picture of the social and religious changes being studied. The Ngram Viewer generates trend lines and longitudinal data that offer a broad overview of major historical trends, and the primary sources in Google Books reveal the rich stories underlying the larger historical trends.

In summary, the Google Ngram Viewer is a powerful and promising research tool that has the capacity to generate large volumes of data for the nineteenth and twentieth centuries. This tool is especially promising for religion, given the lack of measures consistently available over time. Yet, we found that the power of the tool must be balanced with an understanding of the corpus's limitations and the meaning of the measures. As with all research methods, the measures provided by the

Ngram Viewer provide the greatest insights when complemented by the findings of other research methods.

Appendix: Historical Measures in the Current ARDA Ngrams Dataset

Measures from the *Historical Statistics of the United States* (*HSUS*) (Carter et al. 2015)

Variables	Years	Linear Interpolation?
Total population	1800–2000	Yes
Percent urban	1800–2000	Yes
Sex ratio—males per 100 females	1800–2000	Yes
Median age	1800–2000	Yes
Percent foreign born	1850–2000	Yes
GDP, real in 1996 dollars	1800–2000	No
GDP per capita, real in 1996 dollars	1800–2000	No
Percent of 18–24-year-olds enrolled in higher education	1904–1995	Yes
Percent at least 14 years old who are illiterate	1870–1979	Yes
Percentage of workers who are farmers or farm laborers	1860–1990	Yes
Percent of 5–20-year-olds enrolled in school—primary and secondary	1860–1994	Yes
Higher education enrollment, in thousands	1869–1995	Yes
Percent of immigrants who are from Western Europe—Northwestern Europe, Germany, Greece, Italy, Portugal, Spain or Other	1820–1997	No
Percent of immigrants who are from Eastern Europe—Poland, Other Central Europe, Eastern Europe	1820–1997	No
Percent of immigrants who are from Asia	1820–1997	No
Percent of immigrants who are from North America	1820–1997	No
Percent of immigrants who are from South America	1820–1997	No
Percent of immigrants who are from Africa	1820–1997	No
Percent of immigrants who are from Oceania	1820–1997	No
Percent of immigrants who are from Other	1820–1997	No
Total number of immigrants	1820–1997	No
Voter turnout in presidential elections	1824–2000, every four yrs	No

Data from the *Yearbook of American and Canadian Churches* (*YACC*)

Variable	Years	Linear Interpolation?
Number of clergy	1925–2000	No

Data from the National Center for Education Statistics (NCES)

Variables	Years	Linear Interpolation?
Number of higher education institutions	1870–2000	Yes
Percent of higher education enrollment that is in private institutions	1950–2000	Yes

Data calculated from the Association of Theological Schools (ATS) Directory

Variable	Years	Linear Interpolation?
Number of seminaries	1800–2000	No

Calculated variables from multiple data sources

Variables	Years	Linear Interpolation?
Percent of the population that is clergy (*HSUS* and *YACC*)	1925–2000	No
Percent of higher education institutions that are seminaries (NCES and ATS)	1870–2010	No

NOTES

1 The authors would like to thank Roger Geiger, George Marsden, and Grant Wacker for helping educate us on early American higher education and Nathaniel Porter for his assistance in assembling data from the Google Ngram Viewer. This project was made possible through the support of a grant from the John Templeton Foundation. The opinions expressed in this publication are those of the authors and do not necessarily reflect the views of the John Templeton Foundation.

2 The General Social Surveys and National Election Studies are available for download free of charge from the Association of Religion Data Archives (www.theARDA.com).

3 For information on many of the participating libraries, go to the Google Books information page: www.google.com (viewed November 4, 2014). For additional information, including a timeline of related events, go to en.wikipedia.org (viewed November 4, 2014).

4 This article was published in *Science* on Jan. 14, 2011, but an online version of the article was available on December 16, 2010.

5 Michel and his coauthors addressed many of the most frequently asked questions about data collection and the Ngram Viewer here: www.culturomics.org.

6 For more information, see books.google.com (viewed November 4, 2014). By 2012 Google Books included more than twenty million books (googleresearch .blogspot.com, viewed November 4, 2014).

7 For the online supplement to Michel et al. (2011a), go to www.sciencemag.org. Additional information can be found at www.culturomics.org and books.google.com.

8 The Edmunds-Tucker Act was upheld by the Supreme Court on May 19, 1890, and Woodruff's manifesto was announced on Sept. 25, 1890 (Arrington and Bitton 1992:183; Hansen 1981:145).

9 For membership totals for the Church of Jesus Christ of Latter-day Saints from 1925 to 2009, go to theARDA.com.

10 For clergy, congregations, and membership totals for the Assemblies of God from 1925 to 2009, as well recent survey findings and a geographical distribution, go to theARDA.com (www.theARDA.com). For the most recent statistical overviews, go to ag.org

11 Charles Fox Parham is credited with introducing these "new" Pentecostal teachings to Seymour and others, but it was Seymour's Azusa Street Revivals that were most influential in launching the new movement (Wacker 2001).

12 The authors began their graph in 1800 and warned that prior to this date "there aren't enough books to reliably quantify many of the queries" for English-only sources. Since we restrict our search to American English books, our total collection for the early nineteenth century is greatly reduced. To avoid erratic fluctuations due to the small number of books in the early 1800s, we begin our graph in 1840. For additional information on the Ngram Viewer and to review the full quote given above, go to www.culturomics.org.

13 Our Documents, "Morrill Act (1862)," accessed 11/30/16, www.ourdocuments.gov.

14 For an excellent overview of the dramatic transformation of educational institutions during the nineteenth and early twentieth centuries, see David P. Baker's *Schooled Society: The Educational Transformation of Global Culture*, 2014.

15 The Chronicle (chronicle.nytlabs.com) offers search features and graphing tools similar to the Google Ngram Viewer. The authors would like to thank Jonathan Hill for bringing the *New York Times* Chronicle tool to our attention.

16 An even broader online collection of news sources, named Chronicling America, is available through the Library of Congress (chroniclingamerica.loc.gov) and is produced by the National Digital Newspaper Program (NDNP). Unlike Google Ngrams and the *New York Times*, however, this collection does not automatically break out results by year and depict them in a graph. Chronicling America currently provides information on American newspapers from 1836 to 1922.

17 For example, a wild card search of "*fundamentalism" allows users to compare changes in "Christian fundamentalism" and "Islamic fundamentalism." Users can

also examine trends for words that have a similar root with an inflection search; for example, searching "believe_INF" brought up results for "believe," "believed," "believes," and "believing." There is also an option that allows users to do case-sensitive searches; doing so allows users to distinguish between, for example, "Catholic" and "catholic." Users can also differentiate between words that are used as different parts of speech. For example, the search "worship_NOUN,worship_VERB" splits the results by whether the word "worship" was used as a noun or verb. Lastly, users can also combine words into compositions; for example, searching "religion + religions + religious" allows users to see trends of how often these three words have been used. Each of these options is explained in a lengthy footnote on the Ngram Viewer site (books.google.com), and even more information is given on the Culturomics website (www.culturomics.org).

18 This dataset is available at www.theARDA.com.

BIBLIOGRAPHY

Arrington, Leonard J., and Davis Bitton. 1992. *The Mormon Experience: A History of the Latter-Day Saints*, 2nd ed. Urbana: University of Illinois Press.

Axinn, William G., and Lisa D. Pearce. 2006. *Mixed Method Data Collection Strategies.* New York: Cambridge University Press.

Baker, David P. 2014. *The Schooled Society: The Educational Transformation of Global Culture.* Stanford, CA: Stanford University Press.

Bureau of the Census. 1975. *Historical Statistics of the United States, Colonial Times to 1970, Bicentennial Edition.* Washington, DC: U.S. Government Printing Office.

Burke, Colin B. 1982. *American Collegiate Populations: A Test of the Traditional View.* New York: NYU Press.

Burtchaell, James Tunstead. 1998. *The Dying of the Light: The Disengagement of Colleges and Universities from Their Christian Churches.* Grand Rapids, MI: Eerdmans.

Carter, Susan B., Scott Sigmund Gartner, Michael R. Haines, Alan L. Olmstead, Richard Sutch, and Gavin Wright, eds. 2015. *Historical Statistics of the United States: Millennial Edition Online.* New York: Cambridge University Press. Retrieved March 6, 2014, hsus.cambridge.org.

Finke, Roger, and Rodney Stark. 1986. "Turning Pews into People: Estimating 19th-Century Church Membership." *Journal for the Scientific Study of Religion* 25(2): 180–92.

Finke, Roger, and Rodney Stark. 2005. *The Churching of America, 1776–2005: Winners and Losers in Our Religious Economy*, 2nd ed. New Brunswick, NJ: Rutgers University Press.

Gaustad, Edwin. 1976. *Historical Atlas of Religion in America.* New York: Harper and Row.

Hansen, Klaus J. 1981. *Mormonism and the American Experience.* Chicago: University of Chicago Press.

Jenkins, Philip. 2002. *The Next Christendom: The Coming of Global Christianity.* New York: Oxford University Press.

Marsden, George M. 1980. *Fundamentalism and American Culture: The Shaping of Twentieth-Century Evangelicalism, 1870–1925.* New York: Oxford University Press.

Marsden, George M. 1994. *The Soul of the American University: From Protestant Establishment to Established Nonbelief.* New York: Oxford University Press.

Melton, J. Gordon, ed. 1991. *American Religions: A Comprehensive Study of the Major Religious Groups in the United States and Canada*, vol. 1. New York: Gale Research.

Michel, Jean-Baptiste, Yuan Kui Shen, Aviva Presser Aiden, Adrian Veres, Matthew K. Gray, William Brockman, the Google Books Team, Joseph P. Pickett, Dale Hoiberg, Dan Clancy, Peter Norvig, Jon Orwant, Steven Pinker, Martin A. Nowak, and Erez Lieberman Aiden. 2011a. "Quantitative Analysis of Culture Using Millions of Digitized Books." *Science* 331: 176–82. (Published online ahead of print: December 16, 2010.)

Michel, Jean-Baptiste, Yuan Kui Shen, Aviva Presser Aiden, Adrian Veres, Matthew K. Gray, the Google Books Team, Joseph P. Pickett, Dale Hoiberg, Dan Clancy, Peter Norvig, Jon Orwant, Steven Pinker, Martin A. Nowak, and Erez Lieberman Aiden. 2011b. "Supporting Online Material for 'Quantitative Analysis of Culture Using Millions of Digitized Books.'" Accessed November 6, 2014, www.sciencemag.org.

Ringenberg, William C. 1984. *The Christian College: A History of Protestant Higher Education in America.* Grand Rapids, MI: Eerdmans.

Smith, Tom W. 2017. "Improving Cross-National/Cultural Comparability Using the Total Survey Error Paradigm." In *Faithful Measures*, ed. Roger Finke and Christopher D. Bader.

Stark, Rodney, and Roger Finke. 1988. "American Religion in 1776: A Statistical Portrait." *Sociological Analysis* 49(1): 39–51.

Taves, Ann. 2011. "Presidential Address: 'Religion' in the Humanities and the Humanities in the University." *Journal of the American Academy of Religion* 79(2): 287–314.

Thelin, John R. 2011. *A History of American Higher Education*, 2nd ed. Baltimore, MD: John Hopkins University Press.

Wacker, Grant. 2001. *Heaven Below: Early Pentecostals and American Culture.* Cambridge, MA: Harvard University Press.

11.

Pathways to Discovery and Enlightenment

Amazon's Recommendation System as a Source of Information on Religious and Paranormal Consumption Patterns

NATHANIEL D. PORTER AND CHRISTOPHER D. BADER

The authors would count themselves among the many readers who mourn the passing of the traditional bookstore as ever-increasing percentages of book purchases (and purchases of all kinds, for that matter) move online. But as social scientists we can also appreciate the opportunities this sea change in consumption habits provides for new sources of data. Since 1995 Amazon.com, the undisputed leader of online book sales, has been collecting data on the books individuals purchase from its site and, even more importantly, which *other books* that person either purchases or recommends. It is in Amazon's best interests to collect such data. Knowing which books people buy allows Amazon to recommend to other shoppers books that they are more likely to buy. Put more simply, more data = better business.

An unanticipated outcome of Amazon's collection efforts is the creation of an immense and unique set of unobtrusive measures regarding how individuals connect ideas. In the study of religion and spirituality, such data can open up quantitative approaches to many research agendas that are otherwise limited to qualitative study. In particular, co-purchase data can improve the study of small cultural groups and ideas lacking clear boundaries or formal organization. This chapter will demonstrate this value and explore how Amazon's purchasing data can help us clarify the connections and distinctions among religious, paranormal, New Age, and spiritual thought. We begin with a discussion of the existing research on the consumption of religious materials, limited as it is, and the difficulties inherent in quantifying the beliefs of small groups, particularly those lacking clear organizational units, such as the New

Age and paranormal. We then explain how Amazon data can provide data that allow the development of preliminary measures of such diffuse belief systems and the connections among them.

We develop a network map of purchasing patterns using these data in the hopes of clarifying the blurry boundaries among forms of New Age belief, religion, and spirituality.

Research on the Consumption of Religious Materials

In 2004 Mel Gibson's *Passion of the Christ*, based closely on biblical accounts of Jesus' last week, grossed over $370 million in the U.S. box office, becoming the fourteenth-highest-grossing film of all time in the United States. The *Passion of the Christ* phenomenon helped draw the attention of social scientists to documenting and attempting to understand the meaning and importance of the consumption of religious media. The 2005 Baylor Religion Survey devoted several blocks of questions to religiously themed movies, television shows, and books. More than three quarters of respondents (76.7%) had seen one or more of the following popular, Christian-themed television shows and movies of the time: *The Passion of the Christ*, *This Is Your Day* (Benny Hinn), *Joan of Arcadia*, any VeggieTales movies or videos, *7th Heaven*, and/or *Touched by an Angel*. Nearly half of respondents (44.4%) had spent money on some form of religious material good in the preceding month, such as t-shirts with religious messages on them, religiously themed jewelry (crucifixes, etc), bumper stickers, religious art, or other products (Park and Baker 2007).

Book purchases constitute an important aspect of religious consumption and have been the focus of limited research within sociology.[1] In 2013 alone, sales of books by religious presses topped $572 million, or 3.7% of total book sales (Burns 2014).[2] In 2002, the CBA, a trade association for Christian retailers, counted approximately twenty-five hundred member stores specializing in selling Christian materials in the United States (Bader and Lockhart 2006). Bader and Lockhart found that areas with high evangelical Christian adherence rates had proportionally more of these bookstores and fewer astrologers and psychics. This lends support to the idea that conservative religious groups use distinctive consumption to establish cultural boundaries (Park and Draper 2010;

Smith 1998), prevent religious free-riding (Iannaccone 1994; Stark and Finke 2000), and strengthen group identity (Cosgel and Minkler 2004; Wright 2015). Even among the explicitly irreligious, scientists from Richard Dawkins to Bill Nye have achieved increased cultural prominence and high book sales writing about religion.

Religious identity and consumption do not always split people neatly, however. Both strength of religious commitment and individualism in beliefs and practices vary widely within and between self-identified religious groups. Pearce, Foster, and Hardie (2013) inductively identify a sizable group of U.S. adolescents they call "adapters," who "find religion important and report being close to God. This group thinks most about the meaning of life and its members are the most likely to see themselves as spiritual but not religious" (2013:69). Nor are these adolescents merely confused or in the midst of transition between beliefs. Rather, it appears that although the market shares of atheists and evangelicals may be rising (Warner 2010), individuals outside of high-exclusivity groups have increasingly personalized religious and spiritual practices and beliefs. Likewise, in the 2005 Baylor Religion Study, about half (46.7%) of respondents who had read Christian books that were asked about had also read non-Christian religious nonfiction (*Dianetics*, *The Celestine Prophecy*) or the religious conspiracy novel *The da Vinci Code*.

Despite the increasing contemporary prominence of "fuzzy" religion (Voas 2009), sociologists of religion have found some categories of religion and spirituality difficult to quantify, due to the challenge of defining clear categories with high predictive power in traditional survey methods. Person-centered (Pearce and Denton 2011; Pearce, Foster, and Hardie 2013) and longitudinal (Lim, MacGregor, and Putnam 2010) approaches have demonstrated the existence of liminal categories and allowed some classification. But it is difficult to capture any great variety of belief and interest configurations, even in relatively large religion-oriented surveys such as the National Study of Youth and Religion (Smith and Denton 2003) or the Baylor Religion Survey (Baylor University 2005–2011). Religious groups or movements with relatively few adherents in the study area (e.g., anything non-Christian in the United States) tend to be undertheorized because surveys fail to capture enough members of any group to draw reliable statistical conclusions. The relative frequency of interreligious ties among the irreligious and those outside the Judeo-Christian tradition (Scheitle and Smith 2011) further confirms their diffuse nature and suggests a need for data that not only include more people outside dominant religions but also address the interconnection among different groups and modes of thought.

The Challenge of the Paranormal

Decentralized beliefs, such as New Age and paranormal beliefs, present researchers the double challenge of limited scope and a lack of formal organization.[3] Indeed, scholars have struggled with the basic issue of how to define or even label the loose association of beliefs, ideas, phenomena, and experiences that constitute the "New Age," "paranormal," "the supernatural," "occult," "unexplained phenomena," "metaphysics," "pseudo-science," "mysticism," and a host of other terms.[4] Depending upon which definition one uses, crystal balls, Bigfoot, ghosts, and palm reading are similar things; by other definitions they are vastly different. For example, Bader, Mencken, and Baker (2010) use the term "paranormal" to encapsulate any set of beliefs that fall outside the boundaries of conventional science and conventional religion, thereby grouping diverse phenomena from Bigfoot to ESP and holistic healing under the same banner. Goode (2012), on the other hand, distinguishes between *pseudoscience*, which consists of phenomena that *could exist* without entirely overturning conventional science, such as Bigfoot and the Loch Ness Monster, and *paranormalism*, which would include phenomena such as UFOs and ESP that would require radical, wholesale changes to scientific thought in order to be explicable. Further complicating matters is the fact that some scholars explicitly separate the historical "New Age" movement, which traces its history to the 1875 founding of the Theosophical Society, from the occult and paranormal (cf. Melton 1990:ix).

For such diffuse areas of thought, it may behoove scholars to step back and examine the connections that believers (or at least the curious) are making among diverse phenomena *themselves*. Do our abstract, academic definitions reflect the actual thought processes or preferences of the individuals who consume paranormal materials? Purchasing and recommendation information from Amazon.com provides a data source that allows formal inductive exploration of such issues that builds on past research without imposing predetermined categories such as survey response options.

Gathering Amazon Data on Book Copurchases

In order to gather unobtrusive data on the connections individuals make among paranormal subjects, we leverage product recommendations from the "customers who bought this also bought" feature on product pages at Amazon.com. This constitutes a source of copurchasing data, or data on multiple items purchased by the same individuals.

Specifically, for each item in its catalog, Amazon computes the similarity of items not in terms of their content but only in terms of how many customers bought those specific items together (Linden, Smith, and York 2003).[5] This similarity is used to recommend up to a hundred items that are frequently bought by purchasers of the original product. While this method, known as item-to-item collaborative filtering, requires a great deal of computing power, it is able to scale more efficiently than comparing the profiles of users or combining consumption patterns and user ratings of other items, a model that is closer to the Netflix model (Lu et al. 2012). Most importantly from a research perspective, it is relatively simple, connects many different categories of products, is documented by its creator, and reflects actual human behavior; in other words, it is an unobtrusive measure.

The copurchase data that can be gathered in this way are structured as networks of books that are frequently purchased together. To produce the data, we downloaded copies of Amazon product pages for each book we wished to study and of every book in the "customers who bought this also bought" section.[6] Precise data are not available for sales or copurchase quantities, but recommendations are given in rank order from most to least frequently bought together. For questions of general overlap, the rankings are less critical, but they are valuable to help weight relationships in both statistical and graphical approaches.[7]

Typically, recommendations also depend on format; Kindle e-books recommend only other Kindle books, while physical items may recommend any other physical item on the site. We focus on print books here, as data on demographic differences in the customer base of e-books remain limited, and not all books are available electronically. Kindle books, however, have their own unique value as a topic of research, as recommendations are more tightly embedded in the purchase and consumption of books with reader apps. Furthermore, using Kindle books minimizes the number of seemingly unrelated recommendations by removing groceries, clothes, and other typically irrelevant items from the possible pool of recommended copurchases.[8]

In February 2016, we downloaded the Amazon U.S. product pages for the networks of six books identified by Bader, Mencken, and Baker (2010) as prominent on paranormal and New Age subjects. We used a small custom script (program) to collect information embedded in the pages about both the books (title, author, format, sales rank, average review, number of reviews, product categories) and the connections among them (copurchase network). The script, available at the ARDA website (www.theARDA.com), produces text files that can be read in Microsoft Excel or any major statistical or database software.[9] We subsequently recoded the original Amazon categories into groups of related categories, as discussed below. This final step required familiarity with literature in the area and some judgment, but helped produce clear visual and statistical results.

The data from this chapter are available for download at the ARDA (www.theARDA.com), along with other sample data, but we have tried to make the work flow simple to replicate. We used the free web visualization tool d3.js to produce all visualizations. The conclusion provides additional recommendations for successfully implementing copurchase data collection and analysis, including alternative options for network software and guidelines for deciding when copurchase network analysis is most likely to be valuable.

Mapping Out the Paranormal

Copurchase data open up an entire research agenda for in-depth case studies of the copurchasing networks surrounding books of significance within the study of religion. However, broader agendas open up when we engage in content comparisons across books. For example, Amazon data can help us make some sense of the hard-to-quantify realm of the paranormal.

The second author of this chapter (Bader) coauthored the book *Paranormal America* with colleagues in 2010. The goal of the book was to help clarify what constitutes the paranormal, what paranormalists tend to believe, and how paranormal thought relates (if at all) to conventional Christian thought in the United States. In that volume, Bader and colleagues noted three different types of paranormal belief and experience: *enlightenment, discovery,* and *Christian-related.*[10] These three categories, they argued, represent distinctive subareas within the fuzzy area of the paranormal.

Enlightenment refers to aspects of the paranormal that focus upon personal and internal spiritual growth. Fortune telling, astrology, psychic powers, and the like are typically focused upon learning about one's personal past, future, or present or on becoming a better or more powerful person. *Discovery* refers to those paranormal topics wherein believers typically focus upon the documentation of some phenomenon that is not currently recognized by science. Books about UFOs, Bigfoot, and ghosts often focus upon presenting eyewitness testimony and/or evidence for the reality of said phenomena (albeit disputed) (Bader et al. 2010:12–13).

Finally, Bader and colleagues noted that there is a small selection of topics that "are closely connected to Christian beliefs and yet not fully accepted in many Christian settings" (Bader et al. 2010:18). Even though demons and possession, for example, are biblical concepts, not all Christian denominations believe in the reality of such phenomena. Consequently, one can purchase books on demons from a specifically Christian perspective that discuss the theology of demons and how one can achieve "deliverance" from them. But demons and demonic entities also make frequent appearances in non-Christian (or at least not explicitly Christian) books on ghosts and hauntings that appear in the paranormal section of a bookstore.

Bader and colleagues argued that those with an interest in "enlightenment" topics were more interested in personal growth than in proving the reality of phenomena to others. Hence they would tend to be more likely to constrain their interests to other enlightenment topics. On the other hand, those with a strong focus upon *discovery*-related topics could be expected to constrain their interests to similar subjects and eschew the more mystical realm of psychic phenomena. Finally, Bader and colleagues noted that demons, Virgin Mary sightings, and other Christian-related, paranormal topics provided a potential crossover subject. Those with an interest in such phenomena could be expected to distribute their "spiritual capital" between Christianity and the paranormal.

These expected relationships between types of paranormal phenomena represent testable hypotheses. However, finding the data to test such hypotheses, particularly for a subject as fuzzy as the paranormal, is quite difficult. Indeed, due to a lack of available data at the time, *Paranormal America* does not include a quantitative examination of the boundaries of different forms of the paranormal. Rather, the observations included in the book were the result of impressionistic observations made by Bader and his coauthors as they absorbed the source literature and spent considerable time with different types of paranormal enthusiasts.

Using Amazon data, however, we *can* explore the extent to which paranormalists actually group themselves into distinctive subcategories based on the types of content they prefer to consume. These were our hypotheses related to the purchasing of books:

- Readers who purchase an *enlightenment* paranormal book will be more likely to purchase other *enlightenment* books than to purchase *discovery* or *Christian-related* books.
- Readers who purchase a *discovery* paranormal book will be more likely to purchase other *discovery* books than to purchase *enlightenment* or *Christian-related* books.
- Readers who purchase a *Christian-related* paranormal book will be the most likely to also purchase books reflective of conventional Christianity.

What follows is a detailed example of how we examined and compared the copurchasing data of several paranormal books by categorizing those books into broader subject areas.

A Paranormal Library

We compiled Amazon copurchasing data on six books, each qualitatively identified in past research as representative of a prominent area of paranormal interest in one of the three topic types. These six books included two topics we would categorize as *enlightenment* volumes: a popular book about reincarnation (*Many Lives, Many Masters* by Brian Weiss) and a handbook for the development of psychic powers such as ESP (*The Essential Guide to Psychic Powers* by Sarah Bartlett). Also included were three books focused upon the presentation of evidence (*discovery*): *Magicians of the Gods* by Graham Hancock, which argues for the existence of ancient, advanced civilizations; *UFOs: Generals, Pilots, and Government Officials Go on the Record* by Leslie Kean, focused upon contemporary sightings of UFOs and flying saucers; and finally *Sasquatch: Legend Meets Science* by Jeffrey Meldrum, which presents evidence for the reality of Bigfoot. Finally, we include a *Christian-related* item that blurs the boundaries between the paranormal and conventional religion by focusing upon ghosts and demonic entities: *The Demonologist* by Gerald Brittle.

Using Amazon, we can gather copurchasing data for all of these books. For example, our initial dataset consisted of the titles and authors of the eighty-three different books that people who purchased *Many Lives, Many Masters* also tended to buy. Not surprisingly, people who bought Weiss's book purchased books about similar topics, such as Michael Newton's *Journey of Souls: Case Studies of Life between Lives* and twelve others on past lives and reincarnation. But people with an interest in reincarnation also bought books about near-death experiences (stories of experiencing, in some form, the afterlife after being brain dead for some period of time and then returned to life), including *My Life after Death: A Memoir from Heaven* (Erik Medhus), *Imagine Heaven: Near-Death Experiences, God's Promises, and the Exhilarating Future That Awaits You* (John Burke), and *On Life after Death* (Elizabeth Kubler-Ross). Other nonfiction books ranged across a wide variety of topics, from how to deal with "emotional vampires" to healing, nutrition, tarot/oracle cards, Buddhism, Hinduism, and others. And while most of the recommendations are substantively meaningful, some, such as the frequent copurchase of Harper Lee's novel *Go Set a Watchman* (a newly released bestseller when the data were collected) with *Many Lives, Many Masters*, may result more from overall sales trends than associated interests.

However, delving further into Amazon purchasing data and comparing purchasing networks among our books first require an understanding of how Amazon itself categorizes its products.

Categories of Paranormal and Religious Thought

All of Amazon's products are assigned to one or more sets of nested categories, up to three of which are displayed on the product page.[11] For example, *UFOs* by Leslie Kean is listed under Books > Religion & Spirituality > Occult & Paranormal > UFOs. It also has a secondary subject of Books > Science & Math > Astronomy & Space Science and a third of Books > Textbooks > Science & Mathematics. The first decision a researcher will need to make is how to handle multiple categories. For simplicity's sake, we have focused only upon the first assigned category for each book in the copurchasing data.

Of greatest interest to religion researchers are those headings specifically related to religion and spirituality. There are two major categories under which books related to religion are categorized on Amazon: Christian Books & Bibles and Religion & Spirituality. The books most closely related to Christianity end up in Books > Christian Books & Bibles and from there are further categorized into Catholicism, Christian Living, Biographies, Bible Study & Reference, Theology, and many other subcategories. Depending upon the book, these subcategories may go deeper still. For example, *Saints Who Battled Satan* appears under Books > Christian Books & Bibles > Biographies > Saints. The choice of how deeply to delve into these categories depends upon the research question. For our purposes, we wanted to explore the extent to which people interested in paranormal content also expressed interest in conventional Christianity. Therefore we coded all books under Christian Books & Bibles as "Christian."

Books that are not explicitly Christian in content will end up categorized by Amazon under Religion & Spirituality and its subcategories. Two of these subcategories are New Age & Spirituality and Occult & Paranormal. The New Age & Spirituality category includes books about such topics as psychic powers, reincarnation, Wicca/witchcraft, crystals, fortune telling, mysticism, and many others. The Occult & Paranormal includes books about UFOs, mysterious creatures such as Bigfoot and the Loch Ness Monster, advanced ancient civilizations, conspiracies, demons and ghosts, and haunted houses. We used these categories, as is, to code the relevant books. It was immediately intriguing to us that Amazon's categories of New Age & Spirituality and Occult & Paranormal fairly neatly aligned with the definition of *enlightenment* and *discovery* that appeared in *Paranormal America.*

Also contained within the Religion & Spirituality category are books about Other Religions, Practices & Sacred Texts, including Hinduism, Buddhism, and Native American religion. We coded all books within this subcategory as Other Religions. Finally, Religion & Spirituality includes some general books about Worship & Devotion and Religious Studies, which we categorized as such.

Of course, in addition to nonfiction books about religion, Amazon carries nonfiction about a bewildering variety of nonreligious topics, fiction of all types, movies, and everything from air fresheners to vitamins. Since these categories were not of direct interest to our research questions, we simply coded them as "fiction," "movies," "other nonfiction," and "other products." Table 11.1 breaks down the categories of items that purchasers of these six paranormal books tend to also purchase.

Table 11.1. Copurchasing Data for Seven Books on Paranormal Subjects

Category	*Many Lives, Many Masters*	*The Essential Guide to Psychic Powers*	*Magicians of the Gods*	*UFOs: Generals, Pilots and Government Officials*	*Sasquatch: Legend Meets Science*	*The Demonologist*
Christian	3	0	3	0	0	11
New Age & Spirituality	26	10	4	1	2	3
Occult & Paranormal	14	6	23	74	19	36
Other Religions	4	1	4	2	1	24
Religious Studies	1	0	0	0	0	2
Worship & Devotion	1	0	0	0	0	0
Fiction	1	0	7	1	8	8
Movies	0	0	0	5	9	8
Other Nonfiction	28	2	45	15	35	8
Other Products	3	1	7	3	25	1

It is immediately apparent from these results that people who purchased books that would fall into the *enlightenment* category proposed by *Paranormal America* were most likely to purchase other books having to do with enlightenment, confirming our first hypothesis. For example, those who purchased *Many Lives, Many Masters* were more likely to buy another book in the New Age & Spirituality category on Amazon than any other religious or spiritual subject. In a similar vein, those who purchased a book on psychic powers (*The Essential Guide to Psychic Powers*) were most likely to purchase other New Age & Spirituality books. Those with an interest in *discovery*, on the other hand, were most likely to stick with similar subjects. Purchasers of *Magicians of the Gods* (ancient advanced civilizations), *UFOs: Generals, Pilots, and Government Officials Go on the Record*, and *Sasquatch: Legend Meets Science* tended to buy books related to other *discovery* topics.

Also as expected, it was readers of *The Demonologist* who were most likely to branch out into Christian materials. Readers of this book on malevolent entities were most likely to read other Occult & Paranormal books, but they were the most likely of all readers to have purchased Christian books as well.

We can find further evidence of these distinct modes of paranormal thought if we break down our categories further. After all, we would see the patterns present in table 11.1 if people who buy UFO books *only* buy other UFO books and if people who buy books on psychic powers only buy other books on psychic powers. We have better evidence of distinctive domains/groupings of paranormal thought to the extent that people who read a book about one *discovery*-related subject also buy books about a different *discovery*-related subject. Table 11.2 provides more detailed breakdowns of the New Age & Spirituality and Occult & Paranormal categories for four of our paranormal books.

We can see evidence here of interest in one type of paranormal phenomenon inspiring interest in other, conceptually similar types of paranormal phenomena. Readers of *Many Lives, Many Masters* were more likely to purchase other New Age & Spirituality books than to purchase those under Occult & Paranormal. Not surprisingly, they expressed the highest level of interest in other books about reincarnation (nine). But its readers were also intrigued by many other *enlightenment* topics, including angels and spirit guides, channeling, divination, Gaia, mental/

Table 11.2. Detailed Copurchasing Data for Four Paranormal Books

Category	*Many Lives, Many Masters*	*The Essential Guide to Psychic Powers*	*Sasquatch: Legend Meets Science*	*UFOs: Generals, Pilots and Government Officials*
New Age & Spirituality	26	10	2	1
Angels/Spirit Guides	1	0	1	0
Astrology	0	1	0	0
Channeling	2	0	0	0
Divination	1	6	0	0
Gaia	2	0	0	0
Mental/Spiritual Healing	1	0	0	0
New Thought	5	2	0	0
Reference	0	0	1	1
Reincarnation	9	1	0	0
Self-Help	1	0	0	0
Spiritualism	2	0	0	0
Wicca/Witchcraft	1	0	0	0
Yoga	2	0	0	0
Occult & Paranormal	14	6	19	74
Ancient/Controversial Knowledge	0	0	0	2
General	1	0	0	0
Parapsychology	11	6	0	3
Supernatural	2	0	2	1
UFOs	0	0	3	64
Unexplained Mysteries	1	0	14	4

spiritual healing practices, "new thought," spiritualism, Wicca/witchcraft, and yoga. Readers of the *Essential Guide to Psychic Powers* showed an interest in books on astrology, divination, and new thought, and also crossed into reincarnation.

Readers interested in Sasquatch and UFOs (*discovery*-related topics) tended to stay away from subjects such as psychic powers, astrology, and the like. *Sasquatch: Legend Meets Science* readers were most intrigued by other books on "unexplained mysteries" (which is where Amazon tends to categorize books on Bigfoot) but also branched out into UFOs. Readers of *UFOs* purchased many other books on the topic, but showed interest in books on ancient/controversial knowledge, parapsychology, the supernatural, and unexplained mysteries. *Sasquatch* or *UFOs* readers crossed over to also buy books in the New Age & Spirituality category comparatively rarely (two books and one book, respectively).

These exploratory analyses provide some support to the argument put forth in *Paranormal America* that interest in the paranormal can be subdivided into meaningful and distinctive subcategories. The data available from Amazon are deep, and researchers could choose to continue to delve deeper into the connections and relationships among books—deeper than we have the space to do here. One might explore the specific books that are shared between any two paranormal titles. By way of example, one of the "unexplained mysteries" books that tended to be purchased by readers of *UFOs* was, indeed, *Sasquatch: Legend Meets Science*, and the reincarnation book most often purchased with *The Essential Guide to Psychic Powers* was *Many Lives, Many Masters*.

Visualizing the Networks of Paranormal Books and Ideas

The foregoing examples demonstrate how anyone can use copurchase data to explore the relationships of ideas and groups without official organizations or clear boundaries. This type of approach can be extended at least three important ways. First, scholars of comparative and international religion or culture can take advantage of the global ubiquity of Amazon by comparing the networks of similar (or identical) books and topics across the thirteen Amazon international portals representing markets in Europe, Asia, and the Americas. Second, formal statistical models can be used by those with backgrounds in statistics and social network analysis. Statistical models can provide comparisons to random networks (the equivalent of a p-test), investigate specific hypotheses, and even integrate outside data on groups, books, or change over time.

Network visualization, however, is the most helpful and intuitive extension in many situations, and requires no additional training or expertise.[12] There are no formal guidelines for visualizing social network data, although many books and websites provide examples. Rather, the goal is to visualize the structure of the network to complement and enhance other kinds of analysis. Here, we use two different approaches, visualizing each ego-network separately and subsequently combining the networks to help us understand the larger context of the six titles we chose to focus on. To do so, we import the same data we used previously into the free web visualization tool D3.js to produce a force-directed network image that is interactive, customizable, and saveable as a photo or interactive web page. Interactive color versions of figures 11.1 and 11.2 that allow the user to see the title and ties of each book are available at the ARDA (theARDA.com). Books are coded into topical categories as above, and the algorithm positions books so they are closer to books they are most frequently bought with. The seed nodes (the six books we

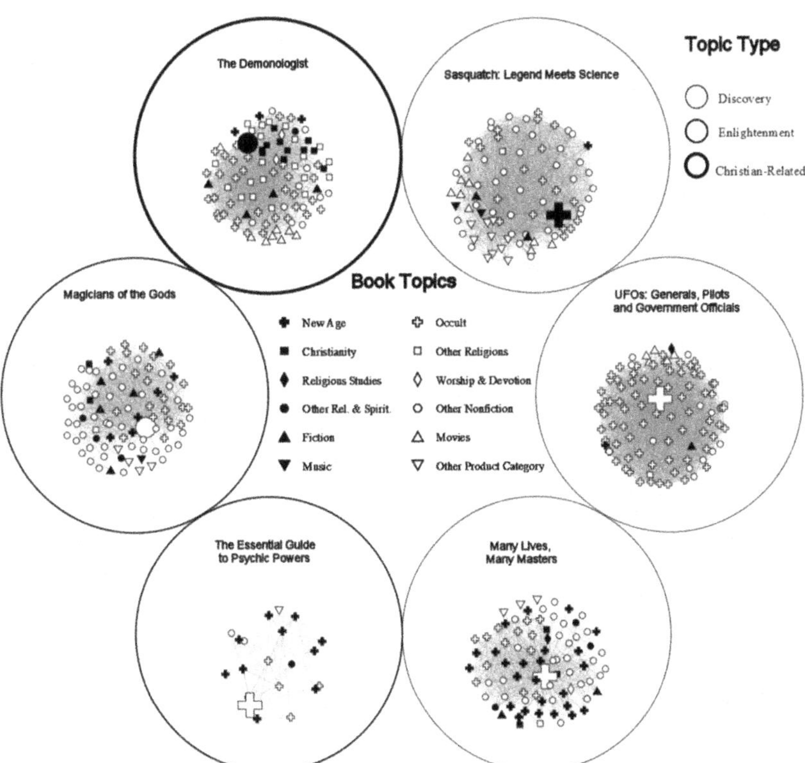

Figure 11.1. Copurchase Networks of Six Paranormal Books.

selected) are enlarged and labeled, and the width of the edges is relative to how frequently those specific books are bought together.

Some differences between the books are immediately apparent in figure 11.1. Books in areas we have classified as *discovery* oriented (Bigfoot, UFOs, and ancient civilization) have dense networks of books on very similar topics in the "occult" and "other nonfiction" categories. The network of *UFOs: Generals, Pilots, and Government Officials*, for example, is a dense cluster of closely related books in the "Occult" and "Other Nonfiction" categories, with other topics, including religion and New Age, relegated to the periphery (meaning they are less interconnected with the books in the central area).

In the case of *Sasquatch: Legend Meets Science*, it is clear that books and other products (t-shirts, car fresheners, etc.) are more densely connected within their groups than between groups. That is, even though buyers of both *Sasquatch* and other related books frequently also bought kitsch (the cluster of white triangles to the lower right), there appear to be at least two subgroups of *Sasquatch* readers, one of which is exclusively or primarily interested in books. The third, *Magicians of the Gods*, has a more intermixed network than that of *Sasquatch* or *UFOs* overall, but is still dominated by the same topics as other *discovery* books, with books on New Age and Christianity, for example, comprising a ring around the core of books on ancient civilizations and related areas in nonfiction and occult.

Enlightenment-oriented books demonstrate a pattern distinct from any of these. *The Essential Guide to Psychic Powers* has the smallest quantity of frequently copurchased books, with New Age, occult, and other topics included. *Many Lives, Many Masters* also has a diverse network consisting of general nonfiction, religion, occult, and New Age books. Both books are network hubs; while some buyers are largely interested in their specific topic, the books also serve to connect that topic to other important subgroups of books. Both books also have fewer and weaker ties to the other books in the network, suggesting that readers may have interest in more diverse topics and a less cohesive canon than our *discovery* books.

In some ways, *The Demonologist*, our example of a *Christian-related* paranormal book, has a similar network to these *enlightenment* books. It, too, connects diverse topics, but with two major differences. First,

Christian and occult books bought with it form very distinct clusters, with little intermixing aside from the generic "other religion" category. That is, *The Demonologist* is a network bridge. Such bridges play a key theoretical role in the diffusion of information and ideas (Rogers 2003). Second, unlike the *enlightenment* books above that primarily connect different paranormal or New Age ideas, *The Demonologist* directly links paranormal or New Age beliefs to more orthodox religious beliefs (in this case Christian).

In summary, our visual analysis suggests that books bought with *discovery*-oriented titles tend to fall within a relatively circumscribed band of similar interests (aside from some crossover with *Magicians of the Gods*), those of *enlightenment*-oriented titles appear to connect a broader range of New Age or occult interests, and only those books with specific ties to Christian ideas or practices attract substantial interest from readers of books associated with organized religion. These findings provide important insights for understanding both the appeal of New Age and paranormal beliefs and the most likely paths by which such beliefs could diffuse to religious practitioners.

A different approach to visually comparing the copurchase networks of books is to combine the networks into a single network and consider how the books and their copurchases fit together in the context of all the books we examined. The image in figure 11.2 was made by combining each of the book networks into a single combined network. It is not representative of all New Age or occult books,[13] and shows less detail about the networks of the individual seed books, but provides other important information we would have missed.

The distinctions we have discussed between *discovery* books (Sasquatch, UFOs, and ancient civilizations), *enlightenment* books (reincarnation and psychic powers), and Christian-related books (angels and demons) is clearly visible. The apparent divide between the core network of *The Demonologist* and that of *Many Lives, Many Masters* is actually bridged by the network of *The Essential Guide to Psychic Powers*, which simply had fewer books frequently bought with it. UFOs and conspiracy theories likewise fall between Bigfoot and advanced ancient civilizations. The primary connection between the groups is via the overlap of books focusing on ancient advanced civilization and books oriented toward New Age practices of self-knowledge, probably driven

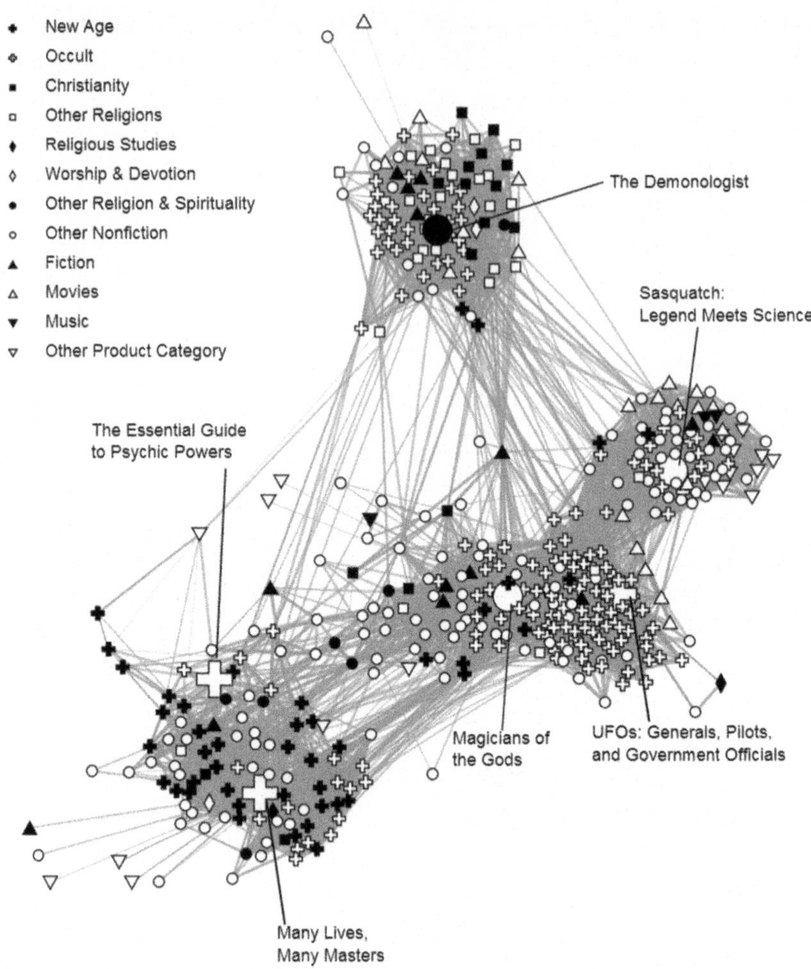

Figure 11.2. Combined Copurchase Networks of Six Paranormal Books.

by a shared openness to unorthodox truth combined with an interest in self-improvement.

Finally, the titles connecting *discovery* directly to the Christian-related cluster demonstrate the potential importance of even a small number of topical bridges in the potential spread of ideas.[14] For example, the black triangle between the *Magicians of the Gods* cluster and the *Demonologist* cluster is densely connected to both groups and also has direct ties to the *Sasquatch* and *UFOs* clusters. It represents *The Books of Enoch*, a collection of so-called forgotten scripture left out of the canon of the Christian Bible but believed by some to be equally valid. It expands on the sparse descriptions of angels, demons, and the devil in the Old Testament and thus appeals to both Christian-related and discovery-oriented interests. Its position as a key bridge suggests that further investigation is merited for those interested in the crossover of paranormal belief and traditional religion. Books on ghosts and apparitions (white squares and triangle in the bottom right of the *Demonologist* cluster) in some cases connect Sasquatch and demons, while books and supplies related to witchcraft (above and to the left of *The Essential Guide to Psychic Powers*) are a secondary path connecting psychic power and demons that could easily be missed given the direct topical tie of exorcism.

Visualizing the book copurchase networks, both individually and in the aggregate, served to confirm the previous findings of distinct groupings of *discovery*, *enlightenment*, and *Christian-related* paranormal books. But whereas topic linking tables provided information primarily on the ties of the specific books we chose, the visualizations allowed us to explore the connections between the other products frequently bought with each of the books. The density of subgroups, the number of links among those subgroups, and (in the aggregate) which topics are "closer" in terms of direct and indirect overlap all help us understand the structure of New Age, occult, and paranormal culture and thought. In particular, these subtleties that are difficult to quantify without visualizing can give us clues as to where to start in studying overlap or diffusion of ideas among groups.

Seeing the Future

There are many more visualization and analysis options for networks of all sizes that we did not have space to explore here, each with its own advantages and disadvantages. We encourage readers to try collecting their own data following this process:

(1) Download local copies of relevant product pages using a private or incognito browser window.[15]
(2) Use our script to extract recommendations and product information.[16]

(3) Recode topics into meaningful groups for your own research.
(4) Import data into your preferred software.
(5) Analyze the networks.

Often, a qualitative analysis of the relationships among different topics for key books (or bestseller lists), like that above, is all that is necessary to provide important evidence for or against the existence of theorized patterns. Networks can also be analyzed quantitatively, using a growing corpus of measures and statistical techniques to help us further understand the roles and positions of individual items, the ways in which topics or items cluster, and even how the networks develop over time (with repeated collection of similar data). Interested readers are encouraged to consult introductory texts in social network analysis (e.g., Borgatti, Everett, and Johnson 2013) and longitudinal network analysis (Snijders 2011).[17] It is even possible to combine copurchase networks with text analysis (e.g., of descriptions or reviews) to compare copurchases in different regions (Amazon sites), or to use ISBNs to connect copurchase data with other public data sources[18] to place copurchased networks in a larger context.

Regardless of the analytic approach, we recommend visualizing every network early in the work flow. Visualization allows investigators to quickly get a feel for the overall structure of a network and discover possible issues with the data. Network graphics also provide for rapid and clear communication to nonspecialists. A variety of social-network-analysis software is available as freeware or at relatively low cost. NodeXL (Smith et al. 2010), a free plugin for modern versions of Microsoft Excel for Windows, provides for easy and flexible network visualization, along with some basic measures of node centrality and clustering. Gephi (Bastian, Heymann, and Jacomy 2009) is a free cross-platform tool for visualizing networks that works quickly and intuitively. UCINET and NETDRAW (Borgatti, Everett, and Freeman 2002) provide a relatively user-friendly menu-driven way to access a wider variety of network measures. For those who want more options and are comfortable with programming, the R statistical environment (R Core Team 2015) is the de facto standard in advanced network visualization and analysis, with key packages including igraph (Csardi and Nepusz 2006) and statnet (Handcock et al. 2008).

Overall, we recommend R (using the visualization script at theARDA.com) for the easiest quick graph and Gephi for the best plug-and-play custom-visualization experience. NodeXL has a similar user experience and will feel more comfortable to Excel users, but the free version requires some manual steps for importing data with node attributes like titles.[19] NodeXL has one additional feature that may be important for presenting results. Each book or group of books can be linked to a custom image, such as a cover photo, to represent it visually, rather than circles or other generic shapes.[20] Regardless of the choice of tool, moving from data to visual is generally painless once the data has been extracted in text format. Most tools also offer options to change the size/color/shape of nodes and edges based on their attributes or network position. Online demos and tutorials are provided at the ARDA (www.theARDA.com).

Sample data, including those used in this chapter, are also available on the ARDA, but the ultimate value of this approach is its flexibility in studying various difficult-to-quantify topics and their relationships. Collecting your own data, whether on the networks of individual products (as here), on the relationships between bestsellers in one or more topics, or on some other collection of items, enables detailed examination of topics salient to your own research.[21] It enables you to set boundaries and choose collections of books that make sense to you or your audience. Even if data on topics of interest to you are publicly available online, collecting your own data makes it possible to gather up-to-the-minute data or even track the networks of objects over time.

Conclusion

We have shown how copurchase networks can be useful to understanding one specific phenomenon, distinctions among types of paranormal topics. Using both tables and network visualizations has allowed us to confirm, using empirical data, the existence of a difference that was previously only informally observed. We have done so despite the lack of formal organizational structures or clear group boundaries that would be necessary for standard survey analysis. Like many of the innovative methods in this volume, however, copurchase network analysis is best suited to specific circumstances.

Studying products that are less frequently sold through online mass retailers may produce unreliable or incorrect conclusions. This includes items that are most often purchased in person, and items sold through specialty retailers or even third-party sellers on Amazon that may produce multiple listings for essentially similar products. The most extreme case of this is items that are most frequently bought offline and for which online and offline purchasing patterns or customer bases differ substantially. Books, music, and movies are among the most natural fits for this type of method, but even they often have multiple editions, both physical and digital, that the investigator must choose between or somehow combine.

The immediacy of the data is both an advantage and a limitation. Data can be collected and analyzed within a period of hours or days, rather than months or years, as is typically the case for sociological survey data. For exploring cultural patterns in contemporary society, this presents an excellent opportunity. However, not only are the data highly specific to a particular time,[22] but there are no general mechanisms in place at present to retrieve past copurchase networks. Unlike social media sites like Twitter, whose APIs are capable of retrieving archived data from any period of time, the methods outlined here only allow users to collect product data as it stands at the time of collection. This also effectively limits the scope of networks collected in this way, as any attempt at large-scale data collection of even a portion of the millions of products Amazon sells would be limited by changes taking place between the beginning and end of data collection.

From a more general substantive perspective, copurchases can be used effectively to study groups when the question of interest relates to the overlap of interests and ideas among products (consumption) or their consumers (culture) in mass society. For difficult-to-quantify interests, such as paranormal and folk religious beliefs, it provides the opportunity to confirm or refine inductive theories reached through observational studies.

Indeed, studying the ego-networks of key products can give insight into the products' roles in the network of customers and ideas, while focusing on top-selling products (i.e., the items on a bestseller list) in a specific area can reveal key divides, commonalities, and bridges in popular perception of that topic. Collecting data at the same time on multiple products or groups allows both direct comparison and study of network overlap. And if nothing else, data on copurchase networks enable concise visual summaries of cultural patterns detected in other ways.

Much has been made of the so-called big data revolution and its impact on how we study society, but the popular conception is that only specialists with advanced knowledge of statistics and programming can take advantage of the digital footprints left by the online activities of everyday people. Modern technology has lowered some of these barriers. In the preparation of this chapter, we have created easily adaptable and freely available tools, including those in the online supplement (www.theARDA.com), that can grow and develop to meet emerging needs in studying how religious groups and ideologies relate to one another.

What is an "evangelical" in today's world? What does it mean to be spiritual but not religious? Does the term "fundamentalist" retain any meaning? Where do nondenominational Christian churches get their theology, absent of traditional organizational forms? And, of course, what is the paranormal and how does it relate to religion? Studying purchasing networks cannot provide definitive answers to such questions, but this approach can most certainly be utilized in an exploratory or confirmatory examination of connections between strands of religious and spiritual thought. By daring to attempt the categorization of the most ephemeral (some might say ghostly) of topics using this technique, we hope to inspire creative practices of data analysis in the social scientific study of contemporary religion.

NOTES

1 Wuthnow (1976) was a rare exception who treated religious books as indicative of religious trends, but used only number of books published (production) rather than number of books purchased (consumption).

2 This figure is a lower bound for religious book sales, as nonreligious presses can and do publish books concerning religion and spirituality, particularly those written outside mainstream Christianity.

3 See the discussion of audience and client cults in Stark and Bainbridge (1985:26ff).

4 See, for example, Lewis (1992); Melton (1992); Melton, Clark, and Kelly (1991).

5 This method, known as item-to-item collaborative filtering, is not the only method Amazon uses for making recommendations on its site.

6 This amounts to no more than 101 pages per ego. We do not recommend large-scale or automatic (robot) data collection, which may violate the Amazon conditions of use.

7 We ignore rankings in the initial tabular analysis below but use them as a parameter later in the visual distance between books.

8 This could remove items relevant to New Age ideas (crystals, singing bowls) but is simpler to interpret in most cases.

9 The script is available as an executable file or Python source file. Companion scripts are also available to recode topics into groups and convert the data into GraphML and Pajek formats.

10 Bader et al. did not explicitly label paranormal topics that were associated with Christianity as "Christian-related" in *Paranormal America*. We do so here for simplicity's sake.

11 Amazon does not explicitly describe how topics are assigned, but it probably uses some combination of topics assigned by publishers, machine coding based on keywords, and assignment by their own expert buyers.

12 Krebs (2008) charted copurchases of political books during election cycles using a similar method. Freeman (2009) provides an overview of network visualization methods. For examples of other types of network images, see the NodeXL Graph Gallery (nodexlgraphgallery.org) or D3 Gallery (github.com).

13 The easiest way to make a semirepresentative network of a topic is to use the network of all books on the bestseller list in that topic, rather than the full networks of a few select books.

14 Interested readers are encouraged to visit the web version of figure 12.2, which allows users to see product titles and isolate only those directly tied to a selected product.

15 This prevents any customization of the recommendation by Amazon based on user profiles that might taint the generalizability of the data. It also prevents the introduction of unusual recommendations into the user's personal profile based on items viewed for the research.

16 Due to variation and potential changes over time in the design of product pages, our script may not function perfectly in all situations. The script is provided without guarantee, although programmers may freely edit the raw Python code to resolve problems or enhance functionality.

17 Caution should be exercised in the selection of statistical techniques for use with this type of data. Because the researcher only has information on the books frequently bought together, but not the individual customers who bought them, the assumptions of many techniques are violated and conclusions may need to be treated as suggestive.

18 The Open Library project (openlibrary.org) of the Internet Archive, for example, provides extensive metadata on millions of books. Citation networks (Google Scholar, Web of Science, etc.) can also be used in the case of scholarly books.

19 At the time of writing, importing of advanced text formats, including Pajek and GraphML files, is only available with a paid NodeXL Pro license.

20 Be aware of copyright and trademark restrictions before including cover photos or related material in any project. Fair-use cover photos for millions of books are available at openlibrary.org.

21 Amazon is not the only source of copurchase data, but it is the largest and most diverse retailer to offer it, and has the best-documented algorithm. More specialized sites may be of interest for studying particular topics, but recommendations can also be based on similar ratings, similar topics, etc.

22 This is important for very new or low-sales items whose networks can develop substantially over a short time due to outside circumstances (holidays, world events, endorsements, discounts, etc.).

WORKS CITED

Bader, Christopher D., and William H. Lockhart. 2006. "Spiritual Shopping: The Effects of State-Level Demographics and Religious Economies on the Locations of Psychics, Astrologers, and Christian Bookstores." *Journal of Media and Religion* 5(2): 91–109. doi: 10.1207/s15328415jmr0502_2.

Bader, Christopher David, Frederick Carson Mencken, and Joe Baker. 2010. *Paranormal America: Ghost Encounters, UFO Sightings, Bigfoot Hunts, and Other Curiosities in Religion and Culture*, 1st ed. New York: NYU Press.

Bartlett, Sarah. 2012. *The Essential Guide to Psychic Powers*. London: Watkins.

Bastian, Mathieu, Sebastien Heymann, and Mathieu Jacomy. 2009. "Gephi: An Open Source Software for Exploring and Manipulating Networks." Paper presented at the International AAAI Conference on Weblogs and Social Media. Accessed November 30, 2016, www.aaai.org.

Baylor University. 2005–2011. "The Baylor Religion Survey." Baylor Institute for the Study of Religion. Waco, TX.

Borgatti, S. P., M. G. Everett, and L. C. Freeman. 2002. "Ucinet for Windows: Software for Social Network Analysis." Cambridge, MA: Analytic Technologies.

Borgatti, Stephen P., Martin G. Everett, and Jeffrey C. Johnson. 2013. *Analyzing Social Networks*. Los Angeles: SAGE.

Brittle, Gerald. 2002. *The Demonologist: The Extraordinary Career of Ed and Lorraine Warren*. Lincoln, NE: iUniverse.

Burns, Jeremy. 2014. "Religious Hardcover Sales Skyrocket over Previous Year," Christian Retailing, April 3. Accessed November 30, 2016, www.christianretailing.com.

Coşgel, Metin M., and Lanse Minkler. 2004. "Religious Identity and Consumption." *Review of Social Economy* 62(3): 339–50. doi: 10.1080/0034676042000253945.

Csardi, G., and T. Nepusz. 2006. "The Igraph Software Package for Complex Network Research." *InterJournal*, Complex Systems: 1695. http://igraph.org.

Freeman, Linton C. 2009. "Methods of Social Network Visualization." In R. A. Meyers, ed., *Encyclopedia of Complexity and Systems Science*. New York: Springer-Verlag. 205.

Goode, Erich. 2012. *The Paranormal: Who Believes, Why They Believe, and Why It Matters*. Amherst, NY: Prometheus Books.

Hancock, Graham. 2015. *Magicians of the Gods: The Forgotten Wisdom of Earth's Lost Civilization*. New York: St. Martin's.

Handcock, M., D. Hunter, C. Butts, S. Goodreau, and M. Morris. 2008. "Statnet: Software Tools for the Representation, Visualization, Analysis, and Simulation of Network Data." *Journal of Statistical Software* 24(1): 1–11.

Iannaccone, Laurence R. 1994. "Why Strict Churches Are Strong." *American Journal of Sociology* 99(5): 1180–1211. doi: 10.1086/230409.

Kean, Leslie. 2010. *UFOs: Generals, Pilots, and Government Officials Go on the Record*, vol. 1. New York: Harmony Books.

Krebs, Valdis. 2008. "New Political Patterns." Orgnet. Accessed May 8, 2015, www.orgnet.com.

Lewis, James R. 1992. "Approaches to the Study of the New Age Movement." In J. R. Lewis and J. G. Melton, eds., *Perspectives on the New Age*. Albany: State University of New York Press. 1–14.

Lim, Chaeyoon, Carol Ann MacGregor, and Robert D. Putnam. 2010. "Secular and Liminal: Discovering Heterogeneity among Religious Nones." *Journal for the Scientific Study of Religion* 49(4): 596–618. doi: 10.1111/j.1468-5906.2010.01533.x.

Linden, G., B. Smith, and J. York. 2003. "Amazon.com Recommendations: Item-to-Item Collaborative Filtering." *IEEE Internet Computing* 7(1): 76–80. doi: 10.1109/MIC.2003.1167344.

Lu, L. Y., M. Medo, C. H. Yeung, Y. C. Zhang, Z. K. Zhang, and T. Zhou. 2012. "Recommender Systems." *Physics Reports–Review Section of Physics Letters* 519(1): 1–49. doi: 10.1016/j.physrep.2012.02.006.

Meldrum, Jeff. 2006. *Sasquatch: Legend Meets Science*. New York: Forge.

Melton, J. Gordon. 1990. *New Age Encyclopedia*. Detroit: Gale.

Melton, J. Gordon. 1992. "New Thought and New Age." In J. R. Lewis and J. G. Melton, eds., *Perspectives on the New Age*. Albany: State University of New York Press. 15–29.

Melton, J. Gordon, Jerome Clark, and Aidan A. Kelly. 1991. *New Age Almanac*. Detroit, MI: Visible Ink Press.

Park, Jerry Z., and Joseph Baker. 2007. "What Would Jesus Buy: American Consumption of Religious and Spiritual Material Goods." *Journal for the Scientific Study of Religion* 46(4): 501–17.

Park, Jerry, and Scott Draper. 2010. "Sunday Celluloid: Visual Media and Protestant Boundaries with Secular Culture." *Sociological Spectrum* 30(4): 433–58. doi: 10.1080/02732171003641032.

Pearce, Lisa D., and Melinda Lundquist Denton. 2011. *A Faith of Their Own: Stability and Change in the Religiosity of America's Adolescents*. New York: Oxford University Press.

Pearce, Lisa D., E. Michael Foster, and Jessica Halliday Hardie. 2013. "A Person-Centered Examination of Adolescent Religiosity Using Latent Class Analysis." *Journal for the Scientific Study of Religion* 52(1): 57–79. doi: 10.1111/jssr.12001.

R Core Team. 2015. "R: A Language and Environment for Statistical Computing." Vienna, Austria: R Foundation for Statistical Computing.

Rogers, Everett M. 2003. *Diffusion of Innovations*, 5th ed. New York: Free Press.

Scheitle, Christopher P., and Buster G. Smith. 2011. "A Note on the Frequency and Sources of Close Interreligious Ties." *Journal for the Scientific Study of Religion* 50(2): 410–21. doi: 10.1111/j.1468-5906.2011.01576.x.

Smith, Christian. 1998. *American Evangelicalism: Embattled and Thriving*. Chicago: University of Chicago Press.

Smith, Christian, and Melinda Lundquist Denton. 2003. "Methodological Design and Procedures for the National Study of Youth and Religion (NSYR)." Chapel Hill, NC: National Study of Youth and Religion.

Smith, M., N. Milic-Frayling, B. Shneiderman, E. Mendes Rodrigues, J. Leskovec, and C. Dunne. 2010. "Nodexl: A Free and Open Network Overview, Discovery, and Exploration Add-in for Excel 2007/2010." *Social Media Research Foundation*, http://smrfoundation.org.

Snijders, Tom A. B. 2011. "Statistical Models for Social Networks." *Annual Review of Sociology* 37: 131–53. doi: 10.1146/annurev.soc.012809.102709.

Stark, Rodney, and William Sims Bainbridge. 1985. *The Future of Religion: Secularization, Revival, and Cult Formation*. Berkeley: University of California Press.

Stark, Rodney, and Roger Finke. 2000. *Acts of Faith: Explaining the Human Side of Religion*. Berkeley: University of California Press.

Voas, David. 2009. "The Rise and Fall of Fuzzy Fidelity in Europe." *European Sociological Review* 25(2): 155–68. doi: 10.1093/esr/jcn044.

Warner, Rob. 2010. *Secularization and Its Discontents*. New York: Continuum.

Weiss, Brian L. 2010. *Many Lives, Many Masters*. New York: Simon & Schuster.

Wright, Hannah. 2015. "YBMs: Religious Identity and Consumption among Young British Muslims." *International Journal of Market Research* 57(1): 151.

Wuthnow, Robert. 1976. "Recent Patterns of Secularization: A Problem of Generations?" *American Sociological Review* 41(5): 850–67.

12.

Lessons Learned from SoulPulse, a Smartphone-Based Experience Sampling Method (S-ESM) Study of Spirituality

BRADLEY R. E. WRIGHT, RICHARD A. BLACKMON, DAVID M. CARREON, AND LUKE KNEPPER

Imagine that you're reading a newspaper, and you come across an article about how people's spiritual experiences vary over the course of their day.[1] The article describes a study that collects data by sending surveys to participants' smartphones, and it says that the study is still enrolling participants. "Why not?" you ask yourself. You're interested in these kinds of things, and you have a smartphone. You go to SoulPulse.org and look over a description of the study. You enter your e-mail address, and you check a box indicating that you agree with an informed consent statement from some university. The website asks you when you wake up and go to sleep each day, so it knows when to send you surveys. Then you take an eight–ten-minute "intake" survey before you start getting the "daily" surveys sent to your smartphone. You think about stopping here because that seems like a lot of time, but you go ahead anyway. The intake survey asks about your personality, health, religious background, spiritual practices, and demographic characteristics. You only have to answer these questions once.

You finish the intake survey, and a few minutes later your smartphone beeps. You have received your first "daily" survey. There's a text message with a link on it, and when you click the link, you go to a webpage with survey questions on it. The first question asks you how aware of God (or a higher power or whatever you think is holy) you are right now. Below it is a slider with the words "Not at all" on the left and "Very much" on the right. You put some thought into it because this is not a question you're used to answering. You touch the slider and a button pops up, and you slide the button a bit to the right. Similar questions follow about love, joy, and peace. Then there are several questions about what you were doing when the text message arrived. One of the questions lists two dozen activities, and each one has a blank checkbox next to it. You happened to have been in the kitchen drinking a cup of coffee and reading the newspaper. So, you check one box next to the words "eating or drinking" and another box next to "watching or listening to the news." After this are several more questions about various topics, including whether you feel sad and whether stressful things have happened to you in the past day. You click a button at the bottom that says "Finished," and that concludes your first daily survey. It had about twenty questions and took about two minutes to complete.

Over the next fourteen days, you receive two surveys a day, always at different times. A few come when you're busy or distracted, so you skip them, but you take most of them—about three out of every four. Several questions are on all the surveys, but most of the questions change from survey to survey. You find this more interesting than answering the same questions over and over again. You answer most of the surveys within twenty minutes of receiving them, but sometimes you wait longer.

After fourteen days of taking these daily surveys, you get an e-mail congratulating you and thanking you for taking part in the study. It has a link to a "personal spiritual report"—something that interested you when you signed up. You click over to the report, and it contains about a dozen graphs that describe how your awareness of God, as well as feelings of love, joy, and peace, varied over the past two weeks. You learn on which days these measures were high and on which they were low. The report also describes how these varied by time of day, how much you slept, what you were doing, exercise, drinking, and other activities. You look it over for a few minutes and think about the findings. With this, you're done with SoulPulse.

The above describes how a typical study participant might experience SoulPulse. To researchers, SoulPulse is an ongoing, smartphone-based experience sampling method (S-ESM) study of spirituality, health, and well-being. About four thousand participants have signed up for it so far, and each participant produces about four–five hundred points of data over twenty-eight surveys in a two-week span.

The ubiquity of smartphones opens up this powerful data-collection methodology. At one time, experience sampling method (ESM) research was limited to local samples who could be contacted using pagers and who would write their answers in diaries (Hektner, Schmidt, and Csikszentmihalyi 2007). With smartphones, however, researchers can now easily reach people nationwide and even worldwide. Smartphone-based ESM (S-ESM) research should make its way into the canon of social science methods, and this chapter discusses some of the issues that arose in the creation of SoulPulse, thus offering guidance to future researchers who would like to use the method. We start with an overall evaluation of this method, highlighting both its advantages and its limitations, and then we turn to issues of measurement, recruitment, participation, and analysis.

General Evaluation of S-ESM

S-ESM research occupies a unique space in social research methodology, for it shares qualities with traditional surveys, qualitative research, and laboratory experiments. Like traditional surveys, S-ESM uses survey questions to collect data; it is scalable to large samples; and it generalizes to larger populations. Like qualitative research, it engages participants' everyday life—measuring what is going on in their world as it is happening. Like laboratory experiments, it focuses on changes in people's states (as opposed to the trait focus in traditional survey research). Thus S-ESM complements these well-established methods. Its constellation of strengths makes it ideal for some research questions.

The foremost advantage of S-ESM is that it measures short-term state changes in everyday life. Some questions in social research apply to causal dynamics that play out over long periods of time. For example, how does childhood socialization affect adult employment? There are other well-established survey methodologies for this type of long-term research. Other questions, however, focus on short-term causal dynamics. For example, how does interpersonal conflict affect one's mood at the moment? Does feeling happy affect altruism? Does feeling emotionally depleted diminish the ability to work? To be examined quantitatively, this type of question requires micro-longitudinal data that measure state changes over short periods of time. These dynamics might not be seen over longer periods of time. For example, it would be unlikely that having a squabble with a friend today would leave us upset in one year, but it might make us feel bad for a day or two. S-ESM records participants' actions, feelings, activities, and states of mind multiple times a day; thus it is suitable for investigating causal processes happening day to day.

Another advantage is that S-ESM measures what participants are doing at that moment in their lives or, depending on the question wording, in the very recent past. This means that participants are not asked to recall events from months or years prior, nor are they prompted to calculate frequencies or averages of what's happening in their lives, staples of traditional surveys. They simply report what they were thinking, feeling, or doing at that moment. This lessens recall bias and gives a more accurate view into participants' lives.

Another potential advantage of S-ESM is its cost structure. Traditional surveys, such as those done by phone, by mail, or in person have some fixed cost to get going and a nontrivial cost per each additional respondent. One has to pay extra for each person contacted. Using the language of regression lines, imagine "cost" on the y axis and "number of participants" on the x axis. Traditional surveys have a moderate intercept and a moderate-to-steep slope. As a result, there is a cap on how many people can be enrolled and how long the survey can be in the field. In contrast, the cost of S-ESM takes a different form. Due to the complex computer programming that it currently requires, it is rather expensive to launch. Before the first participant is surveyed, there are many lines of computer code that need to be written and tested. However, once the program is in place, the maintenance costs are minimal—fixing bugs that arise and making occasional improvements. Thus, S-ESM is expensive to launch, but once it is up, it is inexpensive to maintain. In statistical terms, it has a high intercept but a shallow slope. Furthermore, the initial cost of S-ESM will probably drop over time as standardized S-ESM software becomes available. The cost structure of S-ESM makes it feasible to put an S-ESM study in the field for an extended period and, depending on a researcher's ability to recruit them, include many participants.

As with any research method, S-ESM also has its disadvantages, and they mostly regard sampling. For SoulPulse we chose to use convenience sampling, allowing participants to select themselves into the study. We did this for cost reasons. When we launched SoulPulse we contacted several national polling firms to get quotes for recruiting a random sample of participants, and the prices we were quoted were prohibitively expensive. Thus, we focused on recruiting a diverse, though not representative, sample. Nonetheless, we assume that people who enrolled in SoulPulse are different from those who did not. Those who enrolled in it had heard of it, and thus were reading or listening to the outlets through which SoulPulse was publicized, and any media outlet has its own unique audience profile.

Also, some people may have been aware of SoulPulse and interested in taking it, but they could not because they did not have smartphones. About two thirds of American adults own smartphones (Pew Internet and American Life Project 2014), and people who own smartphones, on average, are different from those who do not. Smartphone users are more likely to live in urban and suburban areas and to be young, well-educated, and wealthy (Pew Internet and American Life Project 2014). Also, they are more likely to be men, extroverts, and people who are not mentally ill (Lane and Manner 2011; Miller 2012). We can compensate for this sample selection, in part, by using sample weights derived from demographic characteristics observed in the population.

As a result of this sample selection bias, SoulPulse data are not suitable for making point estimates about population characteristics. For example, one of the questions in SoulPulse asks participants how much they are aware of God at that moment, and SoulPulse participants average a score of 6.2 out of 10. This does not mean that people in the general population would have the same average score. Indeed, we assume that the true population mean on this variable is lower because SoulPulse participants are disproportionately religious and, by virtue of enrolling in a study about spirituality, they demonstrate an interest in spiritual matters. SoulPulse data are more suitable for estimating the associations between variables, especially using multilevel modeling to estimate within-person effects, because this approach controls for participants' stable characteristics.

Other sample selection biases exist as well. The daily surveys are sent at random times during participants' self-reported waking hours. Some of the surveys arrive at more convenient times than others. For example, if a participant receives a survey when he or she is sitting quietly reading a book, the participant's likelihood of taking it would be rather high. In contrast, if the participant is driving somewhere or late for a meeting, he or she is probably less likely to take the survey. In such situations, participants are instructed to remember the moment when they received the survey and report on it later, but they may just skip it altogether. Accordingly, some types of situations would be better measured than others. The same logic applies to personal states. Some inner states, such as feeling happy or peaceful, might be more conducive to filling out a survey than others, such as feeling rushed or deeply engaged in solving a problem. It is not clear how much these various selection effects would bias analyses, and how much this bias can be ameliorated with sample weights.

Survey Frequency

With this evaluation in mind, let us turn to practical issues of implementing S-ESM research. We start with how often to send daily surveys. When we created SoulPulse, the only other S-ESM study that we knew of was Killingsworth's Track Your Happiness study (Killingsworth and Gilbert 2011). Their study sent participants two surveys a day for thirty days, and so we did that in our pretests. However, some of our beta-testers, friends and colleagues, reported a loss of interest in the study after a couple of weeks. Thus we kept the two-surveys-a-day frequency but cut back the duration to fourteen days. Though this meant fewer surveys sent to each participant, we thought the shortened length would induce more people to participate and reduce attrition out of the study among those who had started it. In retrospect, we should have tested sending three or four surveys a day for that fourteen-day period, for our beta-testers were more sensitive to the duration of the study than the frequency of surveys in a given day.

Measurement Issues

In creating SoulPulse, we encountered several measurement issues as we adjusted common survey practices to fit S-ESM.

Translating Trait Measures into State Measures

We started with various constructs that we wanted to measure—attitudes, beliefs, feelings, experiences, and actions relevant to the study of spirituality and well-being. Then we identified survey items and scales from past research that measured these constructs. In doing this, we realized that we needed to reword them from trait questions to state questions. Traditional surveys take the participants out of their everyday life to talk on the phone or meet with an interviewer. As a result, traditional surveys tend not to ask about that moment since it is a contrived moment. Instead, they ask participants about the frequency or representativeness of momentary states in their lives. For example, participants respond to statements such as "I am the type of person who . . ." or "On average, I . . ." or "In the past, how often have I. . . ." In doing this, traditional surveys focus on traits rather than momentary states.

In SoulPulse, we wanted to ask about what participants were experiencing at that moment or in the recent past, and so we had to alter existing survey questions such that their wording emphasized a momentary state. For example, we started with a seven-item depression subscale from the Depression Anxiety Stress Scales (DASS-21) (Henry and Crawford 2005). This subscale asks respondents to estimate "how much did these apply to you over the past week?" Then it lists various statements about depression, such as "I couldn't seem to experience any positive feelings at all." Respondents, in turn, check one of four boxes, ranging from 0 = "does not apply to me" to 3 = "applied to me very much or most the time." This measures the frequency of depression. For SoulPulse, we did not need to ask about the frequency of depression because we would measure the frequency directly, i.e., in how many of our waves did participants report feeling depressed. Instead, we wanted to measure levels of depression in a given moment. Thus, we altered the DASS Depression Subscale. We changed the question preface to, "How much do each of these apply to you right now?" Then we put each of the seven items into the present tense, for example, "I can't seem to experience any positive feelings at all." Participants answered using a finely graduated slider that ranged from "not at all" to "very much."

We have converted the original frequency question (i.e., how often) to a severity question (how much). In doing so, we assume that our severity question will capture the same underlying construct as the frequency question, but it is possible that the conversion changed the underlying psychometric properties, reducing both validity and reliability. Testing the full impact of this conversion requires in-depth, nuanced analyses.

As a first look, we computed the reliability for DASS depression subscale as measured by SoulPulse, and it was Chronbach's alpha = .92. This compares to the reliability of the original form of this subscale, which is alpha = .82 (Henry and Crawford 2005). This suggests that the conversion from a trait to a state measure does not necessarily attenuate the scale's reliability.

Scale Length

The nature of S-ESM limits how many items can be in any one scale. The daily surveys need to be short enough that participants can take them without too much disruption to their lives. Through the process of beta-testing, we settled on each daily survey having about twenty questions, for participants could do this in about two–three minutes. Unfortunately, several of the scales that we wanted to use had almost that many items themselves. Thus, if we added a scale with that many questions, there was no room to ask other survey questions.

Initially we considered sampling several items from each scale, so that each scale would be at least partially represented in each survey. We chose not to do this, however, because of its unknown impact on the measurement properties of the scales. Instead, we decided to cap the scales in length at about seven to nine questions. Sometimes this meant finding a shorter alternative to a scale that we had initially wanted. At other times we selected only seven to nine items from a longer scale to include on SoulPulse. When we selected a subset of a scale's items, we used two criteria. One, we selected items with high loading scores on the original factor, in order to have high construct validity. Two, we chose items that represented different aspects of the original scale. For example, the original fourteen-item scale for Religious Coping (Pargament, Feuille, and Burdzy 2011) had items for both positive and negative coping. In our seven-item version of it, we chose items representing both positive and negative coping. This provides high content validity.

Sliders

A small, technical, but important measurement issue arose as we developed procedures for recording participants' answers. Many of the questions prompted participants to record their answer by sliding a marker along a horizontal slider. This type of swipe bar is well suited for S-ESM, for it is easy and quick to use, it measures a continuum of responses, and it is frequently used in smartphone apps, so participants are familiar with it.

Initially we created a swipe bar with a circle in the middle. Participants were instructed to move that circle left or right to indicate their response. The software running SoulPulse measures swipe bar answers on a ten-point scale with increments of .1; thus there are one hundred possible levels (.1 through 10.0). Because the choice of levels was done graphically, rather than numerically, these small increments did not place a heavy cognitive load on participants, as would be the case if they had to choose from a list of one hundred separate numbers.

When we downloaded our initial data, we saw a problem. About 10–15 percent of the slider responses were exactly 5.0. What this meant was that the participants were not actually moving the circle. In talking with our beta-testers, we realized that we were seeing an instance of the anchoring and adjustment bias (Epley and Gilovich 2006). When the participants saw the circle initially placed in the middle, and if they thought their actual score was generally in the middle of the range, they would think that the circle was close enough and leave it as their answer. Those who wanted to swipe far left or right would, but many just left the circle where it was, thus creating a preponderance of scores at the default of 5.0 and a significant loss of recorded variation.

To address this, our software programmer created a new measurement bar. Initially it is just a bar without a circle, but when participants touch it, a circle appears where they touched the bar. Then, they can swipe the circle left or right. This avoids the anchoring effect of starting with a circle already in place.

Question Frequency

A difficult measurement question was how many daily survey questions we could include in the study overall. With 28 surveys each 20 questions long, we could have asked 560 separate questions, each question being asked one time only. This would have given us data on many variables. But without repeated measurement, we could not do multilevel modeling. Measuring a variable only once would allow us to analyze variation across people, i.e., how each person scores on that variable. But, a single measurement would not allow us to analyze variation within people, since there are not multiple measures per person, and thus no multilevel modeling. At the other extreme, we could have asked the same twenty questions on every survey. This would have given us very rich data about these twenty questions, but it would not have included enough questions to cover the research interests of the SoulPulse team. Also, we had learned from our beta-testing that participants liked having some variation in the daily survey questions, to keep the surveys more interesting. The same twenty questions time after time would have been repetitive.

We settled between these two extremes by creating a pool of 120 questions for the daily surveys, and each daily survey randomly selected twenty questions from this larger pool using a weighted sampling scheme based on the substantive and methodological importance of the variable. As a result, some questions were asked more often than others.

Of the 120 questions, we asked four of them in every single daily survey. These four variables were of substantive interest, measuring various aspects of daily spirituality. They measured awareness of God and feelings of love, joy, and peace. Also, we used these four questions to generate a personal (automated) report at the end of the study for each participant when he or she finished the study.

Repeatedly measuring the same variable—as we do here—can influence later scores on it, what is termed a testing effect (Campbell and Stanley 1966). We see evidence of this with these variables that were included on every survey. For example, the average score for the awareness of God variable linearly increases across the duration of the study, such that scores at the end of the study are slightly but significantly higher than those at the start. In our analyses, we control for this testing effect by adding the number of the survey (i.e., from one to twenty-eight) as a control variable.

Several other questions were in most daily surveys. These were questions about the immediate situation. They asked "what are you doing now?" "who are you with?" and so forth. These situational questions are useful in papers on a variety of topics, thus meriting their more frequent inclusion.

Many of our questions, however, were included in 20–30 percent of the daily surveys. We chose this frequency because it was about as low as we could go and still have enough data for multilevel modeling. In general terms, if two variables are randomly included in x percent of the daily surveys, then the probability of them co-occurring in the same survey is x*x, and a binomial distribution table gives the expected range of co-occurences. For example, if two variables are each in 30 percent of the surveys, then they should be in the same survey 9 percent (.3*.3) of the time. Using a binomial table, we estimate that with twenty-eight total surveys, the two variables would co-occur in two or more surveys for 55 percent of the participants. This, we deemed, was enough data to conduct meaningful within-person analysis for two variables.

Finally, we asked a handful of questions only once for each participant. These one-time-only questions were of speculative interest for us only. By asking them once, we could conduct between-person but not within-person analyses. If the between-person analyses produced sufficiently interesting results, we could always increase the frequency of asking them at a later point.

Recruitment and Sampling Issues

Our goal in recruiting participants was to obtain a sufficiently large and diverse sample. We are aware of three general approaches for recruiting participants for S-ESM studies. The first approach is to recruit participants from a local population with whom the researcher already has contact. Usually this means recruiting students for a small payment or extra credit (e.g., Spicer 2015). Advantageously, this type of sample is relatively easy to collect, and the great majority of undergraduate students today have smartphones. Several times I have asked my own students how many have smartphones, and invariably all but one or two students do. The problem with this approach, of course, is external generalizability. College students occupy a narrow band of age, education, and other important characteristics, so it is not clear how well observations of college students would extend to the broader population.

A second approach is to hire a professional survey firm to conduct the sampling (if not the research altogether). When we launched SoulPulse, we contacted several such firms, and while they had not previously conducted S-ESM studies, they were willing to undertake the task. Advantageously, these firms are well practiced in drawing nationally representative samples. Unfortunately, at the time we inquired anyway, they were prohibitively expensive. They quoted us prices well into six figures for collecting only one to two thousand subjects. A variation of this second approach is to use Amazon's Mechanical Turk (MTurk). MTurk has a standing group of subcontractors who answer survey questions in exchange for small sums of money. While this approach does not give a representative sample, it does give a diverse sample, unlike studies of undergraduate students. Also, an MTurk study would be substantially cheaper than one done by a professional survey firm, with costs as low as ten dollars per participant (Pew Center Research 2015).

A third approach, and the one we chose for SoulPulse, is to use attraction-based recruitment. This approach was developed by Killingsworth and Gilbert (2010) for the Track Your Happiness study, and it involves offering subjects information about themselves as payment. For SoulPulse, we have attracted participants through various means. Many participants in SoulPulse learned about it through media coverage. After our initial launch, the Associated Press ran a story about SoulPulse in dozens of newspapers nationwide, and this led over a thousand people to sign up for the study. Some months later, the *New Yorker* magazine did a feature story on SoulPulse, and this, too, attracted over a thousand people. Other participants heard about SoulPulse through word of mouth. They had a friend or colleague who took it, or they read about it on social media. Advantageously, this attraction-based approach gathers more diverse participants than a local convenience sample. For SoulPulse, we have participants from all fifty states as well as several other English-speaking countries. Also, this approach has the potential for creating a large pool of data for relatively little money.

Disadvantageously, participants self-select into the study with this approach, and thus it is a convenience sample—a diverse convenience sample but a convenience sample nonetheless. The composition of the SoulPulse study participants varies meaningfully from the national population. SoulPulse participants are disproportionately female (60 percent), with fewer African Americans (3 percent) and Hispanics (7 percent). They are overall better educated (39 percent have some graduate education) and predominantly Protestant (68 percent). Most define themselves as politically independent (48 percent). They are slightly older (median age = forty-five years) and somewhat wealthier (median annual household income = $87,500). As discussed above, it is possible to create sample weights based on these characteristics, but there remain other nonrandom, not-measured selection processes at work.

Our choice of an attraction-based recruitment model put a premium on participants having a good experience. If the SoulPulse site was unattractive or confusing, or if the survey was burdensome, people would not sign up for it, and, if they did, they would be less likely to stay with the study for a full two weeks. This informed many of our decisions. As discussed above, we limited the duration of the study to fourteen days, so as not to outlast participants' interest. We limited the number of questions, and we varied the questions to keep the survey experience fresh. We also hired a graphic artist to give the site a clean, bright, welcoming look.

The biggest draw to SoulPulse, however, is the end-of-study report that the participants receive. This report presents about a dozen graphs that illustrate the participants' spiritual experiences over the previous two weeks. The report describes how awareness of God and feelings of love, joy, and peace varied by life circumstances. Based on interviews with our beta-testers, we identified things that participants might want to know about themselves. For example, how does quality of sleep the night before associate with a participants' awareness of God? How does exercising associate with feeling loving toward others?

Using information as a reward has advantages. It is scalable in that once the software for it is written, it can provide reports for thousands of people as easily as for a few. Also, it provides an incentive for diligent participation in the study, because answering more of the surveys means higher quality of data in the report. As disadvantages, this type of reward works for only a limited number of research topics. Happiness and spirituality are things that people want to know about themselves. However, one can easily imagine other topics that would not draw participants with the promise of self-knowledge. Also, there is added sample selection bias. If people are attracted to the study by the promise of learning about their own spirituality, the study will disproportionately draw people interested in such learning, and these people are presumably different than people not so interested.

Attrition

As with most longitudinal studies, attrition was a concern for SoulPulse. This is especially true given the many places it can happen with S-ESM. Once somebody decides to sign up for SoulPulse, he or she has to find the website, enter an e-mail address, check a box for a consent form, take an intake survey that lasts about ten minutes, enter his or her smartphone number, and enter his or her waking hours. Then, for each of the twenty-eight surveys, participants need to notice the text message, click on the link sent to them, start that daily survey, and finish it.

Initially we anticipated that most of the attrition would happen with the daily surveys, but participation rates in them remains rather high, with about 65–70 percent of daily surveys being answered in full. Rarely do participants start a daily survey without finishing it. Attrition was higher than expected, however, with the intake survey. At the start, almost 40 percent of people who signed up for SoulPulse would start the intake survey but not finish it. In talking to beta-testers, we learned that they were put off by the length of the intake survey. To reduce this problem, we pruned back the number of questions in the intake survey. We also created a status bar at the top of each intake survey page that indicated how far they had to go. Currently, about 70–75 percent of the people who start the intake survey finish it and go on to the daily surveys.

Analyses

So far this chapter has discussed SoulPulse and S-ESM in general terms. Now let us move to a specific empirical example that demonstrates the richness of the data generated by this method. For illustrative purposes, we will describe the relationship between the Daily Spiritual Experience Scale (DSES) and situational activities.

The DSES is a well-known measure of spiritual experiences that has been included in the General Social Survey (GSS). It includes questions such as "I feel God's presence," "I feel thankful for my blessings," and "I desire to be closer to God or in union with the divine." The first step in adapting it to SoulPulse was to translate its wording from trait language to state language. The original DSES scale (Underwood 2011) has sixteen separate items, but this would be too many for SoulPulse, so we pruned it to nine items. We picked the nine items that we thought best captured the breadth of the scale. Then we changed the response categories. In its original form, the DSES asks about the frequency of spiritual experiences. Respondents report how often they have each experience, from "many times a day" to "never or almost never." To change this into an explicit state measure, we asked SoulPulse participants to indicate how much they were experiencing each spiritual experience at that moment, with a slider bar ranging from "not at all" on the left to "very much" on the right. We then set the SoulPulse program to include this revised DSES scale on 25 percent of the daily surveys.

We used participants' responses to the DSES scale to create two variables. The first variable, "DSES–Person Mean," took the average of each participants' DSES-scale scores across daily surveys. For example, suppose that a hypothetical participant answered the revised DSES scale, and the participant's scale-scores were 2, 3, 4, 5, 6, 7, and 8. His or her score for "DSES–Person Mean" would be 5, the average of these seven observations. The second variable, "DSES-Deviation," took each individual observation of DSES and subtracted from participants' "DSES–Person Mean" score. So, our hypothetical participant would have "DSES-Deviation" scores of −3 (i.e., 2−5), −2, −1, 0, 1, 2, and 3 accordingly. If we were to use the DSES as an independent variable, we would use both of these variables in our multilevel analyses to separately estimate between-person and within-person effects of DSES. In the terminology of multilevel modeling, the within-person measure is our L1 (level 1) and the between-person measure is our L2 (level 2).

Most analyses of the DSES, in other surveys, treat it as a trait variable, with each person getting one score to represent the frequency of his or her spiritual experiences. In our analyses, however, we analyze it as a state that can change within a person across observations. To give a sense of how much change is occurring within people, figure 12.1 presents a histogram of the "DSES-Deviation" scores for SoulPulse participants. It is drawn from 8,271 observations recorded from 2,008 participants. As we would expect, the most common deviation score is about zero, simply meaning that participants scored near their overall average score. If participants never varied in their spiritual experiences, i.e., if it were a true, stable trait, then we would expect all values of this

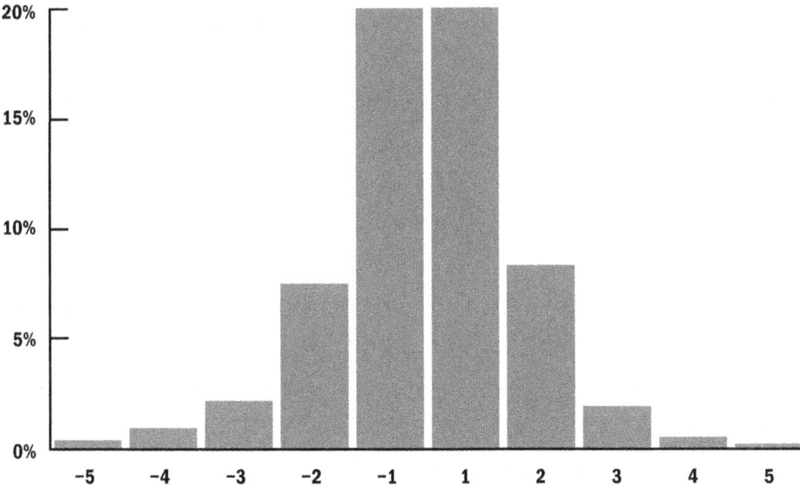

Figure 12.1. Histogram of Within-Person Deviations—DSES.

variable to be near zero (give or take measurement error). As shown in figure 12.1, there is a spread of observations; in fact, about half of all observations were one half-point (on a scale of ten) or more away from zero, i.e., each participant's average score. This suggests that it is meaningful to examine the DSES as both a trait and a state, thus necessitating multilevel modeling.

To link the DSES to day-to-day living, we use a question from SoulPulse that asks participants what activity they are doing at the moment they receive a daily survey. Participants select from a list of two dozen activities. Figure 12.2 plots "DSES-Deviation" scores by daily activities. There are twenty-four activities, and so there are twenty-four bubbles on figure 12.2. Each bubble represents average "DSES-Deviation" scores for when participants are engaging that activity versus when they are not. For example, one of the lower bubbles in the figure is for work, and it is to the left of the midpoint (which is set at zero). This indicates that participants experience lower "DSES-Deviation" scores when they are at work compared to when they are not. At the top of the figure is praying, meditating, or engaging in some other spiritual activity, and it is to the right of the midpoint. This means that, as one would expect, people have higher-than-average spiritual experiences when they are praying, meditating, or doing some other spiritual activity.

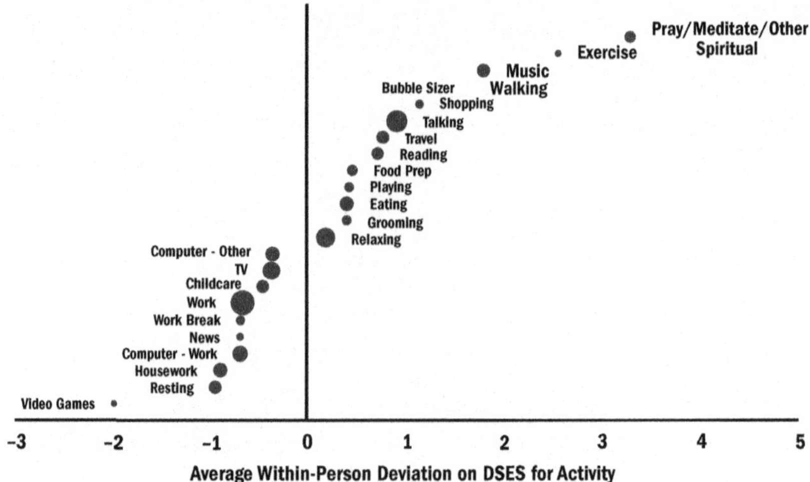

Figure 12.2. Within-Person Deviations in DSES by Daily Activities.
Note: The size of the bubbless represents the frequency with which participants engaged in an activity—larger bubbless indicate more frequently done activities.

Let's take a closer look at the relationship between the DSES and spiritual activities. SoulPulse includes questions about six different spiritually related activities. Four ask about the practice of spiritual disciplines. With the question stem, "In the past 24 hours, have you," they ask participants if they have "read the Bible or other religious text," "prayed," "sought guidance from God in your life–," and "set aside time for solitude to listen to God." Two other questions ask about participation in religious meetings. One asks participants whether, in the preceding twenty-four hours, they have "attended a religious meeting other than weekend services (e.g., Bible study or prayer meeting)." The other, included on only Monday morning surveys, asked if participants had "attended a religious service this past weekend?"

As the spiritual activities ask about behavior in the prior twenty-four hours, they temporally precede the DSES measure. Thus we treat spiritual activities as independent variables and DSES as the dependent variable. This being the case, we create person-mean and deviation scores for each of the spiritual activities and test whether they predict observations of the DSES. With six spiritual activity questions, we will estimate six separate multilevel equations of the following form:

$$y_{ij} = b_0 + \underbrace{b_1(x_{ij} - \overline{x}_j)}_{within\_effects} + \underbrace{b_2(\overline{x}_j)}_{between\_effects} + \underbrace{u_j + e_{ij}}_{random\_effects}$$

Table 12.1 presents the results from these six equations, with each equation being reported in its own row. The numbers in the first column are the within-person effects (i.e., measured as deviations from person-averages) of spiritual activities on the DSES. The second column reports the between-person effect (i.e., measured as a person-average). As shown, the four spiritual disciplines—reading scripture, praying, seeking guidance, and solitude—have both significant within- and between-person effects on DSES scores. The between-person effects are greater in magnitude than the within-person effects. This indicates that the type of people who practice these spiritual disciplines have more spiritual experiences than those who do not; in addition, and to a lesser extent, when people practice these activities, regardless of how often they do so, they have more spiritual experiences.

Table 12.1. Multilevel Models Regressing Daily Spiritual Experiences on Daily Activities

Spiritual activitiy	Zero-order models—Disentangled (6 equations total) (A) Within-effect	(B) Between-effect
Spiritual disciplines		
Read the Bible or other religious text n = 1,677	.008 *** (4.4)	.038 *** (21.0)
Prayed n = 1,560	.017 *** (7.1)	.052 *** (29.7)
Sought guidance from God in your life n = 1,679	.019 *** (8.8)	.056 *** (33.0)
Set aside time for solitude to listen to God n = 1,665	.014 *** (7.3)	.048 *** (24.3)
Religious events		
Attend religious service (weekend) n = 578	-.21 (-.6)	1.80 *** (8.3)
Attend other religious meeting (e.g., Bible study, prayer meeting) n = 435	.43 (1.1)	1.10 *** (3.8)

Note: Cells report coefficient estimate with z-score in parentheses.

The two measures of religious activities tell a different story. Each of the two religious-activity variables has a significant between-person effect on the DSES but an insignificant within-person effect. This finding indicates that the type of people who attend religious services or meetings typically have more spiritual experiences than the type of people who do not attend them. However, among those people who attend religious services and meetings, doing so does not increase spiritual experiences the following day.

Conclusion

This chapter presents an overview of the smartphone-based experience sampling method (S-ESM) as it is applied to collecting data about spiritual and religious experiences. It describes a specific study, SoulPulse, and it examines both strengths and weaknesses of this method.

Smartphone-based experience sampling method studies (S-ESM) are feasible because of the ubiquity of smartphones, and the S-ESM offers a powerful new method for researchers who study spirituality. Many theories of religion and spirituality identify the importance of momentary spiritual states, and S-ESM studies allow for the fine-tuned analyses of these states—whether they be feelings, thoughts, or actions. S-ESM is especially valuable for studying situational effects, such as the effects of specific circumstances on a person.

S-ESM has unique strengths that make it an appropriate method for many research questions. Among its strengths, it measures participants' experiences in the moment; i.e., they are asked about their current experiences rather than being asked to recall the past or to estimate an abstract average experience. Also, the repeated measurement feature of S-ESM readily allows for multilevel modeling in which the experience is level 1 and the person is level 2. This allows for statistical analysis to disentangle between-person and within-person effects related to spirituality. Also, the cost structure of S-ESM studies allows them to potentially be carried on for the long term with a relatively low marginal cost per participant.

S-ESM has weaknesses, some of which can be worked around but some of which would work against this method being used for some research questions. Sampling issues arise when participants are recruited with a convenience sample, as is done with the SoulPulse study. This makes population point estimates difficult. Also, not all people have smartphones, and those who do not have smartphones presumably have different average characteristics than those who do. Another issue is timing. Because S-ESM surveys people in the context of their everyday life, it sometimes surveys them when they either have to delay taking the survey or are unable to do so altogether. Presumably the times when participants are not able to answer immediately are different than those when they are able. Finally, the repeated measurement of items can cause a testing effect where answers given in later surveys are different levels because of the participant having answered the question previously.

As an empirical example, we analyzed participants' scores on the Daily Spiritual Experience Scale (DSES). DSES scores systematically varied across types of types of daily activities, with some activities, such as work, associating with low levels of spiritual experiences. While typically analyzed as a trait measure, the DSES also displays state-like qualities, with participants regularly varying in their DSES scores across measurements.

We estimated several multilevel models to test the impact of spiritual disciplines and religious meeting attendance on spiritual experiences. Both disciplines and attendance have a between-person effect on spiritual experiences, meaning that the type of people who practice spiritual disciplines and who attend religious meetings have greater spiritual experiences. However, only spiritual disciplines also displayed a within-person effect, with participants' spiritual experiences increasing after they practice a spiritual discipline. Religious meeting attendance did not show a within-person effect.

The findings observed with religious service attendance can be interpreted in multiple ways. They could reflect social selection. People who already have more daily spiritual experiences may be more likely to attend religious services, being drawn to that spiritual context. They could also reflect an exposure effect. Perhaps religious services increase spiritual experiences over longer periods of time, but the effect is not sudden enough to capture in a two-week study such as ours.

Regardless of how these findings are interpreted, they highlight the value of data from S-ESM studies for bringing new insight into issues of spirituality and religion. Thus we conclude that this method rightfully belongs in the toolbox of social scientists studying spirituality and religion.

These findings demonstrate the value of using the S-ESM study for studying spirituality. It allows the collection of micro-longitudinal data from many diverse participants on an ongoing basis, and once it is put into the field, this type of data collection method is relatively low cost to maintain.

NOTE

1 This work was supported by grant #48298 from the John Templeton Foundation. We thank John Ortberg, whose idea it was to apply S-ESM to spirituality. For their many contributions to this project, we thank Linda Barker, Charley Scandlyn, John Mumford, Jack Reis, Isaac Gierard, and Tracy Anderson.

REFERENCES

Campbell, D. T., and J. C. Stanley. 1966. *Experiment and Quasi-Experimental Designs for Research.* Boston: Houghton Mifflin.

Epley, Nicholas, and Thomas Gilovich. 2006. "The Anchoring and Adjustment Heuristic: Why the Adjustments Are Insufficient." *Psychological Science* 17(4): 311–18.

Hektner, Joel M., Jennifer A. Schmidt, and Mihaly Csikszentmihalyi. 2007. *Experience Sampling Method: Measuring the Quality of Everyday Life.* Thousand Oaks, CA: Sage.

Henry, Julie D., and John R. Crawford. 2005. "The Short-Form Version of the Depression Anxiety Stress Scales (DASS-21): Construct Validity and Normative Data in a Large Non-Clinical Sample." *British Journal of Clinical Psychology* 44: 227–39.

Killingsworth, Matthew A., and Daniel T. Gilbert. 2010. "A Wandering Mind Is an Unhappy Mind." *Science* 330: 932.

Lane, Wilburn, and Chris Manner. 2011. "The Impact of Personality Traits on Smartphone Ownership and Use." *International Journal of Business and Social Science* 2(17): 22–28.

Miller, Geoffry. 2012. "The Smartphone Psychology Manifesto." *Perspectives on Psychological Science* 7(3): 221–37.

Pargament, Kenneth, Mararet Feuille, and Donna Burdzy. 2011. "The Brief RCOPE: Current Psychometric Status of a Short Measure of Religious Coping." *Religions* (2): 51–76.

Pew Center Research. 2015. "The Smartphone Difference." Accessed January 15, 2016, www.pewinternet.org

Pew Internet and American Life Project. 2014. "Mobile Technology Fact Sheet." Accessed November 8, 2014, www.pewinternet.org.

Spicer, Justina Judy. 2015. "Measuring Student Engagement in Science Classrooms: An Investigation of the Contextual Factors and Longitudinal Outcomes." Dissertation, Michigan State University.

Underwood, Lynn G. 2011. "The Daily Spiritual Experience Scale: Overview and Results." *Religions* 2: 29–50.

Conclusion

Lessons Learned, Challenges Remaining

ROGER FINKE AND CHRISTOPHER D. BADER

The past several decades have witnessed an avalanche of innovations in data analysis. Computers can now quickly calculate improved statistical techniques for addressing correlated error terms, violations of statistical assumptions, multilevel analyses, missing data, and many other refinements for improving statistical estimates. Each improvement in our analytical tools opens new research agendas as scholars replicate and extend findings from past research using the newest technique. During this same time, however, the *measures* used in our analyses have undergone remarkably little change.[1]

This book was designed to allow our authors to explore new measures and methods for the study of religion. We found that each new method and measure allowed us to tap into new dimensions of religion and to uncover new findings. Even when chapters were devoted to evaluating past measures, these evaluations resulted in insights on how our measures shape the stories we tell. We close this book with a brief overview of the lessons we learned and the challenges that remain.

Lessons Learned

First, there is an urgent need for the introduction of new measures for the study of religion.

Given that this was a premise of this project, the first finding might seem unsurprising or even trite. Yet, after working with the authors, we are convinced that the need is even greater than we expected. One of the ongoing changes driving this need is the changing populations being studied by surveys. As the diversity of the samples and the global outreach of surveys increase, the need for revising or replacing measures increases. Smith demonstrated both the importance and the challenges of these changes on multinational surveys where differences in world religions, local cultures, and vocabularies show wide variation. Likewise, Hill and Pargament stressed the importance of taking an "indigenous approach" when developing measures of religion and spirituality. Even when samples are confined to a single nation, Baker, Hill, and Porter show how measures must be revised in response to increasing irreligion.

The need for new and revised measures, however, is driven by more than an increasingly diverse sample. We found that even the most trusted survey items must be questioned and evaluated more thoroughly. Seemingly simple questions on church attendance, importance of religion, and religious affiliation can often be misleading or simply misunderstood. Brenner explained how religious identity can shape the responses given for many of the most common measures of religion and spirituality, Bader and Finke displayed the consequences of subtle changes in question wording and response categories, and Baker, Hill, and Porter found that question format can influence the percentage of respondents classified as religiously affiliated or nonaffiliated.

Moving beyond traditional survey measures, Jong, Zahl, and Sharp and Wright et al. introduce us to entirely new types of measures. Rather than asking respondents to do conscious self-assessment and reflection (where responses may be shaped by religious identity, as discussed by Brenner), Jong, Zahl, and Sharp proposed indirect and implicit measures of religion that can tap into a wider range of religious cognitions. Wright et al. used smartphones and frequent surveys to capture changes in experience and emotion over time. Rather than asking respondents to describe their traits, they asked them to report their current state at the time of the survey, avoiding many of the pitfalls of inaccurate memories and self-assessments that are so common in survey-based research. These new approaches allowed the authors to capture dimensions of religion that are typically ignored by traditional survey measures.

The remaining chapters introduced measures that came from diverse sources, used diverse methods, and studied diverse units of analysis. Once again, however, each of the chapters introduced the need for measures of religion that have been lacking in previous research. Unlike most survey measures, which focus on the self-reported attitudes, beliefs, and behaviors of individuals, these chapters developed religion measures for nations, belief systems, networks, and organizations. They each offered measures that either could not be captured on surveys or would simply be cost prohibitive. Using these measures allowed the authors to study groups that otherwise might be ignored and to cover time periods where religion measures are completely lacking.

Second, there is an urgent need for the use of multiple methods for the study of religion.

We introduced this book as a "venture into the art and science of measuring religion," but it quickly became apparent that the development of new measures, as well as a better understanding of existing measures, relies on the use of multiple research methods. This is not a novel observation. Consider the work of Webb and colleagues from fifty years ago.

> The most persuasive evidence comes through a triangulation of measurement processes. If a proposition can survive the onslaught of a series of imperfect measures, with all their irrelevant error, confidence should be placed in it. Of course, this confidence is increased by minimizing error in each instrument and by a reasonable belief in the different and divergent effects of the sources of error. (Webb et al. 1966:3)

Triangulation of our measurement processes does not mean that we cease using current approaches. Rather, new approaches will complement tried-and-true techniques. Even the development of survey measures benefits from the use of other methods. Brenner turned to quasi-experimental design, using diary-like data collection and cognitive interviews to assess and understand the relationship between overreporting church attendance and religious identity. Baker, Hill, and Porter used quasi-experimental designs to evaluate past measures and test the effectiveness of new measures. Each of the chapters was interested in improving measures for surveys, but they turned to alternative methods to evaluate and test these improvements.

The need for multiple methods, however, was most apparent in the chapters that went beyond surveys. Each of these chapters illustrated how non-survey-based methods facilitated the development of new measures and often resulted in a completely new source of quantitative data. Some of the methods allowed the authors to explore time periods where data or information was previously lacking. Bainbridge used a wide range of sources and methods to offer a more complete story on the Oneida community and to address theory-relevant questions. Finke and McClure relied on Google Books and the Ngram Viewer to produce measures for charting historical trends on religion and for exploring religious events, people, and places in greater depth. Each of the chapters introduced new options for accessing data and information on the past.

But the alternative methods were not confined to delving into the past. Chapters by Scheitle and Bush illustrated how past work on developing measures for nations, organizations, and major events has generated data that open up entirely new lines of research. Scheitle demonstrated how the coding of government documents, newspapers, web pages, court cases, patents, and many other text sources can all offer new measures on religion. Bush discussed the importance of religious NGOs to our understanding of the role religion plays in the secular world and outlined the various means by which researchers can determine whether a nongovernmental organization should be defined as religious in mission. As with religious NGOs, the paranormal can prove difficult to clearly define. Porter and Bader's mapping of Amazon book purchasing networks allowed them to test hypotheses about those following the paranormal that were simply untestable with previous measures and methods. Finally, as reviewed above, Wright et al.'s use of smartphones opened up the option of including measures on current states rather than self-assessed traits.

These methods often did more than simply provide alternative measures; they allowed the authors to understand a part of religion that was previously unexplored, and they provided measures for multiple different units of analysis. In many cases, it was a unit of analysis more appropriate for the theory being tested. For sociologists, the use of multiple methods results in measures on the networks, the organizations, and the larger social context of religion; for political scientists, it offers new measures on the relationship between religion and the state; and for psychologists, it gives insights on the cognition and meaning of the measures. For all social scientists, the alternative methods produce data that allow us to test theoretical propositions that were often untestable in the past.

Third, many opportunities are emerging for the development of new measures and methods for the study of religion.

As we noted in the opening of this chapter, changes in social science measures have failed to keep pace with the rapid advancement of statistical tools. Yet many of the technological advances that allowed for rapid changes in statistical computing have also had an impact on the sources and tools we can use for generating new measures. The authors have reviewed a few of the opportunities for developing new measures, but many more remain.

Some of the new measures rely on established research methods, but they turn to new technologies for executing the methods. The coding of documents offers an obvious example. Scheitle did not create a new research method of content analysis, but did rely on new technology for accessing and coding the documents. As Bainbridge noted, when he first brought census documents to the attention of religion scholars in the 1980s, there were only twelve sites in the entire country where these documents could be reviewed on microfilm. Now anyone can access and search them online. Likewise, newspapers, directories, diaries, and government documents once held in only a few archives are now readily available online. And, as reviewed by Finke and McClure, Google Books now offers access to old books and journals that were once confined to a handful of libraries.

Along with the improved access, the new technologies provide new tools for conducting old methods. For example, the ability to search within and across documents has opened up new opportunities for conducting content analysis and locating primary sources. Whether it is Google's Ngram Viewer allowing us to search millions of books or the Library of Congress's Chronicling America facilitating the search of newspapers, the volume of material that can be covered and the type of data that can be generated has made the collection of new measures more possible than ever before. Even within a single document, directory, or census, basic searches make the collection of new measures more efficient.

Recent developments in technology are also opening up new opportunities for the development, testing, and collection of survey measures. As Bader and Finke note, the ARDA's online Measurement Wizard tool and archive of more than one thousand data collections allows for the effective evaluation of past survey measures; Amazon's Mechanical Turk offers a new method for testing new measures and evaluating old measures; and smartphones allow for new survey measures to be collected. Improved access to past measures and improved tools for assessing and collecting measures are providing new options for improving future measures.

The new technologies also create new sources of data that offer measures previously unavailable. The networks of copurchasing behavior studied by Porter and Bader offer measures that did not exist prior to Amazon's online presence. Websites have produced new data both in the content they offer and in the links they have to other sites. Although not covered in this volume, Google searches, blogs, and social media could all be used to provide new measures of religion. In short, the new technologies are creating new religious content and connections that have largely gone unexplored.

Fourth, regardless of the method used, the criteria for good measures remain the same.

Throughout this volume we and the chapter authors have stressed the use of new measures, new methods, and new sources of data. The focus has often been on the changes to measuring religion. Yet, we would be remiss if we did not stress how the criteria for good measures remain largely unchanged.

The chapters highlighted the importance of clearly defining the concept being measured by providing a definition that sets the standard for what should be included or excluded from a measure. As Hill and Pargament note, such definitions are improved when they emerge from a strong theoretical underpinning. Clearly, researchers should more frequently rely upon theory to set the conceptual boundaries of their measures.

Each of the chapters also stressed the importance of understanding the meaning of the measures. Smith vividly illustrated how meaning can change from one linguistic, religious, and national context to another. Brenner explored how questions on church attendance are interpreted by the respondents and how their responses should be interpreted.

Finke and McClure assessed the meaning of the measures generated by the Ngram Viewer. Even when the meaning of the measures seemed obvious, the authors found that the measures were often being misinterpreted or misunderstood. Rather than selecting measures based on the variance they can explain, and then assigning meaning to them, we should strive for measures that are accurate indicators for the concepts of interest.

Using multiple measures and methods was also stressed by the authors. The use of *multiple measures* is most evident in the Hill and Pargament chapter, in which they review the necessary criteria for developing multi-item measures of religious concepts. Brenner and Bainbridge each used *multiple methods* to better understand key measures and to more fully understand their topics of interest. All of the authors stressed the complexity of understanding and measuring religion, and each called for the creative use of new approaches for developing improved measures.

Fifth, many of the new measures are less intrusive.

It is well known that experiments, surveys, and field research can affect the behavior and responses of those being studied. For this reason, unobtrusive measures offer significant advantages. Yet, finding measures and methods that do not intrude into the life of research subjects, resulting in reactance or impression management, is surprisingly difficult.

The chapters in this book, however, offer several examples of how unobtrusive measures can be constructed. Along with reviewing three examples from his past research, Scheitle suggested other projects where unobtrusive measures could be used. Bainbridge introduced us to a wide range of sources that offer measures on people and events from the past. New tools and data sources for generating unobtrusive measures, such as Google Ngrams and Amazon's copurchasing network data, were also introduced. Other approaches discussed in this volume do require the involvement of the subjects under study, but attempt to reduce intrusiveness, minimize the need for recall, and limit the respondents' efforts to shape their answers. For example, Wright et al.'s use of smartphones to collect "snapshot" data of a respondent's current activities minimized the respondent's need to recall information or to reflect on past behavior.

Sixth, many challenges remain for assessing the new measures and methods.

Whereas the first six chapters were devoted to assessing survey measures and offering strategies for improving these measures, the remaining six chapters were introductions to alternative measures and the methods used to collect them. For many of the methods introduced, the authors readily acknowledge that they have merely provided an initial effort. Some of the methods introduced are in the embryonic stage and will require far more development to reach their full potential; many will require far more effort to generate the data needed for the measures; and virtually all will require researchers to think about both the measures and the methods in new and creative ways.

One of the most significant first steps is to better understand how one method or measure complements or challenges the finding of another. To do so requires that we return to the foundational questions of research methods. How do each of these new measures compare in reliability, validity, and the samples or populations they reach? To what extent can these alternative approaches offer insights that were previously missing? The authors offered brief discussions on the strengths and limitations of their alternative approaches, and the chapters using Google Ngram and Amazon purchasing data each acknowledged challenges in assessing the validity of their measures, but more detailed and critical evaluations are needed. As often happens, preliminary discoveries reveal the need for more discovering, testing, and evaluation.

The New Frontier

Oftentimes discussions of measurement become pessimistic enterprises, as we outline the shortcomings of current approaches and cry out for new ones. With the many challenges facing surveys, especially phone surveys, despair seems appropriate (Wuthnow 2015). At the risk of being contrarian, however, we view the current state of the social scientific study of religion with great optimism. New technologies and new methodological tools have opened up vast opportunities for researchers to gain a better understanding of the predictors of religion and its outcomes in a changing religious world and an increasingly multicultural and cross-cultural context.

Taking advantage of these opportunities will also require support from the entire research community. Institutional gatekeepers will need to welcome innovation too. Reviewers, editors, institutional review boards, and funders often unintentionally erect barriers to new approaches. The safest route is always to fall back upon the methods we know and the measures that seem comfortably familiar, even when they are obviously flawed. But if researchers venture beyond their standard templates for measurement and methods, and if gatekeepers maintain a scholarly skepticism without being dismissive, the decades ahead promise to offer unparalleled levels of creativity and exploration in the study of religion.

NOTE

1 We recognize, of course, the important work of Duane Alwin (2007), Stanley Presser et al. (2004), and others addressing measurement issues in survey design. We argue, however, that measurement issues have received far less attention than data analysis.

BIBLIOGRAPHY

Alwin, Duane. 2007. *Margins of Error: A Study of Reliability in Survey Measurement.* Hoboken, NJ: Wiley.

Presser, Stanley, Jennifer Rothgeb, Mick Couper, Judith Lessler, Elizabeth Martin, Jean Martin, and Eleanor Singer, eds. 2004. *Methods for Testing and Evaluating Survey Questionnaires.* New York: Wiley.

Webb, Eugene J., Donald T. Campbell, Richard D. Schwartz, and Lee Sechrest. 1966. *Unobtrusive Measures: Nonreactive Research in the Social Sciences.* Chicago: Rand McNally.

Wuthnow, Robert. 2015. *Inventing American Religion: Polls, Surveys, and the Tenuous Quest for a Nation's Faith.* Oxford: Oxford University Press.

ABOUT THE EDITORS

Roger Finke is a Distinguished Professor of Sociology, Religious Studies, and International Affairs at the Pennsylvania State University and is Director of the Association of Religion Data Archives (www.theARDA.com).

Christopher D. Bader is a Professor of Sociology at Chapman University and is affiliated with the Institute for Religion, Economics, and Culture (IRES). He is Associate Director of the Association of Religion Data Archives (www.theARDA.com), funded by the John Templeton Foundation and Lilly Foundation, and principal investigator on the Chapman University Survey of American Fears.

ABOUT THE CONTRIBUTORS

William Sims Bainbridge is a director of the Cyber-Human Systems program of the National Science Foundation. He earned his doctorate in sociology from Harvard University with a historical dissertation, *The Spaceflight Movement* (1976). Three studies of religious movements combined history with ethnography: *Satan's Power* (1978), *The Sociology of Religious Movements* (1997), and *The Endtime Family* (2002). In addition to editing *Encyclopedia of Human-Computer Interaction* (2004), he has written several books about online culture, including *The Warcraft Civilization* (2010), *The Virtual Future* (2011), *eGods* (2013), *An Information Technology Surrogate for Religion* (2014), *Virtual Sociocultural Convergence* (2016), and *Star Worlds* (2016).

Joseph O. Baker is Associate Professor in the Department of Sociology and Anthropology at East Tennessee State University, and Senior Research Associate for the Association of Religion Data Archives. He is coauthor of *American Secularism* (NYU Press) and *Paranormal America* (NYU Press). His published research covers topics including religious experiences, practices, and beliefs; religious group dynamics such as strictness, cohesion, and ecstasy; public views of science; theories of deviance; and the sociology of law. He is currently working on a book outlining and testing a parsimonious but powerfully predictive theory of deviance "management" and social movements.

Richard A. Blackmon is a clinical psychologist with a private practice in Westlake Village, California. He has practiced psychotherapy with adults for thirty-five years, specializing in working with clergy and mental health, marital therapy, and adult psychotherapy. In addition, he was an adjunct professor at Fuller Theological Seminary for twenty-one years, teaching classes on clergy mental health. He speaks sporadically around the country on marriage issues and clergy mental health. Lastly, Dr. Blackmon has been one of the principal researchers with SoulPulse on a grant with the Templeton Foundation since 2013. The series of studies with SoulPulse has been investigating the relationship between the daily experience of spirituality and other variables such as mental health, emotional well-being, and relationships.

Philip S. Brenner is Assistant Professor in the Department of Sociology and Senior Research Fellow in the Center for Survey Research at the University of Massachusetts–Boston. His interests in social psychology and survey methodology inform his approach to the study of measurement errors and response biases. His research program examines the function of prominent identities in the survey response process and their contributions to social desirability bias. His recent work has examined the role of identity prominence in the overreporting of religious behaviors like church attendance and prayer, physical exercise and athletics, and voting on self- and interviewer-administered surveys.

Evelyn L. Bush is an Associate Professor in the Department of Sociology and Anthropology at Fordham University. She received her PhD in sociology from Cornell University in 2005. Her research has focused largely on organized religious participation and influence in international and foreign policy institutions that focus on human rights. Her publications have included "Measuring Religion in Global Civil Society" (*Social Forces*), "Explaining Religious Market Failure" (*Sociological Theory*), and several chapters in edited volumes that focus on international relations.

David M. Carreon, M.D., studied civil and environmental engineering at UCLA before going to Stanford Medical School with interests in global health. He took a leave of absence to work with a start-up nonprofit for a year in rural Kenya, setting up a mobile data-collection system with community health workers and community leaders. Upon returning to Stanford, he developed an interest in neuroscience and psychiatry, particularly in how people process information and make choices, both in the lab and in everyday life. He is currently a psychiatry resident at Stanford, using these approaches to better understand conditions like PTSD and addiction.

Jonathan P. Hill is Associate Professor of Sociology at Calvin College. He is author of *Emerging Adulthood and Faith* (2015) and coauthor of

Young Catholic America: Emerging Adults in, out of, and Gone from the Church (2014). He has published articles and book chapters on higher education and religious faith, volunteering, and charitable giving. He also directs the National Study of Religion and Human Origins, a project that explores the social context of beliefs about human origins.

Peter C. Hill, PhD, is Professor of Psychology at Rosemead School of Psychology, Biola University, in La Mirada, California. Dr. Hill is an active researcher in social psychology and the psychology of religion, having authored over one hundred book chapters and articles in peer-reviewed journals. His primary research interests focus on religious fundamentalism, religious/spiritual measurement, positive psychological virtues such as humility and forgiveness, and the role of affect in religious or spiritual experience. He is a past president of Division 36 (Society for the Psychology of Religion and Spirituality) of the American Psychological Association (APA) and was elected Fellow of the APA in 1998.

Jonathan Jong is a Research Fellow at Coventry University, where he co-leads the Brain, Belief, and Behaviour research group. He is also the Research Coordinator of AnthroLab at the University of Oxford. His main research is in the cognitive and cultural coevolution of religious and moral beliefs. He is the author, with Jamin Halberstadt, of *Death Anxiety and Religious Belief: An Existential Psychology of Religion*.

Luke Knepper is a software engineer specializing in web app development. He built the website and technical systems behind SoulPulse: A Smartphone-Based Experience Sampling Method Study of Spirituality. He holds a BS in Computer Science from Stanford and is a lead engineer at the start-up Terrain Data.

Jennifer M. McClure is an Assistant Professor of Religion at Samford University. She received her PhD in sociology from Penn State University in 2015. Her research focuses on religious congregations and examines how they can promote community involvement, informal helping, and charitable giving among their members. In addition, she also conducts applied research for religious congregations and serves as a congregational consultant. She is the Senior Associate for Congregational

Resources at the Association of Religion Data Archives (www.theARDA .com) and is affiliated with the Center for Congregational Resources at Samford University.

Kenneth I. Pargament, PhD, is Professor Emeritus of psychology at Bowling Green State University. He has published over three hundred articles on religion, spirituality, and health, and authored *The Psychology of Religion and Coping: Theory, Research, Practice* and *Spiritually Integrated Psychotherapy: Understanding and Addressing the Sacred.* Dr. Pargament is Editor-in-Chief of the 2013 two-volume *APA Handbook of Psychology, Religion, and Spirituality*. He received the William James Award for excellence in research from Division 36 of the American Psychological Association, the Oskar Pfister Award from the American Psychiatric Association, and an honorary doctorate of letters from Pepperdine University.

Nathaniel D. Porter is a PhD candidate in sociology at Penn State University. His work explores new methods and data sources in the sociology of religion and beyond, with a focus on social network analysis, big data, and analysis of causal processes. His dissertation uses book copurchasing on Amazon.com to study informal ties of shared idea exposure among U.S. Protestant groups. His other projects include a study of the role of parent and friend religiosity in adolescent religiosity and a comparison of ministry outcomes for ELCA pastors holding the traditional Master of Divinity degree and those who complete less academic programs of preparation. He has also designed and implemented a variety of online studies and is actively researching best practices in online data collection for surveys, experiments, web scraping, and data augmentation.

Christopher P. Scheitle is an Assistant Professor in the Department of Sociology and Anthropology at West Virginia University. His research has examined a variety of issues related to the nature and role of religion in the United States. These issues include changes in the way religion is organized, the social dynamics between religion and science, and how religious individuals and organizations are affected by discrimination and criminal victimization. He has published over thirty peer-reviewed articles and two books, and has been awarded two grants by the National Science Foundation.

Carissa A. Sharp, PhD, is a Research Fellow at Newman University's Centre for Science, Knowledge, and Belief in Society. Her primary areas of research are social cognition and the psychology of religion, with a focus on people's cognitive representations of God, the complexity of religious belief, and people's perceptions of the relationship between science and religion. She is principal investigator on the John Templeton Foundation project "Gods in Minds: God-Complexity and the Multiple God-Aspects Framework" and works on the Templeton Religion Trust–funded project "Science and Religion: Exploring the Spectrum" (sciencereligionspectrum.org).

Tom W. Smith is an expert in survey research specializing in the study of societal change and survey methodology. Since 1980 he has been a principal investigator of the National Data Program for the Social Sciences and Director of its General Social Survey (GSS) at NORC at the University of Chicago. Smith was cofounder and Secretary General of the International Social Survey Program (1997–2003). In 2009–2014 he served in the presidency of the World Association for Public Opinion Research.

Bradley R. E. Wright is an Associate Professor of sociology at the University of Connecticut, where he studies American Christianity and spirituality. He received his PhD at the University of Wisconsin, where he specialized in social psychology and criminology. He has authored twenty scholarly articles and two books: *Christians Are Hate-Filled Hypocrites . . . and Other Lies You've Been Told* (2010), and *Upside: Surprising Good News about the State of Our World* (2011). *Hypocrites* won the Christianity Today Book of the Year Award for Christianity and Culture. He lives in Storrs, Connecticut with his wife, sons, and a very small dog. He enjoys bicycle riding, hiking, and nature photography.

Bonnie Poon Zahl is a program consultant to Templeton World Charity Foundation. She received her AB from Harvard College, and her PhD from the University of Cambridge, both in psychology. Her research interests are broadly in religious cognition and religious emotion, and she has published on mental representations of God, anger at God, and attachment to God. She is currently based in Oxford.

INDEX

Lightning Source UK Ltd.
Milton Keynes UK
UKOW04f0415091217
314159UK00002B/205/P